Christian Wisdom

What is Christian wisdom for living in the twenty-first century? Where is it to be found? How can it be learnt? In the midst of diverse religions and worldviews and the urgencies and complexities of contemporary life, David Ford explores a Christian way of uniting love of wisdom with wisdom in love. Core elements of his discussion include the 'discernment of cries', the love and worship of God for God's sake, a wisdom interpretation of scripture, and the education of desire in wise faith. The book includes case studies that deal with inter-faith wisdom among Jews, Christians and Muslims, universities as places of wisdom as well as of knowledge and know-how, and the challenge of learning disabilities. Throughout, there is an attempt to do justice simultaneously to the premodern, modern and postmodern in grappling with scripture, tradition and the cries of the world today.

DAVID F. FORD is Regius Professor of Divinity at the University of Cambridge and a fellow of Selwyn College, Cambridge. He is author of *Self and Salvation: Being Transformed* (1999) and co-editor with Ben Quash and Janet Martin Soskice of *Fields of Faith: Theology and Religious Studies for the Twenty-First Century* (2005).

Cambridge Studies in Christian Doctrine

Edited by
Professor DANIEL W. HARDY, *University of Cambridge*

Cambridge Studies in Christian Doctrine is an important series which aims to engage critically with the traditional doctrines of Christianity, and at the same time to locate and make sense of them within a secular context. Without losing sight of the authority of scripture and the traditions of the church, the books in this series subject pertinent dogmas and credal statements to careful scrutiny, analysing them in light of the insights of both church and society, and thereby practise theology in the fullest sense of the word.

Titles published in the series

Christian Wisdom

Desiring God and Learning in Love

DAVID F. FORD

CAMBRIDGE UNIVERSITY PRESS
Cambridge, New York, Melbourne, Madrid, Cape Town, Singapore, São Paulo

Cambridge University Press
The Edinburgh Building, Cambridge CB2 8RU, UK

Published in the United States of America by Cambridge University Press,
New York

www.cambridge.org
Information on this title: www.cambridge.org/9780521698382

First published 2007

Printed in the United Kingdom at the University Press, Cambridge

A catalogue record for this publication is available from the British Library

ISBN 978-0-521-87545-5 hardback
ISBN 978-0-521-69838-2 paperback

For my mother, Phyllis Ford, in gratitude for her wisdom and love

As when the heart says (sighing to be approved)
O, could I love! And stops; God writeth, Loved.
GEORGE HERBERT

Contents

Acknowledgements

This book began in 1996, stimulated by an invitation from Professor Iain Torrance to deliver the 1998 Scottish Journal of Theology Lectures in the University of Aberdeen. It was a memorable first visit to Aberdeen, with warm hospitality in the home of Iain and Morag and vigorous discussion of the lectures. I came away convinced that they needed a great deal more work before they could be published, but also encouraged to undertake this.

In the intervening years Iain has been very patient as the promised short book of four lectures turned into a longer work that migrated from the Scottish Journal of Theology Monograph series to the Cambridge Studies in Christian Doctrine. In 2005 there was a happy reconnection of the book with its origins when leading ideas from the chapter on scriptural reasoning were explored in an address and discussion during Iain's inauguration as President of Princeton Theological Seminary. I am deeply grateful to Iain for his seminal role in the book and for his generous support of it through many phases.

The conversations to which this book is indebted are innumerable. Some partners, including Daniel Hardy, Micheal O'Siadhail, Peter Ochs, Ben Quash and Tim Jenkins, have been constant, and their influence is pervasive.

Others have had a special influence on particular chapters: my colleagues Nicholas de Lange, Graham Davies, Katherine Dell and, above all, Susannah Ticciati on Job; Frances Young, Sarah Coakley, Donald Allchin, Anthony Thiselton, Richard Bauckham, Miroslav Volf, Robert Morgan, Morna Hooker, Graham Stanton and Brian Hebblethwaite on wisdom in Christian scriptures and traditions; participants in scriptural reasoning, in particular Nicholas Adams, Oliver Davies, James Fodor, Robert Gibbs, Mike Higton, Annabel Keeler, Steven Kepnes, Basit Koshul,

Diana Lipton, Rachel Muers, Aref Nayed, Chad Pecknold, Randi Rashkover, Suheyl Umar, Tim Winter, William Young and Laurie Zoloth; participants in biblical reasoning, including Jon Cooley and Donald McFadyen; Frances Young, Jeffrey Stout, Richard Roberts, Gordon Graham and John Rowett for their engagements about universities; fellow members of the University of Cambridge who have also discussed universities with me, including Nicholas Boyle, Christopher Brooke, Alec Broers, Gordon Johnson, David Livesey, Tim Mead, Onora O'Neill, Alison Richard, David Thompson, David Wilson and Richard Wilson; and members of L'Arche and those who have accompanied it over the years, especially Jean Vanier, Frances Young, Donald Allchin, Christine McGrievy and Jean-Christophe Pascal.

There have been other communities and groups that have helped form the book: St Bene't's Church in Cambridge; the group that has at various times included Hillary Elliott, Alan and Annie Hargrave, Graham and Ali Kings, and Madeleine O'Callaghan; the University of Cambridge Faculty of Divinity and its seminars on Systematic Theology and the Christian God; the postgraduate seminar that meets in my home; the Triangle Club of scientists, philosophers and theologians who discussed a paper on universities; twelve years of fortnightly meetings of the Syndicate of Cambridge University Press, under Alan Cook and Gordon Johnston as chairmen, during which academics from across the disciplines vetted the titles recommended by editors for publication; the Cambridge Theological Federation and its colleges spanning Anglican, Methodist, Orthodox, Roman Catholic and United Reformed traditions, among which I have had closest institutional connections with Westcott House (and am deeply grateful to Michael Roberts, its principal for many years) and Ridley Hall (to whose principals Graham Cray and Christopher Cocksworth I also owe much); the Centre for the study of Jewish–Christian Relations, which, under the leadership of its founding Director, Edward Kessler, has pioneered Cambridge's academic engagement in inter-faith questions; seven years on the Doctrine Commission of the Church of England, chaired by Stephen Sykes and including Michael Banner, Richard Bauckham, Christina Baxter, Jeremy Begbie, Grace Davie, Martin Kitchen, Ann Loades, Al McFadyen, Geoffrey Rowell, Peter Selby, Kenneth Stevenson, Anthony Thiselton, Fraser Watts, John Webster and Linda Woodhead, which produced the 2003 Report *Being Human: A Christian Understanding of Personhood Illustrated with Reference to Power, Money, Sex and Time* in which wisdom is the core category; contributors to the third edition of *The Modern Theologians*, and especially

Rachel Muers, who so generously shared the thinking, the writing and the editing that went into it; four years (2000–2003) attending Primates' Meetings of the Anglican Communion, trying to work out with them in the face of powerful alternatives what a wisdom interpretation of scripture might be; annual meetings of the Society for the Study of Theology, the Society for Biblical Literature and the American Academy of Religion; the Monastery of St Barnabas the Encourager in Wales; the Network of Theological Enquiry (Christian theologians from five continents who gathered in Cambridge, Hong Kong and Madras); members of the Council of 100 Leaders taking part in the World Economic Forum's West–Islamic World Dialogue in Davos and Amman; and my native city of Dublin, which has been flourishing in so many ways and with which there have been not only continuing connections but also new ones.

One especially stimulating thread through these years has been that of postgraduate teaching and continuing relationships with doctoral students. Their varied topics and later works have constantly fed into this book. I particularly thank Michael Barnes SJ, Jeff Bailey, Jon Cooley, Tom Greggs, Mike Higton, David Höhne, Paul Janz, Jason Lam, Riccardo Larini, Rachel Muers, Paul Murray, Ben Quash, Chung Park, Chad Pecknold, Young Hwan Ra, Greg Seach, Gemma Simmonds CJ, Tan-Chow MayLing and Susannah Ticciati.

There have also been several people who have lifted or shared academic or administrative and organisational burdens at critical times and so have provided the time and collegiality without which this book could not have been completed. Dan Hardy has done this repeatedly and with extraordinary generosity in the context of graduate student supervision, examining, scriptural reasoning, inter-faith strategic thinking, reading drafts, and editing the series of which this book is part. Since 2002 I have been Director of the new Cambridge Inter-Faith Programme (CIP), a challenging and exciting responsibility, and one that has both complicated and contributed to the thinking of this book. Julius Lipner was Chair of the Faculty Board of Divinity during CIP's seminal period, and his wise support helped to ensure its flourishing. Tim Jenkins has been unstinting in time, energy and acute advice as chair of the Management Committee of CIP, and his interventions have frequently been crucial. He has been well supported by the other members of that committee, including Janet Martin Soskice, William Horbury, Graham Stanton and Roger Parker. David Thompson as Director of the Centre for Advanced

Religious and Theological Studies has likewise been vital to the developing shape of CIP both in academic design and organisational strategy within and beyond the University of Cambridge. At the core of CIP is its steering group, and there Stefan Reif and Tim Winter have been essential to the way the programme has grown. Among the wider circle of those whose support has been very important to CIP have been Edward McCabe, Tim Ryan, Richard Chartres, Chris Hewer, Emilia Mosseri, Jonathan Sachs, Abraham Levy, Rowan Williams, David Marshall, George Carey, Guy Wilkinson, Alan Ford, William Taylor, Simon Keyes, Amineh Ahmed, Edward Kessler, David Wilson, Peter Agar, Deborah Patterson-Jones, Graham Allen, and Cambridge's Vice-Chancellor, Alison Richard. The day-to-day burden of the programme has been borne by Ben Quash, its Academic Coordinator, and my debt to him is inestimable, especially in taking over as acting director during the sabbatical term needed for this book to reach final draft form.

More recently, the final months of the book's preparation have been greatly helped by the arrival of two outstanding younger colleagues. Catriona Laing has capably taken up the new post of Project Manager of CIP, and her multiple talents, together with her academic and theological understanding, have facilitated progress and liberated much time and energy. To Paul Nimmo I owe deep thanks for his research assistance. He has combined rigorous research backup, footnoting and editing with acute and often challenging comment rooted in a passion for theological truth. The privilege of working with such colleagues has evoked daily gratitude.

There is also the matter of funding. The posts of Ben Quash, Catriona Laing and Paul Nimmo have been financed through generous benefactions given by two very good friends of the University of Cambridge. John Marks (and the Mulberry Trust) was the first to share the vision of CIP to the extent of funding its first post of Academic Coordinator; Mohammed Abdul Latif Jameel (and the Coexist Foundation) brought his vision to unite with ours and helped develop the project combining teaching and research in Cambridge with broad public outreach and education in many modes. With each there has been the added pleasure of a continuing relationship, wide-ranging discussion, and a meeting of minds that has repeatedly led to fresh ideas for how financial resources can be matched with constructive ideas for the good of our world.

Cambridge University Press has, through its long wait for this book, been both patient and helpful. I especially thank Kate Brett, who as

Religious Studies Editor has built impressively on the sound foundations laid by her predecessor Kevin Taylor, and has overseen the final stages of this book, and also Frances Brown and Jackie Warren, who have been of tremendous help in the process of preparing for publication. Within the Faculty of Divinity practical assistance and easing of burdens have come from Ann Munro, Katy Williams, Don Stebbings, Chris Carman, Dorothy Kunze, Rosalind Paul, Nigel Thompson, Peter Harland and Rajashree Dhanaraj, and direct secretarial help with this book from Elisabeth Felter and Beatrice Bertram. Dave Goode's computer assistance has frequently saved the day, always with patience, cheerfulness and willingness to go the extra kilobyte. At the end of the process Jason Fout dedicated many hours to checking the footnotes and copy-editing, resulting in numerous emendations.

Finally, there is the fundamental and pervasive importance of my family. During the writing of the present book my wife Deborah has studied theology, been ordained as a priest in the Church of England, and worked in a parish, in acute hospital chaplaincy, and with many who suffer from severe mental illness. That has opened up new horizons in our marriage and new spheres of joint study, conversation and collaboration through which ideas in the book have been generated and tested. The study of scripture together has been especially fruitful. At the same time our children Rebecca, Rachel and Daniel have been increasingly stimulating conversation partners and companions whose humour, perceptiveness and growing wisdom is a delight as well as a challenging touchstone. My mother-in-law, Perrin Hardy, has frequently been a 'lifesaver' amidst the pressures of busy family life, and she and Dan have shared our practical and other burdens in innumerable ways year after year.

This book is dedicated to my mother, Phyllis Mary Elizabeth Ford, in thanks for her love and wisdom throughout my life. I never fail to be amazed and grateful that she has continued to grow in love and wisdom into her late eighties, and am delighted to be able to respond with this little offering.

David F. Ford
Easter 2006

Introduction: theology as wisdom

Wisdom has on the whole not had an easy time in recent centuries in the West. It has often been associated with old people, the premodern, tradition and conservative caution in a culture of youth, modernisation, innovation and risky exploration. Yet it may be making a comeback. It may be just the heightened alertness that has come from a decade or so spent writing this book, but it has been striking how many references to wisdom I have come upon.

This has been especially evident in areas where knowledge and know-how come up against questions of ethics, values, beauty, the shaping and flourishing of the whole person, the common good, and long-term perspectives. Wisdom is now regularly mentioned in discussions of poverty, the environment, economics, governance, management, leadership, political priorities and policies, education at all levels, family life, the health of our culture, the desire for physical, emotional and mental health, and the resurgence of religion and 'the spiritual'. In most premodern cultures wisdom or its analogues had immense, pervasive and comprehensive importance. It was taken for granted as the crown of education, and as what is most to be desired in a parent, a leader, a counsellor, a teacher. The critiques and crises that all such traditional figures and wisdoms have undergone in recent centuries have not, however, been able to dispense with the elements that went into them at their best.

It is still necessary to try to combine knowledge, understanding, good judgement and far-sighted decision-making. The challenges and dilemmas of prudence, justice and compassion remain urgent. Choosing among possible priorities, each with a well-argued claim, is no simpler today. There is no scientific formula for bringing up children or coping

[1]

with suffering, trauma or death. The shaping over time of communities and their institutions is as complex and demanding as ever. The discernment of meaning, truth and right conduct in religion has not become any easier, despite many confident and well-packaged proposals from religious, non-religious and anti-religious sources. The potential for disastrously foolish judgements, decisions and actions is illustrated daily.

So it is not surprising that wisdom, or the desire for it, crops up more and more, often under those other categories such as good judgement, appropriate decision-making, discernment of priorities, understanding that combines theory and practice, how to cope with complexities, contingencies and difficulties, or how to avoid being foolish. Recognition of the need for wisdom is sometimes partial and restricted to an immediate problem, but if the matter is serious it usually connects with larger issues requiring fuller wisdom. There is also the attraction of wisdom packages with all the answers – religious or ideological formulae that offer clarity, security and certainty in the midst of the confusions and complexities of life. Any wisdom needs to take seriously the desire both for some sense of overall meaning and connectedness and also for guidance in discernment in specific situations.

What if the overall meaning and the discernment in specific situations involve God? That is one way to approach this book's concern with theology as wisdom. What follows is my attempt as a Christian thinker to search out a wisdom for living in the twenty-first century. Christianity, in terms of the sheer number of those who are in some way directly identified with it (a common estimate is around two billion), might be described as at present the largest global wisdom tradition. This means that it is of considerable importance how Christian wisdom is conceived, taught and worked out in practice, both for Christians and for the large number of others who engage with them or are affected by them.

The main thrust of this book is to explore key elements of Christian wisdom and its relevance to contemporary living. Within that, the focus is especially on the Christian scriptures and their interpretation today. The Bible is vital to practically all past and present expressions of Christian identity. Any attempt to articulate Christian faith afresh or to work out its implications in new circumstances also must appeal to the Bible in some way. This is not only a non-negotiable element in Christian wisdom but also the fundamental criterion for its authenticity as Christian. So it makes sense for the Bible to play the leading role in working out Christian wisdom for today.

There is a primary theology that can be distilled from reading and rereading the Bible. This is not simply about information, or even knowledge, but about the sort of wisdom that is gained from reading scripture alert both to its origins, reception and current interpretations and also to contemporary understanding and life. This 'wisdom interpretation' of scripture is the core concern of this book. But it is very important that this is not simply about asking what an ancient book said many hundreds of years ago to its original audience. That 'archaeological' interest (as LaCocque and Ricoeur call it, see chapter 2 below) is important, but the text has also been received by and has nourished readers over the centuries and around the world today through its testimony to God and God's ways with the world. It has continued to be extraordinarily generative for imagining, understanding, believing, hoping and living. Its interpretation has required the making of endless connections with past, present and future, and with a range of disciplines, spheres of life, aspects of self, religions, worldviews and experience. The very abundance of meanings, which are often in tension or even in conflict with one another, calls for continual rereading and discernment.

What sort of theology results from this? It might be described as 'scriptural-expressivist' in its concern to draw from reading scripture a lively idiom of Christian wisdom today, one that forms its expression in sustained engagement with scripture's testimony to God and God's purposes amidst the cries of the world. It is 'postcritical' in its attempt to do justice simultaneously to the premodern, modern and late modern (or postmodern or, perhaps best, 'chastened modern'),[1] taking seriously the critiques of Christianity generated in recent centuries, but not letting them have the last word. It might be termed a 'theology of desire and discernment' in its attempt to unite in a God-centred discourse the love of wisdom and wise loving. It is also a 'theology of learning in the Spirit' in its combination of a pedagogical thrust with an attempt to be alert to the ways God continually opens up texts, situations and people to newness of understanding and life. This learning is dialogical and collegial, located in theological communities understood as 'schools of desire and wisdom'. Above all, the schooling is in loving God for God's sake, resulting in a

1. David F. Ford, 'Holy Spirit and Christian Spirituality' in *The Cambridge Companion to Postmodern Theology*, ed. Kevin J. Vanhoozer (Cambridge: Cambridge University Press, 2003), pp. 269–90.

theology which seeks a wisdom of worship, prayer and discerning desire that is committed to God and the Kingdom of God.

During the final year of writing this book I tried to formulate this sort of theology in thesis form for the epilogue to the third edition of an edited work covering Christian theology from 1918 to the present. The twelve theses that resulted articulate the main elements of what I hope twenty-first-century Christian theology might be about and are the horizon within which this book has been conceived. They are:

1. *God is the One who blesses and loves in wisdom.*
2. *Theology is done for God's sake and for the sake of the Kingdom of God.*
3. *Prayer is the beginning, accompaniment and end of theology: Come, Holy Spirit! Hallelujah! and Maranatha!*
4. *Study of scripture is at the heart of theology.*
5. *Describing reality in the light of God is a basic theological discipline.*
6. *Theology hopes in and seeks God's purposes while immersed in the contingencies, complexities and ambiguities of creation and history.*
7. *Theological wisdom seeks to do justice to many contexts, levels, voices, moods, genres, systems and responsibilities.*
8. *Theology is practised collegially, in conversation and, best of all, in friendship; and, through the communion of saints, it is simultaneously premodern, modern and postmodern.*
9. *Theology is a broker of the arts, humanities, sciences and common sense for the sake of a wisdom that affirms, critiques and transforms each of them.*
10. *Our religious and secular world needs theology with religious studies in its schools and universities.*
11. *Conversation around scriptures is at the heart of interfaith relations.*
12. *Theology is for all who desire to think about God and about reality in relation to God.*[2]

Within that horizon the rationale for the chapters that follow is best understood by surveying their contents.

Two of the key themes took me by surprise. I anticipated neither in the first conception of this book. They arose from grappling with the Bible in the context of life and worship. Chapter 1, 'Wisdom cries', introduces *the first theme of the cry*. The more I have searched for Christian wisdom the more I have been struck by its core connection with cries: the cries for wisdom and the cries by the personified biblical wisdom; cries within

---

2. David F. Ford, 'Epilogue: Twelve Theses for Christian Theology in the Twenty-first Century' in *The Modern Theologians: An Introduction to Christian Theology since 1918*, ed. David F. Ford with Rachel Muers, 3rd edn (Oxford: Blackwell, 2005), p. 761.

and outside scripture that arise from the intensities of life – in joy, suffering, recognition, wonder, bewilderment, gratitude, expectation or acclamation; and cries of people for what they most desire – love, justice, truth, goodness, compassion, children, health, food and drink, education, security, and so on. Christian wisdom is discerned within earshot of such cries, and is above all alert to the cries of Jesus. Doing justice to diverse cries is at the heart of this theological wisdom. The insistence of the cries lends urgency to the search for wisdom. The persistence of the cries, together with the diversity and, often, novelty of their challenges, constantly expands the search and refuses to allow it to rest in any closure.

The *second key theme* is *loving God for God's sake*. It was introduced through the book of Job's question: 'Does Job fear God for nothing?' – 'for nothing' in the sense of gratuitously, as a gift, without expecting a reward. This theme too has become more and more important for my conception of Christian wisdom. It is about letting God be God, acknowledging who God is, and living from that acknowledgement whatever the circumstances and whatever the consequences. It is the nerve of wise living before God. But, since this God hears the cries of the world and is compassionately committed to it, acknowledgement of God for God's sake also involves discernment of cries and living according to what is discerned.

At the end of chapter 1 a third pervasive theme is introduced. Faith is explored in terms of five 'moods' rooted in cries: the indicative that affirms or denies; the imperative of command and obedience; the interrogative that questions, probes, suspects and tests; the subjunctive exploring possibilities of what may or might be, alert to surprises; and the optative of desire. These five run through the book and how they are interrelated is vital to its conception of wisdom. Indeed in formal terms the shaping of wisdom might be seen as the constantly changing interplay of the five moods. *The theological wisdom of faith is grounded in being affirmed, being commanded, being questioned and searched, being surprised and opened to new possibilities, and being desired and loved*. The embracing mood for a wisdom that is involved in the complexities of history while being oriented to God and God's purposes is the optative of desire. The longing for God, and the passion for realising the truth, love, justice and peace of God, are together at the heart of the Christian desire for a wisdom that responds with discernment both to the cries of God and to the cries of the world.

Chapter 2, 'A wisdom interpretation of scripture', attempts both to exemplify and to describe the seeking of this wisdom through scripture. The prologue of the Gospel of John together with the Gospel of Luke and the Acts of the Apostles are the main examples, opening up a set of critical issues: the centrality of God; the horizon of the whole of creation; immersion in history and the contemporary world; the interplay between Jewish scriptures and testimony to Jesus Christ; and the community of those who read scripture and seek to live in its light. Interpretation is a matter of reading and rereading scripture. Yet this apparent simplicity can – and, if the goal is a wisdom that has been open to all available sources of understanding, should – embrace many elements. I explore three of these, scholarship, hermeneutics and doctrinal theology, before summarising some guidelines for a wisdom interpretation of scripture in nine theses and ten maxims.

Chapter 3, 'Job!', and chapter 4, 'Job and post-Holocaust wisdom', are the outcome of years of fascination with a classic of Hebrew wisdom literature, the book of Job. This daring, profound and mysterious work continues to inspire an extraordinary range of responses. *Job is the core wisdom text of the present book*. It resounds with passionate cries: God is to be feared 'for nothing'; creation is of value apart from its human utility; all five moods are vigorously in play; and the most challenging issues, centring on a limit case of human affliction and misery, are wrestled with chapter after chapter. This wisdom pedagogy works through radical searching, debate, controversy and powerful poetry to suggest a way of living wisely before God in the face of extreme testing. There are no neatly packaged answers, and religious tradition is brought face to face with its limitations in coping with cries from the midst of trauma. The wisdom is embodied in someone who cries out, who refuses the friends' packaged traditional answers, who searches and is searched, and whose passionate longing for God is fulfilled in ways that elude conceptual capture.

The book of Job is largely poetry, and I bring it into dialogue with Micheal O'Siadhail's testimony to the Holocaust in poetry, seeking resources for a post-Holocaust wisdom. This leads into one strand of Jewish post-Holocaust thinking and then into its Christian analogue. Christian wisdom in the twenty-first century needs to be sought within earshot of the cries of those who suffered and died in the Shoah; like the tradition of Job and his friends, Christian tradition today is radically tested by this trauma. How might it learn from Jewish post-Holocaust wisdom in seeking its own wisdom?

Such Christian wisdom unavoidably requires an account of Jesus Christ. Chapter 5, 'Jesus, the Spirit and desire: wisdom christology', offers this. It rereads Job, Luke and Acts asking how they might contribute to it, and supplements them with 1 Corinthians. The result is a conception of Jesus as teaching and embodying a prophetic wisdom that integrates law, history, prophecy, wisdom (in the narrower sense of a biblical genre) and praise. He represents a transformation of desire in orientation to God and the Kingdom of God, deeply resonant with Job's God-centred desire. The book of Job's post-traumatic wisdom illuminates the 'wisdom after multiple overwhelmings' distilled in Luke–Acts from crucifixion, resurrection and Pentecost. In 1 Corinthians the crucified and risen Jesus Christ is at the heart of a wisdom in the Spirit for a specific early Christian community. Paul challenges unbalanced understandings of this dynamic wisdom, wrestles with its relevance to other wisdoms, to scripture, to the relations of leaders with followers and to Christian maturity. Above all he portrays a wisdom embodied in lives, practices and communities through the continual improvising of life in the Spirit shaped according to 'the mind of Christ'.

In chapters 6 and 7, the largely scriptural exploration of wisdom in the first five chapters is worked through with reference first to tradition and worship (chapter 6) and second to the God who is loved for God's sake (chapter 7).

In chapter 6, 'Learning to live in the Spirit: tradition and worship', tradition is seen as at best a continual learning to live in the Spirit in the church, drawing from how others have lived in the Spirit. Like scripture, and in line with scripture's own wisdom about tradition, Christian tradition needs to be continually 'reread'.

Among the prime condensations and carriers of tradition is worship, at the centre of which is the identification of God as Trinity. Rather than laying out a doctrine of the Trinity (which would have meant at least another book) this chapter takes soundings on three crucial issues through contemporary thinkers who engage simultaneously with scripture, the classical Christian tradition on God, and modernity. Paul Ricoeur's treatment of being and God leads into a nuanced position on perennially conflictual issues: the Hebraic in relation to the Hellenic; theology in relation to philosophy; and the study of scripture in contexts of worship and of academic debate. Rowan Williams' examination of Arius and of the Council of Nicaea's affirmation of the full divinity of Jesus Christ opens up in a complexly historical way the wisdom of incarnation and its intrinsic relation to God as Trinity. He also offers a Christian theological account of tradition as the task of 're-imagining and recreating continuity at each point of crisis'. Sarah Coakley's scriptural, historical and theological rationale for the Holy Spirit as the third in the Trinity is rooted in Paul's cry-centred evocation of the wisdom of Christian prayer in Romans 8. She suggests how a life of participation in God through the Spirit not only makes deep sense of scripture and the classical Christian tradition but also can have the resources to thrive today, and to cope intellectually with historical, theological, philo- sophical, psychological and gender critiques.

The main thrust of chapter 7, 'Loving the God of wisdom', has already been mentioned above. It is where this book engages most with the traditional Christian dogmatic (or doctrinal or systematic or constructive) theology of God, represented here by Karl Barth. Alongside Barth is placed the distinctly untraditional discourse of Thomas Traherne, and both are drawn upon in seeking Christian wisdom on God. This is traced back through consideration of the five moods to their roots in cries. The wisdom theology of cries then reaches an exegetical crescendo through the book of Revelation, which leads into the conception of the church as a school of desire and wisdom. This also gives a brief historical survey of the precedents for conceiving 'theology as wisdom'.

Chapters 8–10 offer three case studies. Christian wisdom has to engage with other faiths and with secular forces and understanding, contribut- ing to public discussion and deliberation as well as to the teaching of its own communities. These studies seek wisdom in three engagements: between faiths, with universities, and through community with people who have severe learning difficulties.

The number of possible case studies is virtually limitless. These three are chosen partly because I have been involved with each over many years. They also exemplify three challenges to wisdom that are both perennial and also especially acute in the twenty-first century. As conflict related to religions threatens to destroy our world, how might particular faiths come together to draw on their resources for mutual understanding and peacemaking? As higher education expands enormously, as academic disciplines and their applications continue to transform the world, and as 'information age', 'learning society' and 'knowledge economy' become popular terms to describe the results, universities have become more important and at the same time face massive challenges. How might they be wisely shaped for the future? But in a world influenced so much by education, knowledge and know-how, what about those with learning disabilities – is there a wisdom to be learnt through them?

All three case studies draw Christian wisdom-seeking into engagements across the boundaries of its own traditions – although in fact those traditions have themselves already been formed by complex interplay with others from which an immense amount has been learnt. It is taken for granted that the twenty-first-century world is not simply religious or simply secular but complexly both, so that any faith community has to come to terms not only with other faith communities but also with a variety of institutions, understandings and forces that are non-religious or even anti-religious in key respects.[3] The case studies display different types of religious and secular engagements. Inter-faith wisdom-seeking is primarily about interrelating the traditions involved, yet all of these are also coping with secular realities. Universities in the contemporary world are primarily about secular disciplines but they have much to learn from the tradition of Christian wisdom in which they are rooted. The L'Arche communities for those with learning disabilities are complexly religious and secular, and their development and current challenges raise profound questions about how Christian wisdom is to be sought and realised today.

Chapter 8, 'An inter-faith wisdom: scriptural reasoning between Jews, Christians and Muslims', describes and reflects upon joint scriptural study between members of the Abrahamic traditions. This approach to inter-faith wisdom-seeking follows on appropriately after the largely scriptural exploration of earlier chapters. Its emphasis on interdisciplinary study and collegiality among the three faiths also prepares for chapter 9's consideration of universities. Scriptural reasoning is examined both as an interpretative practice and through its institutional location – closely related to the university and also to the religious 'houses' (synagogue, church and mosque) but not assimilable to either setting. It is also seen as having potential to contribute its wisdom to the

---

3. The terms 'religious' and 'secular' are of course subject to much debate and have no agreed meaning. I am using them in a common-sense way, 'religious' referring to the main traditions and communities usually called 'religions' (such as Judaism, Christianity, Islam, Hinduism, Buddhism, Sikhism), and 'secular' to those institutions, understandings and forces that would not identify themselves as religious in that sense. See David F. Ford, 'Faith and Universities in a Religious and Secular World (1)', *Svensk Teologisk Kvartalskrift* 81, no. 2 (2005), pp. 83–91, and 'Faith and Universities in a Religious and Secular World (2)', *Svensk Teologisk Kvartalskrift* 81, no. 3 (2005), pp. 97–106. Theologically, it is especially important not to allow any dualism of the religious and secular to imply that God is not the creator of both.

public sphere, which needs the best resources of the religious communities to help serve the common good.

Chapter 9, 'An interdisciplinary wisdom: knowledge, formation and collegiality in the negotiable university', sees universities as surprising institutions both in their origins and in the transformations represented by the universities of Berlin and Cambridge. Taking Berlin and Cambridge as the main reference points, six key challenges facing universities in the twenty-first century are described: the integration of teaching and research; all-round educational formation; collegiality; polity and control; contributions to society; and, above all, interdisciplinarity. The urgency and scope of these challenges, and the difficulty of coping with them all together, mean that contemporary world-class universities are in danger of failing to meet one or more of them. Universities are also increasingly involved in complex negotiations among diverse stakeholders which can seriously reduce their scope to transform themselves. Yet there is also the possibility of a new 'Berlin surprise', reinventing the university in a way that meets all the challenges. A seventh challenge is therefore to seek the wisdom needed to generate such a surprise, and to draw on the relevant sources – including academically mediated Christian wisdom.

Chapter 10, 'An interpersonal wisdom: L'Arche, learning disability and the Gospel of John', describes and reflects upon the world-wide network of L'Arche communities. They are seen as wisdom-seeking communities facing many fundamental issues of twenty-first-century life, concerning human identity and flourishing, dominant values, faith and faiths, the education of desire, bodiliness, growth and maturity, suffering, trauma, death, institutional governance, celebration and friendship. Elements of earlier chapters are recapitulated and integrated in relation to the prophetic wisdom represented by L'Arche, and in particular by its founder Jean Vanier. As Vanier withdraws from official responsibilities in L'Arche, his remarkable commentary on John's Gospel is taken as a culminating distillation of what he has learnt from the Bible, from L'Arche and from a range of religious and secular sources, offering a wisdom for generational transition. More comprehensively, he invites into a contemplative wisdom, 'the summit of love'.

The Conclusion, 'Love's wisdom', briefly recapitulates the book from the standpoint of love and then celebrates the wisdom of the Song of Songs' desire for love. The Song has been a rich resource for some of the dialogue partners of earlier chapters – Jean Vanier, Paul Ricoeur, Cheryl

Exum, Micheal O'Siadhail and Ellen Davis – and they draw the book to its final focus on the pure cry of lover to lover.

It should be clear from the above survey that this book makes no attempt to be comprehensive. The coverage of scripture, theological *loci*, Christian tradition and case studies is always by example rather than by exhaustive treatment. This inevitably has left many attractive roads untravelled. Several of those have, however, been explored in complementary companion volumes of the Cambridge Studies in Christian Doctrine. Paul Janz's epistemology deals with philosophical and theological questions about knowing in a way that is congenial to my position and in particular highlights the dynamics of desire.[4] At several junctures in the present book what is unwise or foolish, the negative side of wisdom, has been an issue, but has never been pursued to the point of developing it theologically into a doctrine of sin. Again the Cambridge series makes this less necessary because of Alistair McFadyen's perceptive study of sin,[5] which is similarly congenial to the present work. Another topic little explored is wisdom in relation to creation, a connection so prominent in the Bible. In the Cambridge series this is dealt with from different angles by Oliver Davies[6] and Jeremy Begbie.[7] Questions about history and eschatology have also surfaced repeatedly, owing to the conception of Christian wisdom as immersed in history and oriented towards God's future. Here the rich discussion by Ben Quash offers a convincing theological account of history through engagement with some modern theological and literary writers on the topic.[8]

As regards my earlier volume in the same series, *Self and Salvation: Being Transformed*,[9] the present work has from the beginning been conceived as its successor and complement. Wisdom might be seen as the cognitive

---

4. Paul D. Janz, *God, the Mind's Desire: Reference, Reason and Christian Thinking* (Cambridge: Cambridge University Press, 2004). The main reason for my resisting the strong temptation to follow up epistemological questions is because of the recent publication of the second edition of a co-authored treatment of the subject, David F. Ford and Daniel W. Hardy, *Living in Praise: Worshipping and Knowing God* (London: Darton, Longman and Todd, 2005), especially chapters 4 and 7 and the Epilogue.

5. Alistair McFadyen, *Bound to Sin: Abuse, Holocaust and the Christian Doctrine of Sin* (Cambridge: Cambridge University Press, 2000).

6. Oliver Davies, *The Creativity of God: World, Eucharist, Reason* (Cambridge: Cambridge University Press, 2004).

7. Jeremy S. Begbie, *Theology, Music and Time* (Cambridge: Cambridge University Press, 2000).

8. Ben Quash, *Theology and the Drama of History* (Cambridge: Cambridge University Press, 2005).

9. David F. Ford, *Self and Salvation: Being Transformed* (Cambridge: Cambridge University Press, 1999).

dimension inseparable from that book's concern with 'a hospitable self', 'a self without idols', 'a worshipping self', 'a singing self', 'a eucharistic self' and the particular selves of Jesus Christ, Thérèse of Lisieux and Dietrich Bonhoeffer. Pervading that book as well as this one is a fascination with the dynamics of transformation through involvement with God. Much that is only implicit in *Self and Salvation* is opened up in the chapters that follow: the wisdom interpretation of scripture; the interplay of desire, wisdom and love; 'for God's sake' at the heart of wisdom and worship; the approach to other faiths implied by the dialogue between Levinas, Jüngel and Ricoeur; the contemporary university setting within which such dialogues as well as significant aspects of the whole academic theological enterprise can be sustained; and the pervasive conception of theology as wisdom.

There is also a pedagogical point in a treatment through examples and maxims rather than systematic coverage. The hope is to arouse the desire for wisdom and give some guidance on how to search for it. The aim is therefore not so much to hand over a comprehensive package of wisdom as to draw the reader into seeking it in appropriate ways. The interpretation of a few passages of scripture together with some maxims and theses is meant to lead the reader into analogous interpretation of other passages. Likewise the few case studies might perhaps help to generate a similar approach to other topics.

Above all it is hoped that a reader might emerge from this book inspired to read and reread scripture and, with its help, to respond as wisely as possible to the cries of scripture and the cries of the world. If Christian wisdom is concerned to correspond thoughtfully, in many 'moods', to God and God's purposes, the desire for this needs to be aroused; the heart and imagination must be moved as well as the mind. Here the narrative and the poetry of scripture come into their own, together with the sort of prose exemplified by Thomas Traherne. Concepts and metaphors play off each other to evoke the desirability and riches of wisdom and the God of wisdom. The abundance of imagery and ideas flowing from close attention to scripture and to those who have responded to it most wisely create an environment in which the desire for wisdom may grow. Heart and mind are educated together and are stretched to engage passionately in their own search for wisdom. The messy particularities of the Bible and of life refuse to be neatly contained, and the wisdom that copes creatively with them never attains closure but is always alert, searching and desiring more and more of an infinite superabundance. Inseparable from this lavish ramification is a rigorous reserve and *askesis*, the disciplines of mind, heart and body dedicated to One who continually invites, blesses, amazes, challenges and loves. This is the life of theology as wisdom – theology in its most fundamental sense of the mind's desire and love for God and God's ways, inspired by God's Spirit.

1
_____

Wisdom cries

Prophetic scriptural wisdom is inextricably involved with the discernment of cries. This chapter opens up themes and ideas that will be taken up repeatedly in later chapters, such as the wisdom of reserve and ramification, immersion in history with orientation to God's future, the loud cry of Jesus from the cross, what the resurrection opens up, and the 'moods' of faith. These are pursued through the Gospel of Luke and the Acts of the Apostles in order to give an example of a wisdom interpretation of scripture of the sort that will be more reflectively described in the next chapter.[1] Above all the chapter is concerned to explore the significance of cries for Christian wisdom.

> Luke 7:18–35 [18]The disciples of John reported all these things to him. So John summoned two of his disciples [19]and sent them to the Lord to ask, 'Are you the one who is to come, or are we to wait for another?' [20]When the men had come to him, they said, 'John the Baptist has sent us to you to ask, "Are you the one who is to come, or are we to wait for another?"' [21]Jesus had just then cured many people of diseases, plagues, and evil spirits, and had given sight to many who were blind. [22]And he answered them, 'Go and tell John what you have seen and heard: the blind receive their sight, the lame walk, the lepers are cleansed, the deaf hear, the dead are raised, the poor have good news brought to them. [23]And blessed is anyone who takes no offence at me.'

1. Stephen C. Barton suggests that 'distinctive to Luke(–Acts) is a significant connection between the Spirit and wisdom'; in 'Gospel Wisdom' in *Where Shall Wisdom Be Found?*, ed. Stephen C. Barton (Edinburgh: T. & T. Clark, 1999), p. 102. Moreover, he continues that 'for the author of Luke–Acts, wisdom has to be understood eschatologically – that is, in relation to the Holy Spirit. For the coming of (John and) Jesus marks a decisive new stage in the history of salvation and therefore in the history of the revelation of what it means to be truly human, living as the people of God. This represents a distinctive, though not unprecedented understanding of wisdom: a wisdom understood as inspired by the Holy Spirit, taught by Jesus, and available in a remarkably inclusive way to all who become wisdom's children (see 7.35, 36–50)'; ibid. p. 104 [footnotes excised].

²⁴When John's messengers had gone, Jesus began to speak to the crowds about John: 'What did you go out into the wilderness to look at? A reed shaken by the wind? ²⁵What then did you go out to see? Someone dressed in soft robes? Look, those who put on fine clothing and live in luxury are in royal palaces. ²⁶What then did you go out to see? A prophet? Yes, I tell you, and more than a prophet. ²⁷This is the one about whom it is written, "See, I am sending my messenger ahead of you, who will prepare your way before you." ²⁸I tell you, among those born of women no one is greater than John; yet the least in the kingdom of God is greater than he.' ²⁹(And all the people who heard this, including the tax collectors, acknowledged the justice of God, because they had been baptised with John's baptism. ³⁰But by refusing to be baptised by him, the Pharisees and the lawyers rejected God's purpose for themselves.) ³¹'To what then will I compare the people of this generation, and what are they like? ³²They are like children sitting in the marketplace and calling to one another, "We played the flute for you, and you did not dance; we wailed, and you did not weep." ³³For John the Baptist has come eating no bread and drinking no wine, and you say, "He has a demon"; ³⁴the Son of Man has come eating and drinking, and you say, "Look, a glutton and a drunkard, a friend of tax collectors and sinners!" ³⁵Nevertheless, wisdom is vindicated by all her children.'

Jesus, child of wisdom

καὶ ἐδικαιώθη ἡ σοφία ἀπὸ πάντων τῶν τέκνων αὐτῆς
Wisdom is vindicated (or justified) by all her children.

Wisdom is a mother with many children, and Jesus suggests that he himself is one of them. He is talking here to the crowds about John the Baptist, and identifies him too as a child of wisdom. The 'all' implies there are many more in the family. The context stresses the diversity of the children and how hard it can be to see the family likeness: John came 'eating no bread and drinking no wine'; Jesus came 'eating and drinking'; neither was recognised as wise. Yet the difference between them goes deeper than John's ascetic, desert lifestyle versus Jesus' friendship with the tax collectors and sinners, with whom it is hard to imagine John being close.[2] The question John's disciples had asked earlier was whether

2. See G. B. Caird, *Saint Luke* (London: Penguin Books, 1990), p. 112: '[John] must have heard that Jesus was keeping company with the very "*chaff*" on whom he had called down the fire of God.'

Jesus was 'the one who is to come', the Messiah John had taught them to expect. The issue is the shape of history and God's involvement in it. Wisdom is immersed in history and at the same time oriented towards its fulfilment. God desires the discerning action that responds to John's prophetic call to repentance by coming to be baptised. Those who did this '**justified God**' (7:29 – the verb is the same as in v.35), acknowledging God's purpose and moving within it. Those who refused it '**rejected God's purpose for themselves**' (7:30 – the word for purpose, βουλή, is closely connected with wise counsel[3]). But the baptism of John was itself an orientation to 'the one who is to come', opening up to something more. John's prophetic wisdom was to play his particular role in the drama and summon others into their roles.

John the Baptist's purpose right from the start is associated with wisdom, turning '**the disobedient to the wisdom of the righteous**' (Luke 1:17). Even more, Jesus from boyhood was '**filled with wisdom**', amazed the teachers in the temple with his understanding, and '**increased in wisdom**' (Luke 2:40, 47, 52). Luke's opening chapters resound with cries at the overwhelming significance of these two children.

> Luke 1:41–45 [41]When Elizabeth heard Mary's greeting, the child leaped in her womb. And Elizabeth was filled with the Holy Spirit [42]and exclaimed with a loud cry, 'Blessed are you among women, and blessed is the fruit of your womb. [43]And why has this happened to me, that the mother of my Lord comes to me? [44]For as soon as I heard the sound of your greeting, the child in my womb leaped for joy. [45]And blessed is she who believed that there would be a fulfilment of what was spoken to her by the Lord.'

The cry of blessing is fundamental to wise discernment. Whom to bless, what to bless, and when, how and whether to bless are questions whose answers are rooted in core conceptions of God and God's purposes. John's father Zechariah is also filled with the Holy Spirit when he has named John, and his first words after months of silence are: '**Blessed be the God of Israel …**' (Luke 1:68).

Mary's response to Elizabeth's blessing is, like Zechariah's, to bless and praise God: '**My soul magnifies the Lord, and my spirit rejoices in God my saviour …**' (Luke 1:46–47). The main content of both her 'Magnificat' and Zechariah's 'Benedictus' is God's activity in history and the present.

---

3. In the Greek translation of the Hebrew scriptures, the Septuagint (which was Luke's Bible), it is especially common in the wisdom literature.

When Jesus is born the cries are taken up by the angels' praise: **'Glory to God in the highest heaven ...'** (Luke 2:14), and the praise and blessing surrounding his birth is completed by the aged Simeon and Anna. The final, summary sentence of Luke's chapters on the birth and childhood of Jesus is: **'And Jesus increased in wisdom and in years, and in divine and human favour'** (Luke 2:52). So the one who has grown in wisdom comes to John. The people are **'filled with expectation'** and **'questioning in their hearts'** about John's role, and he responds that, while he baptises with water, **'one who is more powerful than I is coming'** who **'will baptise you with the Holy Spirit and fire'** (Luke 3:15ff).

The differentiation is then acted out in Jesus' baptism. There the 'divine favour' is revealed:

> Luke 3:21–22 [21]Now when all the people had been baptised, and when Jesus also had been baptised and was praying, the heaven was opened, [22]and the Holy Spirit descended upon him in bodily form like a dove. And a voice came from heaven, 'You are my Son, the Beloved; with you I am well pleased.'

The one who has grown in wisdom is the beloved (ἀγαπητός), the Son of God, and the Holy Spirit comes upon him in an apocalyptic, heaven-opening event as he is praying.

Then, **'full of the Holy Spirit'** Jesus is **'led by the Spirit into the wilderness'** and tempted for forty days. The core of his identity and vocation as Son of God is the key issue: **'If you are the Son of God ...'** (Luke 4:3, 9). The touchstone of his Spirit-inspired wisdom is clear in each temptation:

> Luke 4:4 Jesus answered him, 'It is written, "One does not live by bread alone."'
>
> 4:8 Jesus answered him, 'It is written, "Worship the Lord your God, and serve only him."'
>
> 4:12 Jesus answered him, 'It is said, "Do not put the Lord your God to the test."'

The Spirit leads him through scripture.

Immediately after the temptations Jesus, **'filled with the power of the Spirit'**, begins to teach in the synagogues, and eventually in his home synagogue at Nazareth. There the whole focus is on the fulfilment of a passage from Isaiah, Luke 4:18–19.[4]

---

4. Though interestingly we are not told that he actually read it, only that he unrolled the scroll and found the place where it was written.

> Luke 4:18–19 [18]'The Spirit of the Lord is upon me,
> because he has anointed me
> to bring the good news to the poor.
> He has sent me to proclaim release to the captives
> and recovery of sight to the blind,
> to let the oppressed go free,
> [19]to proclaim the year of the Lord's favour.'

This is like a working out of the phrase used by John the Baptist's father Zechariah earlier in Luke's Gospel, about the one to come being like the breaking of dawn from on high through 'the compassionate mercy of our God' (διὰ σπλάγχνα ἐλέους θεοῦ ἡμῶν, Luke 1:78).

This compassionate action is at the centre of the passage with which this chapter began, when John's disciples come to Jesus asking whether he is the one they are waiting for. Jesus replies by healing many people and saying:

> Luke 7:22–23 'Go and tell John what you have seen and heard: the blind receive their sight, the lame walk, the lepers are cleansed, the deaf hear, the dead are raised, the poor have good news brought to them. And blessed (μακάριος) is anyone who takes no offence (μὴ σκανδαλισθῇ) at me.'

The message for John is testimony shaped through scripture. It also uses the categories of blessedness and offence. For anyone who hears this testimony what is at stake is their blessedness, their being in the state that God most desires them to be in and that is in fact most desirable. But the terrible danger is that they will be offended, 'scandalised' – that they will find Jesus provokes uncomprehending, gut-level rejection, because he does not fit what is acceptable or expected. These are the stakes in the drama of God's prophetic wisdom.

Cries and discernment

After John's disciples have left, Jesus speaks of both John and himself in ways that press his hearers to stretch their categories and their expectations. It is an exercise in imaginative teaching. There is imagery from the desert, the court and the marketplace. The final picture is of groups of children calling to one another in the marketplace, not able to agree on whether to play at weddings or funerals: **'We played the flute for you,**

and you did not dance; we wailed, and you did not weep' (Luke 7:32). It is a scene of cry and counter-cry in a setting of many other voices. This confusion of cries is like the responses to John and Jesus: neither the call to a change of mind, heart and behaviour nor the good news of a feast-centred Kingdom of God meets the expectations of this generation. So how are these two of wisdom's children vindicated in their mould-breaking activities? One way of exploring this is through focussing on those moments of great intensity when cries, shouts, acclamations, passionate appeals, praises and blessings punctuate Luke's story.[5] *Discernment of cries and crying out with discernment are near to the heart of the meaning of a prophetic wisdom that is involved in history and oriented to God and God's future.*

What is the difference between something said and something cried out? There is obviously no general answer, but in the cries discussed below it is worth bearing in mind what they might mean both for those who cry out and for the content of the message. For the crier the act expresses a profound relationship to what is said. The speaker and the message are powerfully identified with each other. As for the content that is cried out, rather than just spoken, it is highlighted, amplified. It is a sign of the limits of speech, a gesture towards the inadequacy of any words to this content, an indication of the superlative, of breaking the bounds of terms and categories, of transcendence. So it is unsurprising that cries are often associated with address to God – in blessing, praise, thanks, complaint, repentance, petition and sheer joy.

Luke's cry-centred acclamation of John and Jesus in his first two chapters is matched in the third and fourth by the opening of their ministries. John is **'the voice of one crying in the wilderness'** (Luke 3:4), and Luke gives examples of the basic ethical teaching that turned **'the disobedient to ... wisdom'** (Luke 1:17). When Jesus appears the first voice comes with the Holy Spirit **'from heaven'** proclaiming him as Son and Beloved of God (Luke 3:22). In the testing of that identity immediately afterwards, the pressure of temptation repeatedly drives him back to the scriptures for a wisdom that is centred on God; then in his teaching in Nazareth the scripture from Isaiah defines his purpose as centred on the needs of the poor, captives, the blind and the oppressed. These two sets of scriptures unite the orientation to God and to suffering humanity. The wisdom that is embodied here is simultaneously one that hears God's voice (the cry at the heart of

---

5. Not only of Luke's story, of course, but for the sake of simplicity I will concentrate mainly on Luke.

Jewish daily life is God's: '**Hear, O Israel! The Lord your God is one Lord, and you shall love the Lord your God …**' (Deut. 6:4–5)) and worships God, and that hears the cries of the suffering and brings good news to them.

The manifesto from Isaiah echoes through the rest of Luke's Gospel. *If Jesus embodies wisdom, then wisdom is vitally concerned to hear and respond with compassion to the cries of those who are suffering.* The 'cries' are of many sorts: shouting and shrieking demons, a weeping bereaved mother, the hidden sin of a paralysed man, a weeping woman 'sinner', the hunger of a crowd, the touch of a woman with haemorrhages, the beaten and robbed man lying half dead on the Jericho Road, the Prodigal Son in his father's embrace saying '**Father, I have sinned …**', and lepers and blind men shouting '**Have mercy!**'

Alongside the cries of the suffering are cries of amazement, gratitude, praise, blessing, celebration and joy. The culmination of these is the acclamation of Jesus entering Jerusalem, when '**the whole multitude of the disciples began to praise God joyfully with a loud voice for all the deeds of power that they had seen**' (Luke 19:37).

That is on the verge of the climax of the story in the crucifixion, with Jesus' own 'loud cry', which will be discussed below. But first we need to consider perhaps the most significant of Jesus' own cries with a direct reference to wisdom.

Hidden from the wise, revealed to infants

The setting of Luke 10:21–24 is the return of seventy of Jesus' disciples from a mission to the places he was going to visit. They return with joy at their success. Jesus rejoices with them, celebrates the authority they have been exercising, but also says: '**Nevertheless, do not rejoice in this, that the spirits submit to you, but rejoice that your names are written in heaven**' (Luke 10:20). Jesus is teaching discernment in rejoicing. What is the deepest joy? Where does the cry of joy spring from?

> Luke 10:21–24 [21]At that same hour Jesus rejoiced in the Holy Spirit and said, 'I thank you, Father, Lord of heaven and earth, because you have hidden these things from the wise and the intelligent and have revealed them to infants; yes, Father, for such was your gracious will. [22]All things have been handed over to me by my Father; and no one knows who the Son is except the Father, or who the Father is except the Son and anyone to whom the Son chooses to reveal him.' [23]Then turning to the disciples, Jesus said to them privately, 'Blessed are the

eyes that see what you see! [24]For I tell you that many prophets and kings desired to see what you see, but did not see it, and to hear what you hear, but did not hear it.'

He is about to perform the answer to these questions (vv.21–22). For now the message is that there is nothing wrong in achievement and success in the name of Jesus, but to have their names written in heaven is the one thing necessary. It is about their core identity being rooted in God and God's recognition. Jesus' own core identity had been affirmed in his baptism, and in vv.21–22 there are several reminders of that (the Holy Spirit, the Father, heaven, and the 'gracious will', another form of the word rendered as 'well pleased' in Luke 3:22).

Then comes Jesus' own cry of exultation – the word for 'rejoiced' in v.21, ἠγαλλιάσατο, is stronger than the χαίρετε in v.20, and is frequently used in the Psalms.[6] It is rare for Jesus (especially in the Synoptic Gospels[7]) to address his Father directly and intimately like this, and 'in the Holy Spirit' underlines its significance. The form, the language and the content all point to the pivotal nature of the statement. I have already commented on the baptismal echoes; some of those are also present in the climactic affirmation of Jesus by his Father in the story of the transfiguration in the previous chapter (Luke 9:28–36). It is as if the inner meaning of those two critical events, his baptism and transfiguration, is given here in Jesus' exultation; and it can also be linked forwards to him crying out to his Father in Gethsemane and on the cross. Add to this the reference to wisdom and it is clear that there is great potential (as well as difficulty) in these verses for our theme.[8]

The naming of God as 'Father' (five times in these two verses) and 'Lord of heaven and earth' combines intimacy of relationship with universal scope in a way reminiscent of the Prologue of John's Gospel. But also as in John the primary orientation (as vv.23–24 bear out) is neither to interiority nor to the cosmos but to God's purposes being worked out in history.

6. It is sometimes used with special force in conjunction with the strong verb here used for thanks, ἐξομολογοῦμαι. See LXX Psalm 9:2–3.
7. Luke 10:22 (par. Matt. 11:27) is sometimes called the 'Johannine thunderbolt' in the Synoptic sky. It is almost as if sections of John's Gospel are Christian midrashic developments of this rich and mysterious saying.
8. I. Howard Marshall writes in this connection that 'The background of the sayings has been increasingly recognised in recent years as lying in Jewish thinking about wisdom. Divine wisdom is entrusted with the secrets of God and reveals them to men; she is rejected by the mass of men, especially the wise, but is accepted by the poor and unlearned', in *The Gospel of Luke: A Commentary on the Greek Text*, New International Greek Testament Commentary (Exeter: Paternoster, 1978), p. 432.

Then Jesus thanks God '**because you have hidden these things from the wise and intelligent and have revealed them to infants**' (Luke 10:21).[9] How might being hidden from the wise be meant? In the context of Luke's Gospel it is clearly not a complete rejection of wisdom – as we have seen, both Jesus and John are strongly linked with wisdom, and in Jesus' case this will be reinforced in Luke 11 in a passage to be discussed below.[10]

What are 'these things'? The most likely reference is to what Jesus goes on to say in v.22: that all things have been handed over to him by his Father, that only the Father knows who the Son is, and that who the Father is is known only to the Son and to whomever the Son decides to reveal him. This verse will be considered further in due course, but for now it is clear that 'these things' are not likely to be learnt through normal methods of education or investigation. This is 'who' knowledge, deeply personal understanding that is dependent on trust and other qualities of relationship. It is about mutuality and the free self-revelation in reciprocity that can happen in personal interaction. Further, it is about something new, a handing over of all things that, when worked out in history, leads to unprecedented things being seen and heard (see vv.23–24). So it is not just a matter of personal knowledge; it is also about novelty and surprise of a sort to which those who know the past well are likely to be closed or even hostile. Anyone who thinks they have intelligently assessed reality based on the past is likely to find it hard to accommodate such novelty.

Yet these considerations are still not adequate. This verse is not just about persons and history but about God. God is actually being thanked for hiding these things from the wise and intelligent and revealing them to infants. It may even be paradoxical to use wisdom and intelligence to try to make sense of this! But let us take the two positive points: on the one hand, God, who is both Father and unimaginably and incomprehensibly glorious as Creator and Lord of heaven and earth (as portrayed in the Psalms that Jesus liked to quote); and, on the other hand, infants.

---

9. This sharp rejection of the importance and capacity of wisdom and intelligence in relation to God and God's ways has similarities with Paul in 1 Corinthians – 'God chose what is foolish in the world to shame the wise' (1 Cor. 1:27). The latter will be discussed at length in chapter 5 below.

10. For John Nolland, '"wise and understanding" here has no automatically negative overtones; the overtone only becomes negative at the point where the wisdom of "the wise and understanding" will not subordinate itself to the revelation of the divine wisdom', in *Luke 9:21–18:34*, Word Biblical Commentary (Dallas: Word, 1993), p. 572.

Why might it be appropriate for this Father and Creator to reveal these things to infants? They are utterly dependent on what they are given, and so the sheer gift character of God's self-revelation is clearest with them; they are in the most direct relationship with parents; and they are 'all cry' – in relation to this particular knowledge the right human approach is simply wholehearted crying out and then receiving what is given. In the Septuagint, the Psalms speak of praise being shaped out of the mouths of babies and infants (LXX Ps. 8:2) and of the faithful testimony of the Lord making infants wise (σοφίζουσα νήπια, LXX Ps. 18:8). This was a figure of speech in Jesus' and Luke's scriptures, and one with rich possibilities for those who are not infants (and even those with some wisdom and intelligence!) to meditate upon. And any over-literal interpretation is forbidden by the context, where those who might be seen as having had these things revealed to them (apart from Jesus himself) are the disciples, who are not infants, and have been given adult authority.

On the negative side, why might it be appropriate for God to hide these things from the wise and intelligent? The common-sense interpretation is that they are always inclined to rely on their acquired wisdom and their intellectual abilities, and that these can act as a block to receiving something as uncontainable in human categories and faculties as God's fatherly love and divine glory, not to mention the dynamic of reciprocity between the Father, the Son and those who participate in their intimacy. Without being negative about wisdom or intelligence (which Luke certainly is not), it is possible to see the ways in which received wisdom and intellectual formation are likely to offer resistance to the Gospel. Yet it is exactly this that questions the common-sense interpretation, for all its obvious truth. Jesus' exultation requires something further to justify it, and his emphatic addition, '**Yes, Father, for such was your gracious will**', makes us search deeper into that εὐδοκία, the 'good pleasure' of God – what delights God's heart.

This is a difficult text. It is not alone, even on the topic of God confounding the wisdom of the wise (see Isaiah 29:14) or deliberately hiding things from people (see Luke 10:21). But why should God hide what is most important from those who partake of wisdom, which is praised and valued as a gift of God throughout scripture? One obvious answer is that 'human wisdom' is distinguished from the wisdom given by God.[11]

---

11. This is explored further below, in discussing Job in chapters 3 and 4, and 1 Corinthians in chapter 5.

That can take us some way, and is implied in some of the points already made. The good can be enemy of the best, and there is something so radical, comprehensive and all-transforming about the knowledge and love of God that whatever we already know and love can seem more like a hindrance than a help: *the fresh start of infancy seems the only proper analogy.* It may be that we will come to reaffirm some of the wisdom we had before, but it could never have acted as a way into this knowledge of God, and its limitations might well be seen as 'hiding' God.

But none of this grasps the nettle, which is God's active hiding and the particular choosing of his 'gracious will'. We are here at the heart of a biblical theme that is fundamental, inexhaustibly puzzling, and continues to generate profound and apparently irreconcilable controversy. Any wisdom cannot claim to be Christian that has not wrestled with it. When the 'infants' to whom 'these things' have been revealed grow up[12] they have to face it. It runs right through the Bible – Cain and Abel, Noah and those who drowned in the flood, Abraham and his people chosen out of all the nations, Jacob and Esau, Joseph and his brothers, the hardening of Pharaoh's heart, the Israelite houses with the blood of the lamb and the Egyptian houses with dead firstborn, the people of Israel and the peoples of Canaan, Job's passionate sense of injustice before God – and so on up to Jesus and Judas Iscariot, and Paul's anguished grappling with the election and rejection of Israel in Romans 9–11. It also runs through Luke's Gospel, especially in the form of reversals, and is particularly celebrated in his opening chapters and at the conclusion of Acts.

The differences in the cases mentioned are as significant as what they have in common, but there is never a conceptual resolution of the difficulties surrounding God's willing and choosing. The difficulties are conserved and become the material for fresh discernment. In many ways the difficulties are intensified with Jesus, as his final statement to John's messengers suggests: '**And blessed is anyone who takes no offence at me**' (Luke 7:23). Jesus himself is at a crucial juncture as he exults in the Holy Spirit in Luke 10:21–22. On the mountain of his transfiguration he had spoken with Moses and Elijah about '**his departure** (ἔξοδος), **which he was about to accomplish at Jerusalem**' (Luke 9:30); then he had '**set his face to go up to Jerusalem**' (Luke 9:51). The

---

12. This may, however, be applying too literal a meaning to infancy here: it is probably better understood as a permanent state in relation to God, a 'fresh start' day by day and minute by minute.

unfolding of that purpose, doing the will of God to the point of death, is the subject of the rest of the Gospel. But here we have a rare glimpse through the words of Jesus of the inner meaning of God's will.

There are at least three key elements in this meaning. The first, as already discussed, is that, in analogy with a long line of mysterious, provocative discriminations and reversals, it is hidden from the wise and revealed to infants.

The second is that '**all things have been handed over to me by my Father**' (v.22a). Because of the language of knowledge that follows, it is tempting to interpret this as handing on knowledge, but 'handing over' (which is elsewhere used by Luke for passing on the Gospel, granting authority, betraying, and handing over people to authorities) combined with 'all things' has a broader sense and here might best be understood with reference to authority and responsibility, above all for the Kingdom of God. It correlates with Jesus in turn passing on responsibility to his disciples at the Last Supper: '**I confer on you, just as my Father has conferred on me, a kingdom ...**' (Luke 22:29). It is hard to imagine a more radical or comprehensive sense of responsibility.

The third brings us to the spring from which the exultation comes: the reciprocal knowing of Father and Son. *The uniting of joy, responsibility, and the intimate knowing of love centred on full recognition of the other, is simultaneously the source of the cry of rejoicing and the content of divine wisdom.* Sharon Ringe comments on this verse:

> In language that echoes both the style and content of the Gospel of John (see, for example, John 3:31–36; 5:19–38; 17:2–9) Jesus affirms his position as mediator between God and the disciples (Luke 10:22). Jesus' affirmation of this role places him in the tradition of Wisdom or *Sophia* as an expression of God's own reality (Job 28:12–28; Prov. 8:22–36), which is taken up and adapted in the hymn to the Word or *Logos* in John 1:1–18.[13]

There will be more to say in later chapters about Jesus as the wisdom of God, and about the conception of God as Trinity that developed over time. In the present context of Luke's Gospel it is important both to appreciate the extraordinary importance of this passage for the wisdom interpretation of the Gospel and also to follow the theme of wisdom through to the following and subsequent chapters and finally into the Acts of the Apostles.

---

13. Sharon H. Ringe, *Luke* (Louisville, KY: Westminster John Knox Press, 1995), p. 155.

Something greater than Solomon

The cry of the woman to Jesus blessing his mother in Luke 11:27 is responded to by Jesus with an alternative blessing on those who hear the word of God and obey it.

> Luke 11:27–32 [27]While he was saying this, a woman in the crowd raised her voice and said to him, 'Blessed is the womb that bore you and the breasts that nursed you!' [28]But he said, 'Blessed rather are those who hear the word of God and obey it!' [29]When the crowds were increasing, he began to say, 'This generation is an evil generation; it asks for a sign, but no sign will be given to it except the sign of Jonah. [30]For just as Jonah became a sign to the people of Nineveh, so the Son of Man will be to this generation. [31]The queen of the South will rise at the judgement with the people of this generation and condemn them, because she came from the ends of the earth to listen to the wisdom of Solomon, and see, something greater than Solomon is here! [32]The people of Nineveh will rise up at the judgement with this generation and condemn it, because they repented at the proclamation of Jonah, and see, something greater than Jonah is here!'

He has turned her cry into something like a proverb, and it is placed before the following verses about those who hear and do not hear. It is perhaps not surprising that Jonah should be used here: he, like Jesus, delivered a specific message to the people of his time calling for radical response. Luke seems to interpret the 'sign of Jonah' as his proclamation (v.32).

The surprise is v.31 about the queen of the South and Solomon. The word of prophecy of Jonah is juxtaposed with the word of wisdom of Solomon. The Ninevites listening to Jonah the prophet are alongside the Queen of Sheba listening to Solomon.[14]

This greatly expands the horizon of the word of God that is at issue here, culminating in Jesus' exclamatory statement: **'see, something greater than Solomon is here!'** This verse might generate a whole set of maxims.

---

14. Joseph A. Fitzmyer observes that 'By putting the saying about the Queen of the South before that about the Ninevites, Luke enhances the warning with a wisdom-motif. In not heeding Jesus' preaching, the men of his generation have failed to recognize the heaven-sent wisdom which he has come to preach', in *The Gospel According to Luke (X–XXIV)*, The Anchor Bible (New York: Doubleday, 1985), p. 933.

- Let your conception of wisdom be formed by considering Jesus in relationship with Solomon, and meditate on the nature of wisdom, kingship and being 'son of David'.
- Therefore pay attention to Jesus' wisdom sayings (as in Luke 12 immediately after this, where Solomon is again referred to); but also pay attention to Solomon's – Jesus may be greater, but Solomon is also great.
- Remember Jonah as well as Solomon, and let your wisdom be prophetic and your prophecy wise.
- Desire wisdom passionately like the queen, seek it wherever it may be found, and be willing to travel to the ends of the earth to find it.
- Learn from the queen, be open to learning from others like her who come from the ends of the earth, way beyond your usual horizons.
- The queen is not likely to be the only witness at the judgement to accuse you of failing to attend to wisdom: think who the other witnesses down the centuries might be, then try to learn what they learnt – above all what they learnt about Jesus, but also, like Solomon, about the cosmos, nature, family, society, ethics, politics, economics, education, God and love.

That last word suggests a final thought about Solomon's reputation as a lover, the ascription of the Song of Songs to him, and the legends about the love between him and the Queen of Sheba. Of all the Solomonic literature it is the Song that has evoked the most voluminous response to Jesus and Solomon together, and its wisdom of love will appear at the culmination of this book.

Crying out in teaching, prophecy and narrative testimony: Jesus goes to Jerusalem

Solomon's wisdom and Jonah's prophecy are helpful categories for appreciating the second half of Luke's Gospel as Jesus approaches and enters Jerusalem, and they have the advantage of being given by Luke in the words of Jesus. A third key category is narrative testimony, in line with Luke's preface:

> Luke 1:1–4 [1]Since many have undertaken to set down an orderly account of the events that have been fulfilled among us, [2]just as they were handed on to us by those who from the beginning were eyewitnesses and servants of the word, [3]I too decided, after investigating everything carefully from the very first, to write an orderly account for you, most

excellent Theophilus, [4]so that you may know the truth concerning the things about which you have been instructed.

Narrative is the embracing genre, and it comes into its own in the final chapters after Jesus has entered Jerusalem.

The Solomonic strand runs through these chapters in the various types of teaching. There are several parables, including some as part of Jesus' table talk. There are radical wisdom sayings about such things as hypocrisy, greed, providence, food and clothing, faith, discipleship on the way of the cross, prayer, humility, alertness and greatness. The Kingdom of God is overall the main theme, and the teaching often climaxes in cries.

> Luke 11:40 'You fools! Did not the one who made the outside make the inside also?'
> Luke 12:20–21 [20]'But God said to him, "You fool! This very night your life is being demanded of you. And the things you have prepared, whose will they be?" [21]So it is with those who store up treasures for themselves but are not rich towards God.'
> Luke 15:6 'And when he comes home, he calls together his friends and neighbours, saying to them, "Rejoice with me, for I have found my sheep that was lost."'
>   15:9 '"Rejoice with me, for I have found the coin that I had lost."'
>   15:23–24 [23]'"And get the fatted calf and kill it, and let us eat and celebrate; [24]for this son of mine was dead and is alive again; he was lost and is found!"'

Prophetic proclamation and confrontation also occur repeatedly. There are the cries of 'Woe!' to the Pharisees and lawyers (Luke 11:42–52), and of **'You hypocrites!'** to the crowds (Luke 12:56). Jonah-like, he calls to repentance in comment on a recent disaster (Luke 13:1–5). He laments and prophesies over Jerusalem:

> Luke 13:34–35 [34]'Jerusalem, Jerusalem, the city that kills the prophets and stones those who are sent to it! How often have I desired to gather your children together as a hen gathers her brood under her wings, and you were not willing! [35]See, your house is left to you. And I tell you, you will not see me until the time comes when you say, "Blessed is the one who comes in the name of the Lord."'

There is apocalyptic prophecy (Luke 17:22–37; 21:5–33), he foretells his own death and resurrection (Luke 18:31–34), he weeps over Jerusalem and prophesies its fall (Luke 19:41–44), and there is a series of what might be seen as prophetic acts: healings, eating with Zacchaeus the chief tax collector, and driving out the people selling things in the Temple.

Teaching and prophecy are of course often mixed together and they are in any case overlapping categories. One striking passage is in the middle of denouncing the lawyers:

> Luke 11:49–52 [49]Therefore also the Wisdom of God said, 'I will send them prophets and apostles, some of whom they will kill and persecute', [50]so that this generation may be charged with the blood of all the prophets shed since the foundation of the world, [51]from the blood of Abel to the blood of Zechariah, who perished between the altar and the sanctuary. Yes, I tell you, it will be charged against this generation. [52]Woe to you lawyers! For you have taken away the key of knowledge; you did not enter yourselves, and you hindered those who were entering."

This comes as part of an attack that comprehensively indicts the lawyers by appealing to Torah, the prophets and the wisdom writings, thus covering the whole of scripture. In v.52 'the lawyers are charged with removing access to Wisdom's "house" (Prov. 9:1), especially in the form of the salvation of God'.[15] Above all, wisdom and prophecy come together inextricably in the Kingdom of God. That is prophetically proclaimed and enacted, and the quality of its life is largely given in wisdom terms. This is prophecy with a horizon of 'all things', and radical wisdom with the urgency of prophecy. But for all the intensity, expressed most vehemently in cries of Woe! Fools! Repent! Rejoice! Jerusalem, Jerusalem!, there is a further vital dimension – indeed the central one. This is the person of Jesus, 'greater than Solomon', 'greater than Jonah'.

Jesus' proclamation and enactment of the Kingdom of God in word and deed is from the start inseparable from who he is. The opening chapters celebrate him as **'the Son of the Most High'**, occupier of **'the throne of his ancestor David'** (1:32), and **'a Saviour who is the Messiah, the Lord'** (2:11). At his baptism and transfiguration he is affirmed by God as his Son and, as I have suggested above, the inner meaning of that is given in his exultation in 10:21–22, centring on who the Father and the Son are. Immediately before the transfiguration is Peter's confession of Jesus as **'the Messiah of God'** (9:20).

---

15. Ringe, *Luke*, p. 175.

Yet perhaps more important than these verbal affirmations and titles is the narrative testimony of which they are a part. The message of the Kingdom of God and its realisation in teaching, signs and actions is presented together with his suffering, death and resurrection (and with varied responses to all these) in a way that makes the person of Jesus utterly central. The end of the Gospel leaves no doubt about this. Intrinsic to the message is the fate of Jesus who brings it. All four Gospels show this, and the deep structure of their common message is seen in the ministry, death and resurrection of Jesus being testimony to him as living Lord.[16] Their way of achieving this is perceptively analysed by Hans Frei, with a special emphasis on Luke.

Frei describes a three-stage unfolding of who Jesus is. The birth and infancy narratives identify him largely in relation to the people of Israel as a stylised, representative figure. From his baptism he emerges as an individual defined primarily in relation to the Kingdom of God. As he enters Jerusalem the Kingdom of God and its associated titles become less definitive, and are even ironised, and then the story

> beginning with Jesus' arrest, starts to accelerate into an increasingly terse and spare climactic telling, proceeding virtually unimpeded by any didactic material in its final stages. The focus of the story remains on the action by which Jesus' destiny is accomplished, and on Jesus himself as the unsubstitutable person he is. He is shown as an unsubstitutable individual in his own right, his unadorned singularity focussed on both his passion and his resurrection.[17]

Again the cries are indicators of this culminating focus on Jesus himself. As he enters Jerusalem there is the final positive acclamation by his disciples of him as king:

> Luke 19:36–40 [36]As he rode along, people kept spreading their cloaks on the road. [37]As he was now approaching the path down from the Mount of Olives, the whole multitude of the disciples began to praise God joyfully with a loud voice for all the deeds of power that they had seen, [38]saying, 'Blessed is the king who comes in the name of the Lord! Peace in heaven, and glory in the highest heaven!' [39]Some of the Pharisees in

16. David F. Ford, *Self and Salvation: Being Transformed* (Cambridge: Cambridge University Press, 2005), especially pp. 192–3 and 202–9.
17. Hans W. Frei, *The Identity of Jesus Christ: The Hermeneutical Bases of Dogmatic Theology* (Philadelphia: Fortress Press, 1975), p. 135. Frei's treatment of myth, fiction and historical reliability in relation to the Gospels and their ways of portraying the identity of Jesus could be used as a rationale to support the sort of interpretation done in this chapter.

the crowd said to him, 'Teacher, order your disciples to stop.' [40]He
answered, 'I tell you, if these were silent, the stones would shout out.'

This remarkable acceptance of the blessing is followed by weeping over
Jerusalem's inability to recognise him, by cleansing the Temple, and by a
final round of controversy and teaching (including warning about those
who come in his name saying 'I am He!').

From Last Supper to death: wisdom and history

Then comes the Last Supper where the three elements of teaching,
prophecy and narrative come together again, with this 'unsubstitutable
person' at the point of convergence. It is a narrative testimony that moves
the plot forward towards its climax and does so by culminating his
prophecy and his teaching of the Kingdom of God with reference to
Jesus himself. The sharing of the bread as his body and the wine as his
blood can be seen as a prophetic drama;[18] it is closely linked to his 'woe!'
on his betrayer, is later followed by the prophecy of Peter's denial of him,
and finally by instructions to his disciples with the support of a verse of
scripture that 'must be fulfilled in me' (22:37).

> Luke 22:14–27 [14]When the hour came, he took his place at the table, and
> the apostles with him. [15]He said to them, 'I have eagerly desired to eat
> this Passover with you before I suffer; [16]for I tell you, I will not eat it
> until it is fulfilled in the kingdom of God.' [17]Then he took a cup, and
> after giving thanks he said, 'Take this and divide it among yourselves;
> [18]for I tell you that from now on I will not drink of the fruit of the vine
> until the kingdom of God comes.' [19]Then he took a loaf of bread, and
> when he had given thanks, he broke it and gave it to them, saying, 'This
> is my body, which is given for you. Do this in remembrance of me.'
> [20]And he did the same with the cup after supper, saying, 'This cup that
> is poured out for you is the new covenant in my blood. [21]But see, the
> one who betrays me is with me, and his hand is on the table. [22]For the
> Son of Man is going as it has been determined, but woe to that one
> by whom he is betrayed!' [23]Then they began to ask one another, which
> one of them it could be who would do this. [24]A dispute also arose
> among them as to which one of them was to be regarded as the greatest.
> [25]But he said to them, 'The kings of the Gentiles lord it over them;
> and those in authority over them are called benefactors. [26]But not so

18. David Stacey, 'The Lord's Supper as Prophetic Drama', *Epworth Review* 21, no. 1 (January
1994). See my discussion of this in *Self and Salvation*, pp. 150ff.

with you; rather the greatest among you must become like the youngest, and the leader like one who serves. [27]For who is greater, the one who is at the table or the one who serves? Is it not the one at the table? But I am among you as one who serves.'

All of those actions and words have their prime reference to himself, and the same is true of the basic teaching on greatness, giving his wisdom on leadership in the Kingdom of God, which concludes: **'But I am among you as one who serves.'** That is followed by him conferring on his disciples the kingdom (22:28–30), handing it over before he himself goes to his death.

Then, as Frei says, the narrative accelerates. The anguished prayer in Gethsemane crying out to his Father is to do with his own fate. He moves through his arrest, mockery (**'Prophesy! Who is it that struck you!'**), his examination and his trial, whose deciding influence is the shouts of the crowd: **'Away with this fellow! Release Barabbas for us!'** and **'Crucify, crucify him!'** and **'they kept urgently demanding with loud shouts that he should be crucified; and their voices prevailed'** (23:18–23). Then on the cross, amidst scoffing of the leaders, mockery of the soldiers, and deriding by one of the criminals crucified with him, death comes after a loud cry:

> Luke 23:46 Then Jesus, crying with a loud voice, said, 'Father, into your hands I commend my spirit.' Having said this, he breathed his last.

In all three Synoptic Gospels Jesus gives a loud cry at the point of death. Where does this cry spring from? Luke is the only one to attach words to the final cry, a quotation from Psalm 31:5. What does it mean to commend his spirit into his Father's hands? At the very least it means gathering up and handing over his whole life and being. The cry is an expression of the whole person, pouring out what is most intimate, formative and life-giving, what binds him to God, other people and creation. Most of all it comes from the depths of suffering. Luke's is on the surface the least 'agonised' of the four Gospel accounts of Jesus' death, but that is deceptive. There has been his weeping over Jerusalem and his anguish in Gethsemane. On the way to the cross he meets women wailing and beating their breasts:

> Luke 23:28–31 [28]But Jesus turned to them and said, 'Daughters of Jerusalem, do not weep for me, but weep for yourselves and for your children. [29]For the days are surely coming when they will say, "Blessed are the barren, and the wombs that never bore, and the breasts that never nursed." [30]Then they will begin to say to the mountains, "Fall on us"; and to the hills, "Cover us." [31]For if they do this when the wood is green, what will happen when it is dry?'

This note of enveloping catastrophe belies any interpretation of Luke's passion story as non-tragic and smoothly triumphant. The context of the quotation from Psalm 31, for all its trust and praise of God, still plumbs the depths of suffering:

> Psalm 31:9–13 [9]Be gracious to me, O LORD, for I am in distress; my eye wastes away from grief, my soul and body also. [10]For my life is spent with sorrow, and my years with sighing; my strength fails because of my misery, and my bones waste away. [11]I am the scorn of all my adversaries, a horror to my neighbors, an object of dread to my acquaintances; those who see me in the street flee from me. [12]I have passed out of mind like one who is dead; I have become like a broken vessel. [13]For I hear the whispering of many – terror all around! – as they scheme together against me, as they plot to take my life.

If this is where his loud cry springs from, what is its relation to wisdom? Insofar as Jesus has been identified as filled with wisdom, a child of wisdom, greater than Solomon, and even as the very wisdom of God (the only one to know the Father), this death is a wisdom event, a further definition of wisdom. Wisdom can now be informed, energised, directed and tested by this cry, which is the outpouring of Jesus' whole spirit. Jesus' spirit has resisted temptation, has been compassionate towards the cries of the suffering, has exulted in his intimate relationship to his Father, and has now been given up in death for the sake of the Kingdom of God and for the sake of his Father (**'yet, not my will but yours be done'** – Luke 22:42; see **'Father, hallowed be your name. Your kingdom come'** – Luke 11:2). His spirit has also been assaulted by cries of enmity, mockery and accusation. *His wisdom is shaped through the passionate multiple intensities embodied in all the cries that have pervaded his ministry and which climax now in his passion and death.* It is therefore a wisdom involved in relationships of many sorts; immersed in history, including its evils and sufferings; and now swallowed up by death.

The very daring of the identification of Jesus with wisdom means that his death is all the more a crisis and challenge for ideas of wisdom (just as it is for other ideas such as prophecy, Messiahship, leadership, glory and God). Any claim to wisdom can be interrogated from the standpoint of the cross; most find that their categories are inadequate. As emerged above, *the 'infant' approach, starting afresh from Jesus and the cross (which might then as it matures lead to many affirmations as well as critiques and transformations of previous wisdoms), might be more fruitful than beginning from some inherited wisdom and trying to account for the cross in those terms.*

This is in fact the route followed by Luke's Jesus: the main teaching about how Jesus' death makes sense in terms of received understanding in the scriptures is given retrospectively on the road to Emmaus after his resurrection (see further below).

Hence the importance of the narrative testimony. It carries the main weight of announcing what it is that has to be come to terms with. Its referential, pointing function is primary. It has above all to give the crucifixion as news, as a stark event. There is of course interpretation by each narrator of this story, and much has been written about the interests, biases and theologies of the four Gospels. The way the story is told requires a theological wisdom; but part of this wisdom is recognising the need for a basic pointing at the core of any interpretation. It cannot immediately be assimilated to any framework, worldview, explanation or understanding, even a biblical understanding.

Each of the Gospels achieves this self-limitation of interpretation in different ways. Its effect is not just to present the crucifixion as an event that calls for response (immediately Luke recounts the exclamation of the centurion who praises God and said '**Certainly this man was righteous** [or **innocent**, δίκαιος]', and the beating of breasts of the crowds – 23:47–48). It is also, as Frei says, to focus starkly on the person of Jesus. Here is the core reality, always resisting adequate interpretation, inexhaustibly evoking responses in praise, lament, repentance, liturgies, spiritualities, theologies, rejections, polemics, critiques, paintings, sculptures, windows, hymns, poems, buildings, dramas, novels, films, and the shaping of whole communities and individual lives. 'Jesus Christ crucified' is the irreducible centre of each Gospel account, offered to readers in under-interpreted yet definite ways. There is a wisdom of discerning reserve in the relatively bare telling of the story. There is also a wisdom of discernment in coping with the ramifying responses within the New Testament and through the centuries, and in finding what is appropriate and desirable now.[19]

In Christian theology both those wisdoms of reserve and ramification are rooted in acknowledging this crucified man as the wisdom of God. He is not a wisdom that can be turned without remainder into words – even words are driven to transcend themselves in cries. This is wisdom in flesh and blood, in person, in the Holy Spirit, in conflict and decision, in the

---

19. See chapter 5 below on Luke's own use of the Wisdom of Solomon in order to expand on the meaning of the events he narrated.

agonies and joys of life in history, in blessing. Perhaps most surprising of all, Jesus is presented as continuing to teach this embodied wisdom, which is largely the subject of Luke's final chapter.

Open tomb, open scriptures, open eyes, open minds

Luke's account of the resurrection of Jesus in the last chapter of his Gospel begins with more bare description. The women who come with spices are perplexed by the empty tomb, then terrified by the sudden appearance of two men in dazzling clothes, who announce: **'He is not here, but has risen'** (Luke 24:5). After being reminded of what Jesus had said about this the women tell what has happened to the apostles, who do not believe them, though Peter goes to the tomb and is amazed.

Luke leaves things hanging there and switches to two disciples walking to Emmaus who are joined by the risen Jesus. What follows might be seen as the wisdom climax of the Gospel.

> Luke 24:13–53 [13]Now on that same day two of them were going to a village called Emmaus, about seven miles from Jerusalem, [14]and talking with each other about all these things that had happened. [15]While they were talking and discussing, Jesus himself came near and went with them, [16]but their eyes were kept from recognizing him. [17]And he said to them, 'What are you discussing with each other while you walk along?' They stood still, looking sad. [18]Then one of them, whose name was Cleopas, answered him, 'Are you the only stranger in Jerusalem who does not know the things that have taken place there in these days?' [19]He asked them, 'What things?' They replied, 'The things about Jesus of Nazareth, who was a prophet mighty in deed and word before God and all the people, [20]and how our chief priests and leaders handed him over to be condemned to death and crucified him. [21]But we had hoped that he was the one to redeem Israel. Yes, and besides all this, it is now the third day since these things took place. [22]Moreover, some women of our group astounded us. They were at the tomb early this morning, [23]and when they did not find his body there, they came back and told us that they had indeed seen a vision of angels who said that he was alive. [24]Some of those who were with us went to the tomb and found it just as the women had said; but they did not see him.' [25]Then he said to them, 'Oh, how foolish you are, and how slow of heart to believe all that the prophets have declared! [26]Was it not necessary that the Messiah should suffer these things and then enter into his glory?' [27]Then beginning with Moses and all the prophets, he

interpreted to them the things about himself in all the scriptures. [28]As they came near the village to which they were going, he walked ahead as if he were going on. [29]But they urged him strongly, saying, 'Stay with us, because it is almost evening and the day is now nearly over.' So he went in to stay with them. [30]When he was at the table with them, he took bread, blessed and broke it, and gave it to them. [31]Then their eyes were opened, and they recognized him; and he vanished from their sight. [32]They said to each other, 'Were not our hearts burning within us while he was talking to us on the road, while he was opening the scriptures to us?' [33]That same hour they got up and returned to Jerusalem; and they found the eleven and their companions gathered together. [34]They were saying, 'The Lord has risen indeed, and he has appeared to Simon!' [35]Then they told what had happened on the road, and how he had been made known to them in the breaking of the bread. [36]While they were talking about this, Jesus himself stood among them and said to them, 'Peace be with you.' [37]They were startled and terrified, and thought that they were seeing a ghost. [38]He said to them, 'Why are you frightened, and why do doubts arise in your hearts? [39]Look at my hands and my feet; see that it is I myself. Touch me and see; for a ghost does not have flesh and bones as you see that I have.' [40]And when he had said this, he showed them his hands and his feet. [41]While in their joy they were disbelieving and still wondering, he said to them, 'Have you anything here to eat?' [42]They gave him a piece of broiled fish, [43]and he took it and ate in their presence. [44]Then he said to them, 'These are my words that I spoke to you while I was still with you – that everything written about me in the law of Moses, the prophets, and the psalms must be fulfilled.' [45]Then he opened their minds to understand the scriptures, [46]and he said to them, 'Thus it is written, that the Messiah is to suffer and to rise from the dead on the third day, [47]and that repentance and forgiveness of sins is to be proclaimed in his name to all nations, beginning from Jerusalem. [48]You are witnesses of these things. [49]And see, I am sending upon you what my Father promised; so stay here in the city until you have been clothed with power from on high.' [50]Then he led them out as far as Bethany, and, lifting up his hands, he blessed them. [51]While he was blessing them, he withdrew from them and was carried up into heaven. [52]And they worshipped him, and returned to Jerusalem with great joy; [53]and they were continually in the temple blessing God.

The two disciples know all the facts of what has happened, especially the crucifixion and the confirmation that the tomb was empty, but they cannot make sense of it. Jesus' response to their account begins: '**Oh, how**

foolish you are …' (v. 25). It is a clue to hear what he is saying as wisdom.[20] There are other clues too. If the fear of the Lord is the beginning of wisdom then it is wise to pay attention to the role of God in this chapter. The event that opens it, the resurrection, is so obviously attributed to God that this is not even mentioned. The responses to the resurrection include perplexity, amazement, startled terror, fear, wonder and joy. All of this culminates in the disciples worshipping the ascending Jesus and then being continually in the Temple blessing God. And God is literally the last word of this Gospel. So there is the fear, and there is the Lord;[21] and the focus on God is inseparable from the focus on Jesus, who is concerned, among other things, with overcoming foolishness and opening minds to the right understanding of scriptures. *All of this in biblical terms amounts to the conditions for what one might call a new beginning of wisdom in response to what is beyond its previous conceptions.*

So the person who at the beginning of the Gospel is filled with wisdom and amazes the teachers in the Temple, and in the middle has exulted in knowing the Father, and in death has cried out in words from a Psalm, here interprets 'all the scriptures'. Yet, even as he does this and their hearts burn within them, the vital recognition of who he is does not occur through this conversation: it happens only through the breaking of bread. The main point of the teaching about himself is not contained in the teaching: that just opens the way for the recognition and vanishing in the breaking of bread. There is here a wisdom about the limits of verbal wisdom – even when it is taught by Jesus – and *a fortiori* about the limits of textually conveyed wisdom; also about the strange realities of absence and presence, and about what later tradition called word and sacrament. It is a wisdom immersed in events, in community life, and in relating to the risen Jesus, in continuity with the wisdom seen in the life and death of Jesus.

The contemporaneity of the living Jesus Christ (or of the Spirit that, he says, **'I am sending upon you'** – v.49) with all attempts to understand him and what happened to him does not amount to a safe, formulaic rule for sound interpretation of history or of scripture. Forms of theological or

---

20. What follows repeats some of what I wrote in an earlier discussion of this passage, 'Jesus Christ and the Wisdom of God (1)' in *Reading Texts, Seeking Wisdom: Scripture and Theology*, ed. David F. Ford and Graham Stanton (London: SCM Press and Grand Rapids, MI: Eerdmans, 2003), pp. 11ff.
21. There are a number of scriptural references to the fear of the Lord being the beginning of wisdom – Psalm 111:10, Proverbs 9:10 and Sirach 1:14. Other texts which combine the concepts of the fear of the Lord and wisdom are found at Job 28:28, Proverbs 15:33, Micah 6:9 and Sirach 1:16, 1:18, 1:20, 1:27, 19:20 and 21:11.

interpretative closure, whether in method or content, are disturbed and opened up by this living presence, a point Luke repeatedly makes in Acts. Here at the end of his Gospel the ultimate surprise (so great that even explicit foretelling of it is not enough to prepare for it) of the resurrection, signalled by the opened tomb, is followed by the opening of the scriptures (v.32), the opening of eyes (v.31), and the opening of minds (v.45). One might also say that there was an opening up to the whole world ('**to all nations**' – v.47) and an opening of heaven ('**power from on high**' – v.49; '**he withdrew from them and was carried up into heaven**' – v.51). Taken together this amounts to a new transformative dynamic, most vividly described by Luke as the rushing mighty wind and tongues of fire at Pentecost in the first chapter of Acts.

At the heart of this dynamic in Luke 24 is a transformative exchange or transfer. The chapter continues the focus on the person of Jesus but with a new dimension of what happens between him and the disciples, and in the disciples. There is extraordinary intensity of life in relationship: walking together, conversation, blessing, touching, feeding, and great joy. The opening of eyes, minds and scriptures is part of a handing over of responsibility by Jesus to the disciples, a commissioning as witnesses, followed by a blessing that both seals this and begins a new period in which the absence or ascended presence of Jesus leaves them with new responsibility. But it is not only about new responsibility. The ones who carry the responsibility are to be transformed and carry a message that requires repentance and forgiveness of sins. This is a further dimension of what has already been going on during their discipleship, and the decisive event is to be the 'power from on high', the sending of the Holy Spirit.

That is the ultimate transfer, a sharing of life from God, which is about whole persons and communities being transformed; but first, in immediate proximity to his death, the risen Jesus shares his wisdom. So the role of understanding, minds and interpretation is seen by Luke as so important that the teaching of Jesus is the main focus of his Gospel's final chapter. The crucified Jesus gave up his spirit with a loud cry; the risen Jesus cries out at how foolish and 'slow of heart' his disciples are and he prepares them to receive the Holy Spirit by interpreting the scriptures. The meaning of the events they have experienced does not lie on the surface of either the events or the scriptures. In the transfer of responsibility and the transformation of their lives by the coming Holy Spirit, the multiple openings of eyes, minds, world history and heaven are inseparable from the ongoing interpretation of the scriptures. Crying out in witness **'to all nations, beginning from Jerusalem'** (Luke 24:47) is rooted in **'thus it is written'** (Luke 24:46). What sort of hermeneutic is this?

Richard Hays names it 'a hermeneutic of resurrection, the ability to discern in scripture a witness to God's life-giving power'.[22] Having interpreted John 2:13–22 and Mark 12:18–27 his culminating example is Luke 24:13–35, where he sees Jesus trying to teach 'the hermeneutical matrix within which the recent events in Jerusalem become intelligible'[23] through discerning in scripture the pattern of the crucifixion and resurrection of the Messiah: **'Was it not necessary that the Messiah should suffer these things and then enter into his glory?'** (Luke 24:26). Encounter with the risen Jesus and the meaning of 'all the scriptures' mutually interpret each other – this is 'the hermeneutical nexus between scripture and resurrection'.[24]

Hays sums up his hermeneutic of resurrection in a set of 'observations' that in my terms might be termed a Christian wisdom for reading scripture in line with Luke 24 and his other texts. He affirms the centrality of God, the constant possibility of surprises as scriptures are interpreted in new situations, the reading of the Old Testament as Christian scripture in 'respectful controversy' with Jewish readings, the occurrence of epistemological transformation in the readers, the epistemic humility and lack of control required because 'our new understanding depends on an event we cannot possibly understand',[25] the intimate link with practices of shared life, discipleship and mission, and the need to rethink methods of studying the Gospels. Of special importance to the themes of this chapter are his remarks about figural reading and eschatological hope.

On figuration Hays writes:

> Reading in light of the resurrection is figural reading. Because the Old Testament's pointers to the resurrection are indirect and symbolic in character, the resurrection teaches us to read for figuration and latent sense. The Sadducees were literalists, but God seems to have delighted in veiled anticipations of the gospel. For that reason, resurrection is the enemy of textual literalism. Or, more precisely, resurrection

---

22. Richard Hays, 'Reading Scripture in Light of the Resurrection' in *The Art of Reading Scripture*, ed. Ellen F. Davis and Richard B. Hays (Grand Rapids, MI: Eerdmans, 2003), p. 226.
23. Ibid. p. 230.   24. Ibid. p. 232.   25. Ibid. p. 236.

reconfigures the literal sense of Scripture by catalysing new readings that destabilize entrenched interpretations: the resurrection stories teach us always to remain alert to analogical possibilities and surprises. Resurrection-informed reading sees the life-giving power of God manifested and prefigured in unexpected ways throughout Scripture. It would therefore be a mistake to catalogue, say, all the explicitly christological readings of Old Testament texts in Luke–Acts and suppose that we had thereby exhausted the hermeneutical possibilities for understanding Scripture's witness to Jesus Christ. On the contrary, the Jesus who taught the disciples on the Emmaus road that *all* the scriptures bore witness to him continues to teach us to discover figural senses of Scripture that are not developed in the New Testament.[26]

This open process of figuration, which both respects and can go beyond the literal or plain sense, is a vital dimension of what was called above the opening up of forms of theological or interpretative closure. This is an invitation to endless new readings 'alert to analogical possibilities and surprises' between Old and New Testaments, within each Testament, and between them and other texts, understandings, situations, people and events. This is more like wisdom than knowledge, and it also calls for wisdom to test the proliferation of readings. Luke's first twenty-three chapters and what I have developed as a 'hermeneutic of cries' might offer criteria for that testing. The analogical possibilities of (and surprises between) those cries and the cries that sound down the centuries and around the world today provide a critical measure of the adequacy of any prophetic wisdom now.

On hope, Hays writes:

> To read Scripture in the light of the resurrection is to read with emphasis on eschatological hope. The resurrection as a hermeneutical lens brings into focus the Old Testament's propensity to lean forward with eager longing for God to make all things whole. I do not mean simply that texts such as Isa 25:6–8, Ezek 37, and Dan 12:2–3 take on new weight in light of the story of Jesus' resurrection – though of course they do. Rather, I mean that in light of the resurrection, the Old Testament's narrative movement – from sterility to miraculous childbirth, from slavery in Egypt to freedom in the promised land, from exile to return – is to be interpreted as an adumbration of the eschatological hope signified in the New Testament by the resurrection

---

26. Ibid. pp. 233ff.

of the dead. The logic of eschatological hope is structurally fundamental to the Old Testament canon ... Thus the New Testament and the Old Testament are closely analogous in their eschatological orientation and in their posture of awaiting God's deliverance in the midst of suffering.[27]

Such immersion in history and orientation towards the promises and purposes of God has emerged as a key dimension of Luke's Gospel in this chapter. *The eschatological thrust, with its cries of passionate longing, warning, fear, and anticipatory joy, meets the confusion of cries thrown up by the sufferings and joys of ongoing history; and wisdom at the cutting edge of life now is continually challenged, stretched and opened up in contradiction, paradox, offence, agony and exultation.* The Psalms are perhaps the most vivid evocation of this in support of Hays' hermeneutic of resurrection. But the combination of figural and eschatological interpretation amidst the contingencies of life calls for the continual seeking of prophetic wisdom in a scripture-reading community of discernment. That is what Luke's second volume, the Acts of the Apostles, shows in the life of the early church, and my introductory study of Luke will conclude by focussing on just one figure in Acts.

Stephen: 'full of the Spirit and of wisdom'

The giving of the Holy Spirit at Pentecost for Luke completes the handing on of Jesus' ministry to his followers, enabling the fulfilment of what he had told them to do in Luke 24. This happens in many ways, but at the heart of it is an irrepressible crying out in proclamation of the crucified and resurrected Jesus. There is something wild, uncontrollable and 'drunken' about this, symbolised in the story of Pentecost by the imagery of flame, wind and wine. Yet as the crucifixion's loud cry leads into the Emmaus road, so Pentecost's tongues is followed by Peter's scripture-packed sermon (Acts 2:14–36) and by a history in which there is one question for discernment after another. At the very end of Acts the issue, as in Luke 24, is about listening without understanding, looking without perceiving, and hearts that have grown dull, with Paul in prison **'proclaiming the kingdom of God and teaching about the Lord Jesus Christ with all boldness and without hindrance'** (Acts 28:31).

27. Ibid. pp. 234ff.

One person who sums up the union between irrepressible proclamation and scripture-informed wisdom is Stephen. He is the figure in Acts who most resembles Jesus. Like Jesus, Stephen in Acts 6–7 is **'full of the Spirit'**; he acts as a servant; he does **'great wonders and signs among the people'**; he is a powerful controversialist; he is plotted against and accused (with the participation of elders and scribes) of blasphemy and attacking the Temple; he is tried and accused by false witnesses; his face appears transfigured; he accuses the council of repeating the persecutions of their ancestors; the crowd rush on him **'with a loud shout'** to kill him; and while he is being stoned to death his words echo those of Jesus on the cross (in reverse order): he prays **'Lord Jesus, receive my spirit'** and then **'cried out with a loud voice, "Lord, do not hold this sin against them"'** (Acts 7:59–60). His association with wisdom is twice stated by Luke: in giving the qualifications for Stephen being selected as one of seven to wait at table: **'of good standing, full of the Spirit and of wisdom'** (Acts 6:3); and in describing **'the wisdom and the Spirit with which he spoke'** (Acts 6:10). This wisdom in the Spirit is comprehensively about good living, service to others, community-building, personal transfiguration, forgiving enemies, and good dying. It is also radically focussed on the person of Jesus, as seen not only in addressing his dying prayer to Jesus but also in the vision that he announces: **'But filled with the Holy Spirit, he gazed into heaven and saw the glory of God and Jesus standing at the right hand of God. "Look," he said, "I see the heavens opened and the Son of Man standing at the right hand of God!"'** (Acts 7:55–56). This is the supreme instance in Acts of the multiple 'openings' of Luke 24.

By far the greatest amount of space is given by Luke to Stephen's opening of scripture in his speech to the high priest and his council. This partly makes up for Luke's reticence about the contents of Jesus' scriptural interpretation on the Emmaus road. It is an instance of Hays' hermeneutic of resurrection, and Longenecker's exegesis of it shows how in relation to one after another key element in Second Temple Judaism – the land, the Torah and the Temple – Stephen opens it up to what is beyond itself and especially to 'further divine activity'.[28] His is a prophetic scriptural wisdom (and he draws special attention to the role in Israel's history of Joseph's God-given wisdom and the wisdom Moses learnt from

---

28. Richard N. Longenecker, *The Expositor's Bible Commentary with the New International Version: Acts* (Grand Rapids, MI: Zondervan, 1995), p. 142.

the Egyptians – Acts 7:10, 22), inseparable from recent events and from his context, his person, his life and his death, and opening up the future. According to Luke, the most significant person in the church's future was present at Stephen's death and approved of it: Saul, later Paul. His wisdom theology will be discussed in chapter 5 below.

Learning to seek wisdom in the Spirit

This chapter has been seeking Christian wisdom through thinking through scripture, especially Luke's Gospel and a little of Acts. Building on this, the next chapter will further pursue wisdom through scripture and reflect on this as a theological practice. What has been learnt so far?

Our study has tried to follow closely some of the contours of Luke's story. If, as suggested, much of the wisdom is in the way the story is told, then the narrative pattern and detail, the encounters and images, and the key events and statements, yield their meaning by being savoured in their specificity. This has only been possible with selected parts of the text, but the approach could easily be extended. Any 'summary of results' is obviously risky because it is in danger of abstracting from just the specificity which gave rise to them. One of theology's main temptations is to formulate doctrines or other theological conclusions with reference to scripture and then forget that reference, failing to keep open the engagement with scripture that is needed if the theology is to avoid becoming fossilised. What follows takes for granted that the journey through the preceding sections is intrinsic to whatever wisdom there is in the chapter, and that there is no shortcut to the conclusions. It is rather by way of an aide-memoire, a reminder of what needs to be borne in mind, drawing out implications that will be important in later chapters.

A wisdom hermeneutic of cries

The main theme to emerge has been the deep connection in the Gospel between wisdom and cries. Cries preceded Jesus' birth, accompanied it, and preceded his baptism. His ministry was one of compassion in response to the poor and suffering, and it was pervaded with the cries of demons, sufferers, opponents, disciples and crowds, and with Jesus' own cries of exultation, lamentation or woe. The climax of his life in Jerusalem was accompanied by a crescendo of cries focussed on him, and his culminating act was a loud cry from the cross as he died. Then on the

Emmaus road he appeared to disciples, cried out against their foolishness and taught them from the scriptures. His life was a drama punctuated by cries of many sorts, not all of them vocalised – as, in his story of the Good Samaritan, the man left half dead by robbers makes a mute appeal to passers-by (Luke 10:30–37).

At the same time it was a life of wisdom, as Luke stresses beginning with his childhood. Previous sections have elucidated the deep connection between the two. This is prophetic wisdom immersed in the agonies, conflicts and joys of life, whose intensities are often articulated in cries. Jesus continually exercises discernment in temptations, healings, controversies, blessings, and his embodied proclamation of the Kingdom of God. His turning to Jerusalem towards death is in line with the basic act of discernment about his vocation, and Gethsemane is presented as the place where he decisively confirms this. It is, as emerges most clearly on the road to Emmaus and in the rest of the final chapter of Luke, a discernment shaped through the interpretation of scripture in the Spirit.

Jesus' death is the point of deepest interpenetration of his crying out and his understanding of scripture. But there is no suggestion that the loud cry with which he gives up his spirit is exhaustively understandable. There is an excess of the cry over any verbal articulation, knowledge or explanation. In classic terms, it is inextricably cataphatic and apophatic. The cry in its dramatic context signifies powerfully, saying something that continually stretches imagination and thought. It involves the whole self of Jesus, and we read into this gathering and giving up of his spirit all that he is and is related to, including God and 'all things' that have been handed over to him by his Father. This self-involvement, God-involvement and world-involvement are indicated through this cry by this person in this event. Yet the cry also apophatically indicates the limits of language and thought. It is apophatic not just in relation to God but also in relation to the spirit of Jesus and God, to the Kingdom of God, and to death. It gives a new point of orientation for all of these, yet without anything definitive being said. This apophasis is a simultaneity of radical intimacy and unlimited publicity. *Its inarticulable mystery stands as a continual provocation to thought, to the sort of learning through following that Christians call discipleship, and to a responsive crying out in worship and in the agonies and joys of personal and communal living.*

A wisdom that pivots around this cry and the death that follows it can never attain an overview or an integral systematic understanding. It is disruptive or interruptive of such claims, and tries to learn the epistemic humility that Hays approached through the mystery of the resurrection and the hermeneutic appropriate to that. Yet, as with Hays' complementary hermeneutic, this engagement with both cries and the wisdom intrinsic to them can be generative, inspiring interpretations of scripture, history and life that can inform self-involving, God-involving and world-involving life in the Spirit.

Cries and the moods of faith

When Paul was wrestling with the mystery of why his fellow-Jews did not come to faith in Christ through his message he said: '**Faith comes from what is heard, and what is heard comes through the word of Christ**' (Romans 10:17). Luke's Gospel works with a similar assumption. What might my hermeneutic of cries mean for the understanding of faith?

One way into this is to explore the dimensions of faith through the variety of cries: what might that faith be which is formed through hearing these cries? I will consider them with reference to moods, understood grammatically in the first place: indicative, imperative, interrogative, subjunctive and optative. These are not just to be understood literally – it is of course possible effectively to issue a command in the indicative mood, or to raise a question without using a question mark, or to open up subjunctive possibilities without the use of 'may' or might', or, as in the coming sections, to write about all the moods largely in the indicative. Cries themselves are fascinating as parts of speech, calls or acclamations that can be in one mood but resonate with more than one, or exclamations that are not in any particular mood but invite interpretation through several.

Indicative: affirming and affirmed

From before his birth, Luke tells of Jesus being surrounded by cries of affirmation, continuing through his ministry and entry into Jerusalem, until immediately after his death the centurion praises God and says: '**Certainly this man was innocent**' (Luke 23:47). The climactic affirmations come from God his Father in his baptism, in his transfiguration and finally in the act of raising him from death. Jesus' own ministry is one of affirmation, both positive and negative: '**Blessed are you ...**'; '**Woe to you ...**' (Luke 6:20ff). His massive central indicative is proclamation of the Kingdom of God, announced in the synagogue of Nazareth after opening the book of Isaiah: '**Today this scripture has been fulfilled in your hearing**' (Luke 4:21). This happens through word and deed.

I have argued above that the inner theological meaning of his life and work is given in his exultation in Luke 10, when he rejoices in what God has been doing through him and his disciples, and he roots it all in the mutual knowing of Father and Son. *The pattern of affirmation rooted in being affirmed by God is at the core of the confession of Christian faith.* Luke offers a range of ways in which his readers can join in affirming Jesus and God in praise and thanks, and can be addressed by the Gospel story – narrative is the main form of the indicative in historical mode. Telling this story is the basic way of opening up the possibility of faith through hearing. At the beginning and end of his telling of it Luke puts praise – opening with the Magnificat, Benedictus, Nunc Dimittis and the angels, and concluding: '**And they worshipped him, and returned to Jerusalem with great joy; and they were continually in the temple blessing God**' (24:52–53). Blessing God is the core activity of discerning affirmation, and will be explored at length in chapter 7 below.

Imperative: obedience in the Kingdom of God

Jesus himself is under radical obedience, as is clear from the beginning in his temptations – his responses are in terms of the commands of God. He is the Messiah, the Christ, 'anointed' to bring good news, healing and freedom, and his vocation of proclaiming the Kingdom of God culminates in the obedience prayed about in Gethsemane and realised on the cross. Among the core imperatives of faith are his call: '**Follow me!**' (e.g. Luke 5:27; see especially 9:23); the call of his Father: '**Listen to him!**' (Luke 9:35); his commands: '**When you pray, say: "Father …"**' (Luke 11:2); '**Ask … Search … Knock …**' (Luke 11:9ff); '**Do this!**' (e.g. Luke 10:28); and the final commissioning to proclaim repentance and forgiveness and to witness to him (Luke 24:45ff). The encompassing cry here is Jesus' amendment of a blessing: '**While he was saying this a woman in the crowd raised her voice and said to him, "Blessed is the womb that bore you and the breasts that nursed you!" But he said, "Blessed rather are those who hear the word of God and obey it!"**' (Luke 11:28).

The Gospel here invites into an obedience of faith rooted in Jesus' own obedience. The affirmative and imperative converge in Jesus, and Luke's story increasingly concentrates on Jesus going the way of obedience that his Spirit will eventually enable others to follow.

It is arguable that Christian faith has generally been seen largely in terms of indicatives ('This is the good news …') and imperatives ('Do this …'), with a great deal of debate around the nature of each and their relationship. Without denying the truth in that, I want to suggest that the other moods below, while apparently less significant, in fact make an enormous difference to the way faith is understood and lived. Partly that is due to the change in the way indicatives and imperatives operate if they are understood as part of a larger ecology of moods, integrated in the way suggested below.

Interrogative: questioning and questioned

Perhaps the most sensitive of all the moods is the interrogative. Interrogation, testing and critique run through Luke's Gospel, and key events – the annunciation of John the Baptist's and Jesus' births, John's message, Jesus' ministry in Nazareth, his exorcisms, healings, absolutions and confrontations, his provocative proclamation of the Kingdom of God, and finally his actions, teachings, trial and death in Jerusalem – generate a huge amount of questioning, perplexity, doubt, conflict and amazement. There is a loud interrogative note in many of the cries he voices and evokes, and literal questions punctuate the story: '**Is this not Joseph's son?**' (4:22); '**What have you to do with us, Jesus of Nazareth? Have you come to destroy us?**' (4:34); '**Who is this who is speaking blasphemies? Who can forgive sins but God alone? … Which is easier to say, "Your sins are forgiven you," or to say, "Stand up and walk"?**' (5:21, 23); '**Why do you eat and drink with tax collectors and sinners?**' (5:30); '**I ask you, is it lawful to do good or to do harm on the Sabbath, to save life or to destroy it?**' (6:9); '**If you love those who love you, what credit is that to you?**' (6:32); '**What did you go out into the wilderness to look at?**' (7:24); '**Where is your faith?**' … '**Who then is this, that he commands even the winds and the water, and they obey him?**' (8:25); '**But who do you say that I am?**' (9:20); '**Who then is the faithful and prudent manager …?**' (12:42); '**What is the kingdom of God like?**' (13:20); '**Salt is good, but if salt has lost its taste, how can its saltiness be restored?**' (14:34); '**And yet, when the Son of Man comes, will he find faith on earth?**' (18:8); '**Who is it who gave you this authority?**' … '**Did the baptism of John come from men or was it of human origin?**' (20:2–3); '**Who is greater, the one who is at the table or the one who serves?**' (22:27); '**Who is it that struck you?**' (22:64); '**Are you, then, the Son of God?**' (22:70); '**Why do you look for the living among the dead?**' (24:5).

The life, death and resurrection of Jesus can be seen as an interrogation of his generation, his disciples and the leaders of his people, and at the same time their interrogation and testing of him. To hear this story in faith is to receive not just the indicatives and imperatives but also the questions. *In particular the climactic events of his death and his resurrection together form a massive, multifaceted question that goes on generating further questions.* The moment after the disciples see the pierced hands and feet of the risen Jesus remains part of the story: **'in their joy they were disbelieving and still wondering'** (24:41).

Subjunctive: possibilities and surprises

The subjunctive mood of 'may be' and 'might be' is perhaps the one least on the surface of the text. It is the mood in which possibilities are imagined and decisions are made.

It is above all the mood (though rarely the literal verbal mood) of the parables of Jesus. These make vivid the Kingdom of God as evoking a different vision of God and reality, opening up a new future, and inviting into fundamental decisions and reorientations. The parable of the sower holds a mirror up to us as we are faced with different possibilities in responding to Jesus' message (8:5–15); our options in relation to a neighbour in need are played out by the priest, the Levite and the Samaritan on the Jericho road (10:29–37) and by Lazarus and his brothers (16:19–31); the story of those who refused invitations to the banquet make us consider our priorities, and the tower-builder and the king preparing to wage war challenge us to count the cost of our decisions (14:15–33); the elder brother of the Prodigal Son gives an alternative attitude to the compassion of their father (15:11–32); and the parable of the pounds sets before us safer and riskier ways of carrying out our responsibilities before God (19:11–27). The comprehensive catalyst of decision is Jesus himself: the possibility of offence is the mystery at the heart of the good news. Jesus also often avoids the choices with which he is presented – about paying taxes to Caesar or deciding whose wife in the resurrection will be the woman who has married seven brothers (20:20–40), and in the process he opens up different, bewildering and larger possibilities.

The Kingdom of God is full of potentiality for surprise and reversal – a note struck right from the start in Mary's Magnificat (1:46–55); but the ultimate surprise comes in the resurrection of Jesus. That, and the outpouring of the Holy Spirit, generate a superabundance of new possibilities that are global in scope. And, as discussed above in relation to the hermeneutic of resurrection and to the wisdom of Stephen, these are rooted in the possibilities of interpreting scripture in the Spirit in new periods and situations. *The faith that has taken to heart the subjunctive dimension of the Gospel lives in alertness to a Spirit who is inexhaustibly surprising.*

Optative: desiring and desired

In Greek the optative is the mood of desire – 'May it be ...', 'Would that I might ...', 'If only ...'. In Luke Mary uses it in response to the angel announcing that she is to conceive Jesus: **'Let it be** (γένοιτο) **with me according to your word'** (1:38). The theme of desire in Luke's Gospel will be taken up again in chapter 5 below, but it is important now to note in a preliminary way its pervasiveness.

Luke's opening two chapters are a symphony of desire, implicit and explicit. Zechariah and Elizabeth suffer from 'the disgrace' of barrenness (1:25) and are longing for a child. Mary's Magnificat shows a passionate desire for God's blessings for the truly wise (who **'fear him from generation to generation'** – 1:50), the lowly, the hungry, and **'his servant Israel'**, and for the fulfilment of **'the promise he made to our ancestors, to Abraham and to his descendants for ever'** (1:54–55). Zechariah's Benedictus concludes in a burst of hope in God's tender mercy, light and peace. Shepherds race to see the new baby; Simeon in the Temple has been **'looking forward to the consolation of Israel'** (2:25); Anna has spent decades in worship, fasting and prayer **'day and night'** in the Temple as one of those **'looking for the redemption of Jerusalem'** (2:38); and the final story of Jesus' childhood shows him oriented radically to God even to the distress of his parents.

Jesus' baptism is an affirmation of the delight and pleasure of God in his Son: this is the Beloved, the one desired by his Father. The temptations that follow show not only his obedience to the commands of scripture but his wholehearted dedication to God's purposes, overcoming desires for food, power and spectacular success. In his ministry, the Kingdom of God gathers all the other moods together in desire for a fulfilment that is portrayed in terms of feasting, love and sheer joy. At the climax of his ministry the expressions of desire intensify. He laments and weeps over Jerusalem in disappointed longing; the Last Supper is the fulfilment of having **'eagerly desired to eat this Passover with you before I suffer'** (22:15); and his prayer on the Mount of Olives is the final alignment of his desire with his Father's. Interwoven with this story of Jesus desiring and being desired are not only the desires and passions of others but also the constant theme of discernment.

Luke presents the resurrection as the reversal of the disappointed desire of his disciples: '**But we had hoped that he was the one to redeem Israel**' (24:21). *Jesus not only opens their minds and hearts to the way scripture (including that great school of desire, the Psalms) is fulfilled through him, but that fulfilment is the generator of fresh desire for the coming of the Holy Spirit and the sharing of the message of forgiveness with all nations.*

The final verses are filled with blessing – Jesus blessing the disciples as he withdraws from them, and the disciples 'with great joy' worshipping him and blessing God. *Blessing is the ultimate in desiring good for the other, or just celebrating a fulfilment of desire that, when God is its goal and inspiration, can inexhaustibly open up to fresh fulfilments, joys and blessings* (see chapter 7 below).

Theology, the moods of faith, and wisdom

Desire is in many ways the embracing mood of a life immersed in history and oriented towards the fulfilment of God's purposes. In desire the indicatives, imperatives, interrogatives and subjunctives are taken up into a dynamic that orders them towards their fulfilment yet without pretending that we are there yet. This guards against allowing any of them to dominate inappropriately: whether a literalist dogmatism of 'This is so!'; or a moral absolutism of 'Do this!'; or an openness of questioning, doubt and confusion without any definiteness; or an endlessly experimental exploration of attractive possibilities.

This has important consequences for theology. Theology tries to find appropriate affirmations, connections and rich interrelationships, but need not claim some systematically integrated overview of theological knowledge in the indicative mood. It is concerned with practical living and obedience, but need not advocate ethical or political absolutes abstracted from the contingencies of life and history and from a realisation that the ultimate is not yet. It faces doubts, critiques and radical suspicion, without needing to take them as the last word. It opens up possibilities and is alert to surprises, without losing the plot and the core commitment to desiring what God desires, as indicated in scripture.

Above all, theology desires a wisdom that is true to God and God's desires; that lives in the midst of life while hoping in God's future; that takes as its main guide the scriptures interpreted in the Spirit and in community with Christians and with others who seek wisdom; and that seeks to ring true to the great cries that arise in scripture and in life. *Theology is called to be ceaselessly attentive to these cries – articulate, inarticulate or even silent – and to exercise discernment while being gripped by them, with the purpose of shaping life – worship, arts, science, ethics, politics, economics, friendships, and the heart of each person – for the love of humanity, of all creation, and of the God of compassion, wisdom and blessing.*

As far as the theologian and any other seeker of such wisdom is concerned, the core activity is crying out for it. The cry goes first to God. It also goes to anyone who might have wisdom or wants to join in seeking it. But it is not self-generated. It is elicited. *There is a passivity at the core of the cry for this wisdom. It is a response to powerful attraction and attractiveness.* The One who evokes our cry generates wisdom and the desire for it. Our cry is a response to the call of wisdom herself. In the Bible, apart from the desire for God there is no desire that is more passionately and loudly encouraged than the desire for wisdom. **'Wisdom cries out in the street; in the squares she raises her voice. At the busiest corner she cries out; at the entrance of the city gates she speaks'** (Proverbs 1:20–21).

> Proverbs 8:1–4, 10–11
> [1]Does not wisdom call,
>   and does not understanding raise her voice?
> [2]On the heights, beside the way,
>   at the crossroads she takes her stand;
> [3]Beside the gates, in front of the town,
>   at the entrance of the portals she cries out:
> [4]'To you, O people, I call,
>   and my cry is to all that live …
> [10]Take my instruction instead of silver,
>   and knowledge rather than choice gold;
> [11]For wisdom is better than jewels,
>   and all that you may desire
>   cannot compare with her …'

A wisdom interpretation of scripture

Christian theology requires an engagement with scripture whose primary desire is for the wisdom of God in life now. Interpretation with that desire is what is called here a wisdom interpretation of scripture. It tries to do justice to the various dimensions and senses of scripture; to the disciplines and methods through which it has been studied; to the interpretative traditions and communities engaged with it in the past and the present (Christian, cultural and artistic, political, scholarly, inter-faith, critical/polemical, and so on); to the virtues and practices that help wise interpretation; and to the interplay between conversations around the text and other conversations – for example, around God, worship, community formation, historical events and developments, ethical issues, service to society, spiritual and academic disciplines, religious and secular worldviews, or the shaping and healing of lives.

Any one of those topics could be the subject of more than one book. This chapter is an attempt to do just two things: to sketch in broad strokes what a wisdom interpretation of scripture is, using exegeses of biblical passages and analyses of exemplary wisdom interpreters, and distilling the maxims that guide such interpretation; and, in addition, to explain and support the ways in which scripture enters into the other chapters of this book.

The desirability of this task can be seen from various angles. Within Christian theology, biblical interpretation has always been of vital importance. Christianity began within Judaism, and the understanding of Jewish scriptures, which Christians came to call the Old Testament, has always been central to Christian identity. The New Testament's testimony to Jesus Christ is inextricable from its interpretation of the Old Testament. The two testaments together form the complex matrix in relation to which Christianity past, present and future is construed. Many of those construals have been and are deeply problematic, and some are of great practical importance. There are deep splits within Christianity that are generated to a significant degree by these questions. There are also massive inter-faith issues, first of all with Judaism but also with other traditions; and the perception and reception of Christianity in secular settings is deeply affected by how the Bible is regarded and read. For the world's one to two billion Christians, at stake are core issues of faith, worship, mission, community, worldview, and a whole range of practices. Add to this the massive amount of interpretations in the form of academic and popular articles and books, films, radio and television programmes, works of art, educational courses, and so on, and it is clear that this is an area where wise discernment is of great importance.

The starting-point is one of the most influential texts in the history of Christianity, the Prologue of the Gospel of John, read as an example of the interpretation of scripture. This is read in conjunction with John's own statement about the Spirit – that most important and controversial of all aspects of Christian biblical interpretation. Chapter 1, 'Wisdom cries', is next examined to draw out its exegetical and hermeneutical principles. After a discussion of rereading as the core practice of scripture interpretation, the resources offered by scholarship, hermeneutics and doctrinal theology are considered. Finally, the results of the Scripture Project of the Princeton Center of Theological Inquiry are appropriated and briefly discussed in order to come up with a set of core maxims and invitations that it might be helpful to have in mind while seeking wisdom through scripture.

The leading of the Spirit and the Prologue of John

The 'Farewell Discourses' in John's[1] Gospel (chapters 13–17), in which Jesus speaks with his disciples the evening before his crucifixion, are in

---

1. I am calling the author John: For the debate about authorship see any commentary. The ones I have found most useful for this chapter include C. K. Barrett, *The Gospel According to St John: An Introduction with Commentary and Notes on the Greek Text*, 2nd edn (London: SPCK, 1978); Raymond E. Brown, *The Gospel According to John* (Garden City, NY: Doubleday, 1966, 1970); Rudolf Bultmann, *The Gospel of John: A Commentary* (Oxford: Basil Blackwell, 1971); Barnabas Lindars, *The Gospel of John* (London: New Century Bible, 1972); John Marsh, *The Gospel of Saint John* (London: Penguin, 1968); Francis J. Moloney, *The Gospel of John*, Sacra Pagina Series 4, series editor Daniel J. Harrington SJ (Collegeville, MN: The Liturgical Press, 1998); Lesslie Newbigin, *The Light Has Come: An Exposition of the Fourth Gospel* (Edinburgh: The

large part about preparing them for the future beyond his death and
resurrection. In the prominence John gives to these discourses is also to
be seen his concern that his writing enable the Gospel to be passed on to
future generations. There are many notes of encouragement and promise
which open up the prospect that second and later generations might be
more privileged than the first generation of eyewitnesses, above all in
receiving the Holy Spirit (παράκλητος, advocate, helper, comforter,
encourager).

> John 14:12 'Very truly, I tell you, the one who believes in me will also do
> the works that I do and, in fact, will do greater works than these,
> because I am going to the Father.'
> John 16:7 'Nevertheless I tell you the truth: it is to your advantage that
> I go away, for if I do not go away, the Advocate will not come to you;
> but if I go, I will send him to you.'

Just after that assurance comes a remarkable promise about what the
Spirit will do (John 16:12–15).

> [12]'I still have many things to say to you, but you cannot bear them now.
> [13]When the Spirit of truth comes, he will guide you into all the truth;
> for he will not speak on his own, but will speak whatever he hears, and
> he will declare to you the things that are to come. [14]He will glorify me,
> because he will take what is mine and declare it to you. [15]All that the
> Father has is mine. For this reason I said that he will take what is mine
> and declare it to you.'

There are many significant points to be made about this passage, but the
key one for now is to think of the author of the Gospel as one who
received that promise. What does it mean for him (I will treat the author
as male though a case can be made for female authorship) to be guided by
the Spirit into all the truth?

The best way to investigate this is to examine what he in fact wrote,
and in what follows I will consider his most famous passage, the opening
verses of his Gospel.[2]

Handsel Press, 1982); B. F. Westcott, *The Gospel According to St John: The Authorised Version with
Introduction and Notes* (London: John Murray, 1898); and (not strictly a commentary) John
Ashton, *Understanding the Fourth Gospel* (Oxford: Oxford University Press, 1991).
2. Much of what follows on the Prologue of John draws directly on David F. Ford, 'Jesus
Christ in Scripture, Community and Mission: The Wisdom of John 1:1–18' in *Scripture,
Community, and Mission: Essays in Honor of D. Preman Niles*, ed. Philip L. Wickeri (London:
Christian Conference of Asia, Hong Kong and The Council for World Mission, 2002),
pp. 300–11.

'**In the beginning** ('Εν ἀρχῇ) . . .' (John 1:1) is a quotation from what must have been one of the best-known texts in John's Greek Bible (the Septuagint) – the first words of its opening verse, Genesis 1:1. Then comes the surprise: instead of continuing '**God created**' it reads: '**was the Word** (λόγος)'. John is rewriting the opening of his Bible. There are plenty of reminders of Genesis 1 – God, coming into being (ἐγένετο), light, darkness. In this, John's most comprehensive summary statement of truth, John clearly sees himself being led by the Spirit to do biblical interpretation, but of a distinctive sort. He is doing something daringly new, and not only with Genesis 1. In the Prologue he does it with Proverbs, Exodus and other texts too. It is a form of what Jewish interpreters call 'midrash': taking the plain sense seriously but going beyond it, linking it with other texts, asking new questions of it, extending the meaning, discovering depths, resonances and applications of it that have not been suggested before. John's Prologue is Jewish Christian midrash, interpreting scripture in the light of the living Jesus Christ.

In the opening verses John reconceives 'the beginning', and also reconceives God in terms of relationship with the Word. The depth and breadth of all meaning, all wisdom, is traceable to this relationship.

> John 1:1–18 [1]In the beginning was the Word, and the Word was with God, and the Word was God. [2]He was in the beginning with God. [3]All things came into being through him, and without him not one thing came into being. What has come into being [4]in him was life, and the life was the light of all people. [5]The light shines in the darkness, and the darkness did not overcome it. [6]There was a man sent from God, whose name was John. [7]He came as a witness to testify to the light, so that all might believe through him. [8]He himself was not the light, but he came to testify to the light. [9]The true light, which enlightens everyone, was coming into the world. [10]He was in the world, and the world came into being through him; yet the world did not know him. [11]He came to what was his own, and his own people did not accept him. [12]But to all who received him, who believed in his name, he gave power to become children of God, [13]who were born, not of blood or of the will of the flesh or of the will of man, but of God. [14]And the Word became flesh and lived among us, and we have seen his glory, the glory as of a father's only son, full of grace and truth. [15](John testified to him and cried out, 'This was he of whom I said, "He who comes after me ranks ahead of me because he was before me."') [16]From his fullness we have all received, grace upon grace. [17]The law indeed was given through Moses; grace and truth came through Jesus Christ. [18]No one has ever

seen God. It is God the only Son, who is close to the Father's heart, who has made him known.

Wisdom too 'was active in the creation of the world (Wisdom 9:9) and is said to be better than life (Proverbs 8:35) and like light (Ecclesiastes 2:13). Wisdom came into the world and was rejected (1 Enoch 42:2). However she set up her tent among humanity (Sirach 24:8) and dispensed glory and grace (Sirach 24:16).'[3] And into this in the Prologue are woven references to other scriptures, above all to do with Moses in Exodus and the themes of tent-pitching (see Exodus 25:8–9), seeing the glory of the Lord (see Exodus 24:15–16), the law (the whole Sinai story), and grace and truth (see the Hebrew pair *chesed* and *emet* in Exodus 34:6).

This might be described as a Jesus Christ-centred wisdom interpretation of the Bible. It not only does wisdom interpretation in the sense of seeking through scriptures the wisdom of God for contemporary life (John's 'we' and 'us'), but also explicitly uses texts in the wisdom genre (which is not a necessary element in what I am calling wisdom interpretation). There is a sense of the sheer abundance of the meaning of scripture, which is supported by the rest of the Gospel and by the very way John writes. He produces a new Gospel which itself invites this sort of midrash. We can endlessly explore the meaning of key words and phrases such as 'born from above', eternal life, glory, 'I am'; or the signs (water into wine, feeding the multitude, healing the blind man, raising Lazarus); or the farewell discourses; or the way John tells of the climactic events of crucifixion and resurrection. John seems to invite us to meditate, ponder, go deeper, and make new connections. He even builds in multiple meanings and ambiguities (to be born ἄνωθεν – 'from above' or 'again', and so on). Underlying all this is a theology of the abundance that not only came from God in Jesus Christ but continues to come from God. There is '**grace upon grace**' (1:16); the light and truth are inexhaustible because they are generated by God; and the culmination of this for us, as the Farewell Discourses show, is the giving of the Holy Spirit: '**I still have many things to say to you**' (16:12).

The question for readers today is: what might it mean to interpret scripture while learning from John's own rich and daring practice of interpretation and from his Gospel's multilevelled meaning and theology? He clearly saw the giving of the Spirit as a guarantee that this process would continue. In what

---

3. Mark W. G. Stibbe, *John* (Sheffield: Sheffield Academic Press, 1993), p. 23.

follows I will take for granted that the process involves close engagement with scriptural texts, and ask what further wisdom for that engagement might be learned from John's Prologue. The five key elements that emerge will continue as themes in this and later chapters. The elements are:

- *The centrality of God.* The Prologue begins by reconceiving God in relation with the Word (a momentous contribution to the understanding of God that will be explored further in chapters 6 and 7 below) and with all things; and having said that the glory of the Word become flesh has been seen, the Prologue ends by saying that no one has seen God, but that the Son, **'close to the Father's heart'** (v. 18), has made him known. This affirms the priority, ultimacy and comprehensive involvement of God and also the intimacy with God opened up through the relationship of Father and Son; it also indicates the mystery of God visible and invisible, revealed and hidden. Any scriptural interpretation that is not first of all concerned with God is clearly out of line with this – but exploring what that might mean is the key challenge to wisdom in the Spirit.
- *The whole of creation as context.* By including in the opening of his Gospel an intrinsic relationship between Jesus Christ as Word and the creation of all things John sets the horizon for biblical interpretation. Nothing can be ruled out as unrelated to scripture and its understanding – no people, experience, history, culture, event, institution, sphere of knowledge, or religion. How they might figure in the process of the Spirit leading into all the truth is not predictable – there are probably things about them that up to now we have not been **'able to bear'** (16:12). The confidence is that the Word is already involved with them. This is essential to the theological horizon within which the case studies of chapters 8–10 are conceived.
- *Immersion in history and the contemporary world.* The Prologue is realistic about being in a world of light and darkness, acceptance and rejection, and about the importance of time in God's purposes – Moses and John the Baptist are mentioned as key historical agents. The Prologue is also itself a form of communication sensitive to its world: written in Greek, and using as its key term Word (λόγος), whose primary resonance is with the Septuagint (where its range embraces law, prophecy, wisdom and other writings) but which also has a rich content in Hellenistic culture. As one commentator says: 'Here OT, Platonic and Stoic concepts come together in a bewildering unity.'[4] Others see even more

4. Ernst Haenchen, *John 1: A Commentary on the Gospel of John chapters 1–6* (Philadelphia: Fortress Press, 1984), p. 126.

streams of influence pouring into this one oceanic word. It helped to
inspire one of the most fruitful engagements in the history of
Christianity, between the Hebraic and Hellenic strands. Its challenge is
to engage in the same Spirit in new engagements with cultures, traditions and civilisations beyond John's horizon (see especially below
chapter 6 on tradition and chapter 9 on the development of universities). In addition the split between those who reject and those who
accept the Word points to one of the sharp polarisations in John,
including that between Jesus and 'the Jews' (see below chapter 4 on
Judaism and Christianity).

- *The interplay between Jewish scriptures and testimony to Jesus Christ.* I have
already sketched some of the references to the Jewish scriptures and
shown how a distinctive combination of plain sense with midrash is
inspired by the desire to do justice to Jesus Christ. This sets up a
dynamic between those scriptures and testimony to Jesus Christ that
has been at the heart of Christian identity and theology, yet has also
been deeply controversial and – especially in Christian relations with
Jews – at times terrible in what it has encouraged. Wisdom in the
interpretation of Christian scripture has to face this, and in this book it
will be a constant concern, most explicitly in chapter 8 on inter-faith
wisdom.
- *A community of people who seek to live in line with what they are interpreting.*
The situation of Christian understanding of scripture that might
emerge from the Prologue is of 'us' (the first person of the Prologue is
plural), in a family-like community of believers (**'who received him, who
believed in his name'** – v.12), centred on God (**'children of God'** – v.12;
'born of the will of God' – v.13), in the presence and light of the
living Jesus Christ, alert to the relatedness of Jesus Christ to **'all things'**
(v.3) and **'all people'** (vv.4, 9), receiving **'from his fullness'** (v.16) in
ways that can move beyond the literal meaning into an extended or
transformed meaning appropriate to new events, situations and
people, and above all to the fresh **'grace upon grace'** (v. 16) of God. This
community, the church, appears at many points in the following chapters,
and the discussion of it in chapter 7 as a 'school of desire and wisdom' is
pivotal between the early and later parts of the book. *The ever-fresh
wisdom interpretation of scripture in community questions the adequacy of ways
of interpreting scripture whose sole emphasis is on keeping to the literal sense, or to
the historical sense, or to the original author's intention, or whose conception of
scripture is as some sort of container with one limited meaning; and its encompassing presupposition is of the Spirit leading into truth beyond what it has been
possible to cope with before.*

Learning from Luke

The discussion of Luke's Gospel and a little of Acts in the previous chapter gives material to supplement the conclusions drawn above from John's Gospel. Each of the five points just summarised can be confirmed and developed by reference to Luke, and in addition further hermeneutical points can be made in preparation for this chapter's eventual task of trying to distil the most helpful maxims to guide the wisdom interpretation of scripture.

God, creation, history, OT/NT, community
First, there is Luke's approach to the five elements discovered in John's Prologue.

On God, chapter 1 found Luke utterly theocentric. His narrative begins and ends with worship in the Temple; the pivotal events of baptism and transfiguration are about the affirmation of Jesus by his Father; the responsive events of Jesus being tempted in the wilderness and agonising in prayer on the Mount of Olives centre on doing the will of God; Jesus' central message is of the Kingdom of God; the inner meaning of the baptism and transfiguration, given in Jesus' exultation, is centred on the mutual knowing of Father and Son; the crucifixion culminates in the giving up of Jesus' spirit to his Father; and the resurrection is the most comprehensive of all God's acts, leading to blessing God in the Temple with great joy. In terms of the five moods of faith, each is rooted analogously in God, as the one who affirms, commands, questions, surprises, and desires the coming of his Kingdom and the joy of his children. Above all, the cries in Luke's Gospel, which were taken as critical points of intensity and of discernment, leading to a conception of wisdom that is deeply connected with God, the realities of life, and longing for the joy of the Kingdom of God, are dramatic embodiments of how the reality of God and God's activity is primary in relation to creation, suffering, evil, death and life. All of this means that any understanding of Luke (as of John) that does not do justice to the centrality of God is radically defective, and that one of the main challenges of a wisdom interpretation of scripture is to work out what this means in practice.

On the whole of creation as the context for biblical interpretation, Luke too speaks, in Jesus' cry of exultation, of involvement with 'all things'; Jesus' teaching in parables and wisdom sayings is pervaded with perceptions from nature and from social and economic life; and the stories of signs and wonders in nature and in healings embrace the physical world in signifying God and the Kingdom of God. The resurrection of Jesus is the most comprehensive sign of all. Rising from the dead is the most radical conceivable event in creation; Jesus in Luke 24 indicates its relevance to all nations; and, when the Holy Spirit is poured out at Pentecost, it is for **'all flesh'** (Acts 2:17). This horizon is one of the great challenges in Acts and throughout church history, the paradigmatic event being the coming of the Holy Spirit on Cornelius and his household in Acts 10. The embrace of non-Jews within the church, without requiring them to fulfil all the Jewish entry requirements or dietary laws, meant that Peter had to reinterpret his scriptures and let the boundaries of his community be transformed; and analogous challenges have recurred through Christian history regarding boundaries of race, nation, gender, sexuality, slavery and disability.

On immersion in history and the contemporary world, Luke's narrative genre takes this for granted, and it is intensified by the diverse cries that punctuate it. Right from the opening chapters scriptures are being interpreted in relation to current events. Scripture is never seen as a historical document mainly about the past, but as a world of meaning inhabited now, full of resources for understanding and orienting life now in the Spirit. This means that a core concept in Luke is that of prophetic wisdom – Jesus is greater than Jonah the prophet and than Solomon the wise king; but even more important is the person of Jesus as embodying – in encounters, actions, events, sufferings, death and resurrection – a prophetic wisdom that resonates with 'all the scriptures'. Like John in his use of the cross-cultural concept of Word, Luke too is alert to forms of behaviour and expression in his culture that offer the possibility of being affirmed, critiqued and transformed in the light of the Gospel. This complex hermeneutical engagement with his contemporary world is informed on the one hand by being steeped in his Greek Bible, the Septuagint, and on the other by being fluent in the religious, cultural, medical, political and economic languages of his environment.

On the interplay between Jewish scriptures and testimony to Jesus Christ: this pervades Luke's Gospel and Acts and reaches its twin culminations with Jesus on the Emmaus road and Stephen before the council of his accusers. If an 'incarnational hermeneutic' is central to the short Prologue of John, and evident throughout Luke's writings as discussed above in relation to God, creation and immersion in ongoing history, chapter 1's scope of the whole Gospel of Luke and then the church after Pentecost allows three further dimensions of his hermeneutics to unfold, those centred on the crucifixion, the resurrection and the Holy Spirit. They will be commented upon further below, but for now it is important to note that for each of these the double focus on the Old Testament and on the story of Jesus is essential.

Finally, on a community of people who seek to live in line with what they are interpreting: Luke's two volumes are the most detailed and coherent account of the early church. They move from its origins in Israel as the people of God looking for the Messiah, through the gathering of Jesus' disciples and their apprenticeship following him, on to the climax of his death, resurrection and ascension, and then into the giving of the Holy Spirit and the history of the growth and spread of the church told in Acts. Throughout, it is a community that interprets scripture and is shaped by that understanding. Pentecost is a crucial transition, a decisive handing over of responsibility to the church to witness in the Spirit. The need for what I have described as prophetic wisdom is especially evident in Acts as one situation after another calls for discernment.

The answers to such urgent questions cannot simply be read off scriptures, yet scriptures play a vital role. The process leading to Gentile inclusion in the church in Acts 10 and 11 included Cornelius praying and having a vision; Peter praying and having a vision; Peter interpreting the story of Israel, of Jesus and of the church; the coming of the Holy Spirit **'upon all who heard the word'** (Acts 10:44); baptism; extended hospitality; argument and criticism in the mother church in Judea, with Peter accepting the need to be accountable; initial confirmation of what Peter did; later renewed **'dissension and debate'** (Acts 15:2) about the requirement of circumcision, leading to a special council in Jerusalem at which the verdict of James, appealing mainly to scripture, is accepted; and then the sending of a circular letter with the decision, which is recommended as what **'seemed good to the Holy Spirit and to us'** (Acts 15:28). That was not, of course, the end of the matter, and it is arguable that this earliest of the major divisive issues in the church remains the most fundamental for its identity; and this in turn means that the hermeneutical issues inseparable from the relation of the Christians and Jews require constant discernment and fresh wisdom. What 'seems good to the Holy Spirit and to us' here emerges in complex and untidy ways from individual experiences and corporate processes, and without the sort of definitive closure that might do away with the need for continual ongoing debate and discernment.

For a wisdom interpretation of what Luke wrote, appreciating all this is just a beginning. The implicit invitation is not only to be able to understand what he was doing but to attempt something analogous in our period and culture. In this regard it is especially significant that he wrote two volumes, one set in the small geographical region where Jesus lived and died, the other taking the whole Roman Empire as its context and telling of transformations through the church meeting internal and external challenges – but always giving crucial importance to the interpretation of scripture in the light of the Gospel. He encourages a hermeneutic that is centred in the intensities of local living and face to face relationships while having a global vision of God's purposes and the responsibilities that they inspire.

Hermeneutics of the cross, the resurrection and Pentecost
Just as the hermeneutic of incarnation, exemplified above all by John's Prologue and the way Luke in his Gospel and Acts tells the story of the historical involvement of Jesus and the church, will continue to be important in the coming chapters so also will the hermeneutic of the crucifixion, the resurrection and the Holy Spirit. All of them together are essential to any Christian hermeneutic, but not as some sort of formula or method; rather as a reminder to return again and again to the particularities of the testimonies to Jesus Christ seeking the wisdom that he himself inspires in new contexts as the ongoing interpreter of them through his Spirit. Yet, while there may be no formula or method, it is possible to try, as in this chapter, to learn from the experience of repeated engagement with those particularities and to distil some guidelines. What emerges from the study of Luke on the crucifixion, resurrection and Pentecost to contribute to such guidelines beyond what has already been said?

Hermeneutic of the cross
On the crucifixion, the main suggestion has been a hermeneutic of cries centred on the loud cry with which Jesus gave up his spirit on the cross. The simultaneously apophatic and cataphatic nature of that cry; its disruptive and interruptive character; its provocation to thought, discipleship and worship; its identification as closely as possible with the whole life of Jesus that is being given up; its simultaneity of God-involvement, self-involvement and world-involvement; its resonance

with and responsiveness to other cries of suffering, interrogation, long-ing, accusation and hatred; its intimate link with the Psalms and all their cries: all of this together suggests that it is unavoidably and inexhaustibly central to Christian testimony and interpretation of scripture.

Any wisdom interpretation must take place within earshot of this cry and of the cries with which it resonates. What chapter 1 called a 'wisdom of reserve' insists that the plain, underinterpreted realism of the Gospel accounts is returned to again and again; what it called a 'wisdom of ramification' engages in the endless interpretation of this cry in indica-tive, imperative, interrogative, subjunctive and optative moods, and discernment of the wisdom discoverable in millennia of previous inter-pretation. What might be called 'wisdom in the Spirit of Jesus Christ' sees that Spirit as the same that was expelled with Jesus' last cry, given up to his Father, given back in resurrection, and shared in Pentecost: wisdom interpretation is at heart understanding through the same Spirit in which this cry was uttered. In Acts this is above all exemplified in Stephen, 'full of the Spirit and wisdom', who interprets scripture in line with further divine activity in the present and future, and who on the point of death prays: **'Lord Jesus, receive my spirit'** and then dies with a loud cry of forgiveness (Acts 7:59ff). The hermeneutic of the cross in Luke is understanding and living in this Spirit, and this will be discussed further in chapter 5 below. In Luke 9:23–24 its core wisdom is summed up by Jesus:

> [23]Then he said to them all, 'If any want to become my followers, let them deny themselves and take up their cross daily and follow me.
> [24]For those who want to save their life will lose it, and those who lose their life for my sake will save it.'

Hermeneutic of the resurrection

As regards the resurrection, the risen Jesus in Luke 24 is one who, having cried out in death, now teaches 'all the scriptures'. This, as chapter 1 suggested, is the wisdom climax of his Gospel, a new beginning of wisdom in fear, wonder and joy. It is not just about knowledge. It encourages the opening of minds through the opening of scripture in attentiveness to the risen Jesus, and this is part of a multifaceted expe-rience, including walking, conversation, touching, eating and finally blessing. As a hermeneutic of resurrection it has the marks Richard Hays discovered: God's centrality, surprises, the Old Testament read in Christian terms, the epistemological transformation of the readers, an enduring core of mystery beyond our control, close involvement with a community and its vocation, the encouragement of figural reading, and an eschatological orientation. These marks will be gathered into the theses and maxims at the end of this chapter, but for now the point to be made is one that takes the resurrection's position in Luke's narrative seriously: it is not only the culmination of his Gospel but also preparation for the day of Pentecost at the beginning of Acts.

Luke 24 insists that the Holy Spirit has not yet come on the disciples, and the place of the scriptures in preparing for the coming of the Spirit is central. The risen Jesus is incognito during the whole of his teaching on the Emmaus road. The intensive and even lively study of scripture is no guarantee of recognising Jesus or of the coming of the Spirit at Pentecost and the energising of lives in community and mission. The basic orientation to the Spirit, as the end of Luke's Gospel and the opening of Acts make clear, is one of waiting with others, remembering, and calling out to God in blessing and in constant prayer. In the aftermath of Pentecost there is the hermeneutics of Stephen and others 'in the Spirit'. But what of the disciples on the Emmaus road? They are being given interpretation in the Spirit by Jesus, and their hearts burn within them but without recognising him. Even after recognition they still have not yet received the Spirit at Pentecost. Later in the chapter, the rest of the disciples do recognise Jesus and have their minds opened to the scriptures but still are told to wait for Pentecost.

So even those who are well informed, have been in relationship with Jesus before and after his resurrection, and have been instructed by him in the scriptures still simply need to wait and cry out for the Spirit. All the preparation, epistemological transformation, understanding of scripture, fellowship with Jesus and each other, and joyful worship do not amount to a process of development towards the receiving of the Spirit. It remains a complete gift. It is not that the preparation is useless or inappropriate: there is a wisdom of preparation, and the 'foolish' disciples need to learn it. *It is rather that interpretation of scripture in the Spirit recognises that its most essential wisdom is in constantly crying: 'Come, Holy Spirit!'* As the hermeneutic of the cross led back to the invitation of Jesus to take up the cross daily, so the hermeneutic of the resurrection leads back to Jesus' teaching in Luke on insistent asking, searching and knocking.

> Luke 11:9–13 [9]'So I say to you, Ask, and it will be given you; search, and you will find; knock, and the door will be opened for you. [10]For

everyone who asks receives, and everyone who searches finds, and for everyone who knocks, the door will be opened. [11]Is there anyone among you who, if your child asks for a fish, will give a snake instead of a fish? [12]Or if the child asks for an egg, will give a scorpion? [13]If you then, who are evil, know how to give good gifts to your children, how much more will the heavenly Father give the Holy Spirit to those who ask him!'

Hermeneutic of Pentecost

This leads into a hermeneutic of Pentecost. The discussions of both the cross and the resurrection have led into speaking of the Spirit, and each has led back into the teaching ministry of Jesus. Both cross and resurrection have also been simultaneously objects of interpretation and guides of interpretation, reference points in relation to which scripture and life are understood. Hermeneutically, the Spirit is the embracing reality in Luke's Gospel and in Acts. The life of Jesus from before birth is under the sign of the Spirit, which then comes upon him in baptism, leads him into the wilderness to be tempted, and anoints him for his ministry, whose teaching culminates after his resurrection in preparing his disciples for Pentecost.

All of Acts is then under the sign of Pentecost, and at the cutting edge of the history that it recounts is the prophetic, interpretative wisdom in the Spirit exemplified above all by Stephen, but also by Peter, Philip, James, Paul and others. This is constantly related to the scriptures and to testimony to Jesus Christ; it is also constantly opening up new possibilities beyond the literal sense of those scriptures and that testimony. As in Luke's Gospel, this drama of the early church is punctuated by cries, calls, appeals and shouts. The explosion of proclamation on the day of Pentecost sets the tone, and the story is primarily about the course of that proclamation. The dynamic is one of inexhaustible overflow and super-abundance, symbolised by the rushing, violent wind, the tongues 'as of fire', the different languages, and the quotation from Joel about the pouring out of the Spirit on all flesh. Soon afterwards, Peter and John after their release by the authorities gathered with their friends, they 'raised their voices together to God' in prayer, and there was something like a second Pentecost.

> Acts 4:31 When they had prayed, the place in which they were gathered together was shaken; and they were all filled with the Holy Spirit and spoke the word of God with boldness.

The final words of Acts 4:31, 'with boldness' (μετὰ παρρησίας) might stand as a headline for Acts, meaning confident, free, overflowing speech in the Spirit. The term is repeated even more emphatically in the very last verse of Acts about Paul **'proclaiming the Kingdom of God and teaching about the lord Jesus Christ with all boldness and without hindrance'** (Acts 28:31). One filling with the Holy Spirit at Pentecost does not rule out another a while later: this suggests that the hermeneutics of the Spirit is one of an abundance, not least in the interpretation of scripture and of the testimony to Jesus Christ. It is a dynamic that relates to more and more people, regions and spheres of life, but in the process requires more and more discernment. Christian confidence and the mission inspired by texts such as Acts and the commissioning and transfer of responsibility in Luke 24 (as discussed in chapter 1) can be terrible as well as glorious. One of the main concerns of this book is to seek in these matters a wisdom in the Spirit for today, part of which is this chapter's quest for guidelines in interpreting scripture.

Rereading in the Spirit

So far, the previous chapter and this one have approached the theme of scriptural interpretation by doing it and by staying quite close to Luke, Acts and John in any comments. This has assumed a good deal and begged many questions. Before undertaking the culminating task of this chapter – the suggestion of theses and maxims for a wisdom interpretation of scripture – this and the following two sections will step back a little and will deal with a set of key issues in their relationship to wisdom interpretation: the practice of rereading before God; scholarship and hermeneutics; and doctrine and scripture.

The core practice of wisdom interpretation is rereading.

Most of the individual books of the Bible are already steeped in the reading or hearing of other parts of the Bible, or have been edited in the knowledge of them. This is especially true of the New Testament in its multifarious ways of reading the Old Testament, a taste of which has been given already through Luke and John. So the Old and New Testaments are already partly constituted by rereading and are in my terms the primary model for wisdom interpretation. Innumerable acts and processes of reading and rereading, often growing out of hearing and rehearing in oral traditions, have contributed to the scriptures reaching us in their present form. Involved in these acts and processes have been innumerable discernments, assessments, discriminations, selections, writings and rewritings, editings, translations, disputes, critiques, power struggles, communal decisions, and responses to new events and situations – all of which are ingredients in wisdom interpretation.

The process of canonisation might be seen as communal discernment and decision-making about which writings are to be the main focus of rereading in the community. In the early church it was one of a set of elements through which the community articulated its core identity. Others included its patterns of worship and liturgy, especially the eucharist and cycles of readings in lectionaries; its 'rule of faith' – the basic affirmations of Christian belief that developed into the creeds; its structures of church polity, deliberation and authority; its catechesis – the essential teachings, both doctrinal and ethical, and above all scriptural, given to new members before baptism; and its responses to key challenges, both dramatic ones such as persecution and division, and pervasive ones such as how to live as Christians in the Roman Empire. The Bible, both before and after its canonisation as New and Old Testaments, played a vital role in all of these, and they in turn affected it. At every significant point in all those processes scripture was being reread and discussed, and Christian wisdom was being sought in this way on worship, belief, community life, the education of converts and children, and participation in social, economic, legal and cultural life.

Those articulations of core identity might be seen as part of what was called in chapter 1 a 'wisdom of reserve', concerned to discern what is most essential without overspecifying: the understandings, expressions, practices and structures that embody most reliably what Christian faith and living are and ought to be. The reserve, as in the Gospel accounts of the crucifixion, is careful not to overdefine something inexhaustibly rich, not to claim as exclusively normative one among many possible interpretations, and to leave any prescription appropriately open to further specification and improvisation. The very centrality of what results makes it also the object of the most vigorous and sometimes bitter arguments, and not the least of the dimensions of wisdom concerns the ways of coping with these divisions. At the same time the 'wisdom of ramification' allows for the scriptures and the other elements to be endlessly improvised upon and related to new people, ideas, practices and situations.

In relation to scripture, after the canon is initially settled (a question repeatedly reopened through Christian history), the wisdom of reserve is seen in such things as the primary emphasis on the literal or plain sense, in the distillation of the 'rule of faith' as a guide to what is most important, in the selection of liturgical passages and lectionary readings for especially frequent rereading, and in the overarching conceptions of the Trinitarian God and the 'economy of salvation' from creation to the eschaton. The complementary wisdom of ramification is seen in the other 'senses' of scripture that extend its meaning in many directions, in the endless proliferation of interpretations in prayer, song, preaching, catechesis, visual imagery and forms of life, and in the diverse theologies and schools of learning and teaching. Both wisdoms require repeated rereadings, and a further dimension is learning how to combine wisely the disciplines of reserve with ramifying improvisations.

The specifically theological character of the rereading lies in it being done before God, in relationship with God, seeking in the Spirit to follow the purposes of God in the world and finding in scriptures inspired testimony to what all of that involves. If 'the fear of the Lord is the beginning of wisdom' then wisdom interpretation of scripture is done primarily with respect to and for God. The most important thing is to learn to read and reread for the sake of God and the Kingdom of God. This sort of reading is not just a skill to be mastered; it is inseparable from learning to love God, neighbours and enemies, and from transformations of life as well as mind.

This reading will have its solitary side, but at every point (including in solitude) it will be dependent on other people – the authors of scripture, those who have translated and interpreted it, our teachers, and all that the reader relates to in the past, present or future. The question: With and for whom do we read and reread? is, after the question of God, the second (though simultaneous) question for wisdom interpretation. To reread the same passage in company different from usual – in a different community of worship and preaching, a different cultural group, or group of friends, or academic community, or social class, or gender, or age group, or faith community, or with different commentaries – is to find different meanings emerging (see below on regimes of reading). It is also to find that the whole range of moods is relevant. Reading scripture before God with others is occasion for being addressed and for recognising how we are affirmed, commanded, questioned, surprised and loved by God.

The most intense form of address is the cry, or the call of God and of the wisdom of God, and it is both heard and responded to amidst the many other cries from one's own community and from others. The discernment of cries is therefore a fundamental responsibility of communities and their members, and the reading of scripture is a schooling in this discernment as an accompaniment to the cries of praise, joy, thanks, interrogation, repentance, petition, intercession, lament, hope, proclamation, blessing and love in which readers are summoned to join. *To live in the Spirit is to reread with others for the sake of God and the Kingdom of God and to let oneself be addressed, schooled and transformed accordingly.*

Scholarship and hermeneutics as resources for rereading scripture

Among the aids to rereading are scholarship and hermeneutics. They overlap with each other but have somewhat different concerns. *As a thought experiment, imagine someone reading the Gospel of John at school and then again twenty years later.* The text is exactly the same, but it could be a very different experience, depending on what has happened to the reader during those twenty years. It is likely that the most significant factors in the changes will be to do with practices of attentive reading, life experiences and commitments, worship and prayer life (if any), cultural influences, and the company kept over the years. But the later reading might also have been changed by scholarly and hermeneutical factors.

The scholarly factors might include learning Greek and being able to compare the Greek text with the translation being used; studying what scholars have to say about the authorship of the book, the community it was written for, its relation to the other Gospels and to the Septuagint, its context in relation to Judaism and to the Hellenistic world under the Roman Empire, its literary and rhetorical form, its imagery, its theology, and its historical reliability; and reading some of the vast amount that has been written about it by scholars and others over the past two millennia. The main thrust of the scholarly is towards the origins, the 'archaeology' of the text in its context, and the contributions of philology, history, literary analysis and history of thought are especially relevant.

Hermeneutics needs to be alert to all those factors, but adds further dimensions, especially a concern to draw them all together and make sense of the text for now and for the future. It raises questions (including suspicious questions) about the reader and the reader's world of meaning and how that might engage with John's. It refuses to be limited to what the text might have meant to its author or first readers and sees it as having an abundance of potential meaning way beyond those. As one of the most influential texts in Christian history and related cultures it has figured in powerful and often conflicting interpretative strategies, some of which still operate, and hermeneutics wrestles with these to correct or replace them. *Above all, hermeneutics tries to let its questions be commensurate with the subject matter of the text, and in the case of John this will mean taking seriously the horizon John opens up in his prologue: God, the whole of creation, and the meaning of history.*

A reader who has learnt from both the more retrospective view of scholarship and the more comprehensive and prospective view of hermeneutics is likely to have been changed not just in what might come under the heading of knowledge of John's Gospel but in other ways too. Once having entered into the 'common sense' of first-century Jewish Christianity and its environment, one does not then leave it: there is a new dimension to all New Testament interpretation. Once having become critically aware of formative elements in one's own culture that affect one's reading, that carries over into other areas; and, once having been gripped by the questions of God, creation and history, those other areas invite connection with John's message.

Changes such as these can obviously be disturbing, and in fact scholarly and hermeneutical conclusions about John's Gospel have been very controversial in recent centuries, ranging from negative comparisons of its historical reliability in comparison with the other three Gospels, through Bultmann's existentialist hermeneutic, to bitter accusations of anti-Judaism. But for now the question is about scholarship and hermeneutics as resources for rereading scripture wisely as part of Christian theology.

This vast topic has no general answer. There are scholars who are suspicious or hostile towards hermeneutics and theology; hermeneuts who have little to do with scholarship or theology; and theologians who carry on without being much affected by scholarship or hermeneutics; besides many other combinations of hostility, neutrality and ambivalence. My concern is not so much to discuss all the issues between them as to make two modest claims – one negative and one positive.

The negative claim is that insofar as theology is about understanding and truth it is foolish to ignore what scholarship and hermeneutics have to offer, even if it is not always taken on the terms on which it is offered.

The positive claim is that there are good examples of engagement in scholarship and hermeneutics feeding into what I call a wisdom interpretation of scripture.

The best brief way to support those claims is through referring to an example, that of the cooperation between André LaCocque and Paul Ricoeur; but first I will draw on my own experience of similar collaboration.

Example: 2 Corinthians

Over a period of five years in the 1980s I worked with Frances Young, a scholar of the New Testament and early church, on what became the book *Meaning and Truth in 2 Corinthians*,[5] and that was a formative time for the present book's approach to biblical interpretation. Our approach was to study it intensively together, alone, and with classes of students and colleagues, and to use a variety of methods of interpretation which were accompanied by commentary on their rationale, uses and limitations. We produced a translation; used philological and historical-critical methods; made a literary argument about the genre and unity of the letter; made proposals about its overall meaning and coherence; studied the intertextuality between it and Paul's Greek scriptures, the Septuagint; drew on a range of hermeneutical concepts and theories; explored the metaphor of the economy of God; applied to the letter the sociological and historical literature about Corinth and its church; and discussed its contemporary theological contribution to two topics, authority and God.

Among the lessons learnt through this process were the following.

- Rereading is the practice that links all the approaches. The worthwhileness of a method is tested by a rereading that bears in mind the readings done already with other approaches in mind. The result of multiple rereadings in the light of different leading questions, bodies of scholarship, hermeneutical theories and theological positions is to end up with a huge 'surplus of meaning', far too great to be put into any book; and even then to know that future rereadings within and beyond the academy will produce yet more.
- These rereadings are not systematisable under some 'master' theory, theology or metanarrative. If one is convinced that each has some validity, and that they are not simply competitive with each other, then somehow they all have to be kept in play together in their particularity. If this is true of just one short letter, how much more is it the case

---

5. Frances Young and David F. Ford, *Meaning and Truth in 2 Corinthians* (London: SPCK, 1987).

with other, longer scriptural books? Within this ramifying complexity the core simplicity is the practice of rereading.

- Translation is of great theological and hermeneutical as well as scholarly importance. Again and again as we laboured on the translation of the letter the most important hermeneutical and theological questions arose while wrestling over the appropriate English rendering of the Greek. We placed the translation at the end of the book to signify its aim: to enable rereading in the light of what had gone before. 'In translation a book is known for the first time.'[6]
- There is no necessary conflict between the scholarly and the hermeneutical approaches, or between either of them and the theological, but nor is there any overarching integration of them. Rather it is a matter of constant negotiation and discernment, for which my name is wisdom interpretation.

Example: Ricoeur and LaCocque

In 1998 André LaCocque, an Old Testament scholar, and Paul Ricoeur, philosopher and hermeneutical thinker, published their joint studies of a set of Old Testament texts, *Thinking Biblically: Exegetical and Hermeneutical Studies.*[7] It is a remarkable achievement, especially in its articulation of the significance of what they are doing. Their Preface is something of a *tour de force* on how scholarly exegesis and philosophical hermeneutics can come together, refuting convincingly the suggestion of intrinsic opposition between the more archaeological approach of the exegete who uses the historical-critical method to research the production of the text and the more teleological approach of the philosopher who uses concepts, arguments and theories to explore its reception. It describes a double movement through which developments from either side have opened each to the other and made collaboration fruitful.

From the side of exegesis, without disowning the historical-critical method but rather expanding it, there has been a fourfold opening prospectively towards the history of a text's reception. First, it is recognised that writing gives a certain autonomy to the text, so that meaning is continually being born through rereadings – Gregory the Great's saying

---

6. Franz Rosenzweig, in a letter to his cousin Rudolf Ehrenberg on 1 October 1917, found in *Der Mensch und sein Werk – Gesammelte Schriften 1. Briefe und Tagebücher: Band I – 1900–1918*, ed. Rachel Rosenzweig and Edith Rosenzweig-Scheinmann (The Hague: Martinus Nijhoff, 1979), pp. 460–1: 'erst wenn etwas übersetzt ist, ist es wirklich *laut* geworden'.
7. André LaCocque and Paul Ricoeur, *Thinking Biblically: Exegetical and Hermeneutical Studies* (Chicago and London: University of Chicago Press, 1998).

is quoted: 'Scripture grows with its readers.'[8] Second, the text is seen as the outcome of one or often more traditions in which there has been repeated reinventing, refiguring and reorienting, and this continues in the traditions of its reception. Third, perhaps most important of the four, the text is seen as tied to a living community, and the final redaction of its written stage is not seen to bring its life span to an end. The very writing down of a text was done prospectively to meet the needs and expectations of the community, the events it recorded were seen as paradigmatic for the future, the prophecies as open to multiple fulfilments, and the whole text as calling out to be continually completed by being remembered – which in biblical terms means being remodelled and reactualised by the community. Fourth, there is the irreducible plurivocity of the text, open to being read on several levels at once.

From the side of philosophical hermeneutics, some have recognised the desirability of engaging with exegesis in the hope that there is something distinctive to be learnt from the modes of thought in biblical genres such as wisdom, narrative, law, prophecy or psalm. This adds a new corpus of texts to the philosophical repertoire, one where metaphorical discourse is central. Further, these texts are in a unique relationship to the community of faith, and the hermeneut needs to enter, at least imaginatively and with sympathy, into the circle whose principle is that in interpreting their scriptures the community interprets itself – that readers are in the asymmetrical position of learners in relation to the scriptural teacher. That some philosophers are willing to think within this circular relation 'between the elected text and the elected community' brings them closer to the imaginative and intellectual world of the exegete. Finally, there is appreciation of the intersection of biblical modes of thought with those of other cultures, which has become 'the constitutive destiny of our culture',[9] and which calls on thinkers to engage from both sides – again requiring philosophers to be literate in exegesis.

The practical outcome of this convergence of scholarship and hermeneutics is that LaCocque and Ricoeur trace what they call 'trajectories' of the text, taking full account of it in historical critical terms while also doing justice to its augmentations of meaning in reception (as through figuration, typology or allegory, or through intersections with other texts) and, beyond all these, thinking through its significance in contemporary life and thought.

---

8. Ibid. p. xi.   9. Ibid. p. xviii.

What has here been summarised rather densely is in the book eloquently unfolded through actual interpretations of texts, some of which will feature in later chapters (especially Ricoeur on Exodus 3:14 in chapter 6 and on the Song of Songs in the Conclusion). For present purposes two key areas are left implicit by LaCocque and Ricoeur and need to be noted briefly.

Regimes of reading since the Middle Ages

The first is the significance of the institutional settings and regimes of reading within which scriptural interpretation is done. LaCocque and Ricoeur inherit a postmedieval history in which there have been successive dominant regimes of reading. Their approaches can be understood as a new mediation of that history in the interests of a practice of interpretation that draws simultaneously on the premodern, modern and postmodern. They refuse to see the main regimes of reading since the Middle Ages as mutually exclusive but try to demonstrate their fruitfulness and complementarity in the course of dialogical exegesis of particular passages of scripture. It is not a systematic or theoretical integration of regimes (these are often in tension or even contradiction with each other) but rather a set of interpretations that demonstrate, in one case after another, that there is wisdom to be discovered in each regime, at least with regard to some specific texts.

In broad outline, one might distinguish at least six regimes of reading on which they draw, two medieval, one early modern, two modern and a late modern or postmodern polyphony. The patristic and medieval practice of *lectio divina* had its main institutional location in the monastic tradition and fared badly in modernity. Ricoeur shows its contemporary fruitfulness, especially in his critical rehabilitation of an allegorical and liturgical reading of the Song of Songs (see below in the Conclusion). The *lectio* tradition was contested by the scholastic method of using scriptural texts in dialectical dispute, whose main institutional location was the new medieval universities. The scholastics too are drawn upon by Ricoeur, especially in his discussion of '**I am who I am**' in Exodus 3:14 (see below chapter 6). The regime that succeeded the monastic and scholastic was that of the early modern humanist retrieval of the scriptures and their manuscripts in Hebrew and Greek. This flourished in many settings besides universities, and its appreciation of the importance of scholarly study in the original languages and of setting the texts in their original contexts is taken for granted by both LaCocque and

Ricoeur. They also share the humanist suspicion of many theological attempts to use scripture by subsuming it into dogmatic systems or polemics. The two modern regimes are the most obvious ways to differentiate the two. LaCocque represents *wissenschaftlich* historical-critical scholarship while Ricoeur represents modern philosophical hermeneutics; yet each is also committed to, and indeed makes considerable use of, the other. The main intellectual interest of the book is in this interplay, which is internalised by each of them, and whose chief institutional setting is the modern university as it struggles to interrelate very diverse methods of understanding and arriving at knowledge. At the same time they are engaged with a range of what might be called late modern or postmodern approaches (here the diversity, amounting to fragmentation, resists the label 'regime') such as feminism, psychoanalysis, political critique and deconstruction, which have flourished as much outside as within the academy. One might add a seventh approach which is more in the nature of a parallel tradition that has likewise had to grapple with many regimes of reading: throughout their exegeses LaCocque and Ricoeur are frequently in discussion with Jewish thinkers and scholars, both ancient and modern.

It seems to me no accident that, in their attempt to indwell diverse previous worlds of meaning while at the same time being committed to opening up interpretations that can with integrity be inhabited today, they frequently return to the concept of wisdom – and one that, as the next paragraph suggests, is intrinsically theological.

What about theology?

The final question is about theology. The Preface sees 'theological treatises' as complex, highly speculative forms of discourse in which philosophy and biblical thought are 'already inextricably mingled'.[10] The hermeneutical philosopher 'more readily reads works of exegesis'. This has the seeds of a form of theology that, on the one hand, stays close to exegesis, and, on the other hand, continually relates it to contemporary life and thought without producing speculative 'theological treatises'. If one searches through the book for further clues a striking fact is the recurrence of the theme of wisdom – in relation to creation, law, psalms, and above all the Song of Songs. In Ricoeur's section 'Toward a Theological Reading of the Song of Songs'[11] he discovers 'sparks of new meaning' for today by beginning

10. Ibid. p. xv.   11. Ibid. pp. 295ff.

with an intrabiblical reading of the Song in intersection with the cry of jubilation in Genesis 2:23 and the rationale for marriage in Genesis 2:24. The climax is the mutual illumination of the 'sapiential dénouement' of the Song 8:6 and the 'sapiential dénouement' of Genesis 2:24. But such explicit reference to wisdom is not necessary, and may even distract from the more fundamental point that the whole mode of the book's theology, and especially of Ricoeur's, is in line with the sort of wisdom interpretation of scripture being sketched in this chapter.

Yet there is a need to go much further than LaCocque and Ricoeur in giving a theological account of scripture.

Wisdom and doctrine: a theological account of scripture

In the exegesis and theological interpretation done in chapter 1 and the opening sections of this chapter theological positions about the Bible have been implied but not articulated. The classic and unavoidable issues (however they are rephrased or hidden within other topics) include God, revelation and inspiration; church, canon and the formation of Christian readers; and the place of scripture within the teaching of theology and the institutions where this takes place. There is no possibility of treating all those adequately in this section. My approach will be to engage with one recent work which succinctly covers them all, and to postpone to later chapters longer treatments of some of them.

John Webster in *Holy Scripture: A Dogmatic Sketch*[12] offers a provocative contrast to LaCocque and Ricoeur, laying out a Christian doctrinal account of scripture that has little time for either historical criticism or philosophical hermeneutics. His singleminded concentration on the theological in a classic Protestant dogmatic mode sharpens and illuminates the issues even when its treatment of them is not entirely satisfactory.

Webster's core affirmations are in line with our exegesis and discussion in this and other chapters, and it is important to note them, though they need not be expanded upon here.

First, he insists on the priority of God, and on the economy of God's Trinitarian activity as the main doctrinal context within which to consider scripture.

---

12. John Webster, *Holy Scripture: A Dogmatic Sketch* (Cambridge: Cambridge University Press, 2003).

Second, within the economy of God he pays special attention to Jesus Christ and the Holy Spirit. His stress on the Spirit's activity 'in hallowing creaturely processes' makes sure that scripture is not isolated from other spheres and that (together with the process of canonisation and of reception) it is set within the broader dynamics of God's transformative involvement with humanity and all creation. Yet the particularity of the Spirit's work, not least in inspiring what is spoken or written, allows for a strong specific affirmation of God's self-communication coming through the Bible. He perceptively identifies and discusses five key terms that try to do justice to the relationship of divine and human in scripture: accommodation or condescension; the analogy of the hypostatic union of humanity and divinity in Jesus Christ; prophetic and apostolic testimony; means of grace; and the 'servant-form' of scripture; and he makes a strong case for his own suggestion of the text as a 'sanctified' reality, a work of the Holy Spirit that is not at all competitive with human involvement.

Third, he maintains this God-centredness in his understanding of the church as fundamentally a listening community, and with regard to scripture emphasises the receptivity of reading and the requirement for the appropriate formation of readers in the Spirit.

Finally, he argues for the exegesis of scripture as the centre and goal of Christian theology. Theology is a deepened form of reading, it is 'most properly an invitation to read and reread Scripture',[13] and commentary on scripture is theology's basic genre.

I have presented those points without some aspects of Webster's expansion of them that I find more problematic. In my terms he is strongly inclined to a wisdom of reserve (or, perhaps better, a reasoned reserve), supported by a rhetoric dominated by the indicative and imperative. He is concerned to emphasise essentials by polemical means which often result in 'either ... or ...', or 'not ... but ...' dichotomies and confrontations where there might be much to be said for more nuanced discernment. The main strengths are in insisting on the core theological questions and offering an 'insider' appreciation and critique of classic Reformed Protestant theology of scripture – especially in its later tendencies to isolate its doctrines relating to scripture and inspiration from doctrines of God, church and sanctification. It is generous and

---

13. Ibid. p. 130.

appreciative towards that tradition – though perhaps too uncritical of its potential to be untrue to scripture while championing it.

There is not so much in Webster that might come under the heading of a wisdom of ramification. The plurivocity or multiple senses of scripture are not mentioned; tradition is severely constricted in its significance, other than as the continually renewed practice of listening to scripture; the centrality of scripture to theological education does not seem to lead to it having the scope of 'all things' identified above in the Prologue of John; the contributions of history, literature, sociology, philosophy, hermeneutics and other disciplines to the understanding of scripture are seen more under the heading of threat than of potential; there is no hint that Christians living in different cultures all over the world benefit from their contexts in reading scripture; there is no consideration of possible contributions of Jews, Muslims or others to the Christian understanding of scripture (or vice versa); theology in universities is seen as encountering 'some distress', and though it is granted that this 'does not necessarily bespeak the need for theology's withdrawal from public institutions' there seems to be little possibility of it flourishing in them;[14] and no weight is given to the fact that for most of the world's Christians the main engagement with scripture and with improvisations upon it is in worship.

The dominance of the indicative and imperative moods and an accompanying stress on cognitive clarity, sharp divisions and rejections, decisiveness, and focussed concentration have their advantages, but also cause problems. They tend to insulate from history and prescind from eschatology. To make the point in terms of the analogy of linguistic moods: in relation to history, the interrogative mood of Job in the midst of suffering and bewilderment, or the subjunctive mood of exploration and openness to surprise, are both missing from Webster's account of scripture; and, despite several mentions of eschatology, the optative mood of longing, hoping and imaginative anticipation of God's future is far from counterbalancing, let alone embracing, the emphatic indicatives and imperatives.

All this constitutes a challenge not so much to produce an alternative dogmatic account of scripture[15] as to do what Webster suggests needs doing: to exercise 'exegetical reason' (or 'exegetical wisdom') in drawing

---

14. Ibid. p. 134.
15. One rather paradoxical aspect of the book is that while pleading throughout for the primacy of exegesis in theology, and concluding that commentary is the basic genre, it does almost no exegesis. If it is to be seen as commentary it is largely on Protestant dogmatic accounts of scripture and on what are seen as modern aberrations.

on scripture to think both about scripture and about everything else in relation to it and the God to whom it witnesses. As an aid in that practice this chapter concludes with nine theses and ten maxims that might help.

Nine theses and ten maxims for Christian wisdom interpretation

From 1998 to 2002 a group of fifteen people – scripture scholars, theologians and two pastors – met periodically under the auspices of the Princeton Center of Theological Inquiry's Scripture Project. They discussed issues relating to the interpretation of the Bible

> not only in secular culture but also in the church at the beginning of the twenty-first century. Is the Bible authoritative for the faith and practice of the church? If so, in what way? What practices of reading offer the most appropriate approach to understanding the Bible? How does historical criticism illumine or obscure Scripture's message? How are traditional readings to be brought into engagement with historical methodologies, as well as feminist, liberationist, and post-modernist readings?[16]

The book that resulted opened with 'Nine Theses on the Interpretation of Scripture'. These attempted to distil the understanding of scriptural interpretation that was developed in their conversations and in the twenty-one chapters of their book, divided between four sections: How Do We Read and Teach the Scriptures?; A Living Tradition; Reading Difficult Texts; Selected Sermons. In this section I will take each of the nine theses in turn as my starting point for a brief set of comments followed by my own suggested maxims, one corresponding to each thesis, before concluding with an extra tenth.

The movement of this section is from indicative theses to imperative maxims; but the other moods are involved too. Even in the book's presentation of the nine theses each is accompanied by a set of questions for ongoing discussion, and the chapters that generated the theses contain a great deal of vigorous interrogation and grappling with difficult texts and issues. It is also recognised that any such list is exploratory and far from definitive: its theses and my maxims are proposals in an implicit

---

16. Ellen F. Davis and Richard B. Hays, 'Introduction' in *The Art of Reading Scripture*, ed. Ellen F. Davis and Richard B. Hays (Grand Rapids, MI: William B. Eerdmans, 2003), pp. xiv–xv.

subjunctive mood suggesting what may be helpful and recognising that there are dozens of other possible ways of fulfilling this task, each with its own advantages. And they are also all implicitly optative, embodying a desire to practise better what the Scripture Project calls 'the demanding but ultimately joyful art of reading Scripture'.[17] Indeed it is not adequate to see the maxims simply as imperative even though that is grammatically true: they are more like exclamations – in the first place cries to and for the Holy Spirit, and then addressed to others and to oneself.[18] To indicate this, an even briefer exclamation accompanies each maxim, put in the form of an urgent cohortative invitation: 'Let us . . .!'

Thesis 1. Scripture truthfully tells the story of God's action of creating, judging and saving the world.

'The Bible as a whole is relentlessly *theo*centric.'[19] This has been seen in Luke, Acts, John, Webster and others in this and the previous chapter, and this thesis sums up well the main thrust of *The Art of Reading Scripture*. Its main mode of truth-telling is as testimony, often in narrative form, and the authors present this convincingly,[20] though without offering a full theological epistemology.[21]

This truth is inextricable from wisdom, not least in the presentation of the testimony. William Stacy Johnson makes a particularly apt comment:

> there is no such thing as a 'narrative' – whether unified or otherwise – apart from the contingent theological wisdom of those who are doing the narrating. The narrative is not just a given but must be constructed and reconstructed in the life of the community of faith over time. In addition, the biblical narrative must be supplemented and interrogated by the biblical genre of wisdom; the reflections of the wisdom literature of Scripture challenge the all-inclusiveness and tendencies to triumphalism of narrative.[22]

---

17. Ibid. p. xx.
18. Hebrew grammars speak of the cohortative and the jussive as well as the imperative.
19. Ellen F. Davis, 'Teaching the Bible Confessionally in the Church' in *The Art of Reading Scripture*, p. 21.
20. Richard Bauckham in his chapter 'Reading Scripture as a Coherent Story' in *The Art of Reading Scripture* makes a strong case, pp. 38–53.
21. For my own epistemology see David F. Ford and Daniel W. Hardy, *Living in Praise: Worshipping and Knowing God* (London: Darton, Longman and Todd, 2005); see Paul D. Janz, *God, the Mind's Desire: Reference, Reason and Christian Thinking* (Cambridge: Cambridge University Press, 2004).
22. William Stacy Johnson, 'Reading the Scriptures Faithfully in a Postmodern Age' in *The Art of Reading Scripture*, pp. 109–10.

That grasps well the significance of wisdom both in the narrower sense of a biblical genre and in the wider sense of its involvement in the articulation of the whole of scripture.

Yet as has already been suggested and as later exegesis will argue at length, beginning with the next two chapters on Job, biblical wisdom calls for an even more radical recognition of theocentricity: the acknowledgement of God for God's sake. Likewise it calls for a recognition of the intensity of expression and engagement as articulated in cries. My maxim will therefore give primacy to reading scripture for God's sake and discerning the intensity of God's involvement with humanity through cries.

> **Maxim 1.** *Read and reread scripture above all for the sake of God and God's purposes; hear it as God the Creator, Judge and Saviour crying out to humanity; respond to it, in cries, worship, life and thought, with love for God and for the world God loves.*

Let us read for God's sake!

Thesis 2. Scripture is rightly understood in light of the church's rule of faith as a coherent dramatic narrative.

The church's rule of faith, seen above all in its creeds, distils a 'wisdom of reserve' from the whole of scripture, discerning essentials of Christian doctrinal identity. It is vital that the form of this is narrative or dramatic, showing it to be a wisdom immersed in history while oriented to God's future.

In case this seems too smooth a picture, Richard Bauckham in his discussion of what he calls the 'nonmodern metanarrative' of scripture brings out not only its God-centred coherence but also its intractably dialectical aspects seen in tensions such as those between divine moral order and incomprehensible evil, between androcentric and gynocentric perspectives on the story, between the evident activity of God and hidden providence, and between Israel's privilege and God's concern for the nations. These are the sort of tensions that necessitate a wisdom that can, in my terms, work through the full range of 'moods'. Together with other contributors Bauckham also emphasises the story's resistance to closure: 'The church must be constantly retelling the story, never losing sight of the landmark events, never losing touch with the main lines of theological meaning in Scripture's own tellings and commentaries, always remaining open to the never exhausted potential of the texts in their resonances with contemporary life.'[23]

The image of an ongoing drama has some advantages over that of a narrative, and the concept of a theodrama – for example as developed by Quash through critical engagement with Hegel, von Balthasar, Barth and Bonhoeffer – has rich potential.[24]

> **Maxim 2.** *Read scripture guided by the wisdom of the church's rule of faith, participating in its ongoing drama of God's engagement with humanity.*

Let us read theodramatically!

Thesis 3. Faithful interpretation of scripture requires an engagement with the entire narrative: the New Testament cannot be rightly understood apart from the Old, nor can the Old be rightly understood apart from the New.

The Art of Reading Scripture is especially strong on the relation between OT and NT and on the associated question of Christian and Jewish interpretation. Already in interpreting Luke's Gospel (especially chapter 24, whose hermeneutic of resurrection was illuminated by Richard Hays' interpretation of it in *The Art of Reading Scripture*) and the Prologue of John's Gospel the importance of the intertextuality of OT and NT has become clear. In the chapters which follow, the book of Job, together with the Wisdom of Solomon from the Apocrypha, will be the main examples through which this is explored further.

For Christians the resurrection of Jesus and the pouring out of the Holy Spirit together inspire a figural relationship between the two testaments and also between both of them and ongoing history – the theodrama in which we play a role. But Christian conceptions of God's purposes in history have proved extraordinarily oppressive and dangerous to Jews. Is there a way of Christian integrity in interpretation that does not occasion further oppression and danger for Jews or others? My maxim builds this tension into a core element in Christian reading (see also Thesis/Maxim 8 below).

---

23. Bauckham, 'Reading Scripture', p. 44.
24. Ben Quash, *Theology and the Drama of History* (Cambridge: Cambridge University Press, 2004).

Maxim 3. *Read the Old and New Testaments together in the Spirit of the risen Jesus Christ; be alert to their mutual illumination and to the figural potential between and beyond them; be in dialogue especially with Jewish readings.*

Let us always read the OT together with the NT!

Thesis 4. Texts of scripture do not have a single meaning limited to the intent of the original author. In accord with Jewish and Christian traditions, we affirm that scripture has multiple complex senses given by God, the author of the whole drama.

The hermeneutical principles of routinely entertaining more than one possible meaning (Jewish exegesis) or hearing more than one 'voice' speaking in scripture (Augustine) lead to what I have called a ramification of meanings. *The Art of Reading Scripture* is especially good at making the case for multiple senses (drawing on literary, historical, homiletic and theological reasons) while at the same time recognising that the ramification has many dangers and requires even greater discernment than does a dogmatic or historical critical limitation – whether to the plain or to the 'original' sense or to an author's single intention. Difficult texts evoke many possibilities of meaning, and *The Art of Reading Scripture* concentrates especially on them.

A far larger set of texts that invite an abundance of interpretations is those that use symbolic language and rich imagery, and the authors encourage and practise 'total imaginative seriousness' (Walter Moberly)[25] and the slow reading of texts that have been composed with complex literary artistry.

> The Bible speaks often in symbolic, or imaginative, language for the simple reason that the realities of which it speaks exceed the capacity of ordinary, 'commonsense' discourse. Symbols are inherently ambiguous, and necessarily so; their continuing validity depends on their ability to take on new meanings in new situations and in light of new insights and challenges. The nature of biblical language bears on some of the deepest problems with which the church is currently wrestling.[26]

25. R. W. L. Moberly, 'Living Dangerously: Genesis 22 and the Quest for Good Biblical Interpretation' in *The Art of Reading Scripture*, p. 188.
26. Davis, 'Teaching the Bible', p. 12.

In relation to my maxim, such remarks complexify the distinction between plain and other senses and make it all the more important to be concerned about both.

Above all, there is the inevitability of a diverse flowering of meanings when readers 'wonder wisely and deeply'[27] about these rich texts century after century, and around the world. The chapters that follow try to focus such wonder on a few OT and NT texts, open to an abundance of meaning.

> **Maxim 4.** *Seek first the plain sense of scripture in all its literal and metaphorical richness and also be alert for other senses.*

Let us read for plain sense, open to other senses!

Thesis 5. The four canonical Gospels narrate the truth about Jesus.

That there are four different testimonies to Jesus at the heart of Christian faith can be seen as an enrichment, and as a safeguard against fundamentalisms and the idolising of any one 'image' of Jesus. That they converge in the basic pattern of his life, death and resurrection provides the core narrative structure for Christian faith, worship, sacraments and ethics. That the testimony to Jesus is inseparable from testimony to the God of Abraham, Isaac, Jacob, David, Moses and the prophets draws the whole of the Old Testament into the interpretative field of the Gospels. And that that God is also the God of all creation sets an even wider horizon for interpreters. Such considerations lead from *The Art of Reading Scripture*'s fifth thesis to a fifth maxim that sets the Gospels in a wider horizon.

> **Maxim 5.** *Learn who Jesus Christ is for God and for us through following the testimony to his life, death and resurrection, in conversation with all four Gospels, with the diverse voices of the rest of the Bible, and with all truth and wisdom.*

Let us attend to all the witnesses to Jesus Christ!

Thesis 6. Faithful interpretation of scripture invites and presupposes participation in the community brought into being by God's redemptive action – the church.

---

27. Ibid. p. 11.

'The volume we call the Bible, or scripture, is, to belabor a platitude, a *collection* of documents. These documents are extremely diverse – literarily, religiously, culturally, and theologically – and they derive from a long stretch of ancient Near Eastern and Mediterranean political and religious history. What Christians call the Bible, or scripture, exists as a single entity because – and only because – the church gathered these documents for her specific purpose: to aid in preserving her peculiar message, to aid in maintaining across time, from the apostles to the End, the self-identity of her message that the God of Israel has raised his servant Jesus from the dead. Outside the community with this purpose, binding these particular documents into one volume would be pointless' (Robert W. Jenson).[28]

There are massive problems about 'the Bible as the church's book', including some terrible uses to which the church has put it, the deep and often bitter divisions over its interpretation, and the problems about it that the church has often been very reluctant to face. Yet, for the reasons Jenson and others in *The Art of Reading Scripture* give, there is no question what the primary community of its interpretation is, whether or not one is part of that community. 'Primary' in line with Jenson's definition, however, does not mean 'sole' or 'always right' or 'self-sufficient' or 'able to dictate to others': Thesis/Maxim 8 below is the necessary complement to Thesis/Maxim 6. In addition this maxim calls for Christian attention to the realities and cries of the world as a condition for right hearing of scripture.

> **Maxim 6**. *Read scripture as part of the church (past, present and future) in worship and meditation, in study and conversation around the text, and alert to the realities and cries of the world.*

Let Christians read for each other's sake!

Thesis 7. The saints of the church provide guidance in how to interpret and perform scripture.

Discussing St Francis of Assisi in relation to interpreting scripture, James Howell writes:

> The texts are all about trust, living, and following. For interpretation to be appropriate to these texts, wrestling with faith, with discipleship,

28. Robert W. Jenson, 'Scripture's Authority in the Church' in *The Art of Reading Scripture*, pp. 27f.

prayer and devotion, with the God who is in fact the subject of these texts, is unavoidable. [Nicholas] Lash continues [in his essay 'What Might Martyrdom Mean?']: 'Any model of Christian hermeneutics that ignores such questions, or treats them as marginal or merely consequential, is *theoretically* deficient.' There is, indeed, a hermeneutical 'gap.' 'But this "gap" does not lie, in the last resort, between what was once "meant" and what might be "meant" today. It lies, rather, between what was once achieved, intended or "shown," and what might be achieved, intended, or "shown" today.'[29]

Whole lives are the bearers of the wisdom of scripture, and the exposition, in chapter 1 above, of Jesus, 'greater than Solomon', later imitated by Stephen the first Christian martyr, illustrates Lash's point well. This book later explores Jean Vanier's commentary on the Gospel of John, an interpretation inextricable from more than forty years spent founding and living in L'Arche with core members who have severe learning disabilities. That penultimate chapter is an attempt to be apprenticed to Vanier in the wise reading of scripture.

> **Maxim 7.** *Become apprenticed to past and present wise readers of scripture who have lived their lives in response to its message.*

Let us become apprentices of saints!

Thesis 8. Christians need to read the Bible in dialogue with diverse others outside the church.

With whom and for whom scripture is read is of immense importance. *The Art of Reading Scripture* is especially profound on why it is desirable for Christians and Jews to read their scriptures together and what this might mean. Ellen Davis urges Christians

> actively to seek and cultivate theological friendships with Jews . . . Friendship means being forthright and at the same time respectful about our different viewpoints and interpretations. The most positive outcome I know to such a friendship is the recognition that we do not have to figure out which one of us is wrong; indeed, that concept may not even apply. By ordinary logic, if two people or groups disagree, then one is wrong – or it is all relative and does not much matter anyway. But the basis for both disagreement and friendship is something that is neither strictly logical nor strictly relative. Rather,

---

29. James C. Howell, 'Christ was like St Francis' in *The Art of Reading Scripture*, pp. 102–3.

the basis for theological friendship between Christians and Jews is a mystery – the word Paul rightly uses (Rom. 11:25; see 11:33) as he struggles with this most painful new fact of salvation history, the separation of Jews and Gentiles within the household of Israel's faith. The mystery has only deepened over time, as the two communities have over a period of two thousand years sustained an allegiance to the God to whom Israel's Scriptures bear witness, and likewise have experienced the faithfulness of that God to them. This prolonged duality is something neither Paul nor anyone else in the first century anticipated. At the very least, it should caution us all to modesty in our theological assertions. Both Christians and Jews speak with some authority about the nature of God and what it means to worship God truly, authority that comes out of their willingness to study, pray, and to suffer for what they understand to be true. On both sides that understanding is partial, so both Christians and Jews could well learn modesty in their assertions of 'the Truth'.[30]

The number of 'others' with whom scripture might be read is vast, threatening a dissipation of energies: clearly discernment has to be exercised about with whom and for whom scripture is read. In the present work, the main others are Jews, Muslims, practitioners of academic disciplines, and those with learning disabilities. The challenge set by Ellen Davis is to explore the particular theological rationale in each case (Davis' points about the Jews cannot simply be transferred to others) and, even more, to engage in rereading with partners who are, or might become, friends – which, in Christian terms, excludes nobody.

> **Maxim 8**. *Let conversations around scripture be open to all people, religions, cultures, arts, disciplines, media and spheres of life.*

> **Let us read for the sake of friendship with all!**

Thesis 9. We live in the tension between the 'already' and the 'not yet' of the Kingdom of God; consequently, scripture calls the church to ongoing discernment, to continually fresh rereadings of the text in light of the Holy Spirit's ongoing work in the world.

This thesis suggests the most essential elements in wisdom interpretation: God and the Kingdom of God; immersion in history and in what has

---

30. Davis, 'Teaching the Bible' pp. 25f.

already been given, together with orientation towards God's 'not yet'; the continual seeking of discernment in Christ in community; and the activity of the Holy Spirit now at the cutting edge of history leading forward through fresh rereadings. The Holy Spirit has been a continual challenge in the writing of this book: the Johannine breathing of the Spirit who promises to lead into all truth and do 'greater things'; the Pauline Spirit who searches the deep things of God and distributes charismata; and the Lucan Spirit poured out dramatically at Pentecost for a global mission. The elements of Christian wisdom repeatedly involve the Holy Spirit explicitly, just as do the case studies implicitly.

> **Maxim 9.** *Read scripture in the Spirit, immersed in life, desiring God's future, and open to continually fresh rereadings in new situations.*

Let us read in the Spirit for the sake of the Kingdom of God!

The final maxim is on love. 'As we know from other areas of experience, giving careful attention is not just an outcome of love; it is part of the process of growing in love. We love best those for whom we are obligated to give regular, often demanding care: a child, an animal, a sick or elderly person, a plot of land or an old house. Inching patiently through the Greek or Hebrew text is best seen as "an act of charity" – ultimately, charity toward God.'[31]

> Luke 10:25–30 [25]Just then a lawyer stood up to test Jesus. 'Teacher,' he said, 'what must I do to inherit eternal life?' [26]He said to him, 'What is written in the law? What do you read there?' [27]He answered, 'You shall love the Lord your God with all your heart, and with all your soul, and with all your strength, and with all your mind; and your neighbour as yourself.' [28]And he said to him, 'You have given the right answer; do this, and you will live.' [29]But wanting to justify himself, he asked Jesus, 'And who is my neighbour?' [30]Jesus replied, 'A man was going down from Jerusalem to Jericho, and fell into the hands of robbers, who stripped him, beat him, and went away, leaving him half dead . . .

The lawyer in Luke 10:25ff proves a good reader, and Jesus confirms his interpretation of the law. This, as Augustine and many others have agreed, has the most far-reaching implications for reading scripture. The unsurpassable maxim is: *read in love for God and neighbour*. The 'rule of love' (*regula caritatis*) means that any reading has to fulfil the criterion of

31. Ibid. p. 15.

being aligned with love of God and love of neighbour. Then, when the lawyer asks who his neighbour is, Jesus gives his 'rereading' in the parable of the Good Samaritan. The priest and the Levite who passed by the half-dead man without helping him were habitual readers of Torah. The Samaritan too would have known the books of Moses. The one thing that differentiated him was his compassion in response to a mute cry for help. Jesus' parable sets that cry alongside Torah in a contemporary setting with recognisable characters and a message of prophetic wisdom.

Maxim 10. *Let us reread in love!*

3

Job!

> Job 3:20–26 [20]'Why is light given to one in misery, and life to the bitter in soul, [21]who long for death, but it does not come, and dig for it more than for hidden treasures; [22]who rejoice exceedingly, and are glad when they find the grave? [23]Why is light given to one who cannot see the way, whom God has fenced in? [24]for my sighing comes like my bread, and my groanings are poured out like water. [25]Truly the thing that I fear comes upon me, and what I dread befalls me. [26]I am not at ease, nor am I quiet; I have no rest; but trouble comes.'

Job cries out from the depths of the worst imaginable, the fulfilment of what he has dreaded most. He sits covered with **'loathsome sores … from the sole of his foot to the crown of his head'** (2:7). He is bereaved of all his children; he has been deprived of all his possessions; he has lost all his social standing and dignity, and is an outcast despised and jeered at even by those who are themselves despised; his friends 'comfort' him in ways that rub salt into his wounds; his wife urges him: **'Curse God, and die'** (2:9); he cannot find any meaning in his life or suffering; and he is convinced that God has turned against him and is an enemy responsible for all that has happened to him. Physically, materially, socially, psychologically, in his most intimate personal relationships, and most of all religiously, Job embodies extreme affliction and misery. He cannot even find escape in death.

What response can possibly be made to this comprehensive and intensive suffering?

> Job 2:11–13 [11]Now when Job's three friends heard of all these troubles that had come upon him, each of them set out from his home – Eliphaz the Temanite, Bildad the Shuhite, and Zophar the Naamathite. They met together to go and console and comfort him. [12]When they saw him from a distance, they did not recognize him, and they raised their voices and

wept aloud; they tore their robes and threw dust in the air upon their heads. [13]They sat with him on the ground seven days and seven nights, and no one spoke a word to him, for they saw that his suffering was very great.

The friends cry out in solidarity, and sit with him in silence for seven days and nights. Dedicated, self-involved attentiveness to Job in his suffering is the minimal requirement before any word is said. Then when Job **'opened his mouth and cursed the day of his birth'** (3:1) the extraordinary dialogue begins, first between Job and the three friends, then with Elihu, a fourth friend, and finally with God. These speeches, like the whole book, have evoked the most varied interpretations and continue to do so.[1] Indeed, in recent decades Job seems to have exercised a special fascination, perhaps in response to the wars and mass murder that made the twentieth century probably the bloodiest in human history. In line with the concerns of the present book I will read Job as being about searching for wisdom, testing wisdom, and embodying wisdom in the realities of human living.

Wisdom after trauma

That the book of Job is about wise living before God in the face of extreme testing – physical, intellectual, psychological, imaginative, ethical and

---

1. The interpretations most helpful in this and the following chapters include: David J. A. Clines, *Job 1–20* (Dallas: Word Books, 1989); Katharine J. Dell, *The Book of Job as Sceptical Literature* (Berlin: Walter de Gruyter, 1991); E. Dhorme, *A Commentary on the Book of Job* (London: Nelson, 1967); Samuel Rolles Driver and George Buchanan Gray, *A Critical and Exegetical Commentary on the Book of Job: Together with a New Translation* (Edinburgh: T. & T. Clark, 1921); Robert Gordis, *The Book of Job: Commentary, New Translation, Special Study* (New York: Jewish Theological Seminary of America, 1978); Norman Habel, *The Book of Job* (London: SCM, 1985); Marvin H. Pope, *Job: Introduction, Translation and Notes* (New York: Doubleday, 1965).

Perhaps even more than direct commentary on Job this chapter has been shaped by those who seem in their thinking, speaking, writing and living to have done most justice to Job-like cries, in particular Simone Weil, Donald MacKinnon, Sigrid Undsett, Jean Vanier, Frances Young, Peter Ochs, Micheal O'Siadhail and Nicholas Wolterstorff. Most immediately, my own thinking about Job has been shaped by a three-year engagement with the book and its interpreters in the course of co-supervising with Dr Ben Quash the doctoral dissertation of Susannah Ticciati: 'Job: A Hermeneutical and Ethical Interpretation with Reference to Karl Barth' (PhD thesis, Cambridge University, 2003), published as *Job and the Disruption of Identity: Reading beyond Barth* (London and New York: T. & T. Clark, 2005). Her work, together with the years of three-way conversations we had, suggested many of the ideas in what follows. Since the published version differs from the dissertation, I quote from both.

Finally there is the influence of the Septuagint version of Job in Greek. It was clearly based on a Hebrew text that had many differences from what eventually was canonised as the Masoretic Text, and in addition, like all translation, contains a considerable element of interpretation. This was the version that most shaped the New Testament authors and the early church. I have let my reading of it affect the interpretation of this chapter in ways that are often too diffuse to be noted. In particular, study of the Septuagint version has reinforced and developed my conviction of the legitimacy of reading it as a contribution to wisdom.

theological – is supported by its many references to wisdom and related ideas. There is not only the core concern with 'the fear of the Lord' throughout the book, but also the famous treatment of wisdom in chapter 28, and the use of characteristic wisdom terminology.

> Job 1:1 There was once a man in the land of Uz whose name was Job. That man was blameless and upright, one who feared God and turned away from evil.
>
> Job 28:28 And [God] said to humankind, 'Truly, the fear of the Lord, that is wisdom; and to depart from evil is understanding.'
>
> Job 12:1–3 [1]Then Job answered: [2]'No doubt you are the people, and wisdom will die with you. [3]But I have understanding as well as you; I am not inferior to you. Who does not know such things as these?
>
> 12:13 With God are wisdom and strength; he has counsel and understanding.'
>
> Job 15:8 [Eliphaz answered ...] 'Have you listened in the council of God? And do you limit wisdom to yourself?'
>
> Job 32:6–10 [6]Elihu son of Barachel the Buzite answered: 'I am young in years, and you are aged ... [7]I said, "Let days speak, and many years teach wisdom." [8]But truly it is the spirit in a mortal, the breath of the Almighty, that makes for understanding. [9]It is not the old that are wise, nor the aged that understand what is right. [10]Therefore I say, "Listen to me; let me also declare my opinion." '
>
> Job 34:34 [Elihu said ...] 'Those who have sense will say to me, and the wise who hear me will say, [35]"Job speaks without knowledge, his words are without insight." '

More fundamentally there is the way in which Job himself is portrayed as a person who embodies the qualities of wisdom, who seeks it, and who sees it as of supreme importance for living. His friends likewise are deeply concerned about wisdom and make counter-claims to it in their debating with Job. Above all God is seen as concerned with wisdom and understanding. So Job, his four friends and God are all strongly associated with wisdom. Explicitly and implicitly they understand wisdom in different though complexly overlapping ways. They cannot all be right, but neither does anyone seem to be portrayed as simply wrong or foolish.[2]

> Job 38:1–4 [1]Then the LORD answered Job out of the whirlwind: [2]'Who is this that darkens counsel by words without knowledge? [3]Gird up

---

2. Correlative with the language of wisdom throughout the book is that of foolishness and related terms. It is interesting that the Septuagint language intensifies the wisdom/foolishness and θεοσέβεια/ἀσέβεια emphases.

your loins like a man, I will question you, and you shall declare to me. [4]"Where were you when I laid the foundation of the earth? Tell me, if you have understanding ...

38:36–37 [36]Who has put wisdom in the inward parts, or given understanding to the mind? [37]Who has the wisdom to number the clouds?' ... Job 42:1–3 [1]Then Job answered the LORD: [2]'I know that you can do all things, and that no purpose of yours can be thwarted. [3]"Who is this that hides counsel without knowledge?" Therefore I have uttered what I did not understand, things too wonderful for me, which I did not know ...'

Elements of what each says can be related to wisdom traditions within and beyond the middle of a debate in which wisdom and foolishness are intermingled without clear guidelines to distinguish them. Why exactly are the friends judged by God not to have '**spoken of me what is right, as my servant Job has**' (42:7)? The answer has to be found by entering into the debates and seeking discernment. The pedagogy of the book of Job is as far as possible away from Israel (the influence of Mesopotamian wisdom seems especially strong). The reader is brought into the middle of a debate in which wisdom and foolishness are intermingled without clear guidelines to distinguish them. Why are the friends judged by God not to have '**spoken of me what is right, as my servant Job has**' (42:7)? The answer has to be found by entering into the debates and seeking discernment. The wisdom pedagogy of the book of Job is as far as possible away from 'packaged' answers. *It is about the most fundamental questioning and searching, including radical and controversial interrogation of wisdom and its traditions; but even that is not primary: it is above all about being questioned and searched.* Job undergoes this, and the reader is invited to go through a similar process.

The aim is not to arrive at some answer that could be conceptualised: it is rather to draw readers into the way of wisdom, allowing themselves to be questioned and searched and, in response, to question, search, desire and live for the sake of God and goodness – fearing God (the Hebrew word means to fear, reverence, honour; the Septuagint Greek word is θεοσέβεια, meaning relating to God in service, worship, fear and love) and departing from evil (28:28). This is not something that can be achieved once and for all; it is as limitless as the God who is worshipped. The book of Job corresponds to this process by offering endless material for interpretation, and many puzzles. Like other biblical books, it therefore invites frequent rereading, and it might even be a mark of failure were interpretations over the centuries, or across cultures, or through the varied experiences of one lifetime, to remain the same.

Rereading the book of Job frequently might be said to be intrinsic to any biblical wisdom. One never 'moves beyond' this book. It is a way of staying within earshot of the most piercing cries of humanity and our own hearts, and beginning to learn how they might be truthfully related to life in solidarity with others before God. In later chapters Job will be drawn on to contribute to a post-Holocaust wisdom (chapter 4); to help articulate an account of Jesus Christ in relation to wisdom (chapter 5); to explore the understanding of God (chapter 7); to contribute to an Abrahamic wisdom (chapter 8); to raise the question of wisdom in universities (chapter 9); and to connect the cries of Job with the cries of those with mental disabilities (chapter 10).

These extensive implications of Job for the rest of this book make considerable demands on this and the following chapter, both of which are largely on Job. The attempt to meet them is made by moving through Job offering an interpretation that focuses mainly on some key passages. It is not of course possible for even this limited exercise to be very thorough, but it is hoped that it may further two aims: first, to encourage readers to read and reread Job for themselves in preparation for the rest of this book; and second, to give an interpretation of Job rich enough to sustain the main points made in other chapters, both earlier and later. The title of this chapter, Job! is borrowed from Francesca Aran Murphy's interpretation of Job in dramatic terms, suggesting the exclamatory quality found at the heart of the book.[3]

There is also a further dimension in this and the next chapter. To hear and try to interpret the cries of Job while ignoring similar cries in our times would be irresponsible and even inhuman. In the broadest sense it might spell hermeneutical failure not to find, through the process of entering into the anguished meaning of the poetry of this book, resonances with contemporary anguish. One point of connection is with the Shoah or Holocaust, on which there is a substantial literature relevant to Job.[4] My approach will not be to comment directly on those writings but to lay alongside Job a recent response to the Holocaust in poetry. Micheal

3. Francesca Aran Murphy, *The Comedy of Revelation: Paradise Lost and Regained in Biblical Narrative* (Edinburgh: T. & T. Clark, 2000).
4. See D. Blumenthal, *Facing the Abusing God: A Theology of Protest* (Louisville, KY: Westminster John Knox Press, 1993); C. Delbo, *Auschwitz and After* (New Haven: Yale University Press, 1995); D. J. Fasching, *Narrative Theology after Auschwitz: From Alienation to Ethics* (Minneapolis: Fortress Press, 1992); E. L. Fackenheim, *The Jewish Bible after the Holocaust: A Re-reading* (Bloomington: Indiana University Press, 1991); E. Feld, *The Spirit of Renewal: Finding Faith After the Holocaust* (Woodstock, VT: Jewish Lights Publishing, 1994); P. J. Haas, *Morality after Auschwitz: The*

O'Siadhail's *The Gossamer Wall: Poems in Witness to the Holocaust*[5] has been written in the pivotal few years during which there has been sufficient time to build up a considerable literature by both eyewitnesses and others and yet some eyewitnesses to the Holocaust are still alive to respond. He draws on works by survivors, historians, philosophers, novelists and poets.[6] Because the book of Job is largely poetry it is especially appropriate to read it alongside a work of poetry on the Holocaust. The poems cover the historical origins of the Holocaust, the Nazi takeover of Germany as seen through the history of the German town of Northeim, the story of Battalion 101 in its extermination of Jews in Poland, the extermination camps, Jewish resistance, what happened in the French village of Le Chambon, and the aftermath of the Holocaust up to the present.

The core dialogue within which the theology that follows is worked out is, therefore, with the book of Job and *The Gossamer Wall*. As with Job, there cannot be explicit reference to all of *The Gossamer Wall*, but the whole of both texts is implied.

'Summons', the first of a series of sonnets on the extermination camps, expresses the urgency of the contemporary need to heed the cries of Auschwitz and to let our ways of hearing and seeing now be shaped by this remembering.

> *Meditate that this came about.* Imagine.
> Pyjama ghosts tramp the shadow of a chimney.
> Shorn and nameless. Desolation's mad machine
> With endless counts and selections. *Try to see!*
> For each who survived, every numbered
> Arm that tries to hold the wedding guest,
> A thousand urgent stories forever unheard;
> In each testimony a thousand more suppressed.
> A Polish horizon glows with stifled cries:
> Who'll wake us from this infinite nightmare?
> Out of the cone of Vesuvius their lives rise
> To sky-write gaunt silences in the frozen air.
> A summons to *try to look, to try to see.*
> A muted dead demand their debt of memory.[7]

Radical Challenge of the Nazi Ethic (Philadelphia: Fortress Press, 1988); R. P. Scheindlin, *The Book of Job* (New York: W. W. Norton, 1998); E. Wiesel, *The Trial of God* (New York: Random House, 1979).
5. Micheal O'Siadhail, *The Gossamer Wall: Poems in Witness to the Holocaust* (Newcastle: Bloodaxe Books and St Louis: Time Being Books, 2002).
6. For a list of the main sources see ibid. pp. 127f.
7. O'Siadhail, *The Gossamer Wall*, p. 63.

That 'horizon' of 'stifled cries' is one within which Job has to be read today, obeying the summons to meditate and to try to see.

From Prologue to Epilogue: embodied wisdom, fearing God for nothing, and divine experimentation

Job lived in **'the land of Uz'** (1:1). With most commentators, I take this to indicate that he is from outside Israel. There are also many signs that the sort of understanding of God and the covenant with Israel given in the book of Deuteronomy and associated biblical writings is assumed in Job and engaged with critically.[8] This sets up a double perspective whose analogies can still be valuable in seeking wisdom today. The plain sense is that this is a view from outside Israel, that the debate within the book is open to all, and that participation in the covenant of God with Israel need not be assumed. Part of the book's power has been in its appeal to common human experience and its limited religious specificity. At the same time the fact that it is written in Hebrew, sometimes calls God 'YHVH', is in the canon of Jewish scriptures, and has many echoes of other canonical texts means that it also has an insider's perspective. It is therefore a text that is simultaneously set within a tradition to which it contributes, yet also open across its own tradition's boundaries in such a way as both to make itself available to those beyond it and also to open itself to radical critique and transformation. Later chapters will develop an understanding of Christian wisdom for which such communicative, self-critical and transformative interaction across boundaries within the complexities and contingencies of history is crucial – a conception already introduced in the previous two chapters. *Job is a daring experiment in theological imagining and thinking from more than one perspective, offering an incomparable pedagogy in wisdom interpretation of scripture, life and God.*

In what follows I will take the book of Job in its canonical form as a unity and will not speculate about earlier forms, interpolations and redactions.[9] In particular this means seeing the prose Prologue (chapters 1–2)

8. See Ticciati, *Job and the Disruption of Identity*, pp. 58–64; Clines, *Job 1–20*; David Wolfers, *Deep Things out of Darkness: The Book of Job. Essays and a New Translation* (Grand Rapids, MI: Eerdmans, 1995).

9. I am following what Dell calls a 'holistic-type reading of Job' (Katharine J. Dell, *'Get Wisdom, Get Insight': An Introduction to Israel's Wisdom Literature* (London: Darton, Longman and Todd, 2000), p. 35), though she does not follow it herself. I am grateful for conversation with her and with another colleague, Professor Graham Davies, about the advantages and disadvantages of following the course I have chosen.

and Epilogue (chapter 42) as integrated with the poetic dialogues (chapters 3–41). Further, I follow those who see the poetry as revealing and exploring the internal dynamic of the movement from Prologue to Epilogue, with God's speeches from the whirlwind (chapters 39–41) as the integrator (without that implying any straightforward 'answer' to the profound issues raised).[10]

Within the Prologue I will comment on the description of Job, the test agreed to by God and the[11] Satan, and the way in which the complex dynamic of the book's 'moods' is set in motion.

Job as embodied wisdom

I have already (p. 92 above) quoted together Job 1:1 and 28:28 to show that the book intends to portray Job as the embodiment of the wise man who, blameless and upright, fears God and rejects evil. This basic definition of a wisdom that is faithfully oriented towards God and goodness, while being involved with the temptations and complexities of history, is never questioned in the book, but the meaning attached to this wisdom undergoes radical interrogation and transformation. The drama of Job's testing is to be understood as a searching out of wisdom, the dialogue with the friends is a dispute about wisdom and its criteria, and God's speeches interrogatively open up a wisdom that both connects with and transcends the categories of Job and his friends. Finally the Epilogue portrays Job flourishing in a new state of understanding whose continuities and discontinuities with the Prologue are signs of a wisdom tradition that has come through trauma.

Does the new wisdom that emerges in the course of the book mean that Job's initial embodiment of wisdom is not as perfect as is made out? It is easy to be suspicious of it. Is the juxtaposition of impeccable virtue and excessive prosperity meant to lead us to have Satan-like doubts about him? Does he condone what might appear to be conspicuous and self-indulgent consumption by his children? Is Job's pre-emptive sacrificing on behalf of his children just in case they 'have sinned, and cursed God in their hearts' (1:5) a sign of lack of trust, an almost superstitious excess of piety beyond what Israel's Torah required, or even an attempt to

---

10. See Robert Alter, *The Art of Biblical Poetry* (Edinburgh: T. & T. Clark, 1990), ch. IV, pp. 85–110; Ticciati (following Barth) in 'Job: A Hermeneutical and Ethical Interpretation', ch. 2.
11. I call him 'the' Satan throughout as a reminder that this is a very different figure from Satan in other parts of scripture. The Satan in Job is 'the adversary' with a role in heaven, and presents the 'case for the prosecution' in relation to Job.

control God? When the first set of disasters occurs, Job's exemplary reaction might seem like that of someone who (as the Satan suggests) has not yet been touched deeply enough (1:20–22). After the second assault, this time on his body, followed by what he sees as his wife's foolish suggestion, he now begins to question, if mildly.

> Job 2:9–10 [9]Then his wife said to him, 'Do you still persist in your integrity? Curse God, and die.' [10]But he said to her, 'You speak as any foolish woman would speak. Shall we receive the good at the hand of God, and not receive the bad?' In all this Job did not sin with his lips.

And does the phrase 'with his lips' imply that other, sinful things were going on inside him?

Francesca Murphy even offers a dramatic sketch of Job as an 'infernal comedy'. Job is

> too good to be true: the Prologue is setting him up for a fall. The director tells the actor playing Job to go watch some French movie comedies like *Le Cop*, and to play these first scenes like the novice policeman who tries to run his section by the book, is shaken out of his compulsive observance of rules by the disastrous consequences, and falls into his humanity when he falls in love with a prostitute. The director says: the audience is not supposed to *like* the way you carry on. Smirk a bit as you sacrifice, and look over-washed, barbered, slicked back and manicured. 'Few things', says Jacobson, 'are more irreducibly comic than faeces coming out of the sky, and God is going to dump a ton of horse manure on you. Wear a white suit.'[12]

Amidst these and many other interpretations, there is much to be said for taking the Prologue's affirmation of Job in what I take to be its plain sense. He is described in terms of the key characteristics of wisdom (as stated by God in 28:28), and this is reaffirmed by God in 1:8 and 2:3, all without any trace of irony. It is no problem that other interpretations are possible, as suggested by the Satan, but it seems clear that the narrative wants readers to believe in Job's integrity according to the divine criteria for a wise man. Yet while Job is said, as regards his possessions, to be **'the greatest of all the people of the East'** (1:3) and God says **'there is no one like him on earth'** (1:8) it is never said that he is the wisest. It is not at all in tension with the Prologue for him to become wiser. Indeed, as will be argued below, it is very important that such an embodiment of

12. Murphy, *The Comedy of Revelation*, p. 157.

wisdom should be able to learn so much more. In chapter 28 the basic reason for this is clear: the scope of wisdom is the scope of God. What begins in the Prologue is Job's transformation beyond his already exemplary wisdom towards something even more like God's own wisdom. *It is a drama about the 'always more' of a wisdom that is genuinely engaged with God, history and creation.* It is radically critical of elements of the tradition that try to contain wisdom within patterns of retribution or 'just deserts', which fail to do justice to new, unprecedented events, which refuse the challenge to search and be searched through such events, or which (most important of all) do not 'let God be God', relating to him for reasons other than God's own sake. The main clue that the Prologue gives to this God-centred, historical wisdom is in the dialogues between God and the Satan.

Does Job fear God for nothing?

Job 1:6–12 [6]One day the heavenly beings came to present themselves before the Lord, and Satan also came among them. [7]The Lord said to Satan, 'Where have you come from?' Satan answered the Lord, 'From going to and fro on the earth, and from walking up and down on it.' [8]The Lord said to Satan, 'Have you considered my servant Job? There is no one like him on the earth, a blameless and upright man who fears God and turns away from evil.' [9]then Satan answered the Lord, 'Does Job fear God for nothing? [10]Have you not put a fence around him and his house and all that he has, on every side? You have blessed the work of his hands, and his possessions have increased in the land. [11]But stretch out your hand now, and touch all that he has, and he will curse you to your face.' [12]The Lord said to Satan, 'Very well, all that he has is in your power; only do not stretch out your hand against him!' So Satan went out from the presence of the Lord.

The Satan's question about Job in 1:9 indicates what is probably the main point of the book: the wisdom of fearing God for nothing. But what is that? The whole book might be read as a commentary on this verse.[13]

It is important that it is a question; and that it is asked in heaven in address to God; and also that God takes it seriously. One message of this narrative might be that there are open questions in heaven, and even open questions for God. The drama about to unfold is not presented as

---

13. While Ticciati is by no means the only commentator to do this, I am in broad agreement with her way of doing so.

one with a foregone conclusion: it is genuinely underdetermined, and the specific open question at stake focuses on a particular human being's relationship with God amidst the contingencies of history. The only available answer seems to be to see how Job actually behaves within that history. No knowledge of the future and no insight into Job's heart or mind seem to be able to substitute for Job's living of life and his decision-making before God. There is an extraordinary emphasis on the relationship between God and Job; but this is no 'spiritual' bond that can be inspected and comprehensively assessed by either partner: it is, as will appear, unavoidably mediated through Job's historical existence, including his possessions, physical health, marriage, friendships, social and economic life, and relationship to the whole of creation. Yet the core question is not reducible to any of those; it is rather about a relationship to them that is rooted in a quality of relating to God that is called 'fearing God for nothing'. The Hebrew for 'for nothing' is *hinnam*, meaning gratuitously, for no purpose, without cause, and the Septuagint translation is δωρεάν, 'as a gift'.

If, as suggested above, the whole book is needed to explicate the meaning of fearing God for nothing, then the answer must unfold throughout the discussion in this and the following chapter. What emerges as the Prologue unfolds? First, there is Job's response to the loss of his possessions, servants and children.

> Job 1:20–22 [20]Then Job arose, tore his robe, shaved his head, and fell on the ground and worshipped. [21]He said, 'Naked I came from my mother's womb, and naked shall I return there; the Lord gave, and the Lord has taken away; blessed be the name of the Lord.' [22]In all this Job did not sin or charge God with wrongdoing.

That seems like a perfect example of fearing God for nothing. He has lost all his children and all he owns and his first response is to worship God and bless his name. *He is relating to God not for what he receives, but for nothing, for the sake of God's name, for God's own sake.*

This practice of blessing the name of God, or 'hallowing the Name', in the face of overwhelming disaster or suffering goes to the heart of some Jewish responses to the Holocaust. Micheal O'Siadhail captures two such moments in 'Hallowing':

> 1
> At Kelme, the ditch dug, Daniel
> Rabbi asks a commandant's leave

To speak for a while to his people.
Alright speak but make it brief.

Unhurried in the face of the commandant:
The sanctification of the name, trace
And travail of a shadow-desiring servant,
No longer to act, simply to embrace.

Time to end – an officer butts in.
Willingly, lovingly to accept our fate.
The ditch graves gape and wait.
I have finished. You may begin.

2

Ringelblum beaten for nights on end
Refuses to name any gentile friend,
Asks: Can death be so hard to bear?
To deny their gloating over his despair.
A Warsaw bunker someone had betrayed
And all thirty-eight caught in the raid.
A switch of cell? Prisoners contrive
His rescue. Slim chance to stay alive.
And are his children doomed all the same?
So it's the way of Hallow-His-Name.
Kiddush Ha-Shem. Humble acceptance.
For many just the sign of their silence.[14]

Had Job died at this point he would have been a Rabbi Daniel. But instant death is the one thing ruled out for Job. He is to be a survivor. So what more could possibly be required?

The second dialogue between God and the Satan gives a clue. The Satan suggests that Job's traumatic experience has not been comprehensive enough – it has not yet included **'his bone and his flesh'** (2:5). *What is required is the wisdom of fearing God for nothing through the most comprehensive trauma.*

Such wisdom cannot be an immediate reaction on Job's part, something for which he is already prepared – even though he has been as wise as possible in his life to this point. This is something new and extended, and a wisdom appropriate to it is only possible through actually coping as it traumatises every dimension of life, affecting all he has, feels, trusts,

14. O'Siadhail, *The Gossamer Wall*, p. 84.

and is. It calls for a wisdom inseparable from immersion in an ongoing history whose risks and high stakes are acknowledged even in heaven.

The poetic dialogues show Job's way to that wisdom. In chapter 3 he articulates the trauma, crying out in utter anguish. The friends offer an untraumatised wisdom, not rooted in fearing God for nothing amidst suffering or in facing the particularity of who Job is and what he has suffered. Through debating with them he finds himself stripped down, searched and transformed – above all through his hope against hope in God. Then he hears the message of God from the whirlwind, in which the wisdom of fearing God for God's sake is, through a transformation of key elements in Job's earlier cry of anguish, transposed into wondering at and celebrating creation for creation's sake, and a realisation of God that can even be described as: '**now my eye sees you**' (42:5). The rest of the Epilogue then describes an existence embodying wisdom in ordinary life after trauma. As Harold Fisch says: 'The survivors of Auschwitz have been known to establish new families and set themselves up in business. This may not have the aesthetic tidiness of art, but human beings are resilient – and that ... is what the book of Job is saying.'[15]

Before plunging into the poetic dialogues there is one further feature of the Prologue that is important for the interpretation of the whole book and more broadly for the hermeneutics of wisdom.

Theology in the subjunctive: a divine experiment

If the dialogues between God and the Satan are as important as suggested above, this has consequences for what a previous chapter called the 'moods' of the book of Job's wisdom. The Prologue opens with a description in the indicative mood of Job the wise man, his possessions and his family. Yet Job's simultaneous awareness of God and of the contingencies and temptations of human existence introduce a subjunctive, 'may be' note even here:

> Job 1:5 And when the feast days had run their course, Job would send and sanctify them, and he would rise early in the morning and offer burnt offerings according to the number of them all; for Job said, 'It may be that my children have sinned, and cursed God in their hearts.' This is what Job always did.

---

15. Harold Fisch, *Poetry with a Purpose: Biblical Poetics and Interpretation* (Bloomington and Indianapolis: Indiana University Press, 1988), p. 41, quoted in Murphy, *The Comedy of Revelation*, p. 172.

The following verses then effectively frame the whole book in an implicit subjunctive. The experiment agreed by God and the Satan is about whether in certain circumstances Job might curse God (1:12), so demonstrating that he fears God because of the blessings he has received, not 'for nothing'. So this is a subjunctive in search of a decisive indicative, one way or the other. The movement of the book is from the indicative opening of the Prologue, through its comprehensive traumatisation and disruption, to the enhanced indicative ending of the Epilogue in which **'the Lord blessed the latter days of Job more than his beginning …'** and **'Job died, old and full of days'** (42:12, 17).

A wisdom not involved in history and its traumas might perhaps be content with indicatives and imperatives, and with interrogatives that aim at clear answers and directions for living. The book of Job displays such a wisdom through the friends of Job and judges it 'folly' (42:8). Their wisdom is not just about how to respond to trauma; it also represents God as operating mainly in indicatives (especially judgements) and imperatives. But God in the rest of the book is powerfully interrogative. In the Prologue his first two statements are questions, and his whirlwind speeches are pervasively interrogative without much hint of answers or directions. Both history and creation generate more questions than answers. But they also generate cries and desires. Under the pressure of his multiple overwhelmings, Job is stripped down to core desires for justice and above all for direct relationship with God, expressed, as will be seen below, in the many optatives of his speeches. The most comprehensive optative is that of blessing (the implied form of which is: 'May God, or someone or something, be blessed') leading to a new indicative; and the shadow side of that is cursing. From Job's opening sacrifices, offered in case his children might have cursed God in their hearts, through Job's wife urging him to curse God and die, to the Epilogue's account of Job praying for his friends and God blessing Job even more than before, the book is a drama of blessing and cursing. The subjunctive, experimental framing and the radical interrogatives are eventually seen as part of the dynamics of blessing. By the end there is new questioning (42:3, 4) and new commanding (42:8) as well as new desiring and affirming, but it would be foolish ever to forget the subjunctive possibilities and surprises: no guarantee is given to Job that there will be no further traumas, and he and his family are still firmly within historical existence.

So the wisdom of the book insists on all the moods being taken seriously. The ways in which we live with and through affirmations, imperatives, questions, possibilities and desires are opened up to the urgencies and cries of historical existence and to the transformative wisdom of a God of creation and history. *In being offered the possibility of blessing God for God's sake, Job is given a relationship within which he can search and be searched as he wrestles with the worst.*

Into the trauma and out of the whirlwind: chapters 3 and 38–41

The trauma of affliction

Job's initial cry of agony and yearning for death in chapter 3 immediately plunge us into the depths of his trauma.

> Job 3:1–6 [1]After this Job opened his mouth and cursed the day of his birth. [2]Job said: [3]'Let the day perish in which I was born, and the night that said, "A man-child is conceived." [4]Let that day be darkness! May God above not seek it, or light shine on it. [5]Let gloom and deep darkness claim it. Let clouds settle upon it; let the blackness of the day terrify it. [6]That night – let thick darkness seize it! let it not rejoice among the days of the year; let it not come into the number of the months.'

Chapter 3 is an extraordinary sequence of cursing, longing for his life never to have happened, exclamatory interrogatives asking 'Why …? Why …? Why …?' and the final cry of overwhelming misery with which the present chapter opened. It is what Simone Weil named 'affliction' (*malheur*), and is expressed in what she called the language of 'decreation'. Weil, in discussing Job's 'genuine cry of anguish', says: 'The Book of Job is a pure marvel of truth and authenticity from beginning to end. As regards affliction, all that departs from this model is more or less tainted by falsehood. Affliction causes God to be absent for a time, more absent than a dead man, more absent than light in the utter darkness of a cell. A kind of horror submerges the whole soul.'[16] Weil's account of affliction is (in places explicitly) a contemporary commentary on Job by someone deeply sensitive to the trauma in which Europe was engulfed in her time and to the pathologies of European civilisation that allowed the Nazis to thrive.

---

16. Simone Weil, 'The Love of God and Affliction' in *The Simone Weil Reader*, ed. George A. Panichas (New York: David McKay Company, 1977), p. 442.

Job 3:7–26 [7]'Yes, let that night be barren; let no joyful cry be heard in it. [8]Let those curse it who curse the Sea, those who are skilled to rouse up Leviathan. [9]Let the stars of its dawn be dark; let it hope for light, but have none; may it not see the eyelids of the morning – [10]because it did not shut the doors of my mother's womb, and hide trouble from my eyes. [11]Why did I not die at birth, come forth from the womb and expire? [12]Why were there knees to receive me, or breasts for me to suck? [13]Now I would be lying down and quiet; I would be asleep; then I would be at rest [14]with kings and counsellors of the earth who rebuild ruins for themselves, [15]or with princes who have gold, who fill their houses with silver. [16]Or why was I not buried like a stillborn child, like an infant that never sees the light? [17]There the wicked cease from troubling, and there the weary are at rest. [18]There the prisoners are at ease together; they do not hear the voice of the taskmaster. [19]The small and the great are there, and the slaves are free from their masters. [20]Why is light given to one in misery, and life to the bitter in soul, [21]who long for death, but it does not come, and dig for it more than for hidden treasures; [22]who rejoice exceedingly, and are glad when they find the grave? [23]Why is light given to one who cannot see the way, whom God has fenced in? [24]For my sighing comes like my bread, and my groanings are poured out like water. [25]Truly the thing that I fear comes upon me, and what I dread befalls me. [26]I am not at ease, nor am I quiet; I have no rest; but trouble comes.'

'In the case of someone in affliction, all the contempt, revulsion, and hatred are turned inwards; they penetrate to the centre of his soul and from there they colour the whole universe with their poisoned light.'[17]

'Another effect of affliction is, little by little, to make the soul an accomplice, by injecting a poison of inertia into it. In anyone who has suffered affliction for a long enough time there is a complicity with regard to his own affliction; it goes so far as to prevent him from seeking a way of deliverance, sometimes even to the point of preventing him from wishing for deliverance.'[18]

'In affliction, that misfortune itself becomes a man's whole existence and in every other respect he loses all significance, in everybody's eyes including his own. There is something in him that would like to exist, but it is continually pushed back into nothingness, like a drowning man whose head is pushed under the water.'[19]

17. Ibid. p. 443.   18. Ibid.   19. Ibid. p. 460.

'Affliction is not a psychological state; it is a pulverisation of the soul by the mechanical brutality of circumstances. The transformation of a man, in his own eyes, from the human condition into that of a half-crushed worm writhing on the ground is a process which not even a pervert would find attractive. Neither does it attract a sage, a hero, or a saint. Affliction is something which imposes itself upon a man quite against his will. Its essence, the thing it is defined by, is the horror, the revulsion of the whole being, which it inspires in its victim.'[20] 'Those who ask why God permits affliction might as well ask why God created.'[21]

'There is a question which is absolutely meaningless and therefore, of course, unanswerable, and which we normally never ask ourselves, but in affliction the soul is constrained to repeat it incessantly like a sustained, monotonous groan. The question is: Why? Why are things as they are?'[22]

Whatever one makes of Weil's theological response to affliction (which is not something I wish to discuss) her phenomenology of it in the terms just quoted connects it strongly to the experience of those mid-twentieth-century years when the Holocaust was perpetrated. O'Siadhail's distillation in poetry of the experience of victims of the Holocaust strikes similar notes. There is the swallowing up of the whole universe and its meaning in something beyond all categories of sense. O'Siadhail frames the whole historical account in imagery of geological cataclysm. Another recurrent motif is Paul Celan's 'black sun':

> Unwholesome radiance. A devious implacable will
> Outpaces all explanation.
> The black sun shines.
> Quantum leap in some darker mystery of evil.[23]
>
> Black milk, black snow, black sun, black bloom.[24]
>
> A black sun only shines out of a vacuum.[25]

There is the cry of 'Why?' and its pointlessness:

> Each for himself. Father steals from son.
> Parched but denied an icicle Levi asks why?
> *There's no why here.* Shorn and striped biped,
> A tattooed number who'd once been someone.[26]

---

20. Ibid. p. 462.   21. Ibid. p. 463.   22. Ibid. pp. 465–6.
23. O'Siadhail, *The Gossamer Wall*, p. 25.   24. Ibid. p. 114.   25. Ibid. p. 120.
26. Ibid. p. 67.

Above all there is the pervasive 'decreation' of humanity, and the vivid evocation of those corresponding to Weil's writhing, half-crushed worms, such as the 'Muselmänner' who are one stage further than Job in their love for death:

> The submerged or exhausted slow beyond caring.
> A week, at most a month. Then the *laissez-faire*
> Of the overcome and a last ghostly indifference
> To hunger, squalor, beatings or fear. Just staring
> Listless and vacant goners. *Muselmänner.*
> A light in their eye already shines their silence.[27]

What the book of Job does through a poetry of first person testimony Weil analogously does in existential philosophical and theological description and O'Siadhail in realistic narrative poetry. Each of them uncompromisingly faces the reality of affliction. But none of them wants that reality to be the last word about human existence. Weil's way of going through and beyond it is with reference to what Panichas calls her 'criteria of wisdom',[28] including decreation, the love of God, friendship, mediation and beauty – some of these will figure in later chapters below. For now, the main concern is the book of Job, and its contemporary resonance with O'Siadhail's Holocaust poems.

Poetry against despair

In the book of Job each of the main elements – the friends' and Job's speeches, Job's hymn to wisdom, God's speeches, and the Epilogue – plays its part in response to Job's cry in chapter 3. Some of those elements will be discussed below (some in the next chapter) and their role in preparing for the whirlwind speeches will be explored. But what God speaks from the whirlwind in chapters 38–41 stands in the most direct and dramatic relation to the despairing monologue of chapter 3. In the comparison and contrast of these two passages can be found some of the main pointers to the theological sense of the whole book, expressed in poetic terms that continually stretch interpretative capacity and resist conceptual closure – the very imagery is of uncontainability, incomprehensibility, freedom and overflow.[29]

---

27. Ibid. p. 68.
28. See Panichas, *The Simone Weil Reader*, pp. 341–96.
29. In what follows I am indebted mainly to the perceptive analysis (itself owing much to Alter), which includes far more supportive linguistic detail than is mentioned here: Ticciati, 'Job: A Hermeneutical and Ethical Interpretation', pp. 84ff.

Again and again the whirlwind speeches take up language from Job's speech in chapter 3 and transform its significance.[30] Job in his suffering longs for darkness to engulf light, for the stars of the dawn of the day of his birth to be dark, and for birth to lead to immediate death. In God's opening speech Job is interrogated about the whole of creation and its origins. The framework is radically shifted from Job's suffering to the priority of God and the necessity for a wisdom that relates to God, humanity and creation.

> Job 38:4 'Where were you when I laid the foundation of the earth? Tell me, if you have understanding.'

Soon the stars are introduced in a dramatically different way:

> Job 38:7 When the morning stars sang together and all the heavenly beings shouted for joy?

Creation is rooted in joy in contrast to Job's negation of both creation and joy:

> Job 3:7 Yes, let that night be barren; let no joyful cry be heard in it.

The stars later multiply into constellations – Pleiades, Orion, Mazzaroth (38:31–32) – and Job's lack of comprehension and control of them is emphasised by the questioning. These are not likely to be at the service of Job's despair. Before this, chapter 3's swallowing up of light in darkness and life in death is challenged interrogatively with matching imagery:

> Job 38:17–21 [17]Have the gates of death been revealed to you, or have you seen the gates of deep darkness? [18]Have you comprehended the expanse of the earth? Declare, if you know all this. [19]Where is the way to the dwelling of light, and where is the place of darkness, [20]that you may take it to its territory and that you may discern the paths to its home? [21]Surely you know, for you were born then, and the number of your days is great!

The reference to Job's birth takes up one of the fundamental themes of chapter 3, and the imagery of the womb is introduced even earlier in 38:8–11.

---

30. On this see especially Alter, *The Art of Biblical Poetry*, pp. 96ff. He speaks of a 'brilliantly pointed reversal, in structure, image and theme'.

8"Or who shut in the sea with doors when it burst out from the womb? – 9when I made the clouds its garment, and thick darkness its swaddling band, 10and prescribed bounds for it, and set bars and doors, 11and said, "Thus far shall you come, and no farther, and here shall your proud waves be stopped"?'

Ticciati comments on this:

> First, the cloud, which Job invoked in league with darkness to expunge his day (3.5), becomes, in parallel with the 'swaddling bands' of the sea, a procreational and nurturing image (v. 9a), being brought into harmony with the womb of v. 8b, which is freed once more to play its life-giving role. In chapter 3, by contrast, the cloud smothered that which had come forth from the womb (Job's day) in an annihilating act of reversal. Job's desire to remain within the womb (בטן, *beten*, 3.10) then slid seamlessly into a desire for the grave, the equivalence of womb and tomb becoming all but explicit: 'For then I should have lain down and been quiet; I should have slept; then I should have been at rest' (3.13). The womb thus figured as the place of non-existence, or alternatively as that which gives birth to non-existence: 'Why did I not die at birth (מרחם, *merechem*, lit. from the womb), come forth from the womb (מבטן) and expire?' (3.11). In 38.8–11, by contrast, the womb has been reworked into an image of 'the primordial abyss of water (Gen. 7.11) . . . from which the sea issued at creation (Isa. 51.10).'[31] That Job's curse was indeed of cosmic dimensions is confirmed by its reversal here at the cosmic level, the womb of oblivion being converted into the womb of the waters that gushed forth at creation.[32]

The resonances between Job's opening monologue and the whirlwind speeches continue especially through chapters 38–39, and the overall effect is to give a vivid, positive and overwhelming response to Job's despairing cry. Where he contracts all creation to the point of annihilation, God revels in its life, superabundance and uncontainability. Where Job's despairing longings see only death and darkness, God evokes the riotous particularity of creation and the light in which this is appreciated. It is as if an almost unthinkable hope can only be suggested by a delicate opening up of the imagination through reworking the very images that had earlier powerfully expressed despair.

---

31. [Ticciati's note] Gordis, p. 444, who notes the appropriateness of the root גיח, which expresses simultaneously the 'bursting forth of water', 'the rushing forth into battle' and 'the breaking forth from the womb'.
32. Ticciati, *Job and the Disruption of Identity*, pp. 105–6.

O'Siadhail too reintroduces earlier imagery in his final section, 'Prisoners of Hope'. The traumatic effects of Hekla's eruption three millennia ago are traced, but are also interrogatively opened up beyond the catastrophe:

> *'Ten days it rained ashes and the rains were grey',*
> *a chronicler writes with dismay: bitter weather,*
> *dry fogs, dimmed suns, blights and failed harvests,*
> *signs from heaven as the Shang dynasty runs down.*
>
> *A Chinese eyewitness to Hekla's Far East fall-out?*
> *A spewing fireball spreads a dust-veil of desolation,*
> *pall of travail, those broken and scattered peoples.*
> *Destruction turns all their presence into absence*
>
> *unless some testimony breaks their infinite silence.*
> *In remembrance resides the secret of our redemption.*
> *Out of this eruption, can we prepare another climate?*[33]

Earlier in *The Gossamer Wall* the language of earthquakes was used (though always in delicate interplay with that of human responsibility) to evoke overwhelming catastrophe:

> Spasms of precursors. Invisible shivers.
> *Lamentings heard i' th' air, strange screams of death.*
> In the sullen underneath
> Slabs buckle in subduction
> *And prophesying with accents terrible of dire combustion.*
> Rock bends and strains towards its rupture.
> A struck bell, the fabric of a planet quivers.[34]
>
> Wavers on a seismogram, a wider scribble,
> Shifts and jostlings along a seam until
> The moment mother earth bucks and quavers.
>
> Violence spreads out on every side,
> Frenzy of pulses radiates and woe betide
> A jellied soil, any sympathetic ground
>
> That dances to its rhythms. Shocks caught
> And magnified. Even worse havoc wrought
> Far from the epicentre. Consonance of terror.[35]

---

33. O'Siadhail, *The Gossamer Wall*, p. 112.   34. Ibid. p. 17.   35. Ibid. p. 19.

Now in the final section this is taken up into an interrogative and subjunctive hope of repair:

> Never, never again. Pleading remembrance
> Whispers through the gossamer wall:
> *Promise us at least this.* An insisting silence.
> We begin to repair, to overhaul
>
> Soft habits of the psyche, trying to find
> Fault lines, trembling earth-shelves,
> The will overreaching limits of mind
> Grounding worlds in private selves.
>
> Wounds always ajar. In its aftershock
> Our earth still trembles and strains.
> Tentative moves. Even to probe a rock
> Stratum, to map the fault planes?
>
> White noise and quivers. Shifts of geology.
> What might be salvaged? Hesitance
> Of first mendings. Delicate *perhaps* or *maybe*
> Tracing detours of repaired advance.[36]

Even the 'black sun' reappears in an evocation of Passover celebration that hints at

> A light too broad for any black sun to shine.[37]

'Prisoners of Hope', like the whirlwind speeches followed by the Epilogue in Job 42, immerses us in a poetry of life which does not deny, explain, justify or even relativise the preceding trauma and horror. The horrendous suffering and the overflowing life are presented with comparable vividness but without being comparable to each other or embraceable within one conceptual framework. Both *The Gossamer Wall* and the book of Job present many incomparables.

Steven Kepnes affirms Martin Buber's interpretation of Job as offering four irreducibly different responses to innocent suffering.

> These four responses are not stated philosophically, but rather are personified in four figures: Job's wife, his friends, Job himself, and God. They represent highly varied views which find the meaning of Job's suffering alternatively in an unjust God, in a sinful Job, in a

---

36. Ibid. p. 121.   **37.** Ibid. p. 124.

rupture or 'rent' in the universe, and in Job's very power to withstand his suffering.[38]

Yet Kepnes does not, like Buber, order them in a progression. He rather keeps them in play together dialogically, and critiques the limits of philosophical logic in exploring their contradictions:

> Here is where a multi-genre text such as the book of Job which includes plot, character, monologue, dialogue, and poetry fills the clumsy gaps in conceptual thought to respond to suffering not primarily as a logical problem but as an ethical problem, as a religious problem, and, essentially, as a human problem.[39]

O'Siadhail does something similar through portrayals (in different poetic genres) of Holocaust victims, perpetrators, bystanders, collaborators, resisters, chroniclers, 'righteous Gentiles' and survivors, while also evoking other human and natural catastrophes, and continually resonating with poets, historians, musicians, novelists, photographers, thinkers and others who have attempted to testify to the Shoah. His final section is the most challenging. How affirm life and hope, how even write poetry, after Auschwitz? In 'Dust-veil' he interweaves the terrible final weeks of the Third Reich, describing murderous forced marches and tragic endings for many Jews and their rescuers, with glimpses of what happened afterwards to survivors, perpetrators and others. The keynote is unfathomable wickedness:

> No gain or purpose. Just gratuitous hate.[40]

This is the 'for nothing' of evil. In the rest of 'Dust-veil', and in the poems following, there is a painful, interrogative and tentative opening up to the possibilities of life and even of flourishing. Besides reworking the earlier imagery of cataclysm and despair, there emerges – through all the nightmares, the danger and even occurrence of fresh genocides, the insistent memories, 'The crying silence of six million faces',[41] and the fact that 'Dissonant cries of silence refuse to quiesce'[42] – a celebration of life. There are also pervading scriptural references to Babel, the chosen people, paradise, covenants, Abraham, 'Hear, O Israel', Isaiah and Jeremiah.

38. Steven Kepnes, 'Rereading Job as Textual Theodicy' in *Suffering Religion*, ed. Robert Gibbs and Elliot R. Wolfson (London and New York: Routledge, 2002), p. 37.
39. Ibid. p. 39.   40. O'Siadhail, *The Gossamer Wall*, p. 111.
41. Ibid. p. 115.   42. Ibid. p. 118.

There are echoes of other ancient and modern literature (especially in Yiddish), but it is the Hebrew scriptures that bear the main burden: this is a post-Shoah figural interpretation suggesting a fresh rereading of classic texts and themes. It culminates with reference to scripture transmuted into the performance of a celebratory liturgy of remembrance:

Reprise

To remember to break the middle *matzah*
To lean to the left and taste again *maror,*

To pour salt-water on eggs at the Passover,
Share around the untouched cup of Elijah.

Risks. Fugues of detours. Spirals of reprise.
A feast of rich food and well-aged wine.

A light too broad for any black sun to shine.
Scope of conversations, brilliance of what is;

To love the range and fullness yet to recall.
Your golden hair, Margarete, your ashen hair ...

Next year in Jerusalem! Parting toast and prayer.
And still they breathe behind a gossamer wall.[43]

Gratuitous hatred has failed to exterminate gratuitous feasting; but yet Margarete is dead.

God!

Such gratuitousness might also be seen as the crucial theological point of God's whirlwind speeches. Where Job has related everything to his own condition, God celebrates creation for its own sake. Creation is described as of significance in itself, not just in relation to humanity:

Job 39:9–12 [9]Is the wild ox willing to serve you? Will it spend the night at your crib? [10]Can you tie it in the furrow with ropes, or will it harrow the valleys after you? [11]Will you depend on it because its strength is great, and will you hand over your labour to it? [12]Do you have faith in it that it will return, and bring your grain to your threshing floor?

The relationship of God to creation is repeatedly affirmed or implied, above all in the stream of questions. This not only rules out seeing creation in terms of human utility, control or even comprehensibility;

43. Ibid. p. 124.

divine utility, a 'role' for creation in the purposes of God, does not figure either. Creation has a dignity, freedom, beauty, mystery and intense life of its own. It is as if God generates and celebrates creation 'for naught', for its own sake. This is expressed in rich descriptive poetry delighting in observed detail and interrogative urgency. Its effect is to establish the sheer God-given reality of animals and natural phenomena in their own right.

This is an appropriate indirect response to the despair of Job which had sucked all creation into its own suffering and imagined the extinction of light and life; but it is more than that. It is also an indirect affirmation of Job's core orientation towards God: fearing God for nothing. *The logic seems to be: if creation is to be valued for its own sake, how much more is its creator to be revered for his own sake. And the further implication is: humanity as part of God's creation, with Job himself, is similarly precious in and for itself.* The sheer glory of being is celebrated, though without any implication that there is a category embracing God and creation: rather, the interrogatives intensify the sense that, to use later conceptuality, God is in no category. Even as we turn from one created phenomenon to another we are not given any overview but one vivid particular after another, each deserving its own specific praise, each related to God but not to any human framework. The world is a manifold of intensities each with its created integrity, mystery and even untameable wildness, not to be humanly comprehended or controlled. The cumulative impact of all those questions flung at Job by God is to relativise even Job's most profound attempts to question with a view to a comprehensible answer.

What does this mean with regard to the Satan's leading question in chapter 1, 'Does Job fear God for nothing?'? If that question indeed structures the whole 'experiment', and if Job moves from a wisdom of fearing God for nothing (expressed in his initial response: '**The Lord gave and the Lord has taken away; blessed be the name of the Lord**' – 1:21), through trauma, testing and searching, to this culminating confrontation with God, then what happens to Job through the whirlwind speeches is the realisation of a further wisdom of fearing God for nothing. The multifaceted trauma has made his habitual (and, Alter suggests, mournfully resigned[44]) wise response seem empty. Historical events cannot simply be assimilated to pre-existing wisdom. But the

---

44. Alter, *The Art of Biblical Poetry*, p. 85.

affliction does away with resignation and concentrates his attention on his own agony, contracting his whole world into the horizon of his pain. The new wisdom from God offers a different horizon and new objects of attention. It is not just that there is no answer to be found within Job's horizon of chapter 3; the questions and longings in that chapter are not ultimately compatible with what 'the Lord gave' in creation or with the Lord who gave it, however appropriate they are to Job's immediate immersion in trauma.

The new wisdom sets alongside Job's trauma the reality and life of creation appreciated interrogatively for its own sake and, by implication, the reality and life of the Creator who is even more to be acknowledged for his own sake. The logic of Job's repentance in chapter 42 (prepared for in 40:3–5) is of having arrived at a new appreciation of God, exposing the inadequacy of the wisdom learnt in his time of virtuous prosperity. The limits of his previous fearing God have been revealed and surpassed through the testing of history. *There is no denial of the trauma and its terrible inexplicability; but alongside it is an affirmation of a creation that cannot be drawn into trauma without remainder, and of a God who can, through being questioned and questioning, open the eyes of the afflicted to who he is for his own sake: 'Now my eye sees you' (42:5) –* **God!**

As Buber saw, this is the crucial turning point. 'The abyss is bridged the moment [Job] "sees," is permitted to see again.'[45] Yet that 'again' spans the huge distance between Job's first affirmation of God 'for nothing' in the Prologue and his exclamation now in the Epilogue, the traversal of which will be examined in the following chapter in terms of learning wisdom. But first there is the question of the ending.

The sense of the ending: chapter 42

As in *The Gossamer Wall*, the book of Job has a final liturgical moment. God directly rebukes the friends for not having spoken of God '**what is right, as my servant Job has**' (42:7), the friends offer a sacrifice in repentance of their foolishness, Job prays for them, and '**the Lord accepted Job's prayer**' (42:9). Then Job is blessed by God even more than previously. His brothers and sisters and '**all who had known him before**' (42:11) gather round him, and share food, sympathy and money; his herds are double what they were before; as before he has ten children,

45. Martin Buber, *On the Bible*, ed. Nahum Glatzer (Syracuse: Syracuse University Press, 2000), p. 195.

including three beautiful daughters who share with their brothers in the family inheritance; and Job lives another hundred and forty years, seeing four generations of his family, before dying **'old and full of days'** (42:17).

This ending is often criticised. Is it a reassertion of the moral universe of parts of the books of Proverbs or Deuteronomy which the poetic sections seemed to have rendered questionable beyond recall? Is it therefore, in spite of all the earlier protests against a view of God as one who straightforwardly rewards the good and punishes the wicked, a relapse into that retributive conception? Does its simple folk-tale 'happy ever after' conclusion, complete with formulaic doubling of possessions, deny the memory and significance of Job's suffering and wrestling? Does it really suggest that the earlier children could be replaced by the new family? Where does this leave all those sufferers whose 'endings' are far from happy?

I began above to develop an alternative reading, in terms of a wisdom embodied in ordinary life after trauma. At a literary level Alter's preference for seeing the prose frame-story 'as an old tradition artfully reworked by the poet in a consciously archaising style'[46] leads one to be alert for meanings in the Epilogue that resonate with both the Prologue and the poetic chapters in between. What was described above as the Joban 'drama of blessing and cursing' culminates in chapter 42 portraying a blessing that both is in continuity with the Prologue and the poetry and also moves beyond them. Those who are inclined to follow the critical thrust of the previous paragraph's questions need to beware that they are not, for whatever reasons, prejudiced against acknowledging the historical reality of blessing, abundance, good relationships, well-gotten wealth, happy family life and transgenerational flourishing, or even against a God of blessing who creates and sustains such reality.

It is a delicate matter to evoke such blessing after all that has come before, but the Epilogue can be read as an appropriate way of doing so. First, and most obviously, it is a narrative, not a general statement about what can always be expected to happen. It is therefore one historical possibility, and the subjunctive framework of the experiment set up in the Prologue intensifies this sense. Besides, after the hyperbolic picture of Job's prosperity, wisdom and affliction in the Prologue, it should be no surprise to see the Epilogue making its points through a hyperbole of blessing.

---

46. Alter, *The Art of Biblical Poetry*, p. 87.

If we next take Alter's hint and try to see how the folk-tale genre is being 'artfully reworked', a comparison of the Prologue and Epilogue reveals differences suggesting the significance of what has happened in between – this is not just a repetition of traditional formulae.[47] The relationship of Job to God in the Prologue is indirect, and God's dialogue is with the Satan the adversary in heaven; in the Epilogue God speaks directly with Job and with Eliphaz, and the Satan does not appear. Job's piety in the Prologue is wise but also fearful, and his sacrifices are repeated attempts (**'This is what Job always did'** – 1:5) to guard against the possibility that his children might have sinned by cursing God in their hearts. The Epilogue's sacrifice is directly required by God for reconciliation with himself, and the piety is centred on who God is and on obedience rooted in dialogue, recognition, forgiveness and interces-sion. In the Prologue there is feasting in the houses of Job's children, with even a hint of 'conspicuous consumption', and curiously he himself does not seem to take part. The Epilogue has his community gathering round him to share bread in his own house, and the spirit is one of compassion, support and generous gift-giving. There is a transgenerational horizon in the Epilogue that is lacking in the Prologue, conveying historical move-ment in its most fundamental human form.

A further illuminating contrast is between the superlatives of the Prologue and the comparatives of the Epilogue. To set **'the greatest of all the people of the east'** (1:3) and **'there is no one like him on the earth'** (1:8; 2:3) against **'the Lord blessed the latter days of Job more than his beginning'** (42:12) is to be encouraged to think more than a superlative – initially in relation to possessions but also in other respects. Ticciati comments:

> In moving from the superlative to the comparative, it implicitly critiques *any* attempt to define piety within certain boundaries and thus to capture it in a static concept. For the comparative is precisely that which escapes boundaries and does not allow for final definition. It says in effect, 'wherever you set your standard of perfection, I will show you that it can be exceeded, and thus falsify this concept of perfection.' Thus although the epilogue provides a vision that exceeds the perfection of the prologue, it does not claim for itself this status of perfection but rather shifts our perspective from a calculable standard of perfection to that of the movement of exceeding – towards

---

47. Ticciati summarises these well in *Job and the Disruption of Identity*, chapter 3, pp. 65–70.

growth, in other words. In a sense, the way in which the epilogue trumps the prologue is the way in which a process of growth is better than static perfection. These concepts operate on different levels, and it is in this sense that they do not exactly compete. Indeed, the perfection of the prologue can be incorporated into the process of growth as a moment within this. In its portrayal of this growth, the epilogue embodies and fills out the integrity in which Job persists beyond the parameters of the prologue-piety, and hence also the 'for naught' relation to God that this entails.[48]

As with perfection, so with wisdom (which is, of course, essential to Job's integrity); the next chapter will trace how growth is intrinsic to the book of Job's concept of wisdom too.

There is a final, critical issue about the book's ending, one connected to much of what has been said already. Is the book of Job a tragedy whose tragic quality is subverted or contradicted by its ending? Cheryl Exum engages profoundly with the presence of the tragic in the Bible, finding it above all in Saul and Job.[49] She says: 'Tragedy involves catastrophe, and the catastrophic events that bring the tragic tale to closure are irreparable and irreversible.'[50] But if that is so what about the 'closure' of Job's tale? Her answer is as follows:

> Job's restoration to prosperity (with a bonus) at the end of the book is not such stuff as tragedies are made of. Neither is it sufficient in power or conviction to transform the book into a comedy, chiefly because the dialogue brings cosmic terror, as well as human heroism, into such stark relief. In his defiance Job rivals God; comic heroes do not reach such heights. Frye observes of the *Oresteia* that Athena's appearance at the end of the *Eumenides* does not turn the trilogy into a comedy but clarifies its tragic vision. I would make the same claim about Job. God appears to Job in a whirlwind and overwhelms him with questions just as Job predicted he would (9:16–20), holding before him the vision of a beautiful but morally unintelligible universe. The question is: can Job ever again feel secure in such a universe?

To see the Epilogue as a clarification and not a negation of the tragic vision of the book rings true both to the sheer power of the poetic chapters and to aspects of the Epilogue discussed above. Even this blessed

48. Ticciati, 'Job: A Hermeneutical and Ethical Interpretation', pp. 55ff.
49. J. Cheryl Exum, *Tragedy and Biblical Narrative: Arrows of the Almighty* (Cambridge: Cambridge University Press, 1992), p. 12.
50. Ibid. p. 4.

history does not undo the history of suffering. It is still human history ending in death, though as near as might be imagined to complete fulfilment. Exum's final question is also apt: there is no need to deny the continuing subjunctive 'maybe'; there has been no magical change in the character of the world so that Job-like affliction can no longer occur. Yet there is something problematic about her question too. Insecurity is not, in my judgement, the feeling one is left with at the end of the book, and it also seems very far from what Job might be imagined to be feeling. Why?

It has to do with God. In her short but rich conclusion Exum comes tantalisingly near to this:

> Tragedy threatens order by virtue of its recognition of random and unpredictable disorder. The random, the chaotic, the unintelligible, the contingent, are dimensions of reality as we know it, dimensions that the Bible knows also and whose fissures it does not, I have sought to illustrate, try to smooth over. Indeed, the Bible's uncompromising portrayal of reality as embracing dissolution and despair as well as resolution and repair is the source of its extraordinary narrative range and power. Any less expansive, multifaceted, and honest representation of accumulated experience and wisdom would be inadequate and inauthentic. Nor does the tragic vision itself leave us without hope, for if it despairs of knowing the ways of the universe – 'the secrets of God and the limit of the Almighty,' as Zophar puts it (Job 11:7) – at the same time it shows us the dignity and amplitude of human beings coming to terms with the possibilities and limits of mortality.[51]

That is a perceptive description of the biblical witness to what I have called 'immersion in history', and to the orientation of history in hope. But in staying with Zophar on God it stops short of where Job arrives in the Epilogue. As suggested above, this is a 'for nothing' relationship with God for God's sake, reached through trauma, through questioning and being questioned, and through appreciating creation for creation's sake. 'In such a universe', and before such a God, one's own security is not the core concern. Job's wisdom of 'fearing God for nothing' liberates him for a life trusting in God 'for richer, for poorer, in sickness, in health'. The Epilogue shows the enjoyment of riches and other blessings in a long-term community of worship, generosity and compassion. *The cries of*

51. Ibid. p. 152.

suffering have not been forgotten, silenced or ignored; cries of joy and gratitude have greeted the many blessings; and the generative centre of the whole way of living is the cry of awe: 'now my eye sees you' (42:5).

Conclusion

Some leading themes of the present work have been developed through reading the book of Job: the importance for wisdom of cries and of the diverse moods that express the significance of cries; wisdom realised through embodiment in a life immersed in the contingencies, complexities, sufferings and joys of human existence; and above all the wisdom of fearing and adoring God for God's sake, which in turn frees us to acknowledge and value the preciousness of creatures, human and non-human, for their own sake. This chapter has also been this book's most sustained exercise in what the previous chapter called the wisdom interpretation of scripture, and is the only one that deals at length with a text generally recognised as within the genre of 'wisdom literature' in the scholarly sense. Several of chapter 2's maxims for the interpretation of scripture have been exemplified, in particular reading 'for God's sake' and in a 'theodramatic' involvement in history, and reading for the plain and other senses of the text. The extended sense has been sought mainly by reading, alongside the book of Job, Micheal O'Siadhail's *The Gossamer Wall: Poems in Witness to the Holocaust*, and inviting the reader to distil from both a wisdom that might cope with trauma and with the most radical questioning of self, life and God.

But what sort of wisdom is that? The next chapter will continue with Job by attempting to describe the wisdom that has been discovered so far (the main concentration having been on the opening and closing chapters), and by reading the rest of the book of Job in order to learn more about its wisdom pedagogy. It will then relate this both to *The Gossamer Wall* and to Judaism and Christianity after the Shoah.

4

Job and post-Holocaust wisdom

The wisdom of the book of Job, even in those few parts of it discussed in the previous chapter, is difficult to summarise. This is inherent in its intensive particularity, focussed through one 'experiment' on one person, combined with its plurality of voices in dialogue and multiple moods of discourse. Above all it is the cries that cannot be summarised, synthesised or done justice to in prose. The cries ring out again and again, and the poetry imprints them in the heart and memory.

Jean Amery in *At the Mind's Limits: Contemplations by a Survivor of Auschwitz and Its Realities*[1] gives a piercingly graphic and thoughtful account of being tortured. 'Whoever was tortured stays tortured. Torture is ineradicably burned into him, even when no clinically objective traces can be detected.'[2] Amery reflects on the unknown victims and those who are undergoing torture at this minute: 'From other places the screams penetrated as little into the world as did my own strange and uncanny howls from the vault of Breedonk ... Someone, somewhere is crying out under torture. Perhaps in this hour, in this second.'[3] On 17 October 1978, Jean Amery committed suicide. This was no Joban ending; and his writings and his death insist that, whatever the joys and blessings, the cries of Job continue to be heard, and the analogous cries today continue to be listened for.

A wisdom that has really heard Job continues to be tested by its resonance with his cries and those of others; and especially it is tested by one's own sufferings and traumas. Job is a wise man who learns more

---

1. Jean Amery, *At the Mind's Limits: Contemplations by a Survivor of Auschwitz and Its Realities* (Bloomington and Indianapolis: Indiana University Press, 1980).
2. Ibid. p. 34.   3. Ibid. pp. 23–4.

through trauma, and the passionate poetry of the drama opens up for the reader a pedagogy of wisdom whose validity is only likely to be proven through the reader coping with affliction. This is centrally about an individual, and other suffering individuals can learn from it. Yet it is also about this individual in passionate engagement with his community of friends and with the God of their community and its tradition. This makes it appropriate for this and the previous chapter to set alongside Job O'Siadhail's *The Gossamer Wall* with its account of a whole people's trauma. How does Job learn in ways that might shape our learning? What are some of the lessons for traditions and communities faced with new challenges and disturbing, transformative events? I will try to answer that by approaching it from three angles: Job and his friends; Job, his friends and God; and wisdom as searching and being searched. The results of that discussion will then be related to some contemporary Jewish and Christian attempts to develop a post-Shoah wisdom that engages both with each other and with the twenty-first-century world.

Job and friends

The dialogue between Job and his friends in chapters 3–37 can be read as a process of discernment in response to the cry of Job in chapter 3. This parallels the previous chapter's interpretation of what God speaks out of the whirlwind in chapters 38–41 as taking up Job chapter 3's images, categories and content so as to transform them and open a new horizon within which it is possible to appreciate the integrity of creation, God and Job for their own sakes.

The fact that most of the book of Job is taken up with dialogue and argument is worth reflecting upon. It must mean that the author found this to be the most appropriate form through which to convey most of what he or she wanted to say. If the suggestion is valid that this is a book seeking to draw readers into a way of wisdom, then the form of the central thirty-five chapters is significant for that process. How might it work?

The most obvious way it works is to draw readers into a complex argumentative exchange expressed in rich poetry. Both sides make many sensible and even powerful points. But it is an exchange that, as in most passionate discussions, goes beyond argument and counter-argument to invoke whole worlds of meaning, association and feeling. As already discussed, the interrogative, subjunctive and optative moods of questioning, possibility and desire are there alongside indicatives and imperatives; and, to complicate matters further, each mood is used with an array of nuances by different protagonists. It seems designed to resist simplification, summary or overview, in effect saying to us as readers: you have to try to follow this in all its twists and turns, and you are likely to get lost and have to reread again and again. This way of wisdom draws us into a drama of differing positions in which reasoning, feeling and imagining; past, present and future; and God, creation and humanity are all involved. It places considerable responsibility on the reader, who is immersed in this rich material, to grapple with the complexities and make some sense of them. The poetry is far from direct, univocal, 'plain sense' instruction, and invites responses on several levels leading to multiple interpretations. The range of resonances evoked in each reader by this poetry means that it continues to inspire passionate discussion. This provokes further reflection on its sapiential character as creating a way of wisdom that can sustain ongoing debate and argument about important matters that have to be faced afresh by each person and gene-ration and can never be finished with. There can be no clear, neat formula for dealing with trauma; a wise response is likely to encourage each person and community to learn from the past while trying to do full justice to their own specific experience.

Perhaps it is here, in *the attempt to hold together in a community both tradition and new, overwhelming experience,* that we touch on one of the deepest and most widely relevant issues in the book of Job. The book can be read as the attempt of a tradition to face its own limitations and move through a traumatic crisis.[4]

Most traditions (and individuals within them) are adept at dealing with novel situations and assimilating new experiences without too much change, and they have maintained their identities because they have been able do this. Job's friends represent a wisdom tradition that has a well worked out set of responses to suffering, evil, death and other traumas. The core element is that human life and history make sense within a framework of justice implemented by God, ensuring that the

---

4. See Katharine J. Dell, *'Get Wisdom, Get Insight': An Introduction to Israel's Wisdom Literature* (London: Darton, Longman and Todd, 2000) on how Job's 'ideas break outside the bounds of traditional wisdom beliefs, even though they may have their starting-point there' (p. 40). She identifies six key themes (concerning trust in the order of the world, acceptance of a certain ambiguity of events, a clear teaching on punishment and reward, valuing life as the supreme good, confidence in the quest for wisdom, and the personification of wisdom) in Proverbs as characteristic of its traditional wisdom, and shows how each of them is problematised in some way by Job.

good are rewarded and the bad punished. This is stated by Eliphaz in chapter 4 in immediate response to Job's cry in chapter 3.

> Job 4:7–9 [7]Think now, who that was innocent ever perished? Or where were the upright cut off? [8]As I have seen, those who plough iniquity and sow trouble reap the same. [9]By the breath of God they perish, and by the blast of his anger they are consumed.

This theme recurs throughout the book, and Job does not simply reject it. Into his mouth are put words that reflect the same wisdom tradition.

> Job 27:13–23 [13]This is the portion of the wicked with God, and the heritage that oppressors receive from the Almighty: [14]If their children are multiplied, it is for the sword; and their offspring have not enough to eat. [15]Those who survive them the pestilence buries, and their widows make no lamentation. [16]Though they heap up silver like dust, and pile up clothing like clay – [17]they may pile it up, but the just will wear it, and the innocent will divide the silver. [18]They build their houses like nests, like booths made by sentinels of the vineyard. [19]They go to bed with wealth, but will do so no more; they open their eyes, and it is gone. [20]Terrors overtake them like a flood; in the night a whirlwind carries them off. [21]The east wind lifts them up and they are gone; it sweeps them out of their place. [22]It hurls at them without pity; they flee from its power in headlong flight. [23]It claps its hands at them, and hisses at them from its place.

There is no simple reconciliation of this with Job's earlier arguments from experience that the wicked often do flourish.

> Job 21:7–15 [7]Why do the wicked live on, reach old age, and grow mighty in power? [8]Their children are established in their presence, and their offspring before their eyes. [9]Their houses are safe from fear, and no rod of God is upon them. [10]Their bull breeds without fail; their cow calves and never miscarries. [11]They send out their little ones like a flock, and their children dance around. [12]They sing to the tambourine and the lyre, and rejoice to the sound of the pipe. [13]They spend their days in prosperity, and in peace they go down to Sheol. [14]They say to God, 'Leave us alone! We do not desire to know your ways. [15]What is the Almighty, that we should serve him? And what profit do we get if we pray to him?'

The thrust of Job's arguments is not to deny ultimate divine justice or to assert the opposite of what the friends say but to resist applying it like a formula to current events. His reasoning from general experience is one way of challenging the friends' use of the tradition. Far more insistent are the related arguments from his own experience. He maintains that, whatever might be true of others, in his case the generalised use of the tradition is wrong. He has not deserved what has happened to him. He does not fit the ready-made categories used by his friends. They are challenged again and again really to see him, to listen to him.

> Job 6:28 But now, be pleased to look at me; for I will not lie to your face. Job 13:4–12 ⁴As for you, you whitewash with lies; all of you are worthless physicians. ⁵If you would only keep silent, that would be your wisdom! ⁶Hear now my reasoning, and listen to the pleadings of my lips. ⁷Will you speak falsely for God, and speak deceitfully for him? ⁸Will you show partiality towards him, will you plead the case for God? ⁹Will it be well with you when he searches you out? Or can you deceive him, as one person deceives another? ¹⁰He will surely rebuke you if in secret you show partiality. ¹¹Will not his majesty terrify you, and the dread of him fall upon you? ¹²Your maxims are proverbs of ashes, your defences are defences of clay.

He claims a wisdom equal to theirs, but one which is wrestling with something new that challenges what they say.

> Job 12:1–4 ¹Then Job answered: ²'No doubt you are the people, and wisdom will die with you. ³But I have understanding as well as you; I am not inferior to you. Who does not know such things as these? ⁴I am a laughingstock to my friends; I, who called upon God and he answered me, a just and blameless man, I am a laughingstock.'

The core of Job's response is a passionate protest that the friends do not hear and understand his specific cry. This drives him to more detailed accounts of his condition and fuller reflection on how deeply unjust his suffering has been. The culmination comes in chapters 29–31 with his long recollection of his previous life, filled with justice, generosity and deserved social respect, amounting to a vivid portrayal of ordinary life lived wisely – fearing God, doing good and turning away from evil.

Those chapters have another important dimension that has also occurred earlier: the appeal for compassion.

> Job 30:24–31 ²⁴Surely one does not turn against the needy, when in disaster they cry for help. ²⁵Did I not weep for those whose day was hard? Was not my soul grieved for the poor? ²⁶But when I looked for good, evil came; and when I waited for light, darkness came. ²⁷My inward parts are in turmoil, and are never still; days of affliction come

to meet me. [28]I go about in sunless gloom; I stand up in the assembly and cry for help. [29]I am a brother of jackals, and a companion of ostriches. [30]My skin turns black and falls from me, and my bones burn with heat. [31]My lyre is turned to mourning, and my pipe to the voice of those who weep.

Job 6:14–17 [14]Those who withhold kindness from a friend forsake the fear of the Almighty. [15]My companions are treacherous like a torrent-bed, like freshets that pass away, [16]that run dark with ice, turbid with melting snow. [17]In time of heat they disappear; when it is hot, they vanish from their place.

Job 19:19–22 [19]All my intimate friends abhor me, and those whom I loved have turned against me. [20]My bones cling to my skin and to my flesh, and I have escaped by the skin of my teeth. [21]Have pity on me, have pity on me, O you my friends, for the hand of God has touched me! [22]Why do you, like God, pursue me, never satisfied with my flesh?

These and other passages suggest that kindness, love, friendship, pity and responding to the cries of those in need are the practical measure of a wisdom that fears God. The friends began by crying out, weeping aloud and sitting with Job for seven days and nights (2:12–13). But their received wisdom cannot cope with Job's agonised interrogation of his suffering and of their interpretations. They are not able to rethink in line with their initial impulse of compassion. It is compassion that loses out.

As readers we already know that the friends' categories are inadequate. They do not know of the conversation between God and the Satan. Their conception of wisdom cannot allow for a question that is open (even, arguably, for God): whether Job fears God for nothing. Nor can it allow for the consequent significance of what is being worked out in history, and not least between themselves and Job. Something novel, something not to be exhaustively accounted for by precedents, is going on. Even if they failed to understand this, they might have responded to Job with the compassion he appealed for. Instead they made the move that has perennially bedevilled religious, political and other ideologies: they interpreted Job's cry in their own terms, made him fit the procrustean bed of their wisdom, and refused a compassion that endangered the coherence of their system.

But because their wisdom was radically threatened by Job they could not be content with disagreement. They had to attack Job's whole position. This inevitably involved undermining the credibility of his cry. Again, this is a classic move by ideologies that are challenged by the intensity of human sufferings: those who are suffering are feared, suspected, devalued, blamed. They are inscribed in a story in which they are the villains, or subsumed under categories that ensure their marginalisation or rejection.[5] Right from the start in chapter 4 Eliphaz assaults Job's powerful words and their entitlement to be called wise (vv. 1–6), and returns to the subject later (e.g. 15:1–3). Bildad opens his first speech in a similar way (8:1–2):

> [1]Then Bildad the Shuhite answered: [2]'How long will you say these things, and the words of your mouth be a great wind?'

Zophar opens in the same way (11:1–3).

> [1]Then Zophar the Naamathite answered: [2]'Should a multitude of words go unanswered, and should one full of talk be vindicated? [3]Should your babble put others to silence, and when you mock, shall no one shame you?'

Job protests at his cry being emptied of meaning, invalidated and unheard.

> Job 6:26 Do you think that you can reprove words, as if the speech of the desperate were wind?
> Job 16:18 'O earth, do not cover my blood; let my outcry find no resting place.'
> Job 19:7 'Even when I cry out, "Violence!" I am not answered; I call aloud, but there is no justice.'
> Job 31:35 'Oh, that I had one to hear me!'

The late-arriving fourth friend, Elihu, makes an even more comprehensive claim to wisdom and matches this with the ultimate rejection of Job's wisdom and his cry.

> Job 34:34–35 [34]Those who have sense will say to me, and the wise who hear me will say, [35]'Job speaks without knowledge, his words are without insight.'
> Job 35:13 Surely God does not hear an empty cry, nor does the Almighty regard it.

That is a devastating refusal of Job's cry and of the 'wisdom' with which he supports it. It is a final act of discernment, a judgement that irrevocably identifies the cry as empty in God's sight and any justification of it as completely lacking insight. The conflict over the discernment of

---

5. Here the interpretation of the book of Job by René Girard in terms of scapegoating is helpful. See René Girard, *Job the Victim of His People* (London: The Athlone Press, 1987).

Job's opening cry in chapter 3 here reaches its climax, and the vital issues all converge: the authenticity of Job's cry; the claims and counter-claims to wisdom; and God. God is the final court of appeal between Job and his friends, and, having bracketed this out so far, the discussion of their debate now must inquire into what they say of God and to God.

Job, friends and God

When eventually in the prose Epilogue God delivers his verdict on Job and his friends its terms are striking.

> Job 42:7–8 [7]After the LORD had spoken these words to Job, the LORD said to Eliphaz the Temanite: 'My wrath is kindled against you and against your two friends; for you have not spoken of me what is right, as my servant Job has. [8]Now therefore take seven bulls and seven rams, and go to my servant Job, and offer up for yourselves a burnt offering; and my servant Job shall pray for you, for I will accept his prayer not to deal with you according to your folly; for you have not spoken of me what is right, as my servant Job has done.'

The twice-repeated verdict is that the friends, unlike Job, have not spoken what was right *of God*. Further, what they said is described as foolish, the opposite of wisdom. What might that mean?

In line with my decision to take the prose Prologue and Epilogue seriously as the framework for the poetry, and with seeing the Prologue's criterion of whether Job 'fears God for nothing' as the most important hermeneutical key to the book, the vital question to be asked is how what is said by the friends and by Job relates to fearing God for nothing.

The friends seem to be clear and untroubled in their conception of God and God's purposes, while their confidence is continually challenged by Job. It is not that they differ with Job in believing that God is Lord of creation (e.g. friends in chapters 5, 37; Job in chapters 9, 10, 26), is beyond human comprehension and not to be reduced to human dimensions (e.g. friends in chapters 5, 22, 33, 35, 36; Job in chapters 9, 12, 28), is wise and rightly to be feared (e.g. friends in chapters 11, 15, 22; Job in chapters 6, 9, 12, 28), and upholds justice and punishes wrongdoing (friends in chapters 8, 11, 15, 18, 20, 36; Job in chapters 17, 27). The issue is not the existence or attributes of this God. What is it?

I have already described it in terms of different dominant 'moods'. The friends tend to use indicatives and imperatives, and when they use an interrogative the answer is usually clear. Job uses indicatives that raise radical questions and interrogatives that reflect genuine bewilderment, within an optative longing for answers to his questions through direct engagement with God. There is a pervasive subjunctive openness to possibilities regarding God that can hardly be imagined by his friends. His imperatives are in the service of the other moods, all of which are rooted in his cry to God. If the verdict of the book is in favour of Job's way of speaking of God, then this might mean that God is pleased with those who refuse to fit new experience unquestioningly into traditional teaching about God, who ask radical questions about God, their experience and their traditions, who never let their desire for the truth of God and God's justice be quenched, who are open to new possibilities and surprises even in the sphere of their core convictions, and who above all cry out with integrity before God and resist all attempts to misinterpret, marginalise or stifle that cry. That might be too indicative a way of drawing lessons, too binary an analysis of a complex argument in which both sides are needed and neither simply wins, too crude a summary of a way of wisdom to which the process and the poetry are intrinsic. But at least the debate raises such issues as questions. *Reading the book of Job within a community should help to keep its tradition self-critical and open to new developments, and above all enable it, and individuals or groups within it, to cope better with trauma or other radical change.*

But that is too schematic, general and abstracted from the vital question of 'fearing God for nothing' to suffice as an adequate verdict on the debate between Job and his friends. The chief difference between them is in the quality of their relationship with God, which, because it is inseparable from the 'for nothing' relationship, is the pivot of the book taken as a whole.

The friends' God runs the world strictly according to rule, repaying good for good and evil for evil. They are simply repeating the wisdom of their elders.

> Job 15:10 The grey-haired and the aged are on our side, those older than your father.

There is clear affirmation of how things are in line with God's will.

> Job 18:5 Surely the light of the wicked is put out, and the flame of their fire does not shine.
> Job 36:5–7 [5]Surely God is mighty and does not despise any; he is mighty in strength of understanding. [6]He does not keep the wicked

alive, but gives the afflicted their right. ^{7}He does not withdraw his eyes from the righteous, but with kings on the throne he sets them for ever, and they are exalted.

There is a straightforward 'if ... then' understanding of how history works.

> Job 8:5–6 ^{5}If you will seek God and make supplication to the Almighty, ^{6}if you are pure and upright, surely then he will rouse himself for you and restore to you your rightful place.
> Job 22:23–26 ^{23}If you return to the Almighty, you will be restored, if you remove unrighteousness from your tents, ^{24}if you treat gold like dust, and gold of Ophir like the stones of the torrent-bed, ^{25}and if the Almighty is your gold and your precious silver, ^{26}then you will delight yourself in the Almighty, and lift up your face to God.

They are happy to speak confidently for God, Elihu above all.

> Job 36:1–4 ^{1}Elihu continued and said: ^{2}'Bear with me a little, and I will show you, for I have yet something to say on God's behalf. ^{3}I will bring my knowledge from far away, and ascribe righteousness to my Maker. ^{4}For truly my words are not false; one who is perfect in knowledge is with you.'

They see God's transcendence as one of indifference, having no need of people and their goodness, and being unaffected by their wickedness.

> Job 22:1–3 ^{1}Then Eliphaz the Temanite answered: ^{2}'Can a mortal be of use to God? Can even the wisest be of service to him? ^{3}Is it any pleasure to the Almighty if you are righteous, or is it gain to him if you make your ways blameless?'
> Job 35:6–8 ^{6}'If you have sinned, what do you accomplish against him? And if your transgressions are multiplied, what do you do to him? ^{7}If you are righteous, what do you give to him; or what does he receive from your hand? ^{8}Your wickedness affects others like you, and your righteousness, other human beings.'

By contrast, Job finds history, and especially his own story, far less transparent, not at all a matter of 'if ... then', and his speech about God is far from a confident repetition of traditional teaching. Above all, he will not allow that God is indifferent. He is passionate with God, and at the heart of this is his constant crying out to God and against God. Addressing God takes precedence over speaking about him. A hidden, third-person God running the world by rules of retribution is intolerable to him, and again and again he appeals to God to deal with him directly and compassionately. At the heart of this is his desire to be face to face with God; but just because of this the most shocking and intolerable thing of all is his conclusion that God might be his enemy.

> Job 13:15–24 [15]See, he will kill me; I have no hope; but I will defend my ways to his face. [16]This will be my salvation, that the godless shall not come before him. [17]Listen carefully to my words, and let my declaration be in your ears. [18]I have indeed prepared my case; I know that I shall be vindicated. [19]Who is there that will contend with me? For then I would be silent and die. [20]Only grant two things to me, then I will not hide myself from your face: [21]withdraw your hand far from me, and do not let dread of you terrify me. [22]Then call, and I will answer; or let me speak, and you reply to me. [23]How many are my iniquities and my sins? Make me know my transgression and my sin. [24]Why do you hide your face, and count me as your enemy?

Some of the book's most vivid poetry describes this enmity.

> Job 16:6–14 [6]If I speak, my pain is not assuaged, and if I forbear, how much of it leaves me? [7]Surely now God has worn me out; he has made desolate all my company. [8]And he has shrivelled me up, which is a witness against me; my leanness has risen up against me, and it testifies to my face. [9]He has torn me in his wrath, and hated me; he has gnashed his teeth at me; my adversary sharpens his eyes against me. [10]They have gaped at me with their mouths; they have struck me insolently on the cheek; they mass themselves together against me. [11]God gives me up to the ungodly, and casts me into the hands of the wicked. [12]I was at ease, and he broke me in two; he seized me by the neck and dashed me to pieces; he set me up as his target; [13]his archers surround me. He slashes open my kidneys, and shows no mercy; he pours out my gall on the ground. [14]He bursts upon me again and again; he rushes at me like a warrior.

When you are innocent, and yet the one who is the ultimate judge and final court of appeal is your enemy, then your cry is most comprehensively rejected, negated, emptied of meaning or effect. What recourse is there? How can appeal be made against God? The logic of the friends is that by definition no such appeal can be made: God is Creator, is over all, and defines justice. Elihu's culminating speech in chapters 34–37 is especially strong on this, and therefore especially insistent on God's unfathomable transcendence, on the 'if ... then' character of God's activity in history, and on the emptiness of Job's cry.

Job, on the other hand, continues to cry out until answered by God. He confronts his terrible situation but refuses to accept an arbitrary God as the last word. He searches further and never gives up reaching out for more from God even when the only sign of the 'more' is his own crying out. The friends' wisdom negates this searching as pointless and even blasphemous. Yet through the very debate with his friends Job emerges from the sheer agony, darkness and despair of chapter 3. It is not a simple development, but there are key signs of emergence: the very engagement in argument with his friends; the dimensions of justice, life and society that are brought into play; and above all the appeal to an 'umpire', 'mediator', 'redeemer' to intercede with God or set up a fair 'trial' in which Job might be vindicated,[6] together with the desire for a face to face meeting with God.

> Job 9:33 There is no umpire between us, who might lay his hand on us both.
> Job 13:15 See, he will kill me; I have no hope; but I will defend my ways to his face . . .
>   13:24 Why do you hide your face, and count me as your enemy?
> Job 16:19 Even now, in fact, my witness is in heaven, and he that vouches for me is on high.
> Job 19:25–27 [25]For I know that my Redeemer lives, and that at the last he will stand upon the earth; [26]and after my skin has been thus destroyed, then in my flesh I shall see God, [27]whom I shall see on my side, and my eyes shall behold, and not another.

Each of those signs is complex and ambivalent, and gives no simple clarity. But through all Job's agony and confusion the orientation to God is somehow sustained. One utterly vital question is: *Why?* Is Job crying out in order to get back his possessions or his children or his social standing or his health? Surely not. *Job is crying out in order to get God back!* This is 'fearing God for nothing' in the face of traumatic experience and an untraumatised traditional wisdom that discourages searching. Job refuses to cease questioning who God is and how he can relate to God. He refuses to accept a closed retributive system and an ultimately arbitrary God. He seeks something more than that, a God other than that.

---

6. One of the most fascinating and original parts of Ticciati's work is on the figure of the '*mokiach*'. For her complex argument, too lengthy to summarise here, see Susannah Ticciati, *Job and the Disruption of Identity: Reading beyond Barth* (London: T. & T. Clark, 2005), chapter 5.

A second utterly vital question is: *Who is the God he meets?* The previous chapter described the God of the Prologue, whirlwind speeches and Epilogue as one who is to be blessed for his own sake, just as creation, Job and humanity are to be celebrated for their own sake. But there is one further crucial thing to be said about God, springing from the conversation he has with the Satan in the Prologue. There he is seen staking his own name on Job, allowing Job to vindicate his judgement on Job's integrity or not. As discussed above, this is presented as an open question for God as well as for the Satan and Job. *In the openness of life in history, God's name is at stake.* Why? The question about Job is whether he fears God for nothing, gratuitously, and I have just argued that that happens in his debate with his friends. But what does this mean for who God is? Putting his name at stake in history could be seen as arbitrary or an interesting gamble, but the reason that rings true with the preciousness to him of his relationship with Job is that *God does this for the sake of the 'for nothing' relationship with Job.* This is beyond all manipulation, *quid pro quo,* or threat of retribution. It is not only the secret of the possibility of blessing, love, freedom and integrity between God and any human being; it points to the secret of the wisdom of this God. *God's own 'for nothing' is the wisdom of one who risks a relationship without guarantees, and who gives human existence the terrifying dignity of a life and death drama in which wisdom and foolishness really matter.*

A searching wisdom

It is possible now to gather together what has been learnt about wisdom from the book of Job so far.

The essence of the embodied wisdom ascribed to Job is that he **'feared God and turned away from evil'** (1:1). That wisdom was tested to the extreme, the key issue being whether he 'feared God for nothing', for God's sake rather than for what he gained from God. Job's cry of affliction in chapter 3 sounds through the rest of the book. *Is there a friend, a God, a wisdom that can respond to that?* The poetic chapters immerse us in the cries and complexities of creation and history while always asking how God relates to them. This way of wisdom leads through passionate argument and many voices, expressed in poetry whose rich meaning constantly invites renewed efforts to interpret it; through opening up indicatives and imperatives in interrogatives, subjunctives and optatives, and in the process exploring how a wisdom tradition can cope with the novel and the traumatic; through a powerful poetic evocation of the worth of creation for its own sake, in line with God for God's sake, and Job and his friends for their own sake; through Job fearing 'for nothing' the God who 'for nothing', as a gift, risks his name in the contingencies of history; and through the presence of God to Job. Finally, the Epilogue describes a post-traumatic wisdom embodied in an ordinary, 'blessed' life of repentance, forgiveness, prayer, worship, reconciliation, compassion, generosity, shared meals, material prosperity, the birth of children, grandchildren and great grandchildren, responsibility across generations, and death in old age.

Yet within the book too there is in chapter 28 what seems like a summary of its wisdom. Most scholars agree that this appears to be a later insertion in the dialogue section of the book,[7] but they differ widely about its interpretation. I follow Moberly's account of it, which compares Job with Solomon.[8] Of special relevance to this chapter is Moberly's analysis of how, for all the differences between the way wisdom is described in relation to Solomon and Job,[9] the two accounts converge in their understanding of God's wisdom in human life. They do not separate divine and human wisdom but see wisdom as a divine quality that must be humanly embodied. Commenting on the relation to God of justice in Deuteronomy and the interpretation of dreams in Genesis, he says that there the human sphere is set

> within the morally and spiritually demanding context of God . . . So in the light of these parallels, I suggest that the purpose of Job 28 was never to depict a wisdom removed from human life. As justice and the interpretation of dreams are ascribed to God so that they may truly be appropriated by humans, so too with wisdom. The poetic rhetoric of wisdom's elusiveness seeks to remove wisdom from all spheres of human attainment precisely in order to locate it within the context of human life which knows itself responsive and accountable to God. The wisdom which is so elusive is precisely that wisdom which is

---

7. E.g. Gerhard von Rad, *Wisdom in Israel* (London: SCM, 1972), pp. 148ff. Moberly (see below) agrees with von Rad and hears in chapter 28 the voice of the narrator of the prose Prologue.
8. R. W. L. Moberly, 'Solomon and Job: Divine Wisdom in Human Life' in *Where Shall Wisdom Be Found? Wisdom in the Bible, the Church and the Contemporary World*, ed. Stephen C. Barton (Edinburgh: T. & T. Clark, 1999), pp. 3–17.
9. For example, he writes: 'One might say that Solomon's wisdom is wisdom in dealing with other people (in the exercise of his royal responsibilities), while Job's wisdom pertains primarily to himself (in the maintenance of integrity in the face of disaster). Yet one might also say that Solomon shows wisdom in the exercise of power, while Job shows wisdom in the face of powerlessness, either of which may be as significant for others as for self.' Ibid. p. 16.

declared by God to humanity at the end of the poem, that wisdom which Job in the opening story fully embodies and displays. To put it in other terms, the poem, like the story, explores the paradox of living in a world which is creation in relation to a Creator – for in such a world wisdom is like God, both transcendent (i.e. inaccessible) and immanent (i.e. accessible).[10]

Chapter 28 is on this interpretation in line with a portrayal of Job's wisdom as drawing him simultaneously into wrestling with the realities of history, including its traumas, and with God and God's purposes. It is a framework within which the sheer concentration and intensity of the engagement between him and his friends makes sense.

Chapter 28 may also give another clue to the core conception of wisdom in the book. How do its first eleven verses, about mining in the depths of the earth for silver, gold, iron, copper and sapphires, relate to what follows about mortals not knowing the way to wisdom, wisdom being far more valuable than gold, silver, onyx, sapphire, glass, coral, crystal, pearls or chrysolite, and God understanding the way to it and knowing its place?

> Job 28:1–13 [1]Surely there is a mine for silver, and a place for gold to be refined. [2]Iron is taken out of the earth, and copper is smelted from ore. [3]Miners put an end to darkness, and search out to the farthest bound the ore in gloom and deep darkness. [4]They open shafts in a valley away from human habitation; they are forgotten by travellers, they sway suspended, remote from people. [5]As for the earth, out of it comes bread; but underneath it is turned up as by fire. [6]Its stones are the place of sapphires, and its dust contains gold. [7]That path no bird of prey knows, and the falcon's eye has not seen it. [8]The proud wild animals have not trodden it; the lion has not passed over it. [9]They put their hand to the flinty rock, and overturn mountains by the roots. [10]They cut out channels in the rocks, and their eyes see every precious thing. [11]The sources of the rivers they probe; hidden things they bring to light. [12]But where shall wisdom be found? And where is the place of understanding? [13]Mortals do not know the way to it, and it is not found in the land of the living.

It is possible to see these opening verses as a simple denial of human effort in seeking wisdom, recommending complete reliance on God's

---

10. Ibid. p. 15.

initiative and revelation. But that would disconnect it from the rest of the book, with which Moberly convincingly integrates it.[11]

Ticciati takes Moberly's line further in her interpretation of these verses. She concentrates on the theme of 'searching out' (*chaqar*) and related ideas of refining and testing (especially *bachan*). 'I, the Lord, who searches the mind and tries the heart ...' (Jer. 17:10) is a verse that brings together the key terms, and they occur at various points in the dialogues of Job, suggesting a range of related meanings: a process of probing and scrutiny to ascertain Job's true nature; a process of purifying or refining; an exploration of depths; a legal process of investigation, seeking justice. The resonances are with both wisdom and justice, which are so intertwined in the book of Job. She identifies something that is pivotal to the whole drama: the simultaneity of Job being tested and him being led into deeper wisdom. She speaks of 'the character of the self as inextricable from the process of probing – that there is no "self" independently of its being probed'.[12]

In chapter 28 *chaqar* is first used in v.3.

> Job 28:3 Miners put an end to darkness, and search out (חֵקֶר) to the farthest bound the ore in gloom and deep darkness.

The surrounding verses give a vivid picture of the dedication and fruitfulness of this searching out, culminating in its utter radicality.

> Job 28:9–12 [9]They put their hand to the flinty rock, and overturn mountains by the roots. [10]They cut out channels in the rocks, and their eyes see every precious thing. [11]The sources of the rivers they probe; hidden things they bring to light. [12]But where shall wisdom be found?

The opening of v.12 is in Hebrew ו and is more neutral than a contrastive 'but'. As Ticciati, following Moberly, argues, despite an element of negative contrast between human and divine activity because of human inability to reach the place of understanding, the powerful picture of searching out in vv.1–11 is not adequately interpreted as purely negative. The vital clue is in the other use of *chaqar* in v.28.

---

11. Moberly, besides his other points summarised above, identifies five similarities between the Prologue and chapter 28: 'terminology of "fear God and turn from evil" in prime position, serenity of mood or tone, a deceptive simplicity of presentation, the dialectic of wisdom as inaccessible and accessible, the privilege given to the reader to know how wisdom is attained'. Ibid. p. 15.
12. Susannah Ticciati, 'Job: A Hermeneutical and Ethical Interpretation with Reference to Karl Barth' (PhD thesis, University of Cambridge), p. 149.

Job 28:27 then he saw it and declared it; he established it, and searched
it out. (וְגַם־חֲקָרָהּ)

God himself searched out wisdom! There is nothing wrong with searching,
human or divine. Indeed, the ascription of searching to God makes it a
fundamental and necessary part of reality. And v.28 then sums up the
human activity within which human searching comes together with God's –
the activity that has been associated with Job from the book's first verse.

Job 28:28 And he said to humankind, 'Truly, the fear of the Lord, that is
wisdom; and to depart from evil is understanding.'

This drives us back to search vv.1–11 more deeply. This language is used
metaphorically elsewhere in Job and in scripture for a searching and
testing of human minds and hearts. It is hard to imagine that its vivid
use in this context is not meant to resonate in such ways. Moreover, the
words used for darkness here are the same as those used in chapter 3 (3:4,
5, 6) where they are part of Job's self-description. Vv.1–11 then evoke the
'searching self' needed by anyone who is to fear God and depart from evil.
Of course mining does not discover wisdom, but what the miners do is a
profound and encouraging image for those who are concerned with
understanding the depths and darknesses of the self, the world and
God. But there is something even more primary than the searching self:
this is the 'searched self' living before a searching, testing, purifying God.
Ticciati sums this up:

In this deeper dimension that emerges in a rereading of vv.1–11 in the
light of v.28, in other words, the mine (v.1) of human attainment
becomes the self that lies beneath this activity. What are the
implications of this for the relation between human activity in the
world and wisdom? It would seem that wisdom is relocated within
such human activity to the extent that this activity is understood as
emerging out of the probing of the self that is occurring simultaneously
on a deeper level – a probing of self that is carried out by the human
subjects themselves on the one hand, but on the other, and more
fundamentally – the lack of specification of subject in these verses
leaves this possibility of interpretation open – by God. The ascription
of wisdom to God (v.23), and the explicit assertion of the primordial
divine activity of searching out wisdom in v.27, express this
prevenience of God's searching. Indeed, God's searching is the context
and presupposition of his address to humankind in v.28 (which in
turn gives rise to the deeper dimension of vv.1–11):

²⁷Then he saw it and declared it;
he established it, and searched it out (חקרה).
²⁸And he said to humankind,
'Behold, the fear of the Lord, that is wisdom;
And to depart from evil is understanding.'

> What this entails is the fact that genuine human probing (on both levels) always occurs in response to the divine searching – in accountability to God. Indeed, the genuine probing of self *is* this accountability to God. It is to the extent that human endeavour takes place in this accountability (fundamentally to the God **'who searches the mind and tries the heart'**, Jer. 17.10) that it may be said to embody wisdom.[13]

Such a wisdom of being searched and of searching is not something that can be put into a formula. It challenges every aspect and level of the searched and searching self, and even powerful metaphors, passionate arguments, multiple voices and moods, and experiences of traumatic disruption are no guarantee that this way of wisdom will be followed. The book of Job's resistance to straightforward 'plain sense' interpretation and its stimulation of endless disputes about its meaning are perhaps no accident. Its form as well as its content provoke confusion, searching and dispute. But it also invites repeated rereadings in new situations, especially those of deep disturbance and trauma.

This and the previous chapter have accompanied the reading of Job with attention to the Holocaust as an epochal trauma that cries out for Job-like wisdom. In the concluding section we now return to that theme.

Post-Holocaust wisdom

The Gossamer Wall's wisdom of remembering and repair

The final part of O'Siadhail's suite of poems is a penetrating searching of our contemporary world in the aftermath of the Holocaust, a poetic interrogation directed at one dimension of its life after another.

Stretching
So is all history one secret narrative of power
Broken in the brick and rubble of Babel's tower?

13. Ticciati, *Job and the Disruption of Identity*, p. 189.

Hard-bitten Atlas, our hands thrown in the air
Are we too disillusioned now to bother to care?

Our stories become labyrinths of irony that turn
On irony. Fiddlers fiddling while a world may burn.

He breaks me down on every side and I am gone
O you who stalked the barren road to Babylon

Or walked the desert as second Jerusalem fell
And Titus of Vesuvius shattered Herod's Temple

Show us again some end to shape our storyline.
A feast of rich food and well-aged wine...

Isaiah's imagination stretches somehow to cope;
In Jeremiah's darkest scroll a jazz of hope

That stirs even in the deepest cries of silence:
Then shall the young women rejoice in the dance.[14]

There late- or post-modernity's inclination to analyse all history and relationships in terms of power and violence, and to use irony as the dominant trope of a disillusionment that sees through everything and cares responsibly for nothing, is set against the Jewish experience of coping with massive trauma: the exile in Babylon in the sixth century BC, and the destruction of the Temple by the Romans under Titus in AD 70. And the possible sources of hope, resisting meaninglessness and despair, are Isaiah and Jeremiah, two of the biblical authors who addressed the Babylonian exile and its aftermath. Job too is usually seen by scholars as post-exilic, written for a people who knew catastrophic discontinuity and destruction.[15] O'Siadhail evokes this biblical tradition that can show hope stirring 'even in the deepest cries of silence'. It has been one purpose of this and the previous chapter to show such hope in the book of Job.

O'Siadhail's interrogation raises radical issues for contemporary Judaism and Christianity to which I will return below. But impelled by recollecting the Holocaust he also probes specific features of twenty-first-century life. A recurrent image is Babel and its tower (Genesis 11),

14. Michael O'Siadhail, *The Gossamer Wall: Poems in Witness to the Holocaust* (Newcastle: Bloodaxe Books, 2002), p. 116.
15. For a survey of scholarly opinion on the dating of Job see Dell, *'Get Wisdom, Get Insight'*, chapter 3. Her conclusion about Job is: 'It seems most naturally to belong after the Exile, as it attacks the view that suffering must be a direct result of sin and must represent punishment from God, the key theme of exilic theology, but we cannot be more precise than that' Ibid. p. 37.

a symbol not only of human civilisation gone wrong but of this having global implications. He links it with confidence in progress and human ability to control:

> So sure we'd been of plot and *mise-en-scène*,
> A tick-tock dénouement, slow but certain.
>
> Visions of control, primrose track to hell;
> Stoked ovens, gaunt shadows of Babel.[16]

This echoes an earlier, fuller identification of historical fault lines in the opening sequence of poems. 'Hankerings' traces the tragic consequences of Europe's religious wars, and of the Enlightenment's reaction to them with a

>   . . . rage
> For everything certain and hierarchical,
> Three long centuries lusting after order.[17]

The passion for order and control is followed through to the Nazi slogans (and of course reaches beyond them to more recent examples of racism and ethnic cleansing):

> We hunger for overviews, flawless stock,
> Unblurred theories, the pure nightmare
> Of ideal boundaries, *ein Land, ein Volk*.
> *Übermensch* of dark-willed Nietzsche.
> Outcastes, outsiders, freaks, beware
> Our tick-tock reason's overreach.[18]

This is contrasted with an image of Renaissance vitality, a vision of what modern Europe might have been – and presumably still might retrieve:

> What happened to Macbeth's carousing porter,
> Montaigne's wry and carnival knowledge?
> That marvelling at being just as we are,
> Our lovely jumbled here-and-nowness,
> Particular, once-off, centred at the edge,
> This cussed and glorious human mess.[19]

Shakespeare[20] the dramatist and Montaigne the essayist are here the witnesses of multifaceted, uncontrollable human living. In the final

---

16. O'Siadhail, *The Gossamer Wall*, p. 115.   17. Ibid. p. 16.   18. Ibid.   19. Ibid.
20. Allusions to *Macbeth* occur in several poems, letting the Holocaust resonate with Shakespeare's portrayal of gratuitous evil.

sequence the importance of culture and the arts in enabling 'here-and-nowness', memory and hope recurs. The first poem, 'Round-up', meditates on a photographer who

> Zeros on a boy's eyes that want to grow
> Bigger and bigger the more you gaze . . .[21]

The poet Judah Halevi provides the epigraph and a number of quotations, and other poets and novelists are named or quoted, such as Celan, Szymborska and Anne Michaels. Music is especially powerful. The description of Mengele the Auschwitz doctor having the camp cellist Anita Lasker play Schumann leads into a celebration of the powerful music that can spring from terrible suffering, whether of Jews, black slaves or the Irish:

> Depths of survival. Klezmer or jazz or *céilí*,
> A story squeezes at the edge clamours of music;
> Our of darkest histories, profoundest gaiety.
>
> *A feast of rich food and well-aged wine.*
> Visions beyond loosening back into a world
> Too deep and copious for black suns to shine.[22]

In 'Never', facing Adorno's denunciation of poetry-writing after the Holocaust, he gives an apologia not only for his own project but also for other key ingredients in human thriving. Concern about the validity of words, the vision of 'fullness of being', the 'cold narrowings', conversations and dialogues, subversiveness, 'complex yes', 'raucous glory', 'surprise beyond our ken' and feasting: all strike notes that resonate with Job:

> That any poem after Auschwitz is obscene?
> Covenants of silence so broken between us
> Can we still promise or trust what we mean?
>
> Even in the dark of earth, seeds will swell.
> All the interweavings and fullness of being,
> Nothing less may insure against our hell.
>
> A black sun only shines out of a vacuum.
> Cold narrowings and idols of blood and soil.
> And all the more now, we can't sing dumb!

---

21. Ibid. p. 107.   **22.** Ibid. p. 117.

A conversation so rich it knows it never arrives
Or forecloses; in a buzz and cross-ruff of polity
The restless subversive ragtime of what thrives.

Endless dialogues. The criss-cross of flourishings.
Again and over again our complex yes.
A raucous glory and the whole jazz of things.

The sudden riffs of surprise beyond our ken;
Out of control, a music's brimming let-go.
We feast to keep our promise of never again.[23]

Babel comes again in 'Imagine', where the contemporary world is seen to have the potential to generate 'another black sun' through 'New ways of control', oligarchic concentrations of power over information, software and media, and the threat of electronic surveillance.[24] Remembering the Holocaust has simultaneously intensified sensitivity to possibilities of evil and the desire for superabundant life.

What sort of post-Holocaust wisdom emerges from O'Siadhail's poetry? The poems discussed just now show him offering an interrogative wisdom addressed to modernity, both probing the fault lines of its history from the Reformation onwards and also alert to new dangers as this civilisation undergoes unprecedented transformations. Yet interwoven with the interrogation is a more optative strand encouraging a retrieval and renewal of 'the criss-cross of flourishings' which includes ethical, imaginative, intellectual and spiritual dimensions, and notably looks to the Bible, the Renaissance, poetry, music, novels, conversation and the preciousness of each name, each person, in the words of the poem 'Faces', 'Each someone's fondled face'.[25]

Further aspects of this wisdom have been noted in commentary on poems in the previous chapter. O'Siadhail uses the whole range of moods inspired by the urgency and complexity of doing justice to the cries of the victims. Through many voices and forms he opens up the depths of affliction; the dilemmas of historical action; the realities and ambivalences of human conduct, from appalling crimes to courageous resistance; and the possibilities of some repair and healing for deeply damaged communities and traditions. *At the heart of all this is a wisdom of remembering in order to give testimony in the present for the sake of healing the past and opening up a better future.* The final sequence has repeated

---

23. Ibid. p. 120.   24. Ibid. p. 119.   25. Ibid. p. 122.

variations on this theme, summed up in the closing lines of its opening poem:

> *Destruction turns all their presence into absence*
>
> *unless some testimony breaks their infinite silence.*
> *In remembrance resides the secret of our redemption.*
> *Out of this eruption, can we prepare another climate?*[26]

That question matches the later one:

> Can how we remember shape what we become?[27]

which is then given some partial answers with reference to a range of 'testimonies in every medium' and the practices and open-endedness of a witnessing that is above all concerned to keep faith with the cries of the victims:

> Humble siftings, a patient tentative process;
> Angles and tangents of vision, layered witness.
>
> No closure. No Babel's towering overview;
> With each fugitive testimony to begin anew.
>
> *Memory a frequent waking out of forgetfulness;*
> Dissonant cries of silence refuse to quiesce.[28]

The urgency of the responsibility towards those who have cried out reaches a crescendo towards the end of the sequence:

> Never, never again. Pleading remembrance
> Whispers through the gossamer wall:
> *Promise us at least this.* An insisting silence.[29]

The resolution in the final poem (see above chapter 3, p. 111) does not relieve this insistence, but it does integrate it with the Passover's liturgical, communal remembering.

O'Siadhail's poetic wisdom hints at the possibilities of healing for both Jewish and Christian traditions after the Holocaust, but does not (as I will attempt in this and later chapters) venture further in either of those directions. He offers a remembering that is accessible as widely as possible, and a searching wisdom that is mainly concerned with repairing and renewing Western culture and civilisation. It is a deeply humane

---

26. Ibid. p. 112.   **27.** Ibid.   **28.** Ibid. p. 118.   **29.** Ibid. p. 121.

understanding, resonating with much that is concordant, or at least not discordant, in the complex interplay of Hebraic and Hellenic heritages that has shaped so much in the West, both religious and secular.

Judaism after the Holocaust: one response

Job and O'Siadhail together offer some concepts and images through which to approach the responses to the Holocaust by the Jewish people, but the main contributors here must obviously be post-Holocaust Jews. In this brief section there can be no attempt to deal with the vast topic of post-Holocaust Judaism.[30] The point is rather to select one strand of contemporary Jewish thought which connects with the discussion so far, is concerned with Jewish–Christian relations, and prepares the way for later chapters, especially chapter 8 on the inter-faith wisdom of Scriptural Reasoning.

The strand selected is in broad terms that which is associated with the 'Dabru Emet' ('Speak the Truth') statement in 2000 entitled 'A Jewish Statement on Christians and Christianity' and the accompanying book *Christianity in Jewish Terms* edited by Tikva Frymer-Kensky, David Novak, Peter Ochs, David Fox Sandmel and Michael A. Signer.[31] They are written by an interdenominational group of Jewish scholars who say:

> In recent years there has been a dramatic and unprecedented shift in Jewish and Christian relations. Throughout the nearly two millennia of Jewish exile, Christians have tended to characterise Judaism as a failed religion or, at best, a religion that prepared the way for, and is completed in, Christianity. In the decades since the Holocaust, however Christianity has changed dramatically. An increasing number of official church bodies, both Roman Catholic and Protestant, have made public statements of their remorse about Christian mistreatment of Jews and Judaism. These statements have declared, furthermore, that Christian teaching and preaching can and must be reformed so that they acknowledge God's enduring covenant with the Jewish people and celebrate the contribution of Judaism to world civilization and to Christian faith itself.

30. If I were choosing just one from among the huge number of recent publications it would be Eva Hoffmann, *After Such Knowledge: A Meditation on the Aftermath of the Holocaust* (London: Secker & Warburg, 2005). She is especially perceptive on trauma, memory, the relation of the personal to the political, and the need to learn wisdom through all this.
31. *Christianity in Jewish Terms*, ed. Tikva Frymer-Kensky, David Novak, Peter Ochs, David Fox Sandmel and Michael A. Signer (Boulder, Co and Oxford: Westview Press, 2000).

> We believe these changes merit a thoughtful Jewish response ... We
> believe it is time for Jews to reflect on what Judaism may now say about
> Christianity. As a first step, we offer eight brief statements about
> how Jews and Christians may relate to one another.[32]

The eight statements[33] have inevitably been controversial among both
Jews and Christians, but their detailed content is not relevant to the
present section. It is important that the major context recognised by all
of them is post-Holocaust Judaism and Christianity, and there is repeated
reference to the Holocaust or Shoah.[34] In fact the authors represent
among themselves several strands, and of those I want to choose one,
that of Peter Ochs.

In various writings Ochs has sketched a way of living and thinking
after the Shoah (his preferred term) that tries to learn lessons from
previous Jewish catastrophes while also responding to what is specific
in this one. Like O'Siadhail,[35] he draws hope from how the Babylonian
exile stimulated a transformation of Judaism reflected in a new approach
to Torah, in the writing and redacting of Israel's history, in prophetic
writings, and in new forms of worship and wisdom; how the destruction
of the Temple in AD 70 and the consequent diaspora was an occasion for
the development of the Rabbinic Judaism of the Talmud and the
Synagogue; and how the expulsion from Spain was closely connected
with the Kabbalah and other creative responses. Further, he sees renewed
engagement with scripture and Talmud as central to any creative
response today. But this is to be neither a return to traditional forms of
interpretation nor simply modern in its approach: it is necessary to take

32. Ibid. p. xvii.
33. The eight statements are:

1. Jews and Christians worship the same God.
2. Jews and Christians seek authority from the same book – the Bible (what Jews call 'Tanakh' and Christians call the 'Old Testament').
3. Christians respect the claim of the Jewish people upon the land of Israel.
4. Jews and Christians accept the moral principles of Torah.
5. Nazism was not a Christian phenomenon.
6. The humanly irreconcilable difference between Jews and Christians will not be settled until God redeems the entire world as promised in scripture.
7. A new relationship between Jews and Christians will not weaken Jewish practice.
8. Jews and Christians must work together for justice and peace.
   (Ibid. pp. xvii–xx)

34. Ibid. pp. xvii, xix, 23, 25–48, 54–6, 61, 97, 153–8, 164–7, 207, 215–21, 230, 343–4, 362, 367.
35. This is no accident: O'Siadhail in his Acknowledgements says: 'I'm deeply appreciative of the advice and support of my friend Professor Peter Ochs' (*The Gossamer Wall*, p. 127).

full account of both, while also recognising that in the face of the Shoah neither is sufficient. Both the tradition and modernity require critique after the Shoah, not in order to be anti-traditional or post-traditional, nor to be premodern or anti-modern, but in order to try to heal both the tradition and modernity.

An important influence on Ochs has been the leading Talmudic scholar David Weiss Halivni, who survived Auschwitz and went on to develop a postcritical Jewish historiography and theology, relating modern scholarly methods to theological questions.[36] In a foreword to one of Halivni's books Ochs writes of

> the theologically grounded historical scholar's capacity to imagine beyond the limits of explicit, historical documentation, not to supplant history, but in ways consistent with but not reducible to the explicit documentation, to deepen our expectations of what history may reveal. One of the central concerns of postcritical theology is, in fact, to redress the modern academy's tendency to reduce religious history to the terms of a single variety of empiricist historiography.[37]

Halivni himself in a memoir of his time in Auschwitz writes:

> Anyone whose lungs absorbed, on the ramp, on the station platforms of Auschwitz, the smoke effusing from the chimneys of the crematoria ... these are different people who have known a different kind of abandonment ... A sensitive survivor ... should work under the influence of mutually contradictory forces ... On the one hand, one must find fault with what happened, for if there is no fault, there is an indirect affirmation ... On the other hand, if you acknowledge the wrong, then you run the risk of cutting off the branch upon which you rest. A sensitive theologian must work with both sides, for if you take away the tradition, too, you take away the branch upon which you were raised and nurtured ...

36. Halivni was Lucius N. Littauer Professor of Classical Jewish Civilisation at Columbia University, cofounder and rector of the Institute of Traditional Judaism and previously head of the Talmud Department of the Jewish Theological Seminary. Ochs calls him the twentieth century's 'most innovative Talmudist' (in 'Foreword: *Revelation Restored* as Postcritical Theology' to David Weiss Halivni, *Revelation Restored: Divine Writ and Critical Responses* (Boulder, CO: Westview Press, 1997), p. xii).
37. Ibid. p. xv. See Ochs later summary description: 'Halivni's depth historiography draws on the resources of both plain sense history and theology but adds to them the mediatory and interpretive judgments that, lone, add the theological depth missing from empiricist histories, the evidentiary rules missing from ahistorical theologies, and the devout rationality present only when disciplines scholarship and theology meet' (p. xvi).

> Personally, I found this balance in the critical study of Jewish texts,
> in a combination of criticism and belief in the divine origin of the
> text.[38]

Halivni sees the scribe Ezra as a model of the restoration of Israel's Torah
after the destruction of the Babylonian exile, analogous to the restorative
work of the rabbinic sages after the destruction of the Second Temple.
Halivni's own work is seen by Ochs in the same category, responding to
the Shoah of our epoch by addressing his words 'to the perplexed religious Jews of the contemporary academy as well as the perplexed critically minded Jews of the contemporary yeshiva. He seeks to show both
groups how, contrary to their fears, they can lead pious lives at the same
time as they examine with critical clarity the sacred texts on which their
piety rests.'[39]

Yet Ochs insists on a further crucial element: Jews will not be able to
do this alone. He encourages Jews to enter into new partnerships with
others, both religious and secular, and especially with Christians and
Muslims as the other 'children of Abraham'. He recognises that this goes
against two contrasting and dominant Jewish responses. He writes:

> Perhaps because so many of Judaism's great spiritual masters and
> teachers lived in Eastern Europe and therefore died in the Shoah,
> leaving us still weakened in the numbers and depths of our spiritual
> teachers; or perhaps because the enormity of loss – for example, one
> million children and babies gassed or burned alive – overwhelmed our
> traditions of theodicy (or accounting for God's actions); but I really do
> not know why: 'how long, O Lord?' For whatever reason, our people
> appears to have been left, too often, to draw merely logical inferences
> about relations between Jews and Gentiles and, because the data often
> exceeds comprehension, the inferences are often contradictory and the
> net result, despairing. The dominant inference of our parents'
> generation was: if we had reason to fear and mistrust our European and
> Christian neighbors before the Shoah, we have all the more reason
> now; so that, if we had sought a somewhat separate life before the
> Shoah, we should be seeking a fully separate one now. But much of our
> own generation draws the contrary inference from comparable data:
> before the Shoah, it took courage to maintain our separate faith in the

38. Quoted by Ochs in ibid. p. xiv from David Weiss Halivni, *The Book and the Sword: A Life of Learning in the Shadow of Destruction* (New York: Farrar, Straus and Giroux, 1996).
39. Ibid. p. xviii.

face of a world that rejected us; after the evidence of the Shoah, it is simply foolish to try. The lessons of experience, in other words, have pulled Judaism into the contradictory ways of separatism and assimilationism.

Historians might indeed reassure us with the unhappy news that the religion as well as the society of the Jews has suffered yet survived catastrophic loss several times before: after her Babylonian Exile, for example, Israel returned with a renewed but profoundly transformed religion of the Book and of Temple worship; after Rome destroyed the Second Temple, the religion of book gave way to a religion of synagogue prayer and derashah or rabbinic text study. But, as yet, no historian can tell us what new form of rabbinic Judaism may eventually enflame our hearts after these most recently traumatized generations have passed. No one can say when an epoch of despair has passed and one of renewed faith will begin.

Meanwhile, we study, pray, wait, and look for possible signs of a new epoch.[40]

In fact Ochs himself and other Jewish philosophers and text scholars have not only been waiting, but have been trying to discern and offer signs of a new epoch. At the centre of their emerging vision is a post-critical Judaism with three distinguishing marks: rereading of and renewal through classical sources, especially scripture, Talmud and liturgy; a thorough critical and constructive engagement with Western modernity; and a new dialogical and collaborative relationship with Christians and those of other faiths, especially Muslims. This has been seen, for example, in those who wrote, and the larger number who signed, the Dabru Emet statement, and in a group called Textual Reasoning.[41] The inter-faith aspect is exemplified in the Jewish–Christian group that wrote the chapters and responses in *Christianity in Jewish Terms* and in the network of Jews, Christians and Muslims involved in a movement called Scriptural Reasoning.[42] The latter will be the main focus of chapter 8 below on inter-faith wisdom.

40. Peter Ochs, 'Faith in the Third Millennium: Reading Scriptures Together', Address at the Inauguration of Dr Iain Torrance as President of Princeton Theological Seminary, 10 March 2005, p. 39.

41. The most representative publication of this group is *Textual Reasonings*, ed. Peter Ochs and Nancy Levene (London: SCM, 2002).

42. Ochs introduces this into a discussion among the editors of *Christianity in Jewish Terms*, pp. 366–73.

For now, the principal conclusion is that an interpretation of Job as a searching, post-exilic, post-traumatic wisdom,[43] centred on God, critically appropriating tradition, responsive to cries, articulated in many moods, and concerned about the shaping of a full life after destruction, is in line with some fruitful developments in Jewish post-Shoah thought. So too is the status of Job, noted in the previous chapter, as 'a text that is simultaneously set within a tradition to which it contributes, yet also open across its own tradition's boundaries in such a way as both to make itself available to those beyond it and also to open itself to radical critique and transformation.'[44] This combination of being rooted in a tradition and open beyond it has the seeds of a wisdom that might guide distinct scriptural traditions in their internal developments, as well as in their engagements with modernity and with each other. This is especially true of Christianity and Judaism, in each of whose scriptural canons the book of Job is included.

Christianity after the Holocaust: what sort of wisdom?

In a second, Christian foreword, following Ochs' Jewish foreword to Halivni's *Revelation Restored* quoted above, Stanley Hauerwas makes two points:

> First, Christians have awakened to their responsibility to respond to the horrors of the Holocaust. Christians know somewhere in the story that makes them Christian that the Shoah that happened to the Jews

---

43. It is, of course, only one resource among many, both within and beyond scripture. See Irving Greenberg:

> The capacity to resist and criticize contemporary models is a test of the Holocaust as the new orienting experience of Jews and an indication that a new era of Jewish civilization is under way. This new era will not turn its back on modernity; rather, it will reject some of its elements and take from the past (and future) much more fully. Recognizing that ultimate claims and absolute forces are the seedbed of unlimited Holocausts, this era's religious thinking will seek to live with dialectical theological affirmations, with all claims subject to and tested by contradictions.
> There are several theological models for living in contradiction. One such model is that of Job and involves the rejection of easy pieties or denials and the expectation of further revelations of the Presence. Another is the model of the Suffering Servant . . . In a third theological model for a life of contradiction, that of Lamentations 3, there is only anger and pain checked by the flickering memory of past goodness.
> ('The Shoah and the Legacy of Anti-semitism: Judaism, Christianity, and Partnership after the Twentieth Century' in *Christianity in Jewish Terms*, p. 28)

Ochs' alternative to the conceptuality of 'living in contradiction' is articulated philosophically in his critique of the binary logic of contradiction in favour of a triadic logic in line with that of C. S. Peirce – see Peter Ochs, *Peirce, Pragmatism and the Logic of Scripture* (Cambridge: Cambridge University Press, 1998).
44. Above p. 96.

also continues to have its consequences for Christians. There simply cannot be a truthful account of the convictions that make us Christians that does not make it necessary to tell what happened in that time called Holocaust as part of the Christian story. Christians have only begun to explore how such a telling should work, but we know that such exploration cannot be avoided. The tear the Holocaust made in Christian tradition is no doubt different from that for the Jews, but like the Jews, Christians know that the God we worship makes *tikkun* not only possible but necessary.

Second, Christians have awakened to the disestablishment of their religion as an imperial power . . . It is increasingly clear that Christians must learn, like the Jews, to live by learning to read.[45]

In Hauerwas' terms, in response to the tear in Christian tradition made by the Holocaust this and the previous chapter have opened a way through rereading the book of Job. That book is itself about a tear in a tradition faced with extreme, overwhelming affliction. Its lifelines are loud cries and laments, clinging to God for God's sake, revelling in creation, profound debate, radical searching and being searched, passionate desire for God, and testimony to life renewed after trauma. What does this have to teach Christians who desire the mending of the tear, and, as the most critical sign of this, the healing of their relationship with Jews?

As *Christianity in Jewish Terms* acknowledges and exemplifies, a great deal has already been learnt by some Christians and their churches trying to come to terms with the Shoah and with Judaism. The Christian contributors to that volume represent a key dimension of a remarkable, historic development.[46] They have their differences, but generally come together in a postcritical Christianity that both tries to face the Shoah and parallels the three key features of postcritical Judaism described above: rereading classic scriptural and traditional sources so as to be shaped afresh by them; engaging with Western modernity of recent centuries with a view both to learning from it and to healing its pathologies; and deep dialogue with others, both religious and secular, with a special concern for the relationship with Jews as the closest siblings of

45. Stanley M. Hauerwas, 'Foreword: A Christian Perspective' in Halivni, *Revelation Restored*, pp. xix–xx.
46. For a recent volume that charts what has been happening on both the Jewish and the Christian sides across all major topics and gives excellent bibliographies for further study see *A Dictionary of Jewish–Christian Relations*, ed. Edward Kessler and Neil Wenborn (Cambridge: Cambridge University Press, 2005).

Christians. There is no suggestion by them (or by the more numerous Jewish contributors) that there are not wide divergences and deeply problematic issues between Jews and Christians even when they share a postcritical approach. They wrestle with some of the most difficult questions: the Shoah itself, the interpretation of scripture, the Trinity, the image of God, incarnation, redemption, Israel and the church, law and sanctification, suffering and worship. Above all, from various angles they repudiate supersessionism – the position, very common for most of Christian history, that the Christian church has replaced Israel and the Jews in God's purpose of salvation. I do not want to engage with those issues here (though some will figure in later chapters) but rather to draw out one somewhat suppressed theme in relation to my readings of Job and O'Siadhail.

The tone of the chapters in *Christianity in Jewish Terms* is generally, and understandably, sober, measured and generously fair-minded. They contain a caution and reserve that are a natural response to centuries of mistrust, stereotyping and worse, and to many open wounds, especially among Jews. As an initiative by Jews, this is remarkably daring in relation to their fellow-Jews, as the mixed Jewish response showed. The Christian respondents summarise much of the best innovative Christian rereading and rethinking of recent decades. Yet only rarely do they expose the depths or try to evoke the generative intensities that can be part of full engagement before God between Christians and Jews.

The poetry of the book of Job and of O'Siadhail's *The Gossamer Wall* encourages the attempt to articulate such depths. I have especially identified the cries of Job and the cries of Holocaust victims as points of intensity that resonate deeply with each other and call for a theology in many moods. O'Siadhail's non-Jewish response to the Holocaust is an exemplary distillation of a great deal of testimony, commentary and imaginative portrayal of it. His condensation of experience and interpretation sustains intensity without losing realism or historical perspective. It enables a twenty-first-century encounter with it that appreciates the complexity of its historical roots while facing squarely the responsibility of Christians within that history. O'Siadhail also grapples with the Shoah as a modern phenomenon, inseparable from ambivalent and pathological dimensions of the ideas, practices and forces that have shaped modern Europe and its impact on the rest of the world. Yet at the same time he learns from modernity, appreciates its fruitfulness in many spheres, and is a 'prisoner of hope' who trusts in the possibility of new, even fuller life, symbolised in Jewish scripture, liturgy and poetry, as the chief way of ensuring 'never again'.

All of that opens up the space for an explicitly Christian wisdom after the Shoah, and gives a strong intellectual, emotional and imaginative thrust to the search for it. The sort of postcritical understanding developed by the Christian contributors to *Christianity in Jewish Terms* fits this space and embodies something of this thrust. Yet it needs the wisdom of Job too, as understood in this and the previous chapter. Job has been read as a passionate, deeply searching wisdom at whose core is a desire for God for God's sake. Today it can inspire both Jews and Christians to cry to God and to respond in compassion to the cries of each other and of the rest of the world. Perhaps supremely the Psalms invite both into a God-centred world articulated in cries of lament, joy, recognition, gratitude, blessing, cursing and adoration. Seeking ways of inhabiting this world together, passionately and compassionately, without ignoring deep differences, has the promise of leading both Jews and Christians beyond Dabru Emet.[47]

This has implications for all of Christian understanding and practice, and therefore for the whole of this book, which might be seen as seeking a Joban post-Holocaust Christian wisdom. In line with the features of postcritical theology just mentioned, this requires three things: first, a reworking of core elements in Christian thought, which is the main concern of the first seven chapters of this book, and, in line with Hauerwas' injunction quoted above, is mainly about 'learning to read'; and, as attempted in the final three chapters, both an engagement with aspects of modernity (see especially chapter 9 on universities) and a dialogue with other faiths (chapter 8 on scriptural reasoning, another example of learning to read). All three will come together in the discussion of L'Arche and Jean Vanier in chapter 10.

---

47. LaCocque and Ricoeur in *Thinking Biblically* give a relevant example in their interpretation of Psalm 22 ' "My God, My God, Why Have You Forsaken Me?" Lamentation as Prayer', pp. 187–232.

5

Jesus, the Spirit and desire: wisdom christology

Christian wisdom is shaped by and in relation to Jesus Christ. That has already begun to emerge in chapters 1 and 2 above. There the reading of Luke–Acts and the Prologue of the Gospel of John in search of Christian wisdom centred on Jesus Christ. He was seen as both teaching and living out a prophetic wisdom, 'greater than Solomon', 'greater than Jonah', rooted in the reciprocal knowing of himself and his Father. His wisdom was both a discerning of cries and an embodying of them, with his final loud cry from the cross as the central reference point for Christian wisdom. The convergence of Luke and John on key dimensions of this wisdom was explored: it is God-centred, has the whole of creation as its context, is immersed in history and the contemporary world, interprets the Old and New Testaments in relation to each other, and is constantly sought afresh with others in a community whose basic trust is that the Spirit will lead them into further truth. This requires as a core practice what was called a wisdom interpretation of scripture. That was expressed in terms of the hermeneutics of incarnation, crucifixion, resurrection and Pentecost, as ways of rereading in the light of key events that together identify Jesus Christ and his significance. They involve both a wisdom of reserve ('discerning what is most essential without overspecifying') and a wisdom of ramification ('extending meaning in many directions'), all in the service of learning to read scripture in the Spirit of Jesus Christ. Chapter 2 concluded with nine theses and ten maxims on the wisdom interpretation of scripture, which bring these themes together.

One recurrent theme through the first four chapters has been that of desire – what has been called the embracing optative mood of Christian wisdom. Being immersed in ongoing history and also oriented towards

God and God's future is a situation in which discernment of God and God's ways is always incomplete, often confused, yet continually yearns for more wisdom – above all the wisdom of love.

In order to have space to develop the core themes, this chapter will take a good deal for granted. The amount that is written on Jesus is vast. For those who wish to explore the presuppositions, arguments, scriptural interpretations, historical positions, and philosophical and theological discussions that lie behind the thinking in this chapter there is a range of publications of special relevance. My own include a survey of christology;[1] discussions of Jesus in relation to worship and knowledge,[2] to self and salvation,[3] and to the Holy Spirit and Christian spirituality;[4] a Jesus Reader of over three hundred extracts, with introductions and notes, from writings over the past two millennia;[5] two articles that deal with Jesus in relation to the Shoah;[6] a treatment of Jesus Christ as 'the wisdom of God' which is part of a volume on wisdom that takes up many other relevant questions which cannot be dealt with here;[7] and an introduction to Christian theologies since 1918.[8]

There are three further works that give essential background for what follows, putting forward positions with which I am in substantial agreement. One is Frances Young's magisterial opening chapter in the first

---

1. David F. Ford, 'Christology' in *The Oxford Companion to Christian Thought*, ed. Adrian Hastings et al. (Oxford: Oxford University Press, 2000), pp. 114–18.
2. David F. Ford and Daniel W. Hardy, *Living in Praise: Worshipping and Knowing God* (London: Darton, Longman and Todd, 2005; Grand Rapids, MI: Baker Academic Books, 2005) (2nd edn of *Jubilate: Theology in Praise* (London: Darton, Longman and Todd, 1984; US edition, *Praising and Knowing God* (Philadelphia: Westminster Press, 1985)).
3. David F. Ford, *Self and Salvation: Being Transformed* (Cambridge: Cambridge University Press, 1999).
4. David F. Ford, 'Holy Spirit and Christian Spirituality' in *The Cambridge Companion to Postmodern Theology*, ed. Kevin J. Vanhoozer (Cambridge: Cambridge University Press, 2003), pp. 269–90.
5. *Jesus: An Oxford Reader*, ed. David F. Ford and Mike Higton (Oxford: Oxford University Press, 2002).
6. David F. Ford, 'A Messiah for the Third Millennium' in *Modern Theology* 16, no. 1 (January 2000), pp. 75–90; also in *Theology and Eschatology at the Turn of the Millennium*, ed. James Buckley and L. Gregory Jones (Oxford: Blackwell, 2001), pp. 73–88; and David F. Ford, 'Apophasis and the Shoah: Where Was Jesus Christ at Auschwitz?' in *Silence and the Word: Apophasis and Incarnation*, ed. Oliver Davies and Denys Turner (Cambridge: Cambridge University Press, 2002), pp. 185–200.
7. David F. Ford, 'Jesus Christ, the Wisdom of God' in *Reading Texts, Seeking Wisdom: Scripture and Theology*, ed. David F. Ford and Graham Stanton (London: SCM Press, 2003; Grand Rapids, MI: Eerdmans, 2003), pp. 4–21.
8. *The Modern Theologians: An Introduction to Christian Theology since 1918*, ed. David F. Ford with Rachel Muers, with Introduction and Epilogue by David F. Ford, 3rd edn (Oxford and New York: Basil Blackwell, 2005).

volume of *The Cambridge History of Christianity*.[9] There she not only gives a judicious historical account of Jesus of Nazareth but also sets this in the context of two millennia of investigation, study, interpretation and theology, with a special focus on the Western academy in the past two centuries.

A second volume is *The Cambridge Companion to Jesus* edited by Markus Bockmuehl,[10] whose two parts, on the Jesus of history and the history of Jesus, succeed in covering both history and theology in a well-balanced summary way, and include coverage of 'the global Jesus'. Rowan Williams' chapter on 'A history of faith in Jesus' is especially relevant since it can be read as a history of faith in Jesus under the sign of desire.

The third is John David Dawson's *Christian Figural Reading and the Fashioning of Identity*.[11] Dawson focusses mainly on the interpretation of Christian scriptures by Origen of Alexandria, Erich Auerbach, Hans Frei and Daniel Boyarin. Through that lens he explores some critical issues: how Christians read the Old and New Testaments together; how the identity of Jesus is related to the transformation of believers through the Holy Spirit; the nature and significance of historicity in scripture and human existence; and whether Christianity is inescapably supersessionist in relation to Judaism. Dawson will not be explicitly discussed, but his approach to these issues has been influential on this chapter.

The core concerns of this chapter, wisdom in relation to Jesus, the Spirit and desire, will now be pursued through theological interpretation of selected texts, beginning with a rereading of Luke–Acts and continuing with 1 Corinthians, before concluding with a set of maxims for wisdom christology.

Jesus' wisdom of desire according to Luke

Luke's Gospel was seen from the perspective of cries and wisdom in chapter 1 above. Both the cries and the wisdom (in the life and teaching of Jesus) stood out on the surface of the text, but at the end of the chapter a less obvious complementary perspective was explored, focussing on desire. That is now developed further, with special reference to Jesus Christ.

9. Frances M. Young, 'Prelude' in *Cambridge History of Christianity*, vol. 1: *Origins to Constantine*, ed. Margaret M. Mitchell and Frances M. Young (Cambridge: Cambridge University Press, 2006).
10. Cambridge: Cambridge University Press, 2001.
11. Berkeley, Los Angeles and London: University of California Press, 2002.

As with cries and wisdom, the overture to the theme of desire is given in Luke's first three chapters. His own desire in writing his Gospel is stated:

> Luke 1:4 so that you [Theophilus] may know the truth concerning the things about which you have been instructed.

The encompassing purpose of his writing is connected to a project of instruction and learning. Then comes the story of Zechariah and Elizabeth having their desire for a child fulfilled ('... **your prayer has been heard**' – 1:13), followed by the annunciation to Mary. Her optative response became for much subsequent Christian theology and spirituality the core model of human desire attuned to divine desire.

> Luke 1:38 Then Mary said, 'Here am I, the servant of the Lord; let it be with me according to your word.'

When the infant Jesus is brought to the Temple he is received by Simeon ('... **this man was righteous and devout, looking forward to the consolation of Israel**' – 2:25) and by Anna, whose dedicated, patient desire for God and God's promises is even more insistently emphasised:

> Luke 2:36–38 [36]... She was of a great age, having lived with her husband seven years after her marriage, [37]then as a widow to the age of eighty-four. She never left the temple but worshipped there with fasting and prayer night and day. [38]At that moment she came, and began to praise God and to speak about the child to all who were looking for the redemption of Jerusalem.

This sets the coming of Jesus in the context of generations of desiring the fulfilment of God's purposes in Israel's history. The only picture of Jesus as a child is of him seeking out the teachers in the temple, '**listening to them and asking them questions**' (2:46) and then returning to Nazareth where he was '**obedient**' and '**increased in wisdom**' (2:52a). It is the formation of a will and mind through learning in key relationships and in line with the desire of God (see 2:52b). Finally, the ministry of John the Baptist is seen as oriented urgently towards the One who is to come.

One striking feature throughout these chapters is the prominence of the Holy Spirit. John is to be '**filled with the Holy Spirit**' (1:15), Mary is told '**the Holy Spirit will come upon you**' (2:35), Elizabeth '**was filled with the Holy Spirit**' (1:41), Zechariah '**was filled with the Holy Spirit**' (1:67), Simeon had a revelation '**by the Holy Spirit**' (2:26), and John promises that the One who is coming **'will baptise you with the Holy Spirit and fire'** (3:16). The scene has been set for an intensification of both desire and the activity of the Holy Spirit as the narrative shifts back to Jesus.

Desired and tested

Luke 3:21–22 [21]Now when all the people were baptised, and when Jesus also had been baptised and was praying, the heaven was opened, [22]and the Holy Spirit descended upon him in bodily form like a dove. And a voice came from heaven, 'You are my Son, the Beloved; with you I am well pleased.'

Luke 4:1–2 [1]Jesus, full of the Holy Spirit, returned from the Jordan and was led by the Spirit in the wilderness, [2]where for forty days he was tempted by the devil. He ate nothing at all during those days, and when they were over, he was famished.

The baptism and temptation of Jesus act as a sort of headline for what follows in the Gospels of Matthew, Mark and Luke. They are dense with rich symbols: baptism itself, heaven opening, the Holy Spirit in the form of a dove, a voice from heaven, 'my Son, the Beloved', forty days in the wilderness, the devil, and the dramatic images of the temptations – turning stones to bread, surveying all the kingdoms of the world over which authority is offered, and jumping from the pinnacle of the Temple. These resonate in multiple directions within scripture and, according to Matthew and Mark, Jesus' response to each temptation is through quoting scripture.

This is no simple factual account. Its scriptural language recalls creation, the Exodus, the people of Israel's journey for forty years in the wilderness, the content of Torah, apocalypses, revelations by the voice of God, evil confronted, temptation encountered, the extraordinary significance of the Temple, and much else. In its own time it connected with religion, ethics and regional politics (see John the Baptist's message of repentance and his imprisonment for confronting King Herod), with critical decisions about God's purposes in history, and with the authority of the Roman Emperor. This is a narrative that offers readers at the outset a framework of interpretation for the rest of the story – categories that recapitulate key events and dimensions of Israel's history of relating to God and that try to indicate the particular significance and novelty of Jesus.

Luke says that Jesus at his baptism **'was praying'** (3:21). This desire towards God is met by the descent of the Holy Spirit **'in bodily form like** a dove' (3:22). The significance of this is then given by the voice from heaven: **'You are my Son, the Beloved; with you I am well pleased'** (3:22). This suggests the ultimate in desirability: to be loved by God as God's Son, and to please God. Here is the fulfilment of divine desire in human existence. Jesus is ἀγαπητός – one who is loved. This love (ἀγάπη) is at the centre of the core commandment of Torah to love God and neighbour, and of Jesus' own confirmation of that commandment, drawing together the desires of mind, heart, soul and body. It is also the word for love in the Song of Songs in the Septuagint, a love song that has been influential on much Jewish and Christian thought and prayer. At the heart of Luke's wisdom of desire is the mutual loving and knowing of Father and Son in the Spirit (see Jesus' exultation in Luke 10:21–22, discussed above in chapter 1).

But it is desire involved with the conflicts and corruptions of historical existence. The baptism is followed[12] by the temptations when Jesus, **'full of the Holy Spirit'** and **'led by the Spirit'** (4:1) spends forty days fasting in the wilderness. What is tested is his identity as Son of God; the critical focus of the testing is his desire for God and God's purposes. Physical hunger for bread, the attraction of global authority and glory, and the temptation of spectacular success by miraculous means all involve desires that are not necessarily bad. The fundamental criterion for them is their conformity with who God is and what God desires, and, as chapter 1 noted, Jesus' touchstone for discernment is the teaching of scripture. In Luke's story, this wise discernment is in continuity with Jesus' formation since childhood through people inspired by the Spirit in the context of faithfulness to the scriptures, traditions and institutions of Israel. *The core desires are embodied in teachings, long-term practices, and patterns of family and community life. They form what previous chapters have called wisdom about the discernment of cries – cries of God, of one's own mind, heart, soul and body, of other people, of whole groups, interests, societies and traditions, of the natural world.*

Now in his temptations Jesus faces an unprecedented challenge to his identity as beloved Son, to his vocation in relation to God's purposes, and to his life filled with the Holy Spirit, and he responds out of his formation and in particular through his understanding of scripture. The

---

12. Luke, unlike Matthew and Mark, does not tell of the temptations immediately after the baptism. He inserts the genealogy of Jesus through Joseph (3:23–38), which in my terms might be seen as a further sign of the immersion of desire in history.

interweaving of core relational identity, the Holy Spirit and scripture is the nexus through which Luke's wisdom of desire is articulated, and it finds its most concentrated expression in these early baptism and temptation accounts, in the transfiguration and exultation in the middle of his Gospel and in the passion and resurrection narratives at the end.

Transforming desire

In his ministry that begins after the temptations Jesus might be seen as teaching and enacting a God-centred wisdom of desire. At the centre of his teaching is the message of the Kingdom of God. Chapter 1 has already described this in terms of a prophetic wisdom responding to cries. It can also be seen as an invitation to imagine and orient one's life around what is supremely desirable. It meets the desires of the poor, captives, the blind, the oppressed (4:18ff) and many others in need or misery, it offers forgiveness, and it teaches about enmity and reconciliation, prayer, compassion, wealth, generosity, insistent seeking and asking,[13] hospitality, alertness, faithfulness, and much else.

A recurrent theme is the transformation of desire. At its most basic this is about letting the Kingdom of God be one's primary desire and relativising all others.

> Luke 12:29–34 [29]And do not keep striving for what you are to eat and what you are to drink, and do not keep worrying. [30]For it is the nations of the world that strive after all these things, and your Father knows that you need them. [31]Instead, strive for his kingdom, and these things will be given to you as well . . . [34]For where your treasure is, there your heart will be also.

It involves relationships of love and generosity rooted in the compassion of God (6:32–36), and hospitality given to those who need it, not to those who will repay it (14:12–14). At its most drastic it is about a desire to follow Jesus that is greater than the desire for life itself or for the whole world.

> Luke 9: 23–25 [23]Then he said to them all, 'If any want to become my followers, let them deny themselves and take up their cross daily and follow me. [24]For those who want to save their life will lose it, and those who lose their life for my sake will save it. [25]What does it profit them if they gain the whole world, but lose or forfeit themselves?'

---

13. Luke is especially emphatic about the importance of asking, seeking, knocking, searching, even pestering. He alone has the story of the friend at midnight (11:5–8) and the parable of the unjust judge (18:1–8), two dramas of urgent, importunate desire.

In the same category is the hyperbolic encouragement to '**hate father and mother, wife and children, brothers and sisters, yes, and even life itself**' (14:26). This, like the previous radical statement, is about being disciples, μαθηταὶ – 'learners'. *The utterly vital thing to be learnt is the incomparable desirability of God, the Kingdom of God, and how to follow Jesus in his realisation of it.*

Essential to this learning are the parables. Luke shares with other Gospels such parabolic pictures of the Kingdom of God as seed sown in various types of ground, or a great banquet, the latter a classic image of what should obviously be desired. Among his distinctive parables are the Good Samaritan, which puts love and compassion at the heart of being a neighbour (10:25–37), and the set of three in chapter 15 about the lost sheep, lost coin and lost son. These latter give the deepest secret of desire in relation to the Kingdom of God. The desire of the shepherd to find the sheep, of the woman to find the coin and of the father to welcome his son back add up to a picture of God as the one whose loving, faithful desire, even for those who reject him, is at the heart of his Kingdom. The desired Son, the delight of his Father's heart, whose baptism opens the Gospel tells the parable of the desired prodigal who had rejected his father. The teaching that we are wholeheartedly desired by God as part of his family is intensified by Karl Barth's midrashic improvisation on this parable (which frames the christology of the first two parts of his Doctrine of Reconciliation,[14] and which might be read as combining with it the searching shepherd of the earlier parable) according to which Jesus Christ is sent by the father to seek the lost in 'the far country'. And beyond the inner secret of the desire of God yearning for our responsive desire is the celebration, the '**joy in the presence of the angels of God**' (15:10), when that response happens.[15]

The drama of desire in action and passion

Barth's midrash leads into what is christologically more fundamental than Jesus' teaching on the transformation of desire: Jesus' embodiment of that teaching. He resists temptations to focus his desires elsewhere; he shows forgiveness, welcome to the marginalised, compassion to the sick, yearning for the welfare of Jerusalem; he puts the Kingdom of God and

---

14. Karl Barth, *Church Dogmatics*, vol. IV, part 1 (Edinburgh: T. & T. Clark, 1956) and vol. IV, part 2 (Edinburgh: T. & T. Clark, 1958).
15. Such joy might be seen as a fulfilment of desire without being its terminus, since there need be no end to either the desiring or its fulfilment.

doing the will of God ahead of family relationships and everything else; and above all he goes the way of the cross. Amidst the cries of his final days (explored in chapter 1 above), reflecting diverse and often passionately antagonistic desires, Jesus' own desires are focussed on the culmination of his mission. He weeps over Jerusalem in disappointed longing (19:41–44). He introduces the Last Supper with his disciples by saying:

> Luke 22:15–16 [15] . . . 'I have eagerly desired (Ἐπιθυμίᾳ ἐπεθύμησα) to eat this Passover with you before I suffer; [16]for I tell you, I will never eat it again until it is fulfilled in the kingdom of God.'

In this saying, unique to Luke, three key dimensions of Jesus' life come together. The first is his gathering of 'learners' to share his mission, here to share in the Passover.[16] *The second is the orientation to suffering and death. The third is the encompassing purpose of the Kingdom of God.* Here these converge with great intensity under the sign of desire. The meal then gives tangible representations of all three, the bread and wine signifying simultaneously their fellowship (and **'new covenant'** – 22:20), Jesus' imminent death, and the coming Kingdom of God (see 22:18).

After the supper it is the second of those, the suffering and death, that first takes centre stage. Two events especially illuminate the drama of desire that runs through Luke's passion narrative: Jesus' prayer on the Mount of Olives, and his crucifixion.

On the Mount of Olives (Gethsemane in Matthew and Mark) Jesus at the opening and at the end of the scene speaks to his disciples about trial or temptation (πειρασμός):

> Luke 22:40 . . . 'Pray that you may not come into the time of trial' . . .
> 22:46 . . . 'Why are you sleeping? Get up and pray that you may not come into the time of trial.'

This recalls Jesus' own temptations, the testing of his desires in relation to the desires of God. Shortly before, during the Last Supper, Jesus had said to the disciples:

> Luke 22:28 'You are those who have stood by me in my trials . . .'

Now they are sleeping, not standing by him, so everything hangs on his wrestling alone in prayer. What happens is decisive for all that follows.

16. The Passover re-enacts Israel's Exodus from Egypt. In his account of the transfiguration Luke, again uniquely, applies 'exodus' (ἔξοδος) as a description to what Jesus 'was about to accomplish at Jerusalem' (9:31).

> Luke 22:42 'Father, if you are willing (εἰ βούλει), remove this cup from me; yet, not my will (θέλημα) but yours be done.'

The different Greek words for 'are willing' and 'will' both embrace desiring. This is the final resumption of the testing in the wilderness. As the temptations prepared for Jesus' ministry, so this signifies his inner orientation as he prepares for suffering and death. Luke here gives less sense of open possibility and negotiation with God than do Matthew or Mark, yet he still has an 'if...'. Then comes the decisive alignment of Jesus' will with his Father's. If vv.43–44 are original (the manuscript evidence seems to be marginally against them, but I would favour inclusion) then Luke (or a later hand) adds a vivid portrayal of sustained, passionate prayer.

> Luke 22:43–44 [43]Then an angel from heaven appeared to him and gave him strength. [44]In his anguish he prayed more earnestly, and his sweat became like great drops of blood falling down on the ground.

'The word translated as Jesus' "anguish", like the image of the sweat pouring off his body, comes from the realm of athletics. Both point not to hesitancy or uncertainty, but to the intensely focussed energy of an athlete just as a contest is about to begin ... Similarly, the angel's ministry is not a supernatural prop to diminish the cost to Jesus of the struggle. Instead, the angel reminds Luke's readers that what is at stake here is once again the "trial" or "test" of Jesus by Satan – a struggle for Jesus' very identity and life.'[17]

The second key event is the crucifixion. Chapter 1 described this as a 'wisdom event' centred on Jesus' loud cry and open to endlessly ramifying interpretations, beginning with Luke's use of the Wisdom of Solomon. It can also be described as an event of desire and love, both in 'reserved', focussed terms and with ramifying implications, beginning with scripture.

The simple, focussed core is that it is an enactment of obedient, loving desire. Jesus is true to the 'your will be done' of his prayer to his Father on the Mount of Olives. Luke has given abundant material for understanding it in this way, from Jesus' baptism onwards. Key strands of his wisdom christology of desire are woven together in the crucifixion scene. Jesus' compassion for the 'daughters of Jerusalem' as he walks to his death (23:27–31), his forgiveness of those crucifying him (23:34), his enduring of mockery (23:35–37), and his response to the criminal who

---

17. Sharon H. Ringe, *Luke* (Louisville, KY: Westminster John Knox Press, 1995), p. 266.

asks, 'Jesus, remember me when you come into your kingdom' (23:42) all in various ways exemplify what I have called the transformation of desire in line with the Kingdom of God. This death can be seen as the fulfilment of a vocation diametrically opposed to the one set before him in his temptations: acute suffering instead of physical satisfaction; weakness and humiliation instead of power and authority; utter failure inflicted by political and religious authorities instead of spectacular success by miraculous means.

But above all it is the fulfilment of his relationship with his Father. This is graphically represented in his baptism and transfiguration, it is the secret of his resistance to temptation in the wilderness and on the Mount of Olives, and it is the focus of his exultation in the Holy Spirit (10:21–22). On the cross the loud cry articulates it.

> Luke 23:46 Then Jesus, crying with a loud voice, said, 'Father, into your hands I commend my spirit.' Having said this, he breathed his last.

I began to explore the significance of this cry in chapters 1 and 2, culminating in its centrality for a hermeneutic of the cross.[18] Likewise it is central to desire in relation to christology. Psalm 31 (LXX 30) which Jesus quotes (only in Luke)[19] is a passionate prayer of hope and longing addressed to God from a state of extreme suffering in the face of enemies. Especially striking is the Psalmist's relationship of love with God.

> Psalm 31:16 Let your face shine upon your servant; save me in your steadfast love. (See vv.7, 21)

This culminates in the final appeal, which in the Septuagint's use of ἐκζητέω (seek out, search out) has a reciprocity of desire with God.

---

18. The crucial summary paragraph in chapter 2 is: 'On the crucifixion, the main suggestion has been a hermeneutic of cries centred on the loud cry with which Jesus gave up his spirit on the cross. The simultaneously apophatic and cataphatic nature of that cry; its disruptive and interruptive character; its provocation to thought, discipleship and worship; its identification as closely as possible with the whole life of Jesus that is being given up; its simultaneity of God-involvement, self-involvement and world-involvement; its resonance with and responsiveness to other cries of suffering, interrogation, longing, accusation and hatred; its intimate link with the Psalms and all their cries: all of this together suggests that it is unavoidably and inexhaustibly central to Christian testimony and interpretation of scripture.'

19. Why does Luke replace the cry of God-forsakenness from Psalm 22, as given by Matthew and Mark, with this cry of trust and confidence? For a discussion of the possibilities and a judicious conclusion see Peter Doble, *The Paradox of Salvation: Luke's Theology of the Cross* (Cambridge: Cambridge University Press, 1996), chapter 6.

> Psalm 31:23–24 [23]Love the LORD, all you his saints. The LORD preserves the faithful [LXX ἀληθείας ἐκζητεῖ κύριος], but abundantly repays the one who acts haughtily. [24]Be strong, and let your heart take courage, all you who wait for the LORD.

The cry itself, through its use of 'spirit/Spirit' (manuscripts do not distinguish between upper and lower case), recalls all that Jesus has done since the Holy Spirit came upon him at his baptism (see chapter 1 above) and also points forward to the promised coming of the Holy Spirit. It is a final act of orientation to God in hope and confidence, in obedient, loving desire.

The reserved simplicity in Luke's description of Jesus at the Last Supper, on the Mount of Olives and on the cross, seen in this orientation of loving desire, has a counterpart in the characterisation of Jesus as δίκαιος, 'just', 'righteous'. This, in Luke's theology, is what it is most desirable for a person to be. Immediately after Jesus' death the centurion responded with what, in the light of the rest of Luke's Gospel and Acts,[20] is clearly the verdict Luke himself wanted readers to make.

> NIV 23:47 The centurion, seeing what had happened, praised God and said, 'Surely (Ὄντως) this was a righteous man.'

The two pivotal Lucan statements about Jesus' death and resurrection are spotlighted by an adverb not used by Luke elsewhere, ὄντως (surely, really, certainly, actually): here after his death, and in 24:34 after his resurrection – **'The Lord has risen indeed'** (ὄντως ἠγέρθη ὁ Κύριος). Essential to Luke's christology is the just, righteous person who is vindicated by God by being raised from the dead, and his narrative shows the desire of Jesus, aligned with the desire of his Father, being realised ὄντως through crucifixion and resurrection.[21]

This core message invites endlessly ramifying interpretation, starting from scriptures. Luke indicates this in his post-resurrection stories, as described above in chapter 1. In Luke 24 the risen Jesus leads the disciples through all the scriptures interpreting them anew in relation to himself. Their minds are opened as the scriptures are opened; the scriptures are set within a horizon of interpretation that embraces all nations. This sets a pattern that is continued by Peter, Stephen and others in Acts. Luke's

---

20. See ibid. chapters 4, 5, 8.
21. For a perceptive account of Luke's christology see Joel B. Green, *The Theology of the Gospel of Luke* (Cambridge: Cambridge University Press, 1995). On the death of Jesus in Luke with comparisons with the other Gospels see Joel B. Green, *The Death of Jesus: Tradition and Interpretation in the Passion Narrative* (Tübingen: J. C. B. Mohr (Paul Siebeck), 1988).

'wisdom of ramification' is first of all richly scriptural, and it is seen in the way he presents his Gospel as well as in the Acts of the Apostles. In chapter 2 the discussion of the Prologue of John's Gospel saw that remarkable theology as John himself being 'led into all truth' by the Spirit, as taught in his Gospel by Jesus. A key mark of it was the interpretation of his scriptures, with a strong wisdom component. Something similar can be seen in Luke. He sees himself as interpreting scripture after Emmaus and after Pentecost, and it is not surprising to find that his Gospel and Acts are richly intertextual. This could be fruitfully studied through his use of the Psalms, Isaiah, the Pentateuch or other texts, but for my purposes now the Wisdom of Solomon is of most interest. Peter Doble's excellent study of Luke's use of the Wisdom of Solomon is assumed in what follows.[22] It shows Luke, who received the testimonies to Jesus **'handed on to us by those who from the beginning were eyewitnesses and servants of the word'** (Luke 1:2), shaping them with reference to a key wisdom book. It is worth examining this for the light it throws on his Gospel and the connections it makes between a number of concepts that are central to my reading of him and to this chapter's wisdom christology.

A Lucan lens: the Wisdom of Solomon

Doble makes a strong case for Luke having used the Wisdom of Solomon (hereafter called 'Wisdom') in its portrayal of the wise just man (δικαιος) as an interpretative matrix for his Gospel, especially in its account of Jesus' death.[23] This includes features that have been important for my christological discussion, such as the fatherhood of God and the strong emphasis on the testing/temptation of the wise man. But there are many other resonances, naturally with wisdom, but also with the other themes treated in this chapter: Spirit, love and desire.

One of the most powerful passages in Wisdom links spirit/Spirit not only to wisdom but also, through her, to creation, the glory of God, light, holiness, prophecy, beauty, righteousness/justice and love.

> Wisdom of Solomon 7:22–30 [22] . . . for wisdom, the fashioner of all things, taught me. There is in her a spirit that is intelligent, holy, unique, manifold, subtle, mobile, clear, unpolluted, distinct, invulnerable, loving the good, keen, irresistible, [23]beneficent, humane, steadfast, sure, free from anxiety, all-powerful, overseeing all, and

22. Doble, *The Paradox of Salvation*, especially chapter 7.
23. Ibid. especially chapters 4, 5, 7 and 8.

> penetrating through all spirits that are intelligent, pure, and
> altogether subtle. [24]For wisdom is more mobile than any motion;
> because of her pureness she pervades and penetrates all things. [25]For
> she is a breath of the power of God, and a pure emanation of the glory
> of the Almighty; therefore nothing defiled gains entrance into her.
> [26]For she is a reflection of eternal light, a spotless mirror of the
> working of God, and an image of his goodness. [27]Although she is but
> one, she can do all things, and while remaining in herself, she renews
> all things; in every generation she passes into holy souls and makes
> them friends of God, and prophets; [28]for God loves nothing so much as
> the person who lives with wisdom. [29]She is more beautiful than the
> sun, and excels every constellation of the stars. Compared with the
> light she is found to be superior, [30]for it is succeeded by the night, but
> against wisdom evil does not prevail . . .

This and other passages in Wisdom suggest that a focus on wisdom is
inextricable from the spirit/Spirit understood as intimately connected
with God, creation and life in history.

The theme of love is evident in that passage and others. The book opens
with the words 'Love righteousness' (Ἀγαπήσατε δικαιοσύνην), which
might almost be a motto for Luke's Gospel. Love is connected with trust,
truth, faithfulness, grace and mercy (3:9) and with wisdom and the desire
for wisdom (6:12–20), and God is the one who loves all who live (11:26).

Desire pervades the book implicitly and at times explicitly.

> Wisdom 6:11 Therefore set your desire on my words; long for them,
> and you will be instructed . . .
>   6:17 The beginning of wisdom is the most sincere desire for
> instruction, and concern for instruction is love of her . . .
>   6:20 so the desire for wisdom leads to a kingdom.

At the centre of Wisdom in chapter 9 is the prayer in the mouth of
Solomon ardently asking for wisdom. Here God's word and wisdom are
equated in the divine work of creation (vv.1–2), wisdom is the key to
pleasing God and understanding God's commandments (v.9), and in the
culminating verses wisdom is linked with the favourite Lucan themes of
the Spirit and salvation.

> Wisdom 9:17–18 [17]Who has learned your counsel, unless you have given
> wisdom and sent your holy spirit from on high? [18]And thus the paths of
> those on earth were set right, and people were taught what pleases you,
> and were saved by wisdom.

Such verses give a sense of the horizon within which Luke's opening chapters were written, and the whole of his Gospel has echoes of Wisdom even beyond the many instances that Doble notes.

But perhaps the most important parallel between Wisdom and Luke's Gospel and his Acts of the Apostles is in the historical character of wisdom. In Wisdom, creation[24] and the history of the world are read in terms of wisdom's agency. The figure of wisdom is one through which history is interpreted in relation to God and God's purposes. Immediately after Solomon's prayer this wisdom hermeneutic of history is begun and it dominates the rest of the book.

> Wisdom 10:1 Wisdom protected the first-formed father of the world, when he alone had been created; she delivered him from his transgression . . .
> 10:4–5 [4]When the earth was flooded because of him, wisdom again saved it, steering the righteous man by a paltry piece of wood. [5]Wisdom also, when the nations in wicked agreement had been put to confusion, recognized the righteous man and preserved him blameless before God, and kept him strong in the face of his compassion for his child . . .
> 10: 10 When a righteous man fled from his brother's wrath, she guided him on straight paths; she showed him the kingdom of God, and gave him knowledge of holy things; she prospered him in his labours, and increased the fruit of his toil . . .
> 10:13–21 [13]When a righteous man was sold, wisdom did not desert him, but delivered him from sin. She descended with him into the dungeon, [14]and when he was in prison she did not leave him, until she brought him the sceptre of a kingdom and authority over his masters. Those who accused him she showed to be false, and she gave him everlasting honour. [15]A holy people and blameless race wisdom delivered from a nation of oppressors. [16]She entered the soul of a servant of the Lord, and withstood dread kings with wonders and signs. [17]She gave to holy people the reward of their labours; she guided them along a marvellous way, and became a shelter to them by day, and a starry flame through the night. [18]She brought them over the Red Sea, and led them through deep waters; [19]but she drowned their enemies, and cast them up from the depth of the sea. [20]Therefore the righteous plundered the ungodly; they sang hymns, O Lord, to your holy name, and praised with one accord your defending hand; [21]for wisdom opened the

24. See Proverbs 8 on wisdom and creation, which was immensely important in patristic christological discussion and polemic.

mouths of those who were mute, and made the tongues of infants
speak clearly.
Wisdom 11:1 Wisdom prospered their works by the hand of a holy
prophet . . .

The multiple echoes of Luke are clear. Images of the righteous run
through it. There are mentions of saving, deliverance, compassion, the
Kingdom of God, false accusation, servanthood and miracles, and wisdom is linked with prophecy. The theme of the Exodus (which is Luke's
image for the final stage of Jesus' life from his entry into Jerusalem – see
Luke 9:31) is prominent here, and returns at the end of Wisdom as its
supreme image of God's salvation. Both in telling the story of Jesus and in
his account of the early church (Stephen's long speech in Acts 7 is exemplary) the connections between some of Luke's key ideas (wisdom, the
Spirit, love, desire and salvation in history) are better understood, and
the wider ramifications of his story are better appreciated, if he is read
through this lens that he used in writing. The sort of wisdom christology
that this suggests is in line with the broad use of wisdom in the Wisdom
of Solomon. *There wisdom is not just one genre among many but acts as an
integrator for law, history, prophecy, praise, and wisdom in the narrower sense.
This largely intertestamental development is congenial with wisdom playing an
important role in portraying Jesus in the early church, and later centuries were to
take further the idea of wisdom as the leading cognitive integrator of Christian
understanding and practice.*[25]

Job and Jesus

Luke and John nowhere imply that what they are doing in their christological interpretation of scripture should be limited to the instances they
themselves give. On the contrary, they give full encouragement to others
to do analogous readings. Luke's Jesus directs his disciples to '**all the
scriptures**' (Luke 24:27) and the Holy Spirit is promised to be poured out
on '**all flesh**' (Acts 2:17). All people interpreting all scriptures in the Spirit
is a recipe for ramifying interpretations. John's Word is life and '**the
light of all people**' (John 1:4), and the Spirit of truth is promised to
'**abide**' with his followers and '**guide**' them further into truth (John
14:17; 16:13). The task of later interpreters is not just to comment on
what they wrote, but to read 'in the Spirit', learning from how they

25. See below chapter 7 on theology understood as wisdom.

read their scriptures. I will now attempt this with the Book of Job, interpreting it in relation to Luke–Acts. This is a fundamental christological task: taking Jesus' own scriptures as the primary texts through which to interpret the testimonies to him. It is an exercise that needs to be carried out again and again, with one OT and NT book after another, generation after generation, and in one context after another. It faces many problems and risks (with regard to which I find David Dawson's work among the wisest[26]) but these should hardly inhibit attempting it again and again. Without it the mind and desire of Jesus Christ are ignored, and mainstream Christian theology and worship over the centuries lack their central resource.

The book of Job has already, in chapters 3 and 4 above, been read alongside Micheal O'Siadhail's *The Gossamer Wall: Poems in Testimony to the Holocaust*. To place Job now alongside Luke's story of Jesus is in line with a long Christian tradition of relating the two. The points of illumination in this intertextual exercise have differed over the centuries, as have the interpretative approaches and theological frameworks.

Perhaps the most important twentieth-century christological interpretation has been that of Karl Barth. He weaves an interpretation of the book of Job into his discussion of the sin of falsehood in the third part of his Doctrine of Reconciliation.[27] Barth's understanding of sin is closely tied to his christology – for him, only in the light of Jesus Christ does one see sin for what it is. Ticciati, whose work contributed to my interpretation of Job, also offers the most thorough available appreciation and critique of Barth on Job.[28] My interpretation supports her conclusions, in particular on the ways in which Barth's theological concepts, for all

---

26. See above note 11.

27. Karl Barth, *Church Dogmatics*, vol. IV, part 3: first half (Edinburgh: T. & T. Clark, 1961) and second half (Edinburgh: T. & T. Clark, 1962).

28. Susannah Ticciati, *Job and the Disruption of Identity: Reading beyond Barth* (London and New York: T. & T. Clark, 2005). In summary, she starts by noting Barth's unusual concentration on the question of Job's obedience, rather than on the issue of theodicy, in the light of which most read the book. She shows how this allows him to reach an elegant solution to some of the book's most puzzling features, and in particular the relation between prose narrative, dialogue and whirlwind speeches. These 'disjunctions' are read in the light of the threefold christological pattern of election, cross and resurrection. The relation between the prose narrative and the poem (mediated by the whirlwind speeches) is interpreted along these lines as one between eschatology and history, the former being veiled in the latter. The resultant question concerns the form of Job's obedience within the vicissitudes of history, which obscure the pure form of his relation with God as represented in the prose narrative. While Barth thereby pays close attention to the formal structure of the book, she argues that the disjunction he establishes between eschatology and history prevents him from gaining a full appreciation of Job's complexity as a human being; of his growth and development in the course of his dialogue with the friends; in short, of the psychological, social and historical

their richness and depth, still fail to do justice to the history-immersed wisdom of the book. One difference from Barth in my interpretation is that whereas he fruitfully explores the categories of truth and falsehood through the book, I am more concerned with those of desire, wisdom and foolishness.

Of the many possible lines along which to explore christology in relation to Job, I will pursue five.

The desire of God

The first is the parallel between God's approval of Job and of Jesus. The divine commendation of Job is unrivalled in the Old Testament: '**Have you considered my servant Job? There is no one like him on the earth, a blameless and upright man who fears God and turns away from evil**' (Job 1:8; see 2:3). It naturally invites comparison with the commendations of Jesus: '**You are my Son, the Beloved; with you I am well pleased**'; '**This is my Son, my Chosen; listen to him!**' (Luke 3:22; 9:35). Here are two people who are represented as embodying what God desires in humanity, and it should not be surprising if reflection on one illuminates the other.

One who cries out

One point in chapter 3 above was that 'one never "moves beyond" this book. It is a way of staying within earshot of the most piercing cries of humanity and our own hearts.' The previous chapters had focussed more than once on the cries of the Gospel, culminating in Jesus' last 'loud cry' from the cross. One of Simone Weil's insights into the extremity of affliction (see chapter 3, pp. 104–7) is that it is almost impossible to pay full, sustained attention to it. Job, read and reread alongside the Gospel, offers a discipline that might train our attention to concentrate on the

dimensions of the poem. Rather, he reads the book according to a schema or dialectic of obedience/disobedience, in which Job, as obedient, is contrasted with the friends, as disobedient, and the obedient one is recognised secondarily as being simultaneously disobedient, and vice versa – a schema with origins in his doctrine of election, which leads him to a reading of much of the Old Testament in terms of binary pairs of the elect and rejected. This is a complex enough schema to allow him real insight into the book; but it imposes too static a grid on the book, preventing him from grappling with its immanent historical dynamic: Barth's Job is ultimately one-dimensional. His genius in providing such an elegant and compelling reading of Job therefore treads a fine line between attentive exegesis and conceptual closure. More specifically, Ticciati concludes that the unrivalled monopoly of his theological concepts over all other forms of discourse blinds him to the 'wisdom' dimensions of the text, raising the question of whether his theological insight is ultimately tantamount to a 'monotheological' vision.

cries of Jesus and, through him, on the cries he hears now. Job helps to draw attention back again and again to the intractable, unassimilable and unconceptualisable quality of intense suffering as expressed in the cry from the cross. Within the horizon of the book of Job there are rich resources for continually renewed exploration of the ramifying significance of that cry and of what led up to it and followed on from it. 'Never moving beyond Job' parallels the permanent significance of the crucifixion and the continuing reality of suffering, evil and death.

Job is therefore a text of first resort in attempting to do justice to the story of Jesus through the endless search for resonant images, stories, ideas and implications. Three further features stand out as especially fruitful for a wisdom of desire in relation to Jesus.

God-centred desire

One is to do with God. I have described the relationship to God of both Job and Jesus in terms of desire and the testing of desire, and have read each of their stories as pervaded by the optative mood: Job's desire for God and vindication by God; Jesus' desire for God and the Kingdom of God. A vital question is whether Job's 'for nothing' relationship to God, which was taken as a hermeneutical key to the book of Job, also applies to the New Testament. This idea from Job does not appear as such in the New Testament, but through its lens one notices some fundamental features of the Gospel.

Moving through Luke's Gospel, for example, the opening chapters are full of God being glorified, magnified, honoured, praised and obeyed by people who are not doing so for what they can get out of God – Anna's years of night and day worship in the temple are the most vivid example. The whole narrative is focussed on God and God's initiatives, and its key characters have their lives shaped by relating to God. The last verses of this Gospel are also set in the temple, with the disciples worshipping Jesus[29] and blessing God.[30] In between, Jesus himself is the one who lives for God alone, which includes God's Kingdom. The temptations test this at the opening of his ministry, the agony on the Mount of Olives does so at the end, and at the centre of both is Jesus' relationship with his Father,

---

29. They had just been commissioned to proclaim repentance and forgiveness of sins in the name of the Messiah to all nations (Luke 24:47). The 'name of Jesus' becomes an important invocation in Acts, and might be said, in terms of the present discussion, to be the historical expression of the 'for nothing' relationship with God.

30. On God in Luke 24 see Ford, 'Jesus Christ, the Wisdom of God', pp. 12ff.

as seen in his baptism, transfiguration and the exultation of chapter 10. This is a relationship of understanding, intimacy and love, an embodiment of his own teaching of the commandment to love God with all one's heart, mind, soul and strength, and of the leading petition of the prayer he teaches his disciples: 'Hallowed be your name.' This has a radical concern with and orientation towards God for God's sake but is combined with a quality of involvement in the drama of history.

Desire in the contingencies of history

This relation to historical involvement is the fourth, closely related feature important for a christology of desire. Chapters 3 and 4 strained to describe it. 'God for God's sake', 'creation for creation's sake' and 'Job for Job's sake' were seen as key underlying elements in the story, in sharp tension both with the friends' *quid pro quo* view of God in relation to people, and also with Job's cry of despair in Job 3, accompanied by its traumatised understanding of himself, creation and God. But those elements could not be abstracted from the drama going on in Job's life. The critical question of the Satan, 'Does Job fear God for nothing?', cannot be answered by divine knowledge or by argument. 'The only available answer seems to be to see how Job actually behaves within that history' (see p. 100 above). The sense of God's name at stake in the contingencies of history is also there in the Gospel. In order to be true to God Jesus must actually and contingently say no to the Satan in his wilderness temptations, and on the Mount of Olives must likewise say 'Your will be done' to his Father. The desire to live for God's sake is inextricably mediated through historical existence and the decisions Job and Jesus take.

There are huge differences between the two stories and the two men, but the dynamic interplay of fearing God for nothing (or hallowing the name of the Father) with the divine risk of involvement in the contingencies of history is analogous and mutually illuminating. *Desire that has been traumatically tested opens up a future in which others can be drawn into a life of gratuitous abundance.* The condition for this is loving God more than the abundance.

Wisdom after multiple overwhelmings

This leads to the fifth feature: wisdom after trauma. The multiple disasters that strike Job, and the temptations, conflicts and, above all, the passion and death of Jesus, have in this and earlier chapters become intrinsic to a concept of wisdom that is both immersed in the contingencies of history and oriented to God's future. Job has been described as a book of post-traumatic wisdom. How far might that also apply to Luke–Acts?

First, it is worth remarking that if Luke–Acts can be construed in these terms then it is likely *a fortiori* to apply more widely in the New Testament. Luke–Acts is very concerned with continuity and coherence, and among the Synoptic Gospels is least likely to emphasise what is interruptive or disjunctive.

Second, the main candidate for description as a trauma is of course the crucifixion of Jesus. But unlike in Job, where the trauma comes at the beginning of the book, is wrestled with for many chapters and then makes way for a brief picture of life renewed after the trauma, in Luke–Acts the trauma comes near the end of the Gospel and midway through the two-part work, and it is followed by two further overwhelming events, the resurrection of Jesus and the coming of the Holy Spirit at Pentecost. This triple overwhelming marks the most fundamental difference between the stories of Job and Jesus. **'And Job died, old and full of days'** (Job 42:17)[31] stands over against **'He breathed his last'** (Luke 23:46c), followed by **'The Lord has risen indeed!'** (24:34), and then **'All of them were filled with the Holy Spirit'** (Acts 2:4a). The trauma of the crucifixion (whose nature has been discussed already above) happens primarily to Jesus, whose resurrection does not by any means undo it or reverse it, but rather vindicates him as a just or righteous wise person who is associated as closely as possible with his Father (e.g. Stephen, before he is stoned, sees **'the Son of Man standing at the right hand of God'**, and then, as he is dying, prays to Jesus: **'Lord Jesus, receive my spirit'** – Acts 7:56, 59). The traumatised person, transformed through resurrection and ascension but still bearing the marks of his crucifixion (see Luke 24:39–40), becomes a focus not just for allegiance but even for prayer.

This is Luke's way of making unavoidable what later became for many centuries the central doctrinal issue in the church: the humanity and divinity of Jesus Christ. For now, the point is that this threefold event is not simply traumatic; it also transforms the traumatised person into life with God in a new way, and, through the Holy Spirit, generates an ongoing history of analogous transformations. Stephen himself is probably intended by Luke as the archetypal analogy: he is described as full of

---

31. Yet interestingly the Septuagint adds the following to the Hebrew: γέγραπται δὲ αὐτὸν πάλιν ἀναστήσεσθαι μεθ' ὧν ὁ κύριος ἀνίστησιν, promising Job resurrection (Job 42:17a).

the Holy Spirit and wisdom, and the account of his death is dense with parallels to the death of Jesus (see above chapter 1).

Third, what I have called analogous transformations are seen not only in people but also in key dimensions of corporate identity. In chapters 3 and 4 the book of Job was understood as a critique and renewal of the wisdom tradition in the aftermath of the corporate trauma of the Babylonian Exile. Job's friends were heard repeating the answers of their tradition without being open to the possibility that new events might require transformations of traditions. Job, in the midst of trauma, radically questions God and the wisdom associated with God by his friends. The book does not give any formulaic answers, but it vindicates Job over against his friends. It might be seen as encouraging uninhibited interrogation of God and God's purposes, readiness to acknowledge that ready-made answers from the past might be inadequate to cope with new developments, and trust in God beyond all the received ideas of God. Overall, this amounts to a searching wisdom centred on the desire for God and vindication by God, open to being searched, addressed and blessed in new, unprecedented ways.

Such a wisdom is consonant with Luke–Acts. Jesus does not fit within the traditional categories. He is 'greater than Jonah', 'greater than Solomon', a leader who serves, the proclaimer of a Kingdom in which children are central and the poor and disabled are feasted, a welcomer of sinners and outcasts, a Messiah who suffers, the Son whose Father wills that he die. He also asks radical questions of traditions and the upholders of traditions. Then at the end of the Gospel the risen Jesus leads his disciples in rereading their whole scriptural tradition in relation to himself and the events of his life, death and resurrection, challenging their foolishness with a sharpness that echoes Job with his friends. This individual who transcends the usual categories finds analogies in Acts not only in other individuals such as Peter, Stephen and Paul (their failure to fit is indicated dramatically by conflict with authorities, imprisonment, and persecution to the point of death), but also in the innovations of the young church. Its desire to fulfil its call to 'all nations' in the name of Jesus Christ leads it to transform the very boundaries of its own Jewish tradition. What is seen in Acts 10–11 and 15 is a community working out how to handle traditional identity markers (circumcision, food laws) after being multiply overwhelmed by the life and death of Jesus, his resurrection and the outpouring of the Holy Spirit. Luke tells of a fundamental reconception of corporate identity beginning with Cornelius and Peter, continuing with Paul, and involving a conflictual deliberative process.

This culminates in a meeting in Jerusalem (Acts 15). Like Job's friends, the traditionalists are confronted by new, challenging events and respond by repeating past teaching: **'Unless you are circumcised according to the custom of Moses, you cannot be saved'** (Acts 15:1). Peter appeals to his own experience and the coming of the Holy Spirit on Gentiles such as Cornelius; Barnabas and Paul add their testimony of what has been happening; and James finally delivers his verdict. It is a new settlement, crucially appealing to a scriptural vision of the future in which the desire of the nations for God is met by God.

> Acts 15:16–21 [16] "After this I will return, and I will rebuild the dwelling of David, which has fallen; from its ruins I will rebuild it, and I will set it up, [17] so that all other peoples may seek the Lord – even all the Gentiles over whom my name has been called." Thus says the Lord, who has been making these things [18] known from long ago. [19] Therefore I have reached the decision that we should not trouble those Gentiles who are turning to God, [20] but we should write to them to abstain only from things polluted by idols and from fornication and from whatever has been strangled and from blood. [21] For in every city, for generations past, Moses has had those who proclaim him, for he has been read aloud every sabbath in the synagogues.'

That is a 'prophetic wisdom' interpretation of scripture for a specific situation. It is the result of a process that has taken into account current events as well as scripture and tradition, but is above all shaped in the aftermath of the event of Jesus Christ and the giving of the Holy Spirit and through a desire for what God desires, **'that all other peoples may seek the Lord'**. It is a wisdom after trauma that, as in Job, has both individual and corporate implications.

Rereading Job alongside Luke–Acts has gathered material for a christological wisdom of desire through categories and content with regard to cries, God, historical involvement, and 'wisdom after overwhelmings' that include trauma. *Job helps Christian reading that attends to the crucified and risen Jesus Christ as himself God's desire, who lives and dies for the sake of God, who hears and desires to meet the cries of humanity, and whose traumatically tested desires embody God's risky involvement in the contingencies of history.* Job also leads into a further sharp area of interrogation. Chapter 4 opened this up in its discussion of attempts to reconceive Jewish and Christian identities in the aftermath of the Shoah. A critical issue for both is wise discernment with regard to new events that challenge past categories, understandings and practices. Job's suffering, leading into wrestling with his friends and God, was such an event, as was the Shoah, which has raised radical questions for both Jews and Christians. So too was the complex event of Jesus Christ in his life, death, resurrection and the giving of the Holy Spirit, and the reading of Job alongside Luke–Acts enriches Christian post-Shoah wisdom. It can be further enriched by other scriptures, and the next section seeks to do this through Paul's First Letter to the Corinthians.

1 Corinthians and wisdom christology

In the opening chapters of his First Letter to the Corinthians Paul reconceives the Gospel in terms of wisdom. The Corinthian church was suffering from divisions, and from problems concerning sexual behaviour, boundaries between the church and pagan society, the celebration of the Lord's supper and the exercise of spiritual gifts. They also had a resurrection-centred confidence that they had already 'arrived':

> 1 Corinthians 4:8 Already you have all you want! Already you have become rich! Quite apart from us you have become kings! Indeed, I wish that you had become kings, so that we might be kings with you!

This went with confidence in their knowledge, wisdom and spiritual gifts, and the whole complex situation stimulated Paul to respond in their own terms. But their own terms of wisdom were probably also given to them by Paul. Grayston, in his perceptive comments on the letter, sees Paul, 'who had himself offered wisdom', recognising the Corinthian position as a development of his own teaching, and in response

> withdrawing to his primary position of Christ crucified. That Paul should have offered wisdom is not surprising. If the preaching of death and resurrection had the powerful effect of creating a believing community, it would soon become necessary to provide – or encourage the community to provide – an understanding of its existence and an expectation for its future. Thus *sophia* [wisdom] would develop and perhaps get out of hand if the inspiration of 'resurrection' outran the sobering thought of 'death'.[32]

---

32. Kenneth Grayston, *Dying, We Live: A New Enquiry into the Death of Christ in the New Testament* (London: Darton, Longman and Todd, 1990), pp. 24–5.

The letter can therefore be read as Paul being stimulated to work out a more adequate understanding of Christian wisdom in the face of a version of his own message that had, in his judgement, lost its balance – and in particular the balance of doing justice to both crucifixion and resurrection. This is wisdom being shaped in intensive engagement with a lively yet troubled community, one whose spiritual energies Paul wants to encourage but also 'baptise'[33] through fuller identification with the crucified Jesus Christ. The whole letter, not just the parts where wisdom is explicitly a theme, is his wisdom for the church; and, as Grayston suggests, it is a wisdom with a self-critical thrust. Paul is relativising himself along with Apollos and Cephas and any other leader. But what is the conception of wisdom that leads to this?

There is an immense volume of commentary on 1 Corinthians[34] but the limited aim of the present discussion is to supplement the earlier exploration of wisdom and desire in relation to Luke–Acts and Job. With this in mind, there are five key points that emerge.

Desire transformed in love

The first is Paul's concern about the appropriate horizon of desire and hope, and the interplay of 'already' and 'not yet'. The opening of the letter roots his own and the church's identity in the will of God and in calling upon God, and the Corinthians are described as **'waiting for the revealing of our Lord Jesus Christ'** and oriented to **'the day of our Lord Jesus Christ'** (1:7–8). This theme recurs in various forms through the letter. It is critical for the perspective on Christian behaviour.

33. There are more references to baptism in this letter than in any other by Paul.
34. Anthony C. Thiselton, *The First Epistle to the Corinthians: A Commentary on the Greek Text* (Grand Rapids, MI: Eerdmans, and Carlisle: Paternoster, 2000) will be the main guide in what follows. Several reasons make this an attractive aid: it summarises a huge amount of previous scholarship and theology; it pays attention to the reception of the letter in Christian theology over the centuries (both in the course of commenting on specific verses and in separate excursuses on each section of the letter); and its author not only is a perceptive commentator on the text according to contemporary practices in the 'guild' of New Testament scholars but also, unusually, has a rich understanding of philosophy, hermeneutics and systematic theology. Other particularly useful commentaries include C. K. Barrett, *A Commentary on the First Epistle to the Corinthians*, Black's New Testament Commentaries (London: Black, 1968, 2nd edn 1971); H. Conzelmann, *1 Corinthians: A Commentary*, Hermeneia (English translation, Philadelphia: Fortress, 1975); G. D. Fee, *The First Epistle to the Corinthians*, NICNT (Grand Rapids, MI: Eerdmans, 1987); A. T. Robinson and A. Plummer, *A Critical and Exegetical Commentary on the First Epistle of St Paul to the Corinthians*, International Critical Commentary, 2nd edn (Edinburgh: T. & T. Clark, 1914); W. Schrage, *Der erste Brief an die Korinther*, EKKNT 7/1–3 to date (Neukirchen-Vluyn: Neukirchener Verlag, and Zurich and Düsseldorf: Benziger Verlag, 1991, 1995, 1999).

> 1 Corinthians 7:29–31 [29]I mean, brothers and sisters, the appointed
> time has grown short; from now on, let even those who have wives be
> as though they had none, [30]and those who mourn as though they
> were not mourning, and those who rejoice as though they were not
> rejoicing, and those who buy as though they had no possessions, [31]and
> those who deal with the world as though they had no dealings with it.
> For the present form of this world is passing away.

Here the eschatological expectation gives a relativising perspective and
motivates a discipline of detachment in relation to desires and passions.
The positive side of it might be seen in the dispute about whether to eat
food sacrificed to idols.

> 1 Corinthians 10:24 Do not seek your own advantage, but that of the
> other . . .
>   10:31 So, whether you eat or drink, or whatever you do, do everything
> for the glory of God.

This combining of orientation to neighbour and God reaches its climax
in the hymn in chapter 13. There love is both involved with the conflicts
and complexities of historical existence and also never-ending, eschatological, to be completed in face to face loving and knowing.

> 1 Corinthians 13:12 For now we see in a mirror, dimly, but then we
> will see face to face. Now I know only in part; then I will know fully,
> even as I have been fully known.

This is the fulfilment of transformed desire. It is the deepest motivation
for the disciplines of desire and action in ordinary life – the patience, the
kindness, and the refusal of envy, boasting, arrogance, rudeness, insistence on getting one's own way, irritation, resentment and so on – as well
as for the sorts of behaviour Paul has been earlier recommending with
regard to perennial sites of problematic desiring, such as sexual relations,
marriage, eating and drinking, legal disputes and community living. It is
also at the heart of the teaching in chapters 12 and 14 about gifts of the
Spirit and what it is best for a member of the church to seek for himself or
herself – discerning the dynamics of desire that build up the community.

> 1 Corinthians 14:1 Pursue love and strive for the spiritual gifts, and
> especially that you may prophesy.

The seeking of the face of the other, both human and divine, is a central
biblical image for the orientation of desiring, willing, hoping, trusting,

knowing, loving and worshipping,[35] and it unites Paul's 'already' with his 'not yet'. The eschatology is then followed through in chapter 15 with a comprehensive affirmation of the resurrection of both Jesus and believers, completing the movement from the crucifixion in the opening chapters. Jesus Christ, crucified and risen, has been central to this passionate letter aimed at the unity and continuing transformation of the Corinthian community and its members. It gives a wisdom of loving desire immersed in the penultimate and directed towards the ultimate.[36]

The wisdom of this age and the wisdom of God

The character of that wisdom[37] as it is given in the first three chapters of 1 Corinthians is the second key point. It is seen first of all as cutting across two powerful religious and cultural orientations.

> 1 Corinthians 1:22–25 [22]For Jews demand signs and Greeks desire wisdom, [23]but we proclaim Christ crucified, a stumbling block to Jews and foolishness to Gentiles, [24]but to those who are the called, both Jews and Greeks, Christ the power of God and the wisdom of God. [25]For God's foolishness is wiser than human wisdom, and God's weakness is stronger than human strength.

God's desire is expressed in Jesus Christ crucified and also in his choosing and calling as Christians those who in the world's terms are unlikely, and this radically challenges the wisdom (as well as the power) of the world.

> 1 Corinthians 1:26–29 [26]Consider your own call, brothers and sisters: not many of you were wise by human standards, not many were powerful, not many were of noble birth. [27]But God chose what is foolish in the world to shame the wise; God chose what is weak in the world to shame the strong; [28]God chose what is low and despised in the world, things that are not, to reduce to nothing things that are, [29]so that no one might boast in the presence of God.

Is this identification of the wisdom of God with Christ crucified and the **'foolish in the world'** over against human wisdom (elsewhere 'the

---

35. It is a key theme throughout my earlier work in this series, *Self and Salvation*.

36. For a discussion of ultimate and penultimate in relation to intellectual desire see Janz, *God the Mind's Desire*, especially chapter 8.

37. Paul uses wisdom (*sophia*) in close connection with word (*logos*) and knowledge (*gnosis*) and their associated verbs. For a sensitive mapping of the meanings and interrelations see Grayston, *Dying, We Live*, pp. 16–21.

wisdom of the wise, and the discernment of the discerning' – 1:19; 'a wisdom of this age or of the rulers of this age' – 2:6; 'the wisdom of this world' – 3:19) anti-intellectual? That is an important question affecting the very possibility of a wisdom christology. The language strongly contrasting divine and human wisdom and their forms of communication[38] can easily be (and often is) interpreted as rejecting the use of human intelligence and wisdom in matters of faith. This would mean a competitive view of human intellectual activity and divine revelation. Thiselton takes the problem very seriously, and he carefully examines the key passages and the often conflicting interpretations of them to arrive at a decisive judgement, that

> It is not wisdom as such which Paul attacks, but that which is status-seeking, manipulatory, or otherwise flawed in some way which diverts it from the purposes of God.[39]

> Paul constantly strove for wise argument. His respect for reason precludes any anti-intellectualism as such.[40]

38. E.g., expanding on those just referred to: 1:17: '... to proclaim the gospel, not with eloquent wisdom, so that the cross of Christ might not be emptied of its power'; 1:20: 'Has not God made foolish the wisdom of the world?'; 1:25: 'For God's foolishness is wiser than human wisdom ...'; 1:27: 'But God chose what is foolish in the world to shame the wise ...'; 2:1: 'I did not come proclaiming the mystery of God to you in lofty words or wisdom'; 1:4–6: 'My speech and my proclamation were not with plausible words of wisdom, but with a demonstration of the Spirit and of power, so that your faith might rest not on human wisdom but on the power of God. Yet among the mature we do speak wisdom, though it is not a wisdom of this age or of the rulers of this age ...' 1:13: 'And we speak of these things in words not taught by human wisdom but taught by the Spirit ...'; 3:19: 'For the wisdom of this world is foolishness with God.'
39. Thiselton, *The First Epistle to the Corinthians*, p. 165.
40. Ibid. p. 208. See Thiselton's translation of 2:2: 'For I did not resolve to know anything to speak among you except Jesus Christ, and Christ crucified.' That is a somewhat awkward translation, but its intention is to stress the positive resolution to speak of Christ crucified: 'Whether or not he spoke of anything else would be incidental; *to proclaim the crucified Christ, and Christ alone, remains his settled policy*. He did not take a vow of excluding everything else, whatever might happen, but he did make a commitment that nothing would compromise the central place of Christ crucified ... These observations, together with what we know of the rhetorical background at Corinth, release Paul of any hint of an uncharacteristic or obsessional *anti-intellectualism*, or any lack of imagination or *communicative flexibility*. His settled resolve was that he would do only what served the gospel of Christ crucified, regardless of people's expectations or seductive shortcuts to success, most of all the seduction of self-advertisement' – Thiselton, *The First Epistle to the Corinthians*, pp. 211–12. See p. 149 on the value of rhetorical analyses of the letter: 'First, granted Litfin's insistence that rhetoric remains Paul's servant, not his master, and that proclamation and argument remain his primary modes of discourse, Paul does not despise a judicious use of the resources of trained thought in the wider world of his day. Second, this emphasis helps to counter a widespread scepticism among some church people about the extent to which Paul would give such detailed attention to words, phrases, and sentences as biblical specialists tend to suppose.'

This is partly explained by the fact that 'wisdom' (σοφία) is used by Paul in several senses,[41] the two main ones being for worldly wisdom in a negative sense and for divine wisdom. There are two major points to note in order to appreciate what he is saying.

First, everything points to him taking up the theme because it was a favourite of the Corinthians. Sixteen of the nineteen uses of σοφία in the letters undisputedly by Paul occur in 1 Corinthians 1–3 as he appeals to them to stop quarrelling and responds to the issues that divide them, among which are claims to wisdom. So he is listening carefully to what they are saying and trying to give fresh content to their terminology in a vivid, contrastive way. 'Paul wishes to redefine and thus to rescue an important term.'[42]

Second, the redefinition and rescue are achieved by **'the wisdom of God'**, centred on the crucified Jesus Christ. This is a framework that does not make sense, is **'foolishness'**, within the Corinthian conception of wisdom, but that by no means implies that it is unreasonable or anti-intellectual. It is **'the mystery of God'** (2:1), **'God's wisdom, secret and hidden, which God decreed before the ages for our glory'** (2:7); it is **'What no eye has seen, nor ear heard, nor the human heart conceived, what God has prepared for those who love him'** (2:9, quoting Isaiah 64:4, 52:15 and Sirach 1:10). It is this wisdom that created the human mind and everything else, and whose long-term purpose is unimaginable glory and love. This is the only framework within which the cross makes any sort of sense. It takes for granted the wisdom of Sirach, Proverbs, Isaiah, Jeremiah and Job,[43] and in these first three chapters especially uses quotations that stress the transcendent difference and unfathomability of God's wisdom over against what human beings find for themselves. There is no denial of the wisdom literature's encouragement to seek wisdom passionately; the emphasis, however, accords with that literature's more fundamental emphasis on God as the source of wisdom and therefore on right human wisdom having its beginning in **'the fear of the Lord'**.[44] Paul's letters are themselves a performance of his passion for a wisdom and understanding in line

---

41. '... there is a different shade of meaning in the word σοφία (and σοφός) every time it occurs' – C. K. Barrett, *Essays on Paul* (London: SPCK, 1982), p. 7.
42. Thiselton, *The First Epistle to the Corinthians*, p. 230.
43. 1 Cor. 3:19 is the only quotation from Job in the New Testament.
44. In 2:3 Paul says that he came to the Corinthians 'in fear and in much trembling', the attitude appropriate to the presence of God.

with the purposes of God, as his lively intelligence – arguing, reasoning, interpreting scripture, carefully crafting language – is used to shape a community and a way of life that realise the wisdom of God. He exemplifies the non-competitive coexistence in his scriptures of wisdom as gift of God and wisdom as actively sought by human beings in response to God's invitation and command. This resonates deeply with what chapters 3 and 4 above argued about the wisdom of Job, especially as expressed explicitly in Job 28 (see pp. 133–8 above). And as in Job 28 Paul's is a radically 'searching wisdom': **these things God has revealed to us through the Spirit; for the Spirit searches everything, even the depths of God'** (2:10).

That 'everything' (πάντα) recurs in 2:15,[45] and in the daring conclusion of 1 Corinthians 3 discussed below. Paul's 'everything' embraces God and the whole creation and sets an agenda for wisdom-seeking that has inspired a constant stream of writers, beginning with his own followers.[46] Its most distinctive mark is its constant referring of everything to the crucified and risen Jesus Christ, **'who became for us wisdom from God, and righteousness and sanctification and redemption'**(1:30). But at the same time there is the ongoing activity of the Spirit, in this case revealing and searching, and elsewhere in this letter identified with **'demonstration of the Spirit and of power'** (2:4), various **'gifts of God's Spirit'** (2:14; see chapters 12, 14), saying **'"Jesus is Lord" ... by the Holy Spirit'** (12:3), baptism **'in the one Spirit'** (12:13), speaking **'mysteries in the Spirit'** (14:2), praying, praising and blessing **'with the Spirit/spirit'** (14:15), and Jesus Christ, who as **'the last Adam became a life-giving Spirit'** (15:45). This relation of Jesus and the Spirit will be explored further below.

---

45. 'Those who are spiritual discern all things, and they are themselves subject to no one else's scrutiny.' On the difficulties of this verse see Thiselton, *The First Epistle to the Corinthians*, pp. 271ff.

46. In the immediate aftermath of Paul, if the Letter to the Ephesians is taken to be not by Paul but by someone trying to distil his thought for the next generation, Ephesians is a model of creative development of the tradition as regards wisdom. The wisdom of God's purposes gathering up 'everything in heaven and on earth' in Christ is set out right at the beginning of the letter as its horizon (chapter 1, especially vv.8–10; and note the prayer that follows in which the first request is for 'a spirit of wisdom and revelation' – v.17); the cross is pivotal and is applied especially to the fundamental issue of the relation of Jews to Gentiles (chapter 2); in chapter 3 the proclamation of the Gospel by Paul is again linked to 'all things' and 'the wisdom of God' (vv.9–10); and in chapters 4–6 a stream of practical wisdom is offered to the recipients. For my reading of this in relation to the understanding of today, see Ford, *Self and Salvation*, especially chapter 5.

Paul's exegetical wisdom

Inseparable from Paul's testimony to Jesus Christ is the third key point, his interpretation of his scripture. This is a large and complex topic, with many technical scholarly discussions about Paul's scriptural texts, his relation to Hebrew and Greek versions, his Jewish interpretative context, differentiation between Jewish-Christian and other readers of his letters, and so on.[47]

Paul indwells his scripture. As Ulrich Luz says, 'For Paul, the OT is not in the first place something to understand, but it itself creates understanding.'[48] He assumes that, interpreted in the Spirit within the horizon of the glory and purposes of God and the relationship of God to 'all things', the scriptures will speak into the present situation. The Spirit searches the deep things of God (1 Cor. 2:10; see Job 28) and inspires wisdom, knowledge, prophecy, teaching and so on, and reference to scriptures is intrinsic to what is found, taught and prophesied. Interpretation of scripture, testimony to Jesus Christ in the tradition Paul received, and the questions and challenges of life in the Spirit oriented to God's future are all interwoven in Paul's letters. They embody an ever-fresh engagement with scripture and a wide variety of modes of interpretation. '**We have the mind of Christ**' (2:16) does not mean that scripture is replaced by something more immediate: that mind is assumed to be revealed through scripture, as scripture is searched 'in the Spirit'. So, as has already been shown in Luke and John, the scriptures have an openness and orientation to God's future which require continual rereading.

Becoming mature

The fourth key point is that the wisdom of God found in Christ crucified is connected with a specific form of maturity. The theme of maturity is especially prominent in chapters 2–3 and 12–14, and in both passages there is language of childhood and adulthood used metaphorically of Christians.

---

47. See D. Moody Smith, 'The Pauline Literature' in *It Is Written: Scripture Citing Scripture*, ed. D. A. Carson and H. C. M. Williamson (Cambridge: Cambridge University Press, 1988), pp. 265–91; Richard B. Hays, *Echoes of Scripture in the Letters of Paul* (New Haven and London: Yale University Press, 1989); Dietrich-Alex Koch, *Die Schrift als Zeuge des Evangeliums: Untersuchungen zur Verwendung und zum Verständnis der Schrift bei Paulus* (Tübingen: J. C. B. Mohr (Paul Siebeck), 1986); E. Earle Ellis, *Paul's Use of the Old Testament* (Edinburgh: Oliver and Boyd, 1957); Richard N. Longenecker, *Biblical Exegesis in the Apostolic Period* (Grand Rapids, MI: Eerdmans, 1975).
48. Quoted in Thiselton, *The First Epistle to the Corinthians*, p. 160.

Grayston says on chapters 2–3:

> It is clear from the various words used to describe those who heard
> Paul's instruction – *teleioi, pneumatikoi, psychikoi, sarkikoi*
> (1 Cor. 2:6, 13–15; 3:1, 3) – that no fixed terminology was in mind. The
> controlling image is of maturity and immaturity. The *sarkikoi* ('men
> of the flesh') are immature Christians who by jealousy and strife
> show that they are still held by ordinary human desires. The
> *psychikoi* are unreflective non-Christians to whom the divine
> spiritual energies seem unsocially stupid. The *teleioi*[49] are mature
> Christians (not the 'perfect') who can be entrusted with explanatory
> myths of the divine wisdom; and the *pneumatikoi* are experienced
> Christians in whom the divine Spirit is at work to create the structure
> and life-style of the community. Hence, part of the anxiety about
> *sophia* is that the community has accepted it from named leaders
> rather than discovering it by their own endowment of Spirit; and
> Paul is partly to blame, though he says apologetically, 'I could not
> address you as spiritual men' (1 Cor. 3:1).[50]

Taking the earlier and the later chapters of 1 Corinthians together
there appear to be three interwoven strands in this maturity. The first is
having **'God's wisdom, secret and hidden, which God decreed before
the ages for our glory ... revealed to us through the Spirit'** (2:7, 10).
This is summed up as having **'the mind of Christ'** (2:16b), which the
letter has already made clear is the mind of one who was crucified. The
'crucified mind', shaped by the mysteries and depths of God revealed in
Jesus Christ, involves wholehearted participation in the radical transformation begun in Jesus Christ.[51] The measure of maturity is taking
responsibility for one's own part in that transformation.

---

49. [Grayston's note] Paul's use of *teleios* is scarcely technical. In 1 Cor 13:10 *to teleion* is
contrasted with *to ek merous* (what is complete with what is incomplete) in the context of
an illustration from childhood and manhood. 1 Cor 14:20 speaks for itself: 'Do not be
children, ... but in thinking be mature [*teleioi*]'. So probably Phil 3:12, 15. Eph 4:13–14 'mature
manhood ... no longer children'. Col 1:28, 4:12 may be different, but there is nothing else in
Paul (except Rom 12:2, where *teleios* is ascribed to the divine intention).
50. Grayston, *Dying, We Live*, p. 25.
51. Grayston, ibid. pp. 50–1, concludes his discussion of 1 Corinthians with a significant
summary: 'In thus working out the implications of Christ's death, Paul is properly relying on
the imagery, traditional sayings, and cultic formulas already at home within the community.
In the opening chapters of the epistle, however, he breaks new ground. He opposes the word
of the cross to Corinthian wisdom and knowledge for the simple reason that wisdom and
knowledge, however justifiable in themselves, are directed towards the preservation of this
present age and therefore resist the radical transformation God has inaugurated in Christ.
The word of the cross is religiously offensive to Jews and therefore undermines Jewish self-
confidence. It is socially destructive to Gentiles and therefore subverts Gentile social

That leads directly into the second mark of maturity: serving the unity, building up and flourishing of the community. Much of 1 Corinthians is a response to divisions in the community, and Paul makes a direct link between the wisdom of the cross and the unity of the church. On the other hand, the main criterion for immaturity is divisive inclinations and behaviour.

> 1 Corinthians 3:1–4 [1]And so, brothers and sisters, I could not speak to you as spiritual people, but rather as people of the flesh, as infants in Christ. [2]I fed you with milk, not solid food, for you were not ready for solid food. Even now you are still not ready, [3]for you are still of the flesh. For as long as there is jealousy and quarrelling among you, are you not of the flesh, and behaving according to human inclinations? [4]For when one says, 'I belong to Paul,' and another, 'I belong to Apollos,' are you not merely human?

The supreme description of a maturity that builds up the community is in chapters 12–14. After the body of Christ is portrayed in terms of different gifts and responsibilities (apostles, prophets, teachers and so on – 12:27–31) the 'more excellent way' of love is given. Love makes the difference between being a 'child' and an 'adult' (13:9–11).[52] Love is the essential community-builder and needs to govern all use of spiritual gifts.

The main strategy in Paul's wisdom of unity is to call the Corinthians to go deeper into the heart of the Gospel and to conform themselves to the love of Christ and to 'the mind of Christ' that are found there, a love and a mind that are contradicted by their dissension. But it is worth probing further to learn from how Paul went about making his case as well as from what he explicitly said. He is taking the terminology and concerns of the Corinthians (some of which, as mentioned above, may have come originally from himself) and working intensively with them to produce an original reformulation of the Gospel in terms of 'weak power' and 'foolish wisdom'. In doing this he is trying to communicate with them in accordance with 'the mind of Christ', which entailed vulnerability (approaching them 'in weakness' – 2:3), dealing with them on their own terms, refusing manipulative techniques, and appealing

awareness. To those who are caught up in the dissolution of present society it is shockingly stupid, but to those who are sharing in the process of transformation it is God's powerful agent of change. Indeed, it is the hidden mystery of the divine will, which entraps and overthrows the ruling powers of this age and opens up the possibility of God's rule through the crucified and risen Lord.'

52. See Grayston in Thiselton, *The First Epistle to the Corinthians*, p. 160.

passionately to them. There are of course many suspicious interpretations of Paul as exercising his authority (not least through using appeals to weakness) manipulatively and oppressively, but if they are not found convincing[53] then it is possible to read 1 Corinthians as a Gospel-informed practice of peacemaking. Studying the drama of his relationship with the Corinthians – and even trying to sort out the very different reconstructions of it[54] – greatly enriches the sense of the significance and complexity of this practice. The very impossibility of being sure when Paul is quoting the Corinthians and when he is responding to them may be a sign of how successful he has been at entering into their mind-set and taking seriously what they say. His wisdom takes seriously the contingencies of history (whose interrelated particularities never recur but can be learnt from), and helps to repair and redeem the present in the interests of a better community future. Scholarly insights such as those into Paul's way of acknowledging and transforming the Corinthians' terminology help us to understand the quality of his wisdom and give a density and detail that might inspire analogous responses in other situations.

The third element is directly connected with the other two by Paul. It is maturity in relation to leaders. He sharply criticises the sort of dependence on leaders, whether on himself or on others, that leads someone to say '**"I belong to Paul," and another, "I belong to Apollos"**' (3:4). The culmination of his explicit treatment of wisdom in the first three chapters is related to this.

> 1 Corinthians 3:21–23 [21]So let no one boast about human leaders. For all things are yours, [22]whether Paul or Apollos or Cephas or the world or life or death or the present or the future – all belong to you, [23]and you belong to Christ, and Christ belongs to God.

That outflanks the factional divisions of the church by offering a God-oriented 'ecology' of belonging, embracing oppositional confrontation in a higher inclusiveness. Its horizon of wisdom is no less than 'all things' in relation to God, and the language of belonging (expressed in Greek by simple genitives, literally 'all things yours, you Christ's, Christ God's') prepares for the later language of the body of Christ and love. But the most daring move is to turn upside down the relationship of belonging

---

53. For a discussion of Paul's authority and its critics see Young and Ford, *Meaning and Truth in 2 Corinthians*, chapter 8.

54. Thiselton, *The First Epistle to the Corinthians*, particularly pp. 17–29 on 'The Christian Community in Corinth: Beginnings, Nature, and Relations with Paul'.

between leaders and followers. The leaders do not own the followers but rather belong to them. This is at least as counter-cultural as God choosing the foolish, the weak, the low, the despised and the 'nothings' as the majority in the church. The two are also interconnected: those who count for little in society might be especially vulnerable to manipulative leaders who form close-knit factions that give a sense of security and common purpose. Paul meets this with a vision of mature, interdependent members who have internalised 'the wisdom of God', who use their spiritual gifts in mutual love and honour to build up the church, and who hold their leaders accountable before Christ and God just as they themselves are.

Living wisdom christology

Paul meets the Corinthian Christians with more than this vision and teaching. He meets them in person and with testimony to his own ministry. Alongside the message of Christ crucified, the most daring and even scandalous element in what he writes is that he claims to embody what he is talking about.

> 1 Corinthians 4:16 I appeal to you, then, be imitators of me.
> 1 Corinthians 11:1 Be imitators of me, as I am of Christ.

If Christ is the wisdom of God, then part of what those appeals imply is that Paul and the church are to embody God's wisdom. *Indeed, this may be the most important single thing to be said about wisdom christology: that its meaning is found mainly in lives, practices and communities.* That of course includes language, but even the mode of expression, as Paul says, needs to be conformed to Christ crucified.

> 1 Corinthians 2:1–5 [1]When I came to you, brothers and sisters, I did not come proclaiming the mystery of God to you in lofty words of wisdom. [2]For I decided to know nothing among you except Jesus Christ, and him crucified. [3]And I came to you in weakness and in fear and in much trembling. [4]My speech and my proclamation were not with plausible words of wisdom, but with a demonstration of the Spirit and of power, [5]so that your faith might rest not on human wisdom but on the power of God.

Even more than in that linguistic form of 'weak power' the meaning of the crucifixion is seen in Paul's description of what it means to be an apostle, which comes just before his first appeal to be imitated.

> 1 Corinthians 4:9–13 [9]For I think that God has exhibited us apostles as last of all, as though sentenced to death, because we have become a

spectacle to the world, to angels and to mortals. [10]We are fools for the sake of Christ, but you are wise in Christ. We are weak, but you are strong. You are held in honour, but we in disrepute. [11]To the present hour we are hungry and thirsty, we are poorly clothed and beaten and homeless, [12]and we grow weary from the work of our own hands. When reviled, we bless; when persecuted, we endure; [13]when slandered, we speak kindly. We have become like the rubbish of the world, the dregs of all things, to this very day.

In chapter 9 Paul argues at length for his right as an apostle to be accompanied by a wife, or to have his expenses paid so that he does not have to work for a living. His renunciation of those rights (which in my terms might be seen as the transformation of his desires in line with his desire to please Jesus Christ) in the interests of making the Gospel free of charge is then explained in terms that might be described as imitating the incarnation of Christ (his own account of Jesus' self-emptying in Philippians 2 comes to mind).

1 Corinthians 9:19–23 [19]For though I am free with respect to all, I have made myself a slave to all, so that I might win more of them. [20]To the Jews I became as a Jew, in order to win Jews. To those under the law I became as one under the law (though I myself am not under the law) so that I might win those under the law. [21]To those outside the law I became as one outside the law (though I am not free from God's law but am under Christ's law) so that I might win those outside the law. [22]To the weak I became weak, so that I might win the weak. I have become all things to all people, that I might by all means save some. [23]I do it all for the sake of the gospel, so that I may share in its blessings.

It is as if the Spirit of Christ allows his imitator to become multiply incarnate by identifying with many types of people, very different among themselves. The transformation of desire is then described in the image of an athlete's training: **'self-control in all things'** and punishing physical discipline (9:24–27). The most comprehensive rationale for this is given later, just before the second appeal to be imitated.

1 Corinthians 10:31 So, whether you eat or drink, or whatever you do, do everything for the glory of God.

That is what has already been identified as the key to understanding both Job and Jesus: living for God's sake.

Then in the middle of his culminating proclamation and discussion of the resurrection he cries out from his own experience, making sense of the risks he runs by his confidence that death is not the last word.

> 1 Corinthians 15:30–32 [30]And why are we putting ourselves in danger every hour? [31]I die every day! That is as certain, brothers and sisters, as my boasting of you – a boast that I make in Christ Jesus our Lord. [32]If with merely human hopes I fought with wild animals at Ephesus, what would I have gained by it? If the dead are not raised, 'Let us eat and drink, for tomorrow we die.'

The essential picture is of a life conformed to the incarnation, death and resurrection of Jesus Christ while still very much involved with the dangerous and deadly contingencies of historical existence. It is not literal imitation, but like a set of figural variations in the Spirit on the Gospel. It amounts to the letter's fullest presentation of what is meant by Christian maturity, embracing all the marks given above: enacting the 'mind of Christ' centred on the crucifixion; serving the unity and building up of the church; and trying to be the sort of leader who enables the maturity and interdependence of his followers.[55]

The overall orientation of it is towards an inconceivable fulfilment prepared by God **'for those who love him'** (2:9), an ultimate **'face to face'** (13:12), a glorious mystery of transformation: **'We will not all die, but we will all be changed'** (15:51). That is celebrated in a culminating trumpet call and cry.

> 1 Corinthians 15:52–57 [52]For the trumpet will sound, and the dead will be raised imperishable, and we will be changed. [53]For this perishable body must put on imperishability, and this mortal body must put on immortality. [54]When this perishable body puts on imperishability, and this mortal body puts on immortality, then the saying that is written will be fulfilled: 'Death has been swallowed up in victory.' [55]'Where, O death, is your victory? Where, O death, is your sting?' [56]The sting of death is sin, and the power of sin is the law. [57]But thanks be to God, who gives us the victory through our Lord Jesus Christ.

---

55. On Paul's authority and use of power see Young and Ford, *Meaning and Truth in 2 Corinthians*, chapter 8.

That passionate cry is Paul's crowning expression of 'the wisdom of God', uniting immersion in historical existence (body, death, sin, law) with radical transformation, death with resurrection, and all 'through our Lord Jesus Christ'.

Conclusion: maxims of wisdom christology

Christology has been approached in this chapter, as in chapters 1 and 2, through theological commentary on a few scriptural texts with a hinterland of classic formulations and centuries of debates about them. That has produced some primary theology whose concern has been simultaneously to do justice to the texts in that context and to open them up as contemporary Christian wisdom. What are the main lines of christological wisdom that have emerged?

One way of expressing them is, as in chapters 1 and 2, through maxims. These are intended as suggested guidance in the ongoing task of living wisely in the light of Jesus Christ. The abundance of wisdom to be found is assumed, because of its source in God, to be inexhaustible; so the maxims are a pedagogical aid in seeking it, orientations in a search that is never complete. There can be no resting in such maxims: they are signs pointing beyond themselves to the need for further searching. They also assume the discussion and scriptural interpretation in this and previous chapters and what is to follow in chapters 6 and 7. So they are a provisional distillation, focussed through christology, of contemporary Christian wisdom. The maxims are:

- Jesus embodies a God-centred, prophetic wisdom and love in which we are invited to participate by learning it and embodying it.
- It is a wisdom requiring intensive, sustained attention to Jesus through the key events of his life, his death, his resurrection and Pentecost.
- The person of Jesus and those events are fruitfully approached through a hermeneutic of cries – the cries between Jesus and his Father, the cries addressed to them, and the cries of people to each other.
- The fruitfulness also calls for reading and rereading the Old and New Testaments together.
- The drama of desire between Jesus and his Father, and between them and the family of humanity, is a key dynamic in those events, in the rest of history and in the future.
- Within its embracing mood of desire for God and the Kingdom of God the drama calls for other moods in affirmation, injunction, interrogation and experimentation.

- The core practical wisdom of the christological drama of desire is loving God for God's sake, glorifying God, blessing God, hallowing God's name.
- The summary of the human response to Jesus Christ desired by God is to live in the Spirit.

The next two chapters will explore 'learning to live in the Spirit' from various angles, taking up issues emerging from this and previous chapters. These will include tradition, worship, the Trinity, loving God for God's sake, and taking part in the church as a school of desire and wisdom.

6

Learning to live in the Spirit: tradition and worship

Learning to live in the Spirit is the encompassing activity of Christian discipleship after Pentecost.

The first five chapters have so far offered an understanding of Christian wisdom largely through scriptural interpretation. The conception of this wisdom has been as the discernment of cries in the midst of a historical existence summoned towards God's future. Because of that summons, desire for God and God's purposes is wisdom's embracing 'mood'. Indicatives, imperatives, interrogatives and subjunctives are variously in play both in the texts and in their interpretations, but, in responding to the cries of God and of the world, faith's core mood is optative – and first in the passive voice: we are desired by God. This wisdom's main practice is constantly renewed engagement with scripture as summarised in the nine theses and ten maxims at the end of chapter 2. The rereading of scripture in the Spirit as described there connects with a range of engagements that are in principle unlimited – with other people, spheres of life, disciplines, arts, cultures, religions and so on. The succeeding chapters have attempted to give samples of that wisdom interpretation of scripture, mainly through the books of Job, Luke, Acts and 1 Corinthians. There has been no attempt to be exhaustive, the main aim being to exemplify an approach that not only requires further working out through the other books of the Bible and their intertextuality but also requires constant rereading of Job, Luke, Acts and 1 Corinthians.

The last three chapters of the book give three case studies in Christian wisdom chosen from among the many actual engagements important for the twenty-first century. Chapter 8 on inter-faith wisdom is about interpretation of the Christian scriptures alongside those of Judaism and

Islam. Chapter 9 on universities is less explicitly scriptural but draws on the elements of the first seven chapters of this book in order to describe and reconceive a set of institutions with a widely influential global 'ministry of meaning' exercised through academic disciplines and their interrelations and implications. Chapter 10 on L'Arche and its inter-personal wisdom describes a very different arena for the working out of Christian wisdom, and culminates in its articulation by Jean Vanier through his reading of the Gospel of John.

Chapters 6 and 7 connect the earlier chapters with the case studies. This will be done by discussing a series of topics that mediate between them.

Growing out of the interpretation of scripture, this chapter will first sketch a wisdom interpretation of Christian tradition. Tradition has already figured in previous chapters, but not so far as a distinct topic. I will outline (without developing at any length – that would require at least a book) the understanding of tradition with which I am working. I will relate what was said in previous chapters about Job, Jesus and the interpretation of scripture to a wisdom interpretation of tradition. This mediates between the two sets of chapters by bringing the scripture-based elements into relation with two millennia of tradition, culminat-ing in today's challenge to draw on scripture and tradition in facing the sorts of contemporary issues represented by the case studies.

At the heart of living in line with scripture and tradition is worship-ping God, the second topic of this chapter. God is obviously of incompar-able and comprehensive importance for Christian wisdom, and worship is the most direct expression of response to God. Wisdom in worship is at the core of Christian life and thought. Worship sustains and pervades Christian involvement in all spheres of life. But who is worshipped? Right identification of God is vital for Christianity, and in its early centuries its tradition developed a distinctive doctrine of God as Trinity. What is the rationale for this? Rather than offer a full doctrine of the Trinity this chapter takes soundings that test the wisdom of its development, guided by three thinkers who face the difficulties and complexities and also offer a prophetic wisdom on key topics: God and being; incarnation; and the Holy Spirit in the Trinity and in worshippers.

Chapter 7 will continue the theme of living in the Spirit. First, it will explore the core practice that has emerged from earlier chapters: loving God for God's sake – hallowing the name of God whatever the cost. This leads simultaneously deeper into God, exploring the perfections of God and especially the divine wisdom; and deeper into the world God loves, as exemplified in the case studies. The cries of worship and prayer are inseparable from the cries of the world, and it is a perennially crucial task to keep them in fruitful relationship. This requires a school of desire and wisdom where worshippers can learn together to live in the Spirit for the sake of God, of other people and of the world. The final inquiry of Chapter 7 is therefore into a wisdom conception of the church in the context of our religious and secular world.

The church has in fact been presupposed through earlier chapters, and is so especially in the present one. Christian tradition is inextricable from the community that passes it on and continually re-examines it, tests it and improvises on it. Worship is especially a core activity of the church, but this is just the most visible aspect of a sociality that has many other dimensions, including the structuring of practices and relationships that make up a church's polity. This fundamental importance of Christian community and its institutional embodiment is assumed through what follows even though it is not explicitly discussed till towards the end of Chapter 7.

A wisdom interpretation of Christian tradition

Remember!

> Deuteronomy 6:4–9 [4]Hear, O Israel: The LORD is our God, the LORD alone. [5]You shall love the LORD your God with all your heart, and with all your soul, and with all your might. [6]Keep these words that I am commanding you today in your heart. [7]Recite them to your children and talk about them when you are at home and when you are away, when you lie down and when you rise. [8]Bind them as a sign on your hand, fix them as an emblem on your forehead, [9]and write them on the doorposts of your house and on your gates.

> Luke 1:1–4 [1]Since many have undertaken to set down an orderly account of the events that have been fulfilled among us, [2]just as they were handed on to us by those who from the beginning were eyewitnesses and servants of the word, [3]I too decided, after investigating everything carefully from the very first, to write an orderly account for you, most excellent Theophilus, [4]so that you may know the truth concerning the things about which you have been instructed.

> 1 Corinthians 11:23–26 [23]For I received from the Lord what I also handed on to you, that the Lord Jesus on the night when he was betrayed took a loaf of bread, [24]and when he had given thanks, he broke it and said, 'This is my body that is for you. Do this in remembrance of me.'

[25]In the same way he took the cup also, after supper, saying, 'This cup is the new covenant in my blood. Do this, as often as you drink it, in remembrance of me.' [26]For as often as you eat this bread and drink the cup, you proclaim the Lord's death until he comes.

Those texts represent tradition, the process of handing on what is most significant for a community – orally in face to face relationships, in writing and in symbolic action. Tradition is a function of all transgenerational communities, whether religious, cultural, political, legal, scientific or scholarly. At its best it is about passing on what is judged to be important, reliable and essential for a good future for the community.

An examination of traditions immediately shows a range of difficult questions they habitually face. Who judges what is important, reliable and essential for the future? What is the process for deciding? What are the criteria? Is consensus required, and how might that be defined? What sorts of continuity are important, and what sorts of discontinuity are permitted? What are the limits of diversity, of adaptation to new conditions and of dissent? What weight is to be attached to oral over against written traditions? What is the relationship of verbal to behavioural conformity?[1]

Christianity, like any other tradition, has to face these questions, and a huge amount of scholarship and theological debate has engaged with them. My basic point is that the tasks of discerning, preserving and developing Christian tradition are best understood under the heading of wisdom as earlier chapters have portrayed it. It is an ongoing requirement that demands rich, comprehensive understanding, sensitivity to particular circumstances, and the ability both to make appropriate judgements and also to communicate them persuasively to others, if necessary through intensive argument and deliberation.

---

1. For a general account of tradition see Edward Shils, *Tradition* (Chicago: Chicago University Press, 1981). For an account of Christian tradition with special emphasis on its teachings, see Jaroslav Pelikan, *The Christian Tradition: A History of the Development of Doctrine* (Chicago: Chicago University Press, 1971–84) and *The Vindication of Tradition* (New Haven: Yale University Press, 1984). For an account of the early centuries of Christian literature with an integrating concern for hermeneutics – both for the ways in which the literature of the period engaged in interpretation (especially of scripture) and for how we can today appropriately interpret that literature across the intervening centuries, see *The Cambridge History of Early Christian Literature*, ed. Frances Young, Lewis Ayres and Andrew Louth (Cambridge: Cambridge University Press, 2004). Frances Young's introductory and summary chapters are especially relevant to the present discussion: chapter 1 Introduction: The Literary Culture of the Earliest Christianity; chapter 10 Conclusion: Towards a Hermeneutic of Second-Century Texts; chapter 20 The Significance of Third-Century Christian Literature; chapter 21 Classical Genres in Christian Guise: Christian Genres in Classical Guise; chapter 40 Retrospect: Interpretation and Appropriation.

In the early centuries of Christianity the key elements in its identity were slowly worked out. It might be compared to an emerging ecosystem with various niches in symbiosis: deciding on its canon of Old Testament and New Testament scripture; developing structures of church authority and offices; office-holders, ordinary Christians, martyrs, saints and monks interpreting the faith through their lives and words; catechetical teaching leading to baptism; worshipping in a eucharist-centred liturgical pattern; distilling a 'rule of faith' which grew into creeds; and communicating, arguing and negotiating 'settlements' with the surrounding culture, both pagan and Jewish. All of that involved a highly complex process of debate and discernment, continuous century after century. Even landmark decisions about canon or creed never close down the questioning and rethinking about them, let alone about how these are to be interpreted and related to the other elements. Immersed in particular situations, local wisdoms often emerged about such matters, setting the further task of relating them together in a more ecumenical wisdom.

One of the stablest elements for nearly two millennia has been the canon of scripture. There were many problems and conflicts in arriving at it, and the inclusion of some books has often been questioned (the most important being the Apocrypha), but on the whole most Christians over the centuries have been able to appeal to commonly recognised scriptures. This pre-eminent position of the Bible has raised the problem of its relation to tradition: is it better seen as a differentiated part of tradition or as distinct from and superior to it? Inseparable from this is the problem of the relation of both scripture and tradition to the church and its authority. The interrelation of scripture, tradition and church has especially been an issue since the Protestant Reformation emphasis on the authority of 'scripture alone', maintained polemically over against what were judged to be developments incompatible with scripture in tradition and church. Such disputes cannot be done justice here, but it is important that since the twentieth-century ecumenical movement there has been considerable convergence among some of those long divided over these matters.[2] Whatever other elements have been in play in such

---

2. Perhaps the highpoint of convergence thus far has been the ecumenical text 'Baptism, Eucharist and Ministry', which was agreed in 1982, see *Baptism, Eucharist and Ministry: The Agreed Text* (London: CCBI Publications, 1982). In addition, there have been a large number of bilateral dialogues between representatives of different strands of the tradition, including Lutheran–Roman Catholic, Reformed–Orthodox, Anglican–Roman Catholic, Pentecostal–Roman Catholic, and Anglican–Lutheran conversations. A study of ecumenical dialogues shows the need for patient, highly specific discussion and deliberation over

moves towards Christian consensus, wrestling over the interpretation of scripture has been a constant.

The interpretation of tradition needs to be rooted in a wisdom interpretation of scripture, and in this section I draw on previous chapters in order to lay out some of the key considerations that will be borne in mind both in the two other topics dealt with in this chapter and in the case studies in Chapters 8–10.

The Holy Spirit, tradition and innovation

I begin with a strong theological affirmation of the importance of both tradition and innovation, made by an Anglican Old Testament scholar who draws on a Roman Catholic monk:

> One contemporary monastic theologian, Jean Leclercq, identifies the Christian tradition itself as the manifestation of the Holy Spirit; it is 'the stream of life ... coming to us through the Church from the crucified and glorified Christ.'[3] Tradition in that sense can exist only in the stable yet dynamic environment established by active ministry and mission, worship, study, and interactive conversation about the things of God – all that ongoing from generation to generation. In such an environment, we may trust that the work of the Holy Spirit will indeed manifest itself in the periodic emergence of the radically new, which can be accepted and valued because it stands in discernible continuity with what the church has already recognized as God's work.[4]

That might be seen as a statement of the problem of tradition rather than a solution. It affirms both Jesus Christ and the continuing work of the Holy Spirit, both stability and change, both discernible continuity and the radically new. The crucial issue is how those can go together in particular matters. That is what Ellen F. Davis sees being discerned through ministry, mission, worship, study and conversation carried on across generations – in my terms, learning to seek wisdom and to live in

many years, building up relationships as well as mutual understanding and taking far more than doctrinal matters into account. The ecumenical movement might be seen as one of the twentieth century's main contributions to the wisdom tradition of the church, and it is one whose lessons for other fields, especially inter-faith dialogue, have hardly begun to be learnt.

3. [Davis footnote] Jean Leclercq, 'Contemporary Monasticism' in *Fairacres Chronicle* 12, no. 3 (1979), p. 7.
4. Ellen F. Davis, *Wondrous Depth: Preaching the Old Testament* (Louisville, KY: Westminster John Knox Press, 2005), p. 83.

the Spirit in the church. What might be contributed to that process of discernment by Job, by Jesus and by the rereading of scripture?

Job and tradition

Job was described in Chapters 3 and 4 as representing a crisis in the wisdom tradition of Israel. In the face of an unprecedented, traumatic situation, his friends repeat the tradition while Job questions it and questions God. Yet they also enter into wisdom-seeking debate together, and Job's growth in wisdom is inseparable from his wrestling with his friends and with God for truth and vindication. What are some of the lessons from Job for those faced with the task of discerning wise ways forward for the Christian tradition in problematic situations? The first is to reread the book of Job with their situation in mind. Taking the rereading and also the interpretation of Chapters 3 and 4 for granted, some of the lessons from that book's pedagogy in wisdom might include:

- Beware of just repeating a tradition in new situations; be suspicious of simplifications and formulae.
- Learn to read poetry, be open to truth in poetry as well as in prose, and allow it to stretch the imagination and puzzle the mind.
- Scripture itself is self-critical and records many breaks with, as well as renewals of, traditions; any tradition that appeals to it should be open to the possibility of radical revision in new situations.
- Enter into the complexities of arguments, let your assumptions and frameworks be challenged, and sustain ongoing debate even with those who seem to have it very wrong.
- Be attentive to what is going on now, and especially to the cries of those who are suffering.
- Listen especially to those whose wisdom has been tested in trauma and other suffering.
- Practise kindness, compassion and patience as part of a wise way forward.
- Let yourself and your tradition be searched and tested by God as radically as possible.
- Engage with God and with your tradition in all 'moods', and in passive and active voices – affirmed and affirming, summoned and summoning, questioned and questioning, open to possibilities and experiments, desired by God and desiring God and God's purposes.
- Above all, cry out to God and engage with God for God's sake.

Such maxims will prove helpful to bear in mind when considering the practice of scriptural reasoning in Chapter 8, which in relation to

Judaism, Christianity and Islam is both traditional (in its concentration on scriptural interpretation) and untraditional (doing this in dialogue with the other two traditions). They are also relevant to universities which want to do justice to the best in their past while exploring unprecedented possibilities and meeting current challenges. Likewise the L'Arche communities have tried to embody something of Christian faith, hope, love and community while not being a church or a religious order but embracing those of different churches and different religions. More immediately, those maxims, together with the maxims in the next section on Jesus and tradition, have been the criteria for selecting Ricoeur, Williams and Coakley as this chapter's exemplary interpreters of the tradition's development of its understanding of God as Trinity.

Jesus and tradition

Jesus is obviously the central reality of Christian tradition. In Luke's Gospel he is placed firmly in his Jewish tradition.[5]

That Gospel's opening and closing scenes are set in the Temple. His mother, Mary, and uncle, Zechariah, set him in the context of God's history and covenant with Israel. He is seen by Simeon and Anna in the Temple as the fulfilment of Israel's hope for redemption. He takes part in festivals and pilgrimage to Jerusalem with his family. His genealogy goes back through David, Jacob, Isaac and Abraham to Adam. In his ministry he had some differences with the Pharisees (such as over their innovative purity rules) but largely followed their observances, and his attitude to the sabbath is in line with very liberal Pharisees. In his strict attitude to divorce he is nearer to the Qumran sect. Overall, he does not fit fully within any of the religious parties, but his special opponents are the chief priests and Sadducees who run the Temple.

Much of Jesus' teaching can be paralleled in the Judaism of his day, including the use of parables and his summary of the law in the double command of love for God and neighbour. On his prayer Tomson writes:

> Jewish prayers preserved in rabbinic tradition contain emphases similar to Jesus' prayer. The daily main prayer, the *Tefillah* or *Amidah*,

---

5. See Peter J. Tomson, 'Jesus and His Judaism' in *The Cambridge Companion to Jesus*, ed. Markus Bockmuehl (Cambridge: Cambridge University Press, 2001), p. 26: 'Especially Matthew and John are marked by a fierce conflict with contemporary rabbis and, in the case of John, with "the Jews" as a whole. Mark carries only some traces of such a later conflict. Luke is exceptional in that it shows none at all. On the contrary, the author, who also wrote Acts, seems to stress the ties with Judaism at every possible turn.' On the topics of the rest of this paragraph see the rest of Tomson's chapter, culminating in his summary on p. 40.

asks for bread, forgiveness and deliverance from evil; the frequent *Qaddish* prayer for the sanctification of God's name and the execution of His will. In fact, the Lord's Prayer is in no way exclusively 'Christian'. At the same time, the particular combination of motifs appears to be typical of Jesus' teaching.[6]

This picture of Jesus the Jew could be expanded at great length, and the research that supports it has been a major scholarly enterprise since the second half of the twentieth century.[7] From the point of view of this chapter the main significance of the results is that Jesus is firmly identified with his Jewish tradition in such a way that his criticisms and innovations are also recognisably Jewish. Jesus' focus on God and the Kingdom of God are in line with the God-centredness and future orientation found in the Jewish scriptures and the intertestamental period. There are parallels to the book of Job in his use of the resources of his tradition to critique it. As with Job, this is not a matter of simple principles or formulae that can be directly applied whatever the situation. To learn from Jesus' relationship to Jewish tradition involves thinking through its particular aspects and, as with Job, arriving at maxims which are resources for thinking in new circumstances. I will consider some aspects that might be fruitful in this way, assuming the discussions of Luke's Gospel that have already taken place in chapters 1, 2 and 5.

Jesus' relationship with John the Baptist is pivotal for his relationship with his Jewish tradition. John is a desert prophet who confronts complacent traditional identity (**'We have Abraham as our ancestor'**– Luke 3:8) with a call to repentance, but looks beyond his own water baptism to one who **'will baptise you with the Holy Spirit and fire'** (3:16). Here is a decisive sign of the novelty of Jesus, confirmed in the account of his baptism: the coming of the Holy Spirit, which was believed by fellow-Jews to have been quenched since the last biblical prophet. The baptism combines this sign with affirmation of Jesus by God as **'my Son, the Beloved'** (3:22). One who is in intimate and ultimate relationship with

6. Ibid. p. 32.
7. Among the major works are: E. P. Sanders, *Jesus and Judaism* (London: SCM, 1985); Geza Vermes, *Jesus the Jew* (London: SCM, 2001); John P. Meier, *A Marginal Jew: Rethinking the Historical Jesus*: vol. 1: *The Roots of the Problem and the Person*; vol. 2: *Mentor, Message, and Miracles*; vol. 3: *Companions and Competitors* (New York: Anchor Bible Commentary, 1991, 1994, 2001); Hyam Maccoby, *Jesus the Pharisee* (London: SCM, 2003); Paula Frederiksen, *Jesus of Nazareth, King of the Jews: A Jewish Life and the Emergence of Christianity* (New York: Knopf, 1999); Bruce D. Chilton, *Rabbi Jesus – An Intimate Biography: The Jewish Life and Teachings That Inspired Christianity* (New York: Doubleday, 2000).

the God of Israel both has, and has come in order to share, the Holy Spirit. This is innovation as fulfilment, not discontinuity, the image of a tradition come to fruition. When in the temptations Jesus' identity as Son is tested it is to the scriptures of his tradition that Jesus appeals. In the transfiguration (9:28–36) scripture and tradition are represented in person by Moses and Elijah, with the fulfilling focus again on Jesus as the chosen Son (echoing Abraham and his son Isaac) and on his future as he makes his 'exodus' in Jerusalem (9:31). The transfiguration is a dense symbol uniting the presence of God, recapitulation of the tradition, Jesus as its embodied fulfilment, his disciples as the nucleus of its future transmission, and orientation towards the climactic events of a new Exodus. At the heart of it is literally living tradition – Moses and Elijah – in the presence of God in conversation with the present about the future.

The Last Supper has a similar combination: the re-enactment of the Exodus tradition in the Passover meal; the future orientation to the Kingdom of God; the dramatic focus on Jesus himself, his body and blood, and on the imminence of the climactic events; and the community of disciples who are commissioned to carry on this tradition ('**Do this in remembrance of me**' – 22:19), instructed in an ethos of greatness through service, and promised that they '**will sit on thrones judging the twelve tribes of Israel**' (22:30). This generation of a renewed[8] tradition which judges but does not reject the tradition it renews (22:30 makes it clear that Jesus is envisaging an Israel-centred eschaton with twelve Jewish judges – the Gentiles will be a surprise) has posed a fundamental challenge throughout Christian history in relation to Judaism. In terms of the transfiguration, the question is whether today's Christians and Jews can try to discern God's desire for them in conversation with each other as well as with Moses and Elijah.

Luke's culminating example of such intensive convergence is given in the final chapter of his Gospel. It comes after the discontinuity of the crucifixion and resurrection, and it retrospectively relates those events to God, the events of Jesus' life, the eucharist-like practice of blessing and breaking bread together, all the scriptures, the community of disciples, all nations and worship in the Temple. These strands are drawn together in a finale oriented immediately towards the coming of the Holy Spirit.

8. See 22:20 'new covenant in my blood' where new, *kaine*, means renewed, not a replacement.

This is the transformative opening up of a tradition in the aftermath of over-whelming events. The multiple opening of tomb, minds, hearts, eyes, scriptures, all nations and the future (see above Chapter 1) is yet not discontinuous or lacking in definition. The openness and transformation go with a continuity of identity that is focussed on the main subject of the events, Jesus Christ, and received in a community that, both before and after, eats, walks, reads scripture, witnesses and worships together. The gift of the Holy Spirit is promised to energise and sustain this Christ-centred identity in a new way.

After Pentecost, Jesus Christ and the Holy Spirit are decisively at the heart of the ongoing tradition whose early years are narrated by Luke in the Acts of the Apostles. *One striking feature of that story is the daring innovation that is possible beyond any precedents in the lifetime of Jesus.* This is not a conception of tradition as continuing to repeat literally the sorts of things that Jesus did. The main example is in the mission beyond Judaism to the Gentiles. Jesus largely restricted his ministry to Israel; Acts tells the story of the opening up of full membership in the church to Gentiles who have not fulfilled the conditions of entry to Judaism, such as circumcision and keeping the Torah's purity and food laws. Acts also tells of a tradition being formed not only by Jesus' disciples but also even more by new converts such as Stephen and Paul, with accompanying innovation, debate and conflict.

Which maxims, supplementing those above from Job, might distil some-thing of what Luke's Gospel and Acts offer to those shaping Christian tradition today? The following are some that have contributed to the choice of Ricoeur, Williams and Coakley as models in this chapter and to the thinking in chapters 8–10 on inter-faith scripture study, the reinvention of universities, and communities for those with learning disabilities.

- Value and learn from the Jewish Torah, along with Jewish rituals, feasts, transgenerational community, institutions, forms of prayer and worship, and scriptural interpretation.
- Continually reread the Old Testament in the light of the New Testament and vice versa, alert to the potential of figural interpretation.
- Draw on scripture as the best teacher of tradition, offering a wisdom of continuity and discontinuity.
- Figure yourself and your community into the drama of God's involvement with the world, and be open to surprises on the scale of resurrection from the dead or Peter's baptism of Cornelius.

- Since tradition is both habitable and challengeable above all from the standpoint of a future in which Jesus Christ is the final judge, rethink and renew the Christian tradition's identification of and with Jesus Christ while at the same time seeking God's future in the Spirit beyond constriction to literal repetition of what Jesus did or said.
- Let the intensive convergence of vital elements of tradition and innovation, as seen in Jesus' baptism, transfiguration, Last Supper and walk to Emmaus, inspire analogous intensities today.
- Let exemplary persons – martyrs, saints and other witnesses – be understood as living embodiments of the interpretation of scripture and tradition.
- Take advantage of overwhelming events and challenges to Christian tradition to seek renewal and transformation.

Rereading scripture, rereading tradition

Chapter 2 concluded with nine theses and ten maxims on the wisdom interpretation of scripture. In the light of the maxim above, that scripture is the best teacher of tradition, it is not surprising that, *mutatis mutandis*, an understanding of tradition can appropriate those theses and maxims. Most indeed have already figured in the two sets of maxims drawing on Job and Luke–Acts: reading for God's sake; reading theodramatically; reading Old and New Testaments together; reading for the plain sense and other senses; reading within the church; being apprenticed to saints; and reading 'in the Spirit, immersed in life, desiring God's future, and open to continually fresh rereadings in new situations' (see p. 188 above). Those can be applied both to scripture and to the texts, practices and events of tradition, with allowance for the special status of scripture.[9] I will now comment briefly on the implications for tradition of the three remaining maxims, concerning the diverse witnesses to Jesus, especially the four Gospels; dialogue with diverse others, especially 'moderns' with a bias against tradition; and rereading in love.

Four different Gospels First, there is the injunction to 'attend to all the witnesses to Jesus'. The diversity of scripture has been a major

---

9. How this specialness is defined has been a matter of great debate and division within Christianity. This is not, of course, something on which scripture itself can directly adjudicate. A wisdom approach to this tends to pay more attention to the ways scripture is actually used in tradition, worship, theology, ethics and so on than to definitions of its authority in relation to tradition. For a perceptive analysis of both the concept of authority and how scripture is used in a number of modern theologies see David H. Kelsey, *The Uses of Scripture in Recent Theology* (London: SCM, 1976).

preoccupation of biblical scholars, especially in the past two centuries.[10] The tendency has been to emphasise the variety of voices, often in tension or even contradiction, and histories of dispute, polemic and division have been discerned within and behind the texts. Interpretations from the standpoint of particular interests (such as women, Jews, heretics, the poor and marginalised) have illuminated further these texts as sites of diversity and of frequent struggles for power. There has been a similar preoccupation with the Christian tradition. Predictably, all this has stimulated counter-moves to show scripture and tradition as having coherence or unity.

For Christianity, the most critical biblical issue is the testimonies to Jesus, especially in the four Gospels. Stephen Barton sees the decision to canonise the four as a vital development in Christian tradition, and he summarises what I judge to be a convincing position:

> One of the most striking features of the history of the early church is the decision to include four gospels in the canon of Christian Scripture ... [My] main argument will be that the four gospel texts bear witness in distinctive ways to the one gospel message at the heart of which is the one person, Jesus of Nazareth. That there are four gospels standing side by side in the canon, none of which has been subordinated to another, is an invitation to recognize that the truth about Jesus to which the gospels bear witness is *irreducibly plural* without being either incoherent or completely elastic. The fourfold gospel points to the profundity of Jesus' impact on his followers, the inexhaustibility of the truth about him, and the way in which knowledge of Jesus is necessarily self-involving.[11]

Barton later sums up the motives not only of the authors of the Gospel writers but also of Old Testament authors and editors (and those who wrote improvisations on biblical books such as the *Book of Jubilees* or *Joseph and Asenath*) as being 'not to give a single, fixed account of the past, but to provide authoritative, scriptural resources to enable Israel (and subsequently the Jews) to live *from the past in the present and with a view to the future*. For this to be possible, multiple retellings and ongoing elaborations of the oral and literary inheritance were essential.'[12] This is

---

10. For a survey of various modern approaches to biblical interpretation together with accounts of specific biblical books in modern interpretation see *The Cambridge Companion to Biblical Interpretation*, ed. John Barton (Cambridge: Cambridge University Press, 1998).
11. Stephen C. Barton, 'Many Gospels, One Jesus?' in *The Cambridge Companion to Jesus*, ed. Bockmuehl, p. 170.
12. Ibid. pp. 177–8.

what I would call a wisdom interpretation both of the authorship of the Old and New Testaments and of the tradition's reception of them. The concern is for a reliability that is in the service of faithful and wise living within the tradition and orientation towards the future. That of course is vulnerable to all sorts of distortions and corruptions, but the appropriate response is to be continually alert for distortions and corruptions, yet not to expect that there is some way of arriving at an authoritative, complete and commonly agreed account from which all possibility of error, bias and subjectivity has been excluded.

Barton's conclusion stresses the positive side of the plurality of Gospels, and he uses the category of wisdom:

> [W]hat a plurality of gospels offers is a complex repetition and multiple elaboration that *intensifies and complicates*. The Jesus of whom the gospels tell is not fully known in the first encounter. We have to return again and again, not just to one gospel but to all four, and not just to the gospels but to the whole scriptural witness. And theological wisdom suggests that we will gain most out of successive encounters if we come to the gospels, not just on our own, but in good company: the good company of the communion of saints past and present, who embody in their lives and in their worship what true knowledge of Jesus, mediated by the gospels, is all about.[13]

That is a wisdom approach to the diversity of a scripture-centred tradition,[14] offering a framework and spirit in which to engage in the many tough problems the tradition faces, and encouraging continual, thoughtful rereading in a long-term community of worship, conversation and deliberation.

Reading across boundaries Next is the maxim to read in dialogue with diverse others – people, religions, cultures, arts, disciplines, media and spheres of life. The Christian warrants for this are thoroughly scriptural – God's creation of and love for the whole of creation, Jesus Christ as the wisdom of God related to all things and people, the Holy Spirit poured out 'on all flesh', the longed for 'recapitulation of all things',[15]

13. Ibid. pp. 182–3.
14. In the present work I have limited my range of reference to scripture, tradition and contemporary life in attempting to search out the riches of a few chosen texts and topics. The approach is mostly through particular examples which invite analogous thinking in relation to other examples rather than through an attempt at comprehensive coverage.
15. For an interpretation of this idea from the Letter to the Ephesians with regard to Jews and others, see David F. Ford, 'A Messiah for the Third Millennium', *Modern Theology* 16, no. 1 (January 2000), pp. 75–90.

and so on. But, because Christian scripture only covers a little of Christian history, the subsequent tradition, during which most of the Christian experience of diverse others has taken place, is especially important in this regard. The Bible is more adequate in giving an account of the key elements of Christian identity than it is in giving direct guidance about which are appropriate transformations of that identity in new situations around the world century after century.

In a world where Christians are present in every region and sphere of life, and where there is unprecedented interaction across geographical, cultural, religious, disciplinary and other boundaries, one of the most urgent tasks of Christian thought is to take dialogues across such boundaries seriously. Each of the three case studies in chapters 8–10 sharply raises boundary issues and, correlative with them, questions of identities in transformation. How might Judaism, Christianity and Islam engage in dialogue that both takes their traditional core identities seriously and yet is peacemaking? How might twenty-first-century universities be true to the best in their religious origins and be places where wisdom is pursued, as well as knowledge and know-how? How might the Gospel of John and the experience of friendship with people having severe learning difficulties illuminate each other?

Those are some of the leading questions faced in chapters 8–10, and each of them involves what has perhaps been the most prominent and widespread debate about tradition in recent centuries: what does modernity mean for tradition? The questioning of tradition, both its general authority and its specific contents, has been one of the distinguishing marks of Western thought and culture in recent centuries. The diverse others with whom one might have to engage in interpreting the Christian tradition today include those who belong to a modern tradition (though that is not their favourite self-designation) of critically and radically questioning premodern tradition – its authority, reliability, beneficial effects, continuity, coherence and relevance. For many, critique and rejection of tradition is one of the main benefits brought by modernity. In their sense, when speaking of Christianity, tradition includes the Bible as a central element. So all that is said in chapters 1–7 about scripture is relevant, and perhaps the most important lesson from that is the wisdom to be gained from appreciating the different 'regimes of reading', premodern, modern and late modern, as discussed in chapter 2 above. The dialogue between *lectio divina*, scholasticism, humanism, historical critical and other approaches (literary, sociological, psychological, political, feminist, poststructuralist, and so on) and hermeneutics is a vital arena for wisdom-seeking with regard to other elements of the tradition besides scripture.[16] There is no one 'answer' to multiple modern critiques of Christian tradition: the critical questions need to be taken one by one and assessed. But the resources that enable self-critique (such as Job and Jesus) also help the Christian tradition question back and assess modernity. In the final three chapters both scriptural reasoning and contemporary universities give examples of such mutual critique.

Rereading in love The final maxim is: 'Let us reread in love'. The Christian tradition, as Barton says, invites readers to share the company of the whole communion of saints, those who people the Old and New Testaments and those who have been the Bible's most inspired and receptive readers over the centuries and around the world today. To receive their readings, and the testimonies to their lives, as offerings of love is the deepest secret of the wisdom of the tradition. In recognition of this, the main focus of the third case study is on Jean Vanier's reading of John's Gospel in relation to the L'Arche communities to which he has dedicated his life.

Christian teaching about love is not confined to its own community or even those friendly towards it; it includes love of enemies too. What might it mean to read Christian scripture and tradition through the eyes of its unsympathetic or hostile interpreters, or even its enemies? The engagement with other faiths, especially Judaism and Islam, may allow this to happen to some extent; so does participation in a university tradition that historically had to struggle for its academic freedom and integrity against a coercive imposition of Christianity.

The overriding Christian maxim about love is to love God with all one's heart, mind, soul and strength. The prime setting for reading is 'before God'. To reread in love means above all rereading in love for God, and the place where this happens most explicitly is in prayer and worship, to which we now turn.

Wisdom in worship: discerning who God is

Scripture and tradition come together most explicitly, intensively and influentially in prayer and worship. Worship is a performance of the two

---

16. See the discussion of Ricoeur on readings of Exodus 3:14 below.

together that helps shape the life of the present community in relation to God, each other and the world. Christian worship at its best has something of that fruitful combination in the Spirit of key elements that have been seen in the book of Job, the Prologue of John, Paul's First Letter to the Corinthians and Luke's accounts of Jesus' baptism, transfiguration, exultation, Last Supper and walk to Emmaus: deep engagement with scripture and tradition; the centrality of the Father's relationship to Jesus in the Spirit; crying out to God; loving God for God's sake; remembering the events of Jesus' life and identifying with him in his death and resurrection; commitment and compassion in community; and orientation to God's future, which includes the future of all people and all creation.

Week by week around the world hundreds of millions of people take part in Christian worship in congregations. How should they pray? Why? How often? With whom? Where? Who leads it and how are they to train and prepare? Which parts of scripture should be read or chanted? Should a set liturgy be used or not? If a liturgy is used, what is an acceptable range of improvisation on it? What is the role and significance of the eucharist? What part should singing and music play? What about intercession, petition, confession? If there is a sermon or homily, who should give it, what should it be on, and how long should it be? How take into account the local culture, languages, concerns? How provide for children, young people, those with disabilities, singles, married, well-educated, those with little education, old people? What funding is needed and how is it to be gathered? What relation does this worship have to other activities and spheres of life? What are the conditions for full participation? What theology informs it and is it appropriate? Do some people exercise authority and power in damaging ways? What is the appropriate location for discussing and deciding upon such matters? What structures are needed to enable worship to be sustained over years and generations? How might rising generations best be taught to worship?

For those praying alone some of the questions may not be relevant, but yet the basic ones remain, asking how, why, how often, where, which scriptures, what balance of praise, thanks, confession, intercession and petition, which modes of learning, and what relation to the rest of life.

The questions could go on. The purpose in raising them is not to give answers, which will of course vary widely in different traditions and situations. *The main point is that a good deal of wisdom is needed to sustain a worship tradition. It is indeed a prime example of Christian wisdom.* To shape

worship well requires an understanding of many things, and all in relation to God. It relates to scripture and tradition; church and world;
individual and community; personal and public; leading and following;
body, mind and imagination; past, present and future; silence, speech
and music; the oral and the written; teaching and learning; timing and
movement; clothing and gesture; money and buildings; the immediate
and the long term; and a vast number of obvious and subtle signs. These
elements need to be understood in such a way as to bring them all
together in an event among a specific group of people at a set time.
That calls for an array of judgements and decisions. Many of these are
made implicitly by deciding to follow a particular tradition, so that key
decisions have been taken, often over a long period of time and centuries
earlier, by that tradition. But even in a form of traditional worship that
insists on as exact a repetition of the set form as possible there is scope for
choice, improvisation and initiative in leading and following.

Graham Hughes' reflections on why he chooses 'meaning', with its
vast range of reference (from entries in dictionaries to 'the meaning of
life'), as a key term through which to approach worship might also
support the use of 'wisdom'.

> Yet it does seem to me that [meaning] *is* the word, in all its breadth and
> complexity, which we want – for the reason that the subject matter in
> which we are interested, worship, itself contains this great range of
> senses and references. Sometimes the question a worshipper asks is
> with respect to our most sharply defined sort of meaning: that of the
> preacher's words or concerning the arcane language of the prayers. On
> other occasions it will be more equivocal: why does the priest move
> to this place in the sanctuary for this part of the liturgy? And on yet
> other occasions the question of meaning will be as large as the
> worshipper's life – what would it mean for her to try to live in the
> way suggested. At some points what is at stake perhaps has more to do
> with what we might call 'disposition' or 'ambience' or 'feeling' – for
> example the effects of the architecture, or the way in which the space is
> lit, or the style and arrangement of the furnishings. The music will
> always have been of central importance. And hardly less significant will
> have been the style, the manner, the bearing or the leader(s) – whether
> this communicated distance, officialdom, ritual propriety or pastoral
> warmth; or perhaps, at an opposite extreme, informality and
> conviviality. In the end, each of these things will have contributed
> directly to the meaning – and the 'meaningfulness' or otherwise – of
> the event. Enveloping all of these – that is, on its largest and most

daunting scale – is the question whether 'God', as represented in the Judaeo-Christian tradition, can 'mean' anything for people living in our thoroughly secularised age. All these angles are held within the question of 'the meaning of worship'.[17]

Christian wisdom is concerned with a similar breadth of questions and with the intellectual, aesthetic and practical judgements that contribute to worship and, especially, shape its performance today. With regard to the present chapter, the key question will be about the truth and wisdom of identifying God as Trinity. *Who is God?*

God as Trinity: scriptural, classical, contemporary

The doctrine of the Trinity might be seen as the most concentrated distillation of Christian wisdom. That Christian worship in all its main traditions names 'one God, Father, Son and Holy Spirit' is its most distinctive feature in comparison with its nearest monotheistic neighbours, Judaism and Islam. The two central Christian innovations in relation to Judaism, Jesus as Messiah (Christ) and the outpouring of the Holy Spirit, were part of Christian teaching, baptism, worship and scriptural interpretation for centuries before the Trinity was defined as a doctrine. To be doctrinally explicit in this way was a huge step for a faith that insisted on its continuity with Judaism and with the testimony of the Jewish scriptures to God.

I have written at some length elsewhere about this 'Trinitarian revolution' and its relation to worship.[18] There are several key elements: discerning the 'grammar of God' in scripture and worship; various rationales for the doctrine of the Trinity; and the renewal of the doctrine in the past century.

The Trinitarian 'grammar' might be discerned in the narrative testimonies of scripture. Jesus' baptism has the Father acknowledging his Son as the Spirit comes upon him, and the baptismal formula in the final chapter of Matthew's Gospel is 'in the name of the Father and of the Son and of the Holy Spirit' (Matt. 28:19). The resurrection is a 'God-sized' event – the Father raising the Son in the power of the Spirit, the Son as the

---

17. Graham Hughes, *Worship as Meaning: A Liturgical Theology for Late Modernity* (Cambridge: Cambridge University Press, 2003), pp. 4ff.
18. See David F. Ford and Daniel W. Hardy, *Living in Praise: Worshipping and Knowing God* (London: Darton, Longman and Todd, 2005), chapters 4 and 7; also David F. Ford, *Self and Salvation: Being Transformed* (Cambridge: Cambridge University Press, 1999), chapters 1, 3, 5, 6, 7, 8.

content of the Father's act, and the sharing of it and in it through the Spirit. The three climactic events of the death of Jesus, the resurrection of Jesus and Pentecost might be seen as having a similar grammar – the cross centred on the crucified Son, the resurrection on the act of the Father in raising the Son, and Pentecost on the outpouring of the Holy Spirit.

Paul and John, the most influential New Testament contributors to the development of the doctrine of the Trinity, both have numerous relevant passages, of which I will take one from each. Paul's account of Christian prayer in Romans 8 interweaves Father, Son and Spirit in ways that both make each intrinsic to who God is and also resist any simple identification of one with the other.

> Romans 8:14–17 [14]For all who are led by the Spirit of God are children of God. [15]For you did not receive a spirit of slavery to fall back into fear, but you have received a spirit of adoption. When we cry, 'Abba! Father!' [16]it is that very Spirit bearing witness with our spirit that we are children of God, [17]and if children, then heirs, heirs of God and joint heirs with Christ – if, in fact, we suffer with him so that we may also be glorified with him.
>
> 8:26–28 [26]Likewise the Spirit helps us in our weakness; for we do not know how to pray as we ought, but that very Spirit intercedes with sighs too deep for words. [27]And God, who searches the heart, knows what is the mind of the Spirit, because the Spirit intercedes for the saints according to the will of God. [28]We know that all things work together for good for those who love God, who are called according to his purpose.

That cry-centred description of the wisdom of Christian prayer will be discussed further below in relation to Sarah Coakley's interpretation of it.

Jesus' farewell discourses in John's Gospel (chapters 13–17) combine statements about the sending of the Spirit of truth, the παράκλητος (advocate, comforter, strengthener, helper, one who can be cried out to and will come alongside to help), with statements of the unity of Father and Son – and the latter is a unity of love and of glory (**'the glory which I had with you before the world began'** – 17:5) that is open to embrace others who are consecrated by the truth.

> John 17:20–23 [20]'I ask not only on behalf of these, but also on behalf of those who will believe in me through their word, [21]that they may all be one. As you, Father, are in me and I am in you, may they also be in us, so

that the world may believe that you have sent me. [22]The glory that you have given me I have given them, so that they may be one, as we are one, [23] I in them and you in me, that they may become completely one, so that the world may know that you have sent me and have loved them even as you have loved me.

Again the context is that of prayer. The cumulative picture of these discourses together with the Prologue's identification of Jesus the Word with God and the resurrection stories of Jesus breathing the Holy Spirit into his disciples is of elements open to Trinitarian developments.

More general considerations point in the same direction. As Christian worship developed in continuity with Jewish scriptures and traditions (with their strong concern about idolatry) and also shaped by texts such as Romans and John's Gospel in the setting of a pagan world with many gods, the negative concern to avoid idolatry also gives a rationale for the doctrine of the Trinity. Three basic ways to identify God wrongly are to absolutise one of the three in separation from the others: a transcendent Creator who is not involved in history; or a divine human being; or an immanent presence or principle of some sort. The negative rule is that no one member of the Trinity should be conceived apart from interrelation with the other two.[19] The positive side of that might be seen as a desire to do justice simultaneously to three essential dimensions of transcendence – transcending creation as its maker 'from nothing', the ethical transcendence of love embodied within history, and the eschatological transcendence of God's future anticipated now in the Spirit.

It is not that the eventual doctrine of the Trinity is a necessary deduction from any New Testament text or from concern to avoid idolatry or from reflections on the dimensions of transcendence. Rather, a profound

19. See Ford and Hardy, *Living in Praise*, pp. 69–70: 'The Trinitarian pattern was acted out in baptism and worship long before it became a doctrine. As a doctrine, it was partly worked out to correct unacceptable distinctions and emphases. Perhaps the most helpful way of seeing its negative function (vital both in worship and the whole Roman and Hellenistic religious context) is as a guard against various forms of idolatry. The idol could be a transcendent God who is not really free to take a personal part in history; or a divine human being who himself receives all worship; or a God who is within human beings or in some other way immanent in the world. Those three basic ways of absolutising one dimension of the Christian God roughly correspond to the Father, Son and Holy Spirit. Taken as a unity, the Trinity continually dispels illusions and fantasies about God. It applies a corrective to any one type of language, whether talk about the transcendence of God in analogies, or sacramental and historical accounts of God's character and presence, or subjective, experiential witness to the immediacy of God. So the Trinity is a comprehensive "negative way", refusing to let one rest in any image of God. It offers a ground rule: never conceive the Father apart from the Son and Holy Spirit, or the Son without Father and Spirit, or the Spirit without Father and Son.'

question about the identification of God in the aftermath of the death and resurrection of Jesus and the giving of the Holy Spirit insists on an answer. The 'I am who I am', 'I will be who I will be' of Exodus 3:14 has had a new self-identification added besides the 'God of Abraham, Isaac and Jacob': the God of Jesus Christ with the eschatological gift of the Spirit. The effort to do justice to this new event stretches previous conceptions of God with an optative and interrogative urgency. But this stretching happens in a thoroughly historical way, through the development of forms of baptism, prayer and worship, catechesis, scriptural interpretation, arguments and theological positions. The critical decision point is the Council of Nicea in AD 325, when Jesus Christ is affirmed as 'of one substance' with the Father (see below on Rowan Williams). But beyond that there is the Council of Constantinople in AD 381 when the Holy Spirit is also affirmed as of one substance with the Son and the Spirit (see below on Sarah Coakley). Neither of these affirmations can be seen in retrospect as inevitable, and they were certainly not seen as such by their contemporaries. *They were discernments of a wisdom that presupposed not only a deep involvement with scripture, tradition, prayer and worship but also a rigour of thought and a Job-like openness to questioning and going beyond tradition in order to be true to God.*

It is just this character of the doctrine of the Trinity (and in this it is no different from any other doctrine) as a wisdom worked out before God in the complexities and ambiguities of history that calls for it to be rethought continually if it is to be held wisely. In recent decades it has been as much in contention as ever. Indeed, one of the striking features of the period from 1918 to the present (in contrast to the previous hundred years) is the extraordinary fascination exercised by the Trinity on Christians from most parts of the church and with varied key concerns – through all the traditional Christian churches, Pentecostals, feminists, liberation theologians, Asians, Africans, Europeans, North and South Americans, Australians, New Zealanders, ecumenists, conservative evangelicals, philosophical theologians, historical theologians, political theologians, inter-faith theologians and theologians working through the arts, the natural sciences and the human sciences.[20]

20. See *The Modern Theologians: An Introduction to Christian Theology since 1918*, ed. David F. Ford with Rachel Muers, 3rd edn (Oxford and New York: Basil Blackwell, 2005), *passim*.

God as Trinity: critical discernments on being, incarnation and the Holy Spirit

What, then, does it mean to rethink the Trinity wisely today? For some it has meant reworking the whole doctrine, but here I want to draw attention to three quite brief but rich contributions which display something of a prophetic wisdom. They are chosen to take soundings in three key issues: God's being and the relation of Hebraic to Hellenic wisdom; the divinity of Jesus Christ; and the divinity of the Holy Spirit.

God and being; Hebraic and Hellenic; *lectio* and *quaestio*; worship and philosophy: Paul Ricoeur on Exodus 3:14

For over fifteen hundred years the impact of what Ricoeur calls the 'event that consisted in conjoining God and Being'[21] shaped the conception of reality in Christianity, Judaism and Islam, with roots deep in the composition and translations of the Hebrew scriptures. Recently that tradition has been fundamentally challenged both from within Jewish, Christian and Islamic thought and from outside, through philosophers such as Martin Heidegger. As Ricoeur makes clear, a great deal is at stake: the relation of the Hebraic to the Hellenic, and of philosophy to scripture, theology and worship; the significance of centuries of vigorous interpretation of scripture and thinking about God both as Trinity and in philosophical terms; the way Christianity is related to Judaism and the God of Jewish scriptures, which are also Christianity's Old Testament; and the question as to whether to be content with Heidegger's 'expulsion

---

21. Paul Ricoeur, 'From Interpretation to Translation' in *Thinking Biblically: Exegetical and Hermeneutical Studies*, by André LaCocque and Paul Ricoeur (Chicago and London: University of Chicago Press, 1998), p. 356. See in the opening paragraph of his essay: 'because the LXX (Septuagint) translated [Exodus] 3.14 as *ego eimi ho on*, and the Latins by *sum qui sum*, Exodus 3.14 was to exercise on all of Western thought the influence whose breadth and depth I shall refer to below. The Greek translation has to be considered a veritable event in thinking. The semantic field of the Hebrew verb *hyh* found itself linked in an enduring manner to that of the Greek verb *einai*, then to the Latin verb *esse*, where these verbs bring into the field of translation a broad conceptual history, stemming principally from the philosophies of Plato and Aristotle, and therefore from modes of thought that antedate the translation of the LXX. This history of meaning continued on, interconnected with that of the Hebrew and Christian Bibles, through the Greek and Latin fathers, then by way of the age of Scholasticism and its giants (Bonaventure, Thomas Aquinas, Duns Scotus), to include even Descartes and the Cartesians, up to Kant and beyond; that is, until it reaches us, readers of the Bible, situated at the end of this tumultuous history of the relationship between God and Being', p. 331. For a recent discussion of Aquinas that is congenial to Ricoeur's position and (not least through its use of wisdom as an integrating concept and its contemplative focus on God for God's sake) also to my own, see Matthew Levering, *Scripture and Metaphysics: Aquinas and the Renewal of Trinitarian Theology* (Oxford: Blackwell, 2004).

of Judaism and Christianity from the sphere of Western culture',[22] his effective marginalisation of them in an increasingly secularised context.

Into this millennia-long debate Ricoeur inserts his essay on Exodus 3:14, which I read as a contribution of prophetic wisdom. It is exemplary both in his range of relevant reference and in the quality of perception and judgement that he brings to the material. It is prophetic in addressing the issues listed in the previous paragraph in such a way as to open a wise way forward.

Ricoeur's breadth of reference is required by the topic (and the other two examples discussed below reach towards a somewhat similar range). He engages with classical Greek philosophers, Philo, Augustine, Pseudo-Dionysius, leading medieval thinkers, and modern and late modern Western thought – Christian, Jewish and secular. He also examines Exodus 3:14 with exegetical precision, both in its Hebrew form and in the long history of its translation and reception. Throughout, his readings are simultaneously critical and generous, and most critical when identifying those (for example, Heidegger in his condescending approach to Christian theology, or those who accuse thinkers such as Aquinas of advocating an 'ontotheology' that confuses God and Being) whose interpretations, in the interests of furthering their own theses, are insufficiently rigorous or generous in the quality of their attention to others.

Of special relevance to this chapter's concern with tradition, God and worship are three of his judgements.

The first is his recognition of the need to preserve the classical Christian tradition's balance between, on the one hand, the affirmative way of saying positive things about God through the use of analogies within creation, and, on the other hand, the negative or apophatic way of recognising the radical inadequacy of all affirmations.[23]

The second is his insistence, for the maintenance of this balance, on the centrality of biblical interpretation and the naming of God in prayer

22. Ricoeur, 'From Interpretation to Translation', p. 357; see p. 359 on the possibility of 'a new pact with Western reason'.
23. On Augustine's achievement of a wise balance he says (ibid. pp. 346–7): 'However it is not necessary to overemphasise the opposition of this affirmative and this apophatic theology. The way of eminence, marked by use of analogy, does not take place without the negation of lower-order attributes, and the apophatic way, with its battery of negations, distinguishes itself from a purely privative unknowing only if it continues to be a kind of overthrown affirmation.' See ibid. p. 350, on 'the subtle equilibrium between ontologism and apophatism' that Aquinas inherited.

and worship. His striking verdict on leading medieval scholastic Christian theologians (Aquinas, Scotus) is that

> the most independent theological speculation, on the epistemological
> plane of argumentation, with regard to biblical interpretation
> continued to be intimately bound to this interpretation as regards its
> inquiry into the concept of Being, as though the question *quid est?* (what
> is God?) were still driven by the question *qui est?* (who is God?), where
> the personal pronoun attests to the deep kinship, for Christian
> understanding, between the *quaestio* and *lectio divina*. In this sense, the
> Christianization of Hellenism is secretly more powerful than the
> Hellenization of Christianity.[24]

Closely allied to this is his observation that medieval thinkers always related their discourse about God as One with Trinitarian discourse, the naming of God that was central to Christian worship.

Yet the 'secrecy' in that 'secretly more powerful than …' risks misconstrual and losing the opportunity for constant renewal through rereading scripture. Ricoeur notes the dangers of a logical, dialectical and strongly philosophical method in theology (the *quaestio*) becoming divorced from 'the hermeneutic interpretation of the biblical text, governed by its *lectio* and the order that the text imposes'.[25] His own constructive way forward is to set both the monastic *lectio* and the scholastic *quaestio* in a longer history of readings of scripture. As described in my terms in chapter 2 above, he draws on resources from the other main 'regimes of reading' in the Western academy: the humanist return to original languages and sources; the historical critical probing of the archaeology of the text and its original context (Ricoeur's essay follows and is in dialogue with André LaCocque's historical critical essay on Exodus 3:14) and a hermeneutics that takes account of both the history of readings and the text's present significance.

The third judgement is that, for all the danger of losing sight of 'the order that the text imposes', it is also unwise to fail to bring philosophical rationality into engagement with the text of scripture. The succession of regimes of reading testifies to the continual fruitfulness of this. Ricoeur's critiques of some ontological readings of Exodus 3:14 are balanced by an

---

24. Ibid. p. 348. For a similar point drawing attention to the significance of worship and prayer, see p. 349 on Anselm's ontological argument.
25. Ibid. p. 348.

emphasis on 'certain features of our text, which, despite the quasi obses-
sive distrust of exegetes as regards what to them seems to be only a
speculative abstraction, give rise to a perplexity of such a nature as to
make, if not legitimate, at least plausible, the so-called ontological reading'.[26] Beyond such cautious claims he also vigorously confronts those
Jewish and Christian thinkers who 'attempt to think God apart from
being',[27] and who use concepts such as redemption, ethics, gift and love
to do so. His main worries are that they risk 'reinforcing the current
vogue for irrationalism'[28] and consenting to marginalisation in
Western culture. But he also challenges them to go deeper into
Exodus 3:14 both in its relation to Jewish and Christian scriptures
(notably Deuteronomy and John's Gospel) and in its conception of
'being', which in Greek, Latin, German, French and English cries out
for the use of the verb 'to be' and its cognates, and is not done justice to
without them. 'Why not say that the Hebrews thought being in a new
way?' 'Ehyeh Aser Ehyeh continues to give rise to thought, at the
bounds of every translation.'[29]

Ricoeur's tracing of the meanings of Exodus 3:14 (which could be
elaborated upon and supported extensively by reference to his other
writings[30]) offers a multifaceted discernment of how God might be
appropriately named and conceptualised through that verse by drawing
on Hebraic and Hellenic resources. *The wisdom is in the way he differentiates, interrelates and rebalances several pairs of elements: Exodus 3:14 in its
original language and context in conjunction with the history of its translations
and interpretations; biblical interpretation with theology; theology with philosophy; Judaism with Christianity; Old Testament with New Testament;
Christianity with Western culture. All this is in the service of rethinking God
in such a way as simultaneously to do justice to past thought and worship, to
address current issues prophetically, and to open the tradition up to yet further
development: in short, the intellectual dimension of learning to live in the Spirit
today.*

26. Ibid. p. 332.   27. Ibid. p. 358.   28. Ibid. p. 359.   29. Ibid. pp. 360, 361.
30. See Paul Ricoeur, *Symbolism of Evil* (Uckfield: Beacon Press, 1986); *Figuring the Sacred:
Religion, Narrative and the Imagination*, trans. David Pellauer (Minneapolis: Augsburg, 1995);
Essays on Biblical Interpretation (Minneapolis: Fortress, 1980); *Time and Narrative*, vols. 1–3,
trans. Kathleen Blamey, Kathleen McLaughlin and David Pellauer (Chicago: University
of Chicago Press, 1990); *Oneself as Another*, trans. Kathleen Blamey (Chicago: University of
Chicago Press, 1992); *Memory, History, Forgetting*, trans. Kathleen Blamey and David Pellauer
(Chicago: University of Chicago Press, 2004).

Innovation, incarnation and the intimate otherness of God:
Rowan Williams on Arius and Athanasius

In the 'Postscript (Theological)' to his book on Arius,[31] Rowan Williams reflects on contemporary lessons that might be drawn from his account of the Christian controversies surrounding the denial by Arius of fully divine status to Jesus Christ. The book carefully follows the currents of fourth-century imperial and church history and shows how theological and philosophical positions were worked out in the midst of them.

It is a messy, conflictual story, complex in events and in thought, and offers a wisdom on the divinity of Jesus Christ that is more explicitly immersed in the contingencies of history than Ricoeur's discussion of God and being in relation to Exodus 3:14. Ricoeur largely focusses on 'events of thought'; here, as is appropriate to a controversy about incarnation, the thought is involved with political and institutional events and clashes of opponents who mobilise temporal as well as spiritual and intellectual power. Some of the philosophical issues dealt with by Ricoeur figure in the Arian controversy too, but largely Williams' account turns on the interpretation in their historical context of scripture, liturgy and traditional doctrinal language. Ricoeur concentrates mainly on the unity of God and God as Creator, and his reference to the Trinity is largely to differentiate the 'who' (*qui est*) of the Christian God from the 'what' (*quid est*) of God's being. Williams explores the central 'scandal' of the Trinity, the incarnation of God in Jesus Christ, rereading the Arian controversy in the light of the intervening centuries, and trying to discern its significance now. Neither Ricoeur nor Williams sees faithfulness to scriptural and theological truth being maintained simply by repeating past formulae, and both give accounts of innovations in how God is identified. Ricoeur's are about new readings of Exodus 3:14 in different linguistic, intellectual and cultural settings; Williams pays some attention to those but mainly examines situations where public, institutional and political issues are also at stake – his main parallel to Athanasius and the champions of Nicene orthodoxy is found in Karl Barth, Dietrich Bonhoeffer and others who stood for the Barmen Declaration against the 'German Christian' supporters of the Nazis in the 1930s, with Emanuel Hirsch a very distant parallel to Arius.

---

31. Rowan Williams, *Arius: Heresy and Tradition*, 2nd edn (London: Darton, Longman and Todd, 1987), pp. 233–45.

One of the most striking conclusions of Williams is that Arius, despite some conceptual innovations in the interests of clarity and consistency, was basically a conservative, wanting to repeat the past. Athanasius and others who took up Arius' challenge were seeking new formulations that might

> do justice not only to the requirements of intellectual clarity but to the
> wholeness of the worshipping and reflecting experience of the Church.
> The doctrinal debate of the fourth century is thus in considerable
> measure about how the Church is to become intellectually self-aware
> and to move from a 'theology of repetition' to something more
> exploratory and constructive. Athanasius' task is to show how the
> break in continuity generally felt to be involved in the credal *homoousios*
> [the term used by the Council of Nicea for the unity of being or
> substance between God the Father and Jesus Christ] is a necessary
> moment in the deeper understanding and securing of tradition; more
> yet, it is to persuade Christians that strict adherence to archaic and
> 'neutral' terms alone is in fact a potential betrayal of the historic faith.
> The Church's theology begins in the language of worship, which
> rightly conserves metaphors and titles that are both ancient and
> ambiguous; but it does not stop there. The openness, the 'impropriety',
> the *play* of liturgical imagery is anchored to a specific set of
> commitments as to the limits and defining conditions within which
> the believing life is lived, and the metaphorical or narrative beginnings
> of theological reflection necessarily generate new attempts to
> characterise those defining conditions ... Although the radical words
> of Nicaea became in turn a new set of formulae to be defended
> (intelligently or unintelligently), the actual history of the Church
> in the succeeding centuries shows that some kind of doctrinal
> hermeneutics had come to stay; continuity was something that had to
> be re-imagined and recreated at each point of crisis.[32]

That has much in common with the prophetic wisdom of Job and Jesus as described in previous chapters, especially the re-imagining and re-creating of continuity at each point of crisis. It is distilled from complex historical developments, and it invites, as Williams himself shows, application in analogous situations: 'Barmen demanded not a mindless confessional conservatism (though some caricatured its tone in just such terms), but a re-engagement with authentic theology: a "making difficult" of a gospel buried under the familiarities of folk piety.'[33] Williams'

---

32. Ibid. pp. 235–7.   33. Ibid. p. 237.

prophetic discernment is not just directed against theologies of repetition. It also reaches back to the Bible, from which questions are raised about Athanasius' triumphalist, unscrupulous and possibly brutal way of championing his cause.[34] Learning to live in the Spirit in the church is not only about being theologically right and discerning appropriate doctrinal innovation; it is also about the spirit in which controversy is carried on, and about reflecting in one's exercise or acceptance of authority a vulnerability that corresponds to the centrality of the cross of Christ.[35]

At the heart of his theological reflection is Williams' discernment of the key insight in Athanasius' affirmation of Jesus Christ's full divinity. This insight is intrinsically rich and has ramifying consequences for teachings about God, creation, humanity, sin, salvation, church and eschatology,[36] but at its heart is the perception of the logic of incarnation.

> [W]hat matters theologically is not what God 'can' do in the abstract, but what is appropriate to the reality of the human condition. The only *decisive* redemption – as opposed to continual divine acts of grace or pardon – is the transfiguration of the human condition from within, the union of grace with the body, as Athanasius puts it. The argument returns to the point of the absolute newness and difference of redeemed humanity; *for this newness to make sense, we must suppose a critical rupture in the continuities of the world; for this, God alone is adequate – yet God acting upon us not 'from outside', but in union with human flesh.*[37]

The implications of this are illustrated in several ways, two of which are of special interest here. First, there is the change in how affirmative and negative (apophatic) ways in theology and prayer are related.[38] Williams is here in line with Ricoeur but explores more deeply the specifically theological rationale. He says of the apophatic theology of the Cappadocian fathers, Victorinus, Pseudo-Dionysius, Maximus the Confessor, Thomas Aquinas and John of the Cross, that

---

34. Ibid. p. 239.
35. See ibid. p. 239: 'Theologically speaking, an appeal to the Church's charter of foundation in the saving act of God, rooted in the eternal act of God, can never be made without the deepest moral ambiguities, unless it involves an awareness of the *mode* of that saving act as intrinsic to its authoritative quality and as requiring its own kind of obedience. That is to say, the God who works in *disponibilité*, vulnerability and mortality is not to be "obeyed" by the exercise *or* the acceptance of an ecclesial authority that pretends to overcome those limits.'
36. All of these topics figure in Williams' discussion, which might be seen as doing systematic theology in a wisdom mode.
37. Ibid. pp. 240–1, my italics.
38. For a fuller discussion of this that sets it in the context of the whole history of faith in Jesus see Rowan Williams, 'A History of Faith in Jesus' in *The Cambridge Companion to Jesus*, ed. Bockmuehl, pp. 220–36. This is especially relevant to the theme of desire in chapter 5 above.

it is no less serious in its negativity than Arius or Plotinus. The crucial difference, however, is that this energy of conceptual negation is bound up with a sense of intimate involvement in the life of God, rather than of absolute disjunction. The disjunction *is* there, in the fact that created sharing in the life of the divine is precisely a ceaseless growing into what is always and already greater and does not itself either grow or diminish: the fulness of the divine eludes us because it is further 'back' than our furthest and remotest origins, and beyond all imaginable futures. Yet this is a disjunction of a different kind from that envisaged by Plotinus, for instance, where, however fully we become *nous*, the One remains an inaccessible other, over against us, except in those fleeting moments of something like dissolution when we drop into its depths. Set this beside Gregory of Nyssa's or Augustine's account of *a steady and endless enlarging of the heart through union in prayer and virtue with the Word, which is also a steady and endless growth in knowledge of the Father,* and you can perhaps see the fundamental difference made by Nicea.[39]

That places the 'negative way' within a continual, prayer-centred process of learning to live in the Spirit.

Second, there are the consequences of this for the understanding of God as Trinity.

Because [God's] activity and life are self-differentiating, a pattern of initiating gift, perfect response, and the distinct and 'new' energy that is the harmony of these two movements, created difference, otherness, multiplicity, may find place in God. If the life of God is eternally in response as well as initiating, then created response is not necessarily 'external' to God but somehow capable of being attuned to and caught up in God's own movement in and to himself.[40]

Here responsive living in the Spirit, grounded in incarnation, is embraced within the dynamics of Trinitarian life. Williams also touches lightly on the 'second difference' in God, that of the Holy Spirit, for a fuller exploration of which I turn to Sarah Coakley.

39. Williams, *Arius*, pp. 242–3, my italics.
40. Ibid. p. 243. Williams goes on to quote Donald MacKinnon's conception of Jesus transcribing divine receptivity into history, made possible by a divine relation to time such as is misunderstood if the God so related is not seen as triune. This leads into a reflection on how Nicene Christianity 'does something to secure a certain seriousness about the conditions of human history' (p. 244), a seriousness which I have tried throughout this book to maintain in the way wisdom is understood.

God the Holy Spirit: Sarah Coakley on Romans 8, prayer, desire
and incorporative or contemplative Trinitarianism

Why 'hypostatise' the Holy Spirit as a distinct third member of the
Trinity? Sarah Coakley, in her essay on 'Why Three? Some Further
Reflections on the Origins of the Doctrine of the Trinity',[41] tackles the
historical and theological deconstruction of the doctrine of the Trinity
attempted by Maurice Wiles. One of his main arguments is that the
mesmeric hold of the triadic baptismal formula, together with a *lex orandi*
('law of prayer') that influenced early Christian doctrine out of line with
what was warranted by scripture, experience or reason, led the church
into an illogical and inappropriate affirmation of the distinguishable
divinity of the Holy Spirit.

Coakley sees Wiles' critique of the hypostatisation of the Spirit as so
effective that most recent doctrines of the Trinity fail to provide adequate
answers to it. She analyses five types of modern Trinitarianism with
regard to their conceptions of the Spirit. First is 'Dismantling the
Trinity: why "hypostatize" the Spirit at all?'[42] Second is 'The "economic"
Trinity is the "immanent" Trinity: the Spirit as completer and commu-
nicator of revelation'.[43] Third is 'The Trinity construed from reflection
on the death of Christ: the Spirit as the uniting bond between Father and
Son'.[44] Fourth is 'The Trinity as prototype of persons-in-relation'.[45]
These four types are found wanting in different ways as regards the
Spirit, and in the rest of the article Coakley advocates her distinctive
version of the fifth: 'The Holy Spirit as a means of incorporation into
the trinitarian life of God'.[46]

At the heart of her case for the incorporative type is Romans 8:9–30,
which I called above Paul's cry-centred description of the wisdom of
Christian prayer. Here the Spirit is not just extending the revelation of
Christ or enabling recognition of him but is 'actually catching up and
incorporating the created realm into the life of God (or rather "the
redeemed life of sonship", to use Pauline terminology)'.[47] She weaves
many other strands into her argument. She argues from the implicit logic

41. In *The Making and Remaking of Christian Doctrine: Essays in Honour of Maurice Wiles*, ed.
Sarah Coakley and David Pailin (Oxford: Clarendon Press, 1993).
42. Ibid. pp. 32–3, including Wiles, Geoffrey Lampe, James Mackey and Schleiermacher.
43. Ibid. pp. 33–4, including Karl Barth, Karl Rahner, Paul Tillich and David Brown.
44. Ibid. pp. 34–5, including Jürgen Moltmann and Hans Urs von Balthasar.
45. Ibid. pp. 35–6, including John Zizioulas and Colin Gunton.
46. Ibid. pp. 36ff., including, with various reservations, Michael Ramsey, von Balthasar,
Vladimir Lossky and Yves Congar.
47. Ibid. p. 36.

of eucharistic worship and from Luke's account of Jesus' baptism and his theology of the Spirit in the Acts of the Apostles. She challenges Wiles' reading of the *lex orandi* and of pneumatology in the second and third centuries, drawing on Irenaeus, Tertullian and Origen among others. She explains why the Spirit was seen as dangerously unmanageable through its association with ecstasy, visions, prophecy, sectarianism and the power of women, leading to the case for its hypostatisation being down-played. In the post-Nicene period she shows the 'reflexive subtlety' of Athanasius' case for the hypostatisation drawing on Romans 8, and the Cappadocian version as less convincing because of its more linear, hier-archical dimension. She refers to a number of other Christian thinkers and mystics down the centuries as representatives of incorporative or contemplative Trinitarianism, culminating in contemporary contempla-tives, worshippers in the Pentecostal/charismatic traditions and some theologians.

Her constructive case is summarised in a paragraph that might serve as a culmination both to my previous chapter's scriptural account of desire in relation to Jesus Christ and the Spirit and to the present series of three examples of theological wisdom on the Trinity:

> The 'Son', we note, in this model is released from a narrow extrinsicism. The term connotes not just the past earthly Jesus, nor even yet the risen person of 'Christ' (if that is individualistically conceived), but rather the transformed divine life to which the whole creation, animate and inanimate, is tending, and into which it is being progressively transformed (Rom. 8:19–25). Moreover, it is important to underscore that the 'experience' claimed of the Spirit here is not that of some different quality, or emotional tonality, from the (simultaneously experienced) 'Father' and 'Son'; it is not that different *sorts* of discrete 'experience' attend the three persons. (Perhaps, indeed, this is why Paul notoriously slides between 'God', 'Christ', and 'Spirit' in straining to express the almost inexpressible in Romans 8:9–11.) Rather, what I am claiming here is that the pray-er's total 'experience' of *God* is here found to be ineluctably tri-faceted. *The 'Father' is both source and ultimate object of divine desire; the 'Spirit' is that (irreducibly distinct) enabler and incorporater of that desire in creation – that which makes the creation divine; the 'Son' is that divine and perfected creation.*[48]

48. Ibid. pp. 37–8, my italics.

Conclusion

This chapter has extended wisdom interpretation from scripture to tradition. This has been done partly by offering a scriptural understanding
of tradition and further developing maxims previously used to express
biblical wisdom. Partly, too, it has been done through drawing on
exemplary contemporary interpreters of scripture and tradition. In line
with this book's concern with God-related wisdom the main focus has
been upon the Christian tradition of worship and its identification of
God as Trinity, Father, Son and Holy Spirit.

Ricoeur, Williams and Coakley have together exemplified theological
wisdom on the Trinity that has a strikingly wide range of reference and
rich combination of elements. They draw on many disciplines; they are
alert to the relevance of prayer and worship; they respond to a wide range
of critiques of theology, of incarnation and of the Trinity; they give
insightful accounts of continuity and innovation; they situate discourse
about the Trinity in the context of historical and contemporary events
and of ecclesial, political, psychological and gender dynamics; and they
make argued judgements on fundamental disputes.

Each of them has more to say about these matters in other works.[49]
There in varying degrees they demonstrate many of the characteristics of
the sort of theology the present book is also attempting: a scriptural-
expressivist concern to offer a lively idiom for wise Christian understanding and action, drawing on scripture and alert to the cries of our
world; a postcritical attempt to take seriously the premodern, modern
and postmodern; sensitive discernment of the dynamics of desire and the
leading of the Spirit amidst the complexities of life; dedication to a
pedagogy that encourages passionate searching, intensive conversation
and disciplined prayer; and, throughout, 'letting God be God'.

For now, I hope sufficient has been drawn from them to give a
representative taste of that theology and, in particular, some sense of
what it means today to discern who God is with reference to Christian
scriptures and tradition, and why that discernment deserves to be seen as
essential to a Christian wisdom that desires to worship God **'in spirit
and truth'** (John 4:24).

---

49. In addition to the Ricoeur texts listed above, see Rowan Williams, *On Christian Theology*
(Oxford: Blackwell, 2000) and *Why Study the Past? The Quest for the Historical Church* (Grand
Rapids, MI: Eerdmans, 2005); Sarah Coakley, *Powers and Submissions: Spirituality, Philosophy
and Gender* (Oxford: Blackwell, 2002).

7

Loving the God of wisdom

There is a core insight into the nature of wisdom that has been discovered in Old Testament, New Testament and the Christian tradition. This is: *God is to be loved for God's sake.*

The present chapter opens with an exploration of that maxim. Its implications are followed through in the rest of the chapter: on the one hand, attempting to appreciate God as God through considering the divine perfections; and, on the other hand, recognising that to love God for God's sake is, inseparably, to love the people and the world God loves. Yet this double involvement with God and neighbour is not done in isolation, it requires a community, a school of desire and wisdom that is concerned for both God and the world, and within which people can be formed in faith, hope and love. So the later sections of the chapter will consider the church, concluding with a brief survey of the ways in which its theology can be embraced within the concept of wisdom. Throughout, the overarching theme of this chapter, as of chapter 6, is learning to live in the Spirit.

Hallowing the name: loving God for God's sake

The centrality to Christian wisdom of relating to God for God's sake – hallowing, fearing, loving, praising, blessing, glorifying God's name simply because God is God – has been indicated in previous chapters mainly by reference to Job and Jesus and reading scripture for God's sake. Paradigmatic texts are the Satan's question, '**Does Job fear God for nothing?**' (*hinnam*, δωρεαν, as a gift); and the prayer Jesus taught his disciples, '**Father, hallowed be your name. Your kingdom come, your will be done**', which is re-enacted at the climax of Jesus' own life in his prayer on the Mount of Olives: '**Father, if you are willing, remove this cup from me; yet, not my will but yours be done.**' Job's cries express a desire directed to God for God's sake, not just for his lost possessions, children and reputation; and Jesus' life and teaching are integrated around his desire for God and God's Kingdom.

In later chapters Christian participation with Jews and Muslims in scriptural reasoning will be described as a practice that flourishes best when each tradition is reading their scriptures and those of others before God (as each identifies God) and for God's sake – the latter being an idea to which, for all their different ways of identifying God, many Jews and Muslims have given comparable centrality. The integrity of university research and teaching amidst the pressures to serve the interests of money or power will be seen as dependent on an alliance of those who stand for the importance of valuing truth for truth's sake, the Christian rationale for which is intrinsically related to the interrelation of loving God for God's sake and creation for creation's sake. The account of Jean Vanier's teaching and the practices of the L'Arche communities will show a radical honouring of each person for their own sake, whose most complete expression is in friendship with each other and in communion with God for God's sake.

So the present section faces the most important question in this chapter: how to think through the hallowing of God's name, the loving of God for God's sake, as central to Christian wisdom.

From Abraham and Isaac to Shadrach, Meshach and Abednego

I begin from Gerhard von Rad's magisterial conclusion to his book on Old Testament wisdom.[1] He notes many features of Israel's wisdom, in its various books and periods, that have been important for previous chapters: the fundamental relationship with fear of Yahweh; concern about the contingency of historical events and the search for elements of stability and continuity within events; the nature of innovations in wisdom and in understandings of history; widespread borrowing from foreign sources; the relation of the genre of wisdom with wisdom communicated in other genres such as historical narrative, law, hymns, prophecy and apocalyptic; the connection of trust in the hidden Yahweh with trust in

---

1. Gerhard von Rad, *Wisdom in Israel*, tr. James D. Martin (London: SCM Press, 1972), pp. 287–319.

creation; and wisdom's resistance to comprehensive systematising and theorising in favour of the pervasive importance of discussion and dialectic: 'Can one then understand all these works, with their varied teachings, other than as part of a great dialogue in which truth can be opposed to truth?'[2]

At the heart of von Rad's account of wisdom is desiring and striving to work out, in both ordinary life and amidst conflicts and large events, a way of being human before God.

> But this humanity could not be protected by a handful of clever rules. Again and again it had to be established anew from the very heart of Yahwism. More and more we saw the wise men involved in a struggle with fundamental problems which threatened to darken their relationship with God and which called for fairly decisive theological reflection. And finally we even saw them – bordering on hubris – summoned and wooed by the mystery of the world itself and responding to that wooing with an intellectual love. Thus wide, then, was the theological framework stretched within which the wise men in Israel believed they could begin to understand themselves correctly. To live intellectually in such spheres, to be able to handle such knowledge, really required a *rōhab lēb*, a 'width', a 'breadth' of heart and mind (1 Kings 5:9). In this concept, what was both the task and, at the same time, the presupposition of Israel's humanity found admirable expression. As weapons in the conflict with theological problems, in later wisdom especially, hymnic traditions were mobilized against the attacks.[3]

This breadth of mind and heart, continually renewed from the heart of Yahwism (which must mean in relationship with Yahweh and in re-engagement with different strands of testimony to him), developing a passionate intellectual life, and drawing increasingly on literature such as the Psalms, is found in the Wisdom of Solomon and the book of Sirach. Von Rad then offers a daring insight into the two-part development of Israel's wisdom-thinking, suggesting that

> within Israel's didactic achievement one can discern a movement which has a certain logical consistency. Dissociating itself sharply from a sacral understanding of the world, this way of thinking placed man and his created environment in a measure of secularity with which Israel had never before been thus confronted. With wonderful

---

2. Ibid. p. 312.   3. Ibid. pp. 309–10.

open-mindedness, the older teachers' way of thinking circles round a man who has been, to a certain extent, newly discovered, man with all his psychological realities and imponderables, his possibilities and his limitations. In later wisdom, on the other hand, there appears what can almost be called a counter-movement. More specialized, theological questions had arisen, and later wisdom saw itself faced with the task, without sacrificing to the secularity of creation the knowledge that had been acquired, the task of bringing the world and man back once again into the centre of God's sphere of activity. This, of course, raised new and difficult questions which demanded answers. It is difficult to decide which of these two movements was threatened with the greater dangers, the placing of creation within the sphere of secularity or the bringing of it back within the sphere of direct, divine action towards man and the world.[4]

It is hard not to suspect that von Rad sees in this double movement of secular differentiation followed by reintegration with the divine what he hopes might be a possibility for his own time. It certainly fits with what I see as the task of Christian wisdom today in what will be described below as our 'religious and secular world': constant re-engagement with scripture and tradition, openmindedness in many directions, and seeking to combine the gains of modern academic disciplines with a theological wisdom that is most intensively expressed in worship.

But von Rad does not quite follow through on the God-centred logic of his insight. All the indicators are there, but he stops short. His verdict on what is most decisive in the tradition is: 'But almost more important than the differentiation of strong movements within wisdom, is what has continued in it from the very beginning, namely the unwavering certainty that creation herself will reveal her truth to the man who becomes involved with her and trusts her, because this is what she continually does. It is this self-revelation of the orders of creation, and not the convictions of the teachers or their zeal, that has the last decisive word.'[5] This appears to revert to the main characteristic of the first movement without doing justice to the theological and doxological thrust of the second.

The 'last decisive word' in Sirach is praise of God.

Sirach 43:27–33 [27]We could say more but could never say enough; let the final word be: 'He is the all.' [28]Where can we find the strength

4. Ibid. pp. 316–17.   5. Ibid. p. 317.

to praise him? For he is greater than all his works. [29]Awesome is the Lord and very great, and marvellous is his power. [30]Glorify the Lord and exalt him as much as you can, for he surpasses even that. When you exalt him, summon all your strength, and do not grow weary, for you cannot praise him enough. [31]Who has seen him and can describe him? Or who can extol him as he is? [32]Many things greater than these lie hidden, for I have seen but few of his works. [33]For the Lord has made all things, and to the godly he has given wisdom.

'**For he is greater than all his works**' is one of the core insights of worship. Whatever the glories of creation, or what von Rad calls the 'self-revelation of the orders of creation', and whatever the benefits received or expected from God, there is a wisdom which recognises that God is to be glorified over and above and apart from the relationship to creation or ourselves.

The joyful, ecstatic side of this is in the delighted leap from the wonder, beauty, truth or goodness of creation to amazement at its Creator, or in the astonishment of gratitude that moves into appreciation of the One whose very being is to love, to be generous, to be. There can be a dawning realisation that no necessary chain of causality leads back to the origin of our world, but that across the unimaginable chasm of divine freedom creation is the gift of One who calls it out of nothing. Beyond the fascination of atoms, trees, people and stars, this One is the ultimate and inexhaustible fascination for heart and mind. To try to think God in God's self is to have our language stretched beyond all analogies, sometimes to revel in an abundance of names and attributes, each of them inadequate, and sometimes to accept their inadequacy in silence. It is to generate images and concepts that try to do justice simultaneously to an infinity of wisdom, goodness, understanding, peace and love. It is to rejoice in their failure because this points beyond them to who God is as God. It is to explore the deepest sense of loving God with all of one's heart, mind, soul and strength. The simple core is: God is to be praised and loved for God's sake.

One scriptural text after another leads into this path.

> 1 Samuel 12:22 For the LORD will not cast away his people, for his great name's sake, because it has pleased the LORD to make you a people for himself.
>
> Isaiah 42:8 I am the LORD, that is my name; my glory I give to no other, nor my praise to idols.
> Isaiah 48:11 For my own sake, for my own sake, I do it, for why should my name be profaned? My glory I will not give to another.

Ezekiel 20:44 And you shall know that I am the Lord, when I deal with you for my name's sake, not according to your evil ways, or corrupt deeds, O house of Israel, says the Lord God.

Ezekiel 36:23 I will sanctify my great name, which has been profaned among the nations, and which you have profaned among them; and the nations shall know that I am the Lord, says the Lord God, when through you I display my holiness before their eyes.

Psalm 22:23 You who fear the Lord, praise him! All you offspring of Jacob, glorify him; stand in awe of him, all you offspring of Israel!
Psalm 27:8 'Come,' my heart says, 'seek his face!' Your face, Lord, do I seek.
Psalm 72:19 Blessed be his glorious name for ever; may his glory fill the whole earth. Amen and Amen.

John 17:5 So now, Father, glorify me in your own presence with the glory that I had in your presence before the world existed.

Philippians 4:4 Rejoice in the Lord always; again I will say, Rejoice.

Ephesians 3:18–21 [18]I pray that you may have the power to comprehend, with all the saints, what is the breadth and length and height and depth, [19]and to know the love of Christ that surpasses knowledge, so that you may be filled with all the fullness of God. [20]Now to him who by the power at work within us is able to accomplish abundantly far more than all we can ask or imagine, [21]to him be glory in the church and in Christ Jesus to all generations, for ever and ever. Amen.

Revelation 5:13–14 [13]Then I heard every creature in heaven and on earth and under the earth and in the sea, and all that is in them, singing, 'To the one seated on the throne and to the Lamb be blessing and honour and glory and might for ever and ever!' [14]And the four living creatures said, 'Amen!' And the elders fell down and worshipped.
Revelation 15:4 Lord, who will not fear and glorify your name? For you alone are holy.

There is another side too. The nearest biblical parallel to the testing of Job[6] to see whether he fears God 'for nothing' is the sacrifice, or binding,

---

6. Von Rad's discussion of Job parallels his discussion of wisdom in general that has just been quoted in that there is a formal recognition of what I have identified as its hermeneutical key (fearing God for nothing), but this is not followed through in his final verdict. He offers fresh insight into the meaning of Job's relationship with God (ibid. pp. 217–26), but the final emphasis is on 'Yahweh *pro me*' (p. 221) rather than God for God's sake.

of Isaac. '**God tested Abraham**' (Gen. 22.1). Abraham had been given his heart's desire, Isaac, by God and promised a future of unimaginable blessing through him, but now he is asked to offer him as a sacrifice. Does he trust God only so far, only when he benefits? Will he sacrifice what is most precious to him for the sake of God? This story has been of immense significance for both Jews and Christians (and to a lesser extent for Muslims), being at the origins of the history of Israel as chosen by God and a type of God's offering of Jesus.[7] In the story, God's verdict is clear: '**for now I know that you fear God, since you have not withheld your son, your only son, from me**' (Gen. 22:12). 'The narrative concerns Abraham's anguished acknowledgement that God is God … Like Job, Abraham is prepared to trust fully the God who gives and the God who takes away.'[8]

The practical implication of fearing God is the conformity of one's life to God, even if that means dying. *God is more important than life itself, whether one's own life or that of those who may be dearer than one's own life.* Hallowing the name of God means being holy as God is holy, following through the consequences of this utter dedication to God even to the point of death. The culmination of this in both Jewish and Christian traditions is martyrdom.

> Daniel 3:16–18 [16]Shadrach, Meshach, and Abednego answered the king, 'O Nebuchadnezzar, we have no need to present a defence to you in this matter. [17]If our God whom we serve is able to deliver us from the furnace of blazing fire and out of your hand, O king, let him deliver us. [18]But if not, be it known to you, O king, that we will not serve your gods and we will not worship the golden statue that you have set up.'

The '**But if not**' is a sign of the '**for nothing**'. When Abednego, whose original name was Azariah, is later represented as praising God in the furnace with the others the leading emphasis is on blessing God and glorifying his name.

---

7. See A. R. E. Agus, *The Binding of Isaac and Messiah* (Albany, NY: SUNY, 1988); J. I. Gellman, *Abraham! Abraham! Kierkegaard and the Hasidim on the Binding of Isaac* (Aldershot: Ashgate, 2003); Edward Kessler, *Bound by the Bible: Jews, Christians and the Sacrifice of Isaac* (Cambridge: Cambridge University Press, 2004); J. D. Levenson, *The Death and Resurrection of the Beloved Son: The Transformation of Child Sacrifice in Judaism and Christianity* (New Haven and London: Yale University Press, 1993), and *The Sacrifice of Isaac in the Three Monotheistic Religions* (Jerusalem: Franciscan Printing Press, 1995); E. Noort et al. (eds.), *The Sacrifice of Isaac: The Aqedah (Genesis 22) and Its Interpretations* (Leiden: Brill, 2002).
8. Walter Brueggemann, *Genesis* (Atlanta, GA: John Knox Press, 1982), pp. 189–90. Brueggemann is led to reflect on the meaning of the word 'God' in serious faith and in 'the innocuous single-dimensional piety of civil religion'.

Prayer of Azariah 1:1–3 [1]They walked around in the midst of the flames, singing hymns to God and blessing the Lord. [2]Then Azariah stood still in the fire and prayed aloud: [3]'Blessed are you, O Lord, God of our ancestors, and worthy of praise; and glorious is your name for ever!

1:11 For your name's sake do not give us up for ever, and do not annul your covenant . . .'

1:28–35 [28]Then the three with one voice praised and glorified and blessed God in the furnace: [29]'Blessed are you, O Lord, God of our ancestors, and to be praised and highly exalted for ever; [30]And blessed is your glorious, holy name, and to be highly praised and highly exalted for ever. [31]Blessed are you in the temple of your holy glory, and to be extolled and highly glorified for ever. [32]Blessed are you who look into the depths from your throne on the cherubim, and to be praised and highly exalted for ever. [33]Blessed are you on the throne of your kingdom, and to be extolled and highly exalted for ever. [34]Blessed are you in the firmament of heaven, and to be sung and glorified for ever. [35]Bless the Lord, all you works of the Lord; sing praise to him and highly exalt him for ever . . .

1:67–68 [67]Give thanks to the Lord, for he is good, for his mercy endures for ever. [68]All who worship the Lord, bless the God of gods, sing praise to him and give thanks to him, for his mercy endures for ever.'

Here, as elsewhere in the Bible and Jewish and Christian tradition, there is no contradiction between looking to God for mercy, salvation or other blessings and blessing God for God's sake, but nor is there an identification of the two, and the priority is clear. It was a distinction and priority that became more important in situations of pressure and persecution, and discerning its appropriate application required wisdom.[9]

---

9. See Jonathan Sacks, 'Sanctifying the Name' in *To Heal a Fractured World: The Ethics of Responsibility* (London and New York: Continuum, 2005), pp. 57–70, for a contemporary Jewish exploration of the theme of *kiddush ha-Shem*, defined as behaviour that creates respect for God, including loving God more than life itself. 'At stake is the very nature of God and the definition of the children of Israel as "a kingdom of priests and a holy nation" . . . "sanctifying the name" is a metaprinciple of Judaism . . . "Sanctifying the name" is no mere marginal addendum to the script of Jewish life but its very point: to bring God's presence into the world by making others aware that God's word sanctifies life' (pp. 64, 67, 68). Yet in a time of war, genocide, oppression and suicide bombing (sometimes 'in God's name') he lays alongside the traditional teachings and examples of martyrdom one that provocatively reinterprets its meaning in the face of oppression and genocide. He quotes Rabbi Isaac Nissenbaum on the night of the Warsaw ghetto uprising against the German army in April 1943 saying: 'This is a time for the sanctification of life, *kiddush ha-hayyim*, and not for the holiness of martyrdom, *kiddush ha-Shem*. Previously, the Jew's enemy sought his soul, and the

At the same time, the wisdom tradition in Israel was, as von Rad tells it, becoming more theological, and the very concept of the fear of God was being elaborated and made more embracing.

> What a profusion Sirach needs in order to develop what he understands by the fear of God! . . . The fear of God is joy (1.11), the fear of God is humility (1.27), the fear of God is love for God (2.15f.) . . . The fear of God seeks God, is orientated towards God (32.14f.), and it trusts in him and hopes in him (2.6). Unquestionably the term appears in Sirach in a much broader and more general sense. Above all, however, the fear of God complies with the Torah.[10]

So keeping Torah is the main sign of wisdom and discernment, inseparable from crying out to God:

> Deuteronomy 4:6–8 [6]You must observe them diligently, for this will show your wisdom and discernment to the peoples, who, when they hear all these statutes, will say, 'Surely this great nation is a wise and discerning people!' [7]For what other great nation has a god so near to it as the LORD our God is whenever we call to him? [8]And what other great nation has statutes and ordinances as just as this entire law that I am setting before you today?

And the leading command of Torah, daily repeated, is the cry of God:

> Deuteronomy 6:4–5 [4]Hear, O Israel: The LORD is our God, the LORD alone. [5]You shall love the LORD your God with all your heart, and with all your soul, and with all your might.

Loving God in the Spirit of Abraham, Moses, Job and Azariah is the fulfilment of fear of God and the essence of wisdom.

From Jesus to the Gulag

Christianity inherited both the expanded wisdom tradition (see chapter 5 on the Wisdom of Solomon in relation to the Gospel of Luke) and the example of witnessing to God even at the risk of one's life. Its supreme example was the death of Jesus, and early in the Acts of the Apostles the martyrdom of Stephen, **'full of the Spirit and of wisdom'**, is portrayed in terms reminiscent of Jesus' crucifixion (see p. 42 above). Martyrdom was

---

Jew sanctified his body in martyrdom [i.e. he denied his enemy what he wished to take from him]. Now the oppressor demands the Jew's body, and the Jew is therefore obliged to defend it, to preserve his life' (p. 68).

10. Von Rad, *Wisdom in Israel*, pp. 243–4.

a key focus for Christian identity in the early centuries of persecution, and the last book of the New Testament, the book of Revelation, gives the ultimate picture of worship in heaven: those who have given their lives as witnesses to Jesus Christ cry out in worship to God and the Lamb (Jesus, who has given his life) on the throne. The twentieth century probably had more Christian martyrs than any other, and perhaps the largest single group died in the prison camps of the Soviet Union's Gulag.[11]

Martyrdom has always been complemented by many less dramatic yet costly practices whose core meaning is to be traced to hallowing God's name, doing 'in the name of Jesus' things that embody the incomparable priority and glory of God: consecrated virginity and celibacy, asceticism of many sorts, pacifism, sacrificial and secret giving, poverty, canonical obedience, disciplines of prayer, taking on burdens, responsibilities and vocations for the sake of God and God's Kingdom and, encompassingly, loving God and loving other people for God's sake. The very importance of such practices means that they are especially vulnerable to distortion – 'the corruption of the best is the worst'. So in relation to all of them wisdom is at a premium, summed up in the wisdom of love.

The New Testament writings that engage most richly with the glory of God, the death of Jesus and the wisdom of love are the letters by Paul and his followers and the Gospel and letters of John. In Paul's letters the three especially come together in Romans and 2 Corinthians, and in the latter are closely woven into Paul's presentation of his own life and ministry.[12] Perhaps the most thorough interweaving of the three is in the Letter to the Ephesians.[13] John's Gospel redefines the concepts of glory and of love by reference to the death of Jesus, and Jesus himself is identified with God and God's glory.[14] In later tradition John's Gospel was the main scriptural influence on the developing doctrine of the Trinity, and that has been central to centuries of thought, worship, meditation and contemplation focussed through praising, blessing, glorifying, adoring and hallowing God's name.

The Trinity has inspired not only a fascination with God's being as God but also theologies and spiritualities, such as those of Coakley (see

11. See Anne Applebaum, *Gulag: A History of the Soviet Camps* (London: Penguin Books, 2003).
12. On 2 Corinthians see Ford and Young, *Meaning and Truth in 2 Corinthians*, especially chapters 1, 8 and 9.
13. See David F. Ford, *Self and Salvation: Being Transformed* (Cambridge: Cambridge University Press, 1999), chapter 5.
14. For more on John's Gospel see chapter 10 below.

chapter 6 above) and others, that invite worshippers into communion
with God in the Spirit. Key terms that are used in relation to human
affirmation of God for God's sake are seen as most appropriate for the life
of God in God's Trinitarian life: the mutual glorification of Father, Son
and Holy Spirit in the 'glorious' Trinity; the mutual love of Father and
Son in the Spirit; or the mutual blessing and enjoyment of the three in the
'blessed' Trinity.

Not surprisingly it is best expressed in poetry, such as the final canto
of Dante's *Divine Comedy*,[15] hymns such as St Patrick's Breastplate ('I bind
unto myself the name, the strong name of the Trinity') and prose that
transcends itself towards poetry. I conclude this section with an example
of the latter that has recently been discovered, Thomas Traherne's discourse on life in the Kingdom of God. Having earlier celebrated God
through meditating on 'the Sun: how Glorious a Creature it is: What
an Image of the Divine Essence, how great an Emblem of the Holy
Trinity',[16] he later evokes God as One to be loved 'ten thousand times
more, then we lov our selvs', and improvises on Paul and John to give an
intoxicating taste of what it means to be made in the image of this God
and incorporated into God's life and love (and suggesting that the 'for
nothing' might here coincide with 'for everything'). He then concludes
with the Queen of Sheba, the kingdom and wisdom of Solomon, and the
incomparablility of the Kingdom of God as the fulfilment of human and
divine desires:

> The Enjoyment of God in his Kingdom, is the Life and Glory of it, and
> the Soul, it is the utmost Height of which any Kingdom, or Soul is
> Capable: Tis worthily Mentioned under the Head of its formal Cause,
> because the offices and Employments, the Estate of the Realm the
> Condition of the Nobilitie, the order, and Degree of the Attendants
> especialy, difference one Kingdom from another. for which cause the
> Queen of Sheba so admired Solomon, that when she had Seen all his
> Wisdom and House that he had built, and the Meat of his table, and the
> Sitting of his Servants, and the Attendance of his Ministers, and their
> Apparrel, and his Cup bearers, and his Ascent by which he went up
> unto the House of the Lord; there was no more Spirit in her. And She

---

15. See David F. Ford and Daniel W. Hardy, *Living in Praise: Worshipping and Knowing God*
(London: Darton, Longman and Todd, 2005), chapter 4.
16. Thomas Traherne, *The Works of Thomas Traherne*, vol. 1: *Inducements to Retirednes, A Sober View
of Dr Twisses his Considerations, Seeds of Eternity or the Nature of the Soul, The Kingdom of God*, ed.
Jan Ross (Cambridge: D. S. Brewer, 2005), pp. 356–61. See Ford *Self and Salvation*, pp. 275–80.

Said to the King. It was a true Report which I heard in mine own Land
of thy Acts, and they Wisdom: Howbeit I believed not the words untill
I came, and mine Eys had seen it: and behold the half was not told
me, thy Wisdom and Prosperity Exceedeth the fame which I heard.
Happy are thy Men, Happy are these they Servants that stand
continualy before thee, and hear thy Wisdom! Blessed be the Lord thy
God which delighteth in thee to set thee on the Throne of Israel:
Because the Lord Loved Israel for ever, therefore made he thee King to
do Judgment and Justice. If it be So Happy to attend upon a Wise King,
what is it to sit in the Throne of Glory! GODS Kingdom is Such a
Kingdom, that Evry Subject Sitteth on a Throne. If Solomons Throne
were So Glorious, which was Made of Ivory, and overlayd with Gold,
that there was not the like in any Kingdom. what may Eternity be
which is the Throne of GOD! And What will that Kingdom be where all
Attendants are Celestial Kings, where all the offices are to Reign, and
Enjoy, and Rejoyce, and Sing Praise; and Lov and Honor and Adore,
and to sit down at the Heavenly Table, and feast while the Son of Man
cometh forth to Serv them that live in the Same. Verily there is no
Kingdom like unto this, which is cast into such a Model of Perfection,
that all his Soveraignty and Supremacy therin: Nothing being to be seen,
but the Perfection of Beauty, with Joy unspeakable and full of Glory.[17]

Perfecting perfection: the God of blessing who loves in wisdom

In teaching about the Christian God a classic accompaniment to the
doctrine of the Trinity is discussion of the qualities, the attributes or, to
use Barth's preferred term, the perfections of God. Looking through
Traherne's rich embroidery of language in the quotation above suggests
an array of perfections, some traditional (love, wisdom, goodness) and
some not so common (beauty, felicity, joy). Christian theology over the
centuries has shown great variety in the lists of key attributes of God that
have been proposed, and no normative selection has prevailed. It is therefore up to each theologian and tradition to work out their own list of
attributes and how to interrelate them. The arbitrariness of this is limited
not only by common appeals to scripture but also by a classic maxim of
Augustine: that with regard to God each attribute is essentially identical
with the others, and there can be no contradiction between, for example,

17. Ibid. p. 280.

God's justice and God's mercy.[18] This section does not propose a full doctrine of God's attributes but, in line with the present chapter's pivotal role in the book, is attempting three things: to set the attributes of God in the context of worship (which is being understood as a key context for learning and expressing Christian wisdom); to suggest blessedness, love and wisdom as three leading attributes consonant with the God already identified; and to say something about wisdom as an attribute of God. Since I have written at some length about these topics elsewhere, they will be dealt with briefly and more in the mode of summary than of exposition.

Perfecting perfection

The classical Christian wisdom about attributing specific perfections to God has already featured in Ricoeur's discussion of God and being. It is about discerning the appropriate articulation of and balance between, on the one hand, the way of analogical affirmation – that, for example, God is wise in a way analogous to human wisdom but yet very differently, 'supereminently'; and, on the other hand, the way of negation – already, as Ricoeur argued, presupposed at the limits of analogy, and also, as Williams argued, reconceived in the light of the incarnation. The mainstream balance seen in Ricoeur, Williams and Coakley is performed in prayer and worship.

Ascribing a perfection to God is best seen first of all as a way of hallowing God's name, praising God as God, rejoicing in God as God. 'Praise perfects perfection.'[19] The analogy of personal relationships is the most helpful. Recognising someone's worth and responding with wholehearted appreciation creates a new dimension of the relationship. The amazement, acknowledgement, respect and delight that are at the heart of praise can overflow continually. There can be a longing for larger capacities of expression and responsiveness, and it can lead into all sorts of generosity and creativity.

> It is not basically a matter of comparison with anyone else: the focus of fascination is this person in all his or her individuality. The appreciation that is poured out is concerned to do justice to what seems like a unique miracle, which has a rightness and perfection that can

---

18. See Augustine, *Trin.* 15.5(7).
19. Ford and Hardy, *Living in Praise*, p. 8. Praise as perfecting perfection is a key concept in this book. See especially chapters 2, 7 and Epilogue.

only be responded to with astonishment. It has simply to be recognized for what it is, quite apart from any consequences or intentions. There may be all sorts of hopes and fears but the essence of the matter is being true to what is there to be amazed at, quite apart from oneself.[20]

This strange logic can be stretched to God as the One who both inspires and receives worship. The God who is praised for being loving is in relationship with the worshipper, and lovingly delights in the response. The perfection of God's love includes responding to it being appreciated for its own sake, and one way of seeing this is as God's perfection being perfected. There is a similar logic in thanks, the companion of praise. The more perfect a gift or action or event is, the more thanks are appropriate. The more decisively complete it is the more thanks are evoked. A whole life can be lived in grateful response. What is added to the completeness by gratitude? What is added to perfection by praise? Addition is hardly the right image. In relation to God we are in the realm of what Coakley called participation or incorporation, and she linked it with contemplation, in the Spirit, of who God is, One whose Trinitarian life is constituted by mutual glorifying, blessing and loving. Entering into this is a transformative process of participation in line with what Williams described as 'a steady and endless enlarging of the heart through union in prayer and virtue with the Word, which is also a steady and endless growth in knowledge of the Father'[21]

That knowledge[22] is what the mind endlessly stretches towards in order to fulfil its desire to do more justice to God through praise and thanks. Worship that is not concerned about truth becomes corrupt and idolatrous,[23] or at least repetitious and unable to respond to the guiding of the Spirit into newness. So there is a call to think and rethink God as adequately as possible, and part of that is stretching the mind to conceive and reconceive God's perfections.

20. Ibid. p. 9.
21. Rowan Williams, *Arius: Heresy and Tradition* (London: Darton, Longman and Todd, 1987), p. 243.
22. For the relation of praising God to knowing God see Ford and Hardy, *Living in Praise*, especially chapters 4 and 7. See Paul D. Janz, *God, the Mind's Desire: Reference, Reason and Christian Thinking* (Cambridge: Cambridge University Press, 2004), chapters 7 and 8.
23. Matthew Levering in *Scripture and Metaphysics: Aquinas and the Renewal of Trinitarian Theology* (Oxford: Blackwell, 2004) gives a perceptive account of Thomas Aquinas as concerned both negatively about idolatry and positively about 'knowing and loving God's name for his sake' (p. 22), uniting scripture and metaphysics in a theology that is best described as 'contemplative wisdom'.

The God of blessing who loves in wisdom

There have, as mentioned above, been many lists of key perfections of God proposed over the centuries. The coordinating set of three that I propose in the summary phrase, 'the God of blessing who loves in wisdom', is a variation on Barth's in his doctrine of God, 'the being of God as the One who loves in freedom'.[24] Barth uses this to coordinate twelve perfections of God (grace, holiness, mercy, righteousness, patience, wisdom, unity, omnipresence, constancy, omnipotence, eternity and glory) in relation to God's love and freedom. I have discussed aspects of Barth with special reference to the thought of Eberhard Jüngel elsewhere;[25] the concern now is to relate it to this chapter. God's wisdom, as the perfection central to the concerns of this book, will be singled out for discussion below, and Barth's treatment of it will be critically developed. God's love, which has already been a leading theme in chapter 5 and will appear again in chapter 10, will be represented by a fragment from the newly discovered and recently published manuscript by Thomas Traherne already quoted above, and he will also contribute a substantial meditation on the blessedness of God. But the first topic is the rationale for the choice of blessing, love and wisdom together.

Why these three? Love and wisdom are present in the lists of nearly every major theologian, often in coordinating roles. They represent core aspects of personhood, fundamental forms of self-transcendence. Love is more to do with will and affectivity, wisdom more with intelligence and judgement, and both are shaped through desire and vision. It is idiosyncratic of Barth to place so much emphasis on the side of willing by using love and freedom as his coordinating pair; and his account of wisdom as one of the perfections of the divine loving is, as will be suggested below, somewhat unsatisfactory.[26] Love and wisdom have the advantage that a strong biblical case can be made for linking each of them both with God (as θεός, Yahweh) and with the Father, with Jesus Christ and with the Holy Spirit.[27] Within the tradition, there are those who especially

24. Karl Barth, *Church Dogmatics*, vol. II, part 1 (Edinburgh: T. & T. Clark, 1957), §28, pp. 257–321.

25. David F. Ford, 'The God of Blessing Who Loves in Wisdom' in *Denkwürdiges Geheimnis: Beiträge zur Gotteslehre*, ed. Ingolf U. Dalferth, Johannes Fischer and Hans-Peter Grosshans (Tübingen: Mohr Siebeck, 2004), pp. 113–26.

26. On some of the problems posed by his use of freedom in this role see Ford, 'The God of Blessing Who Loves in Wisdom', p. 124.

27. Freedom is more difficult in this respect, and recourse has to be had to deducing it from other terms such as lordship, grace or power.

connect wisdom with Jesus Christ and love with the Holy Spirit, but that
can also be reversed; and all recognise that love and wisdom are also to be
attributed to the Father. Within the Trinity, the interrelation of persons
in coinherence is conceivable analogously through the union imaginable
between friends or lovers who share as deeply as possible in each other's
lives and have full mutual communication, understanding and wise
judgement, though this analogy is always qualified by the need to affirm
God's unity and exclude tritheism.

Overall, as one works with the whole of scripture and the tradition,
these two perfections prove their worth again and again as headings under
which to think of God and God's relation to the world, and they also
resonate with the most important dimensions of human existence today.
They can be applied to God 'supereminently' by analogy; at the same time
their association with inexhaustible richness and unfathomable mystery,
even as terms applied to humans, is well suited to the apophatic recognition of radical inadequacy, discontinuity and ignorance, combined with a
passionate desire to go deeper into this 'bright darkness'.

Traherne combines them both (as above, with many others, including
blessedness) in a classic move from human to divine love. The Empress
falls wildly and extravagantly in love and she lives only for the sake of the
beloved. How much more does God love us! Traherne daringly follows
the logic of God's love:

> Let us ascend from temporal to Eternal Love. If these Petite and finite
> Lovers can be thus ardent, and by meer Instinct understand their
> Interest: If they desire Beauty for these Ends, and to make themselves
> more amiable, wash, perfume, and powder and Curle; appear in Gay
> Attires, Embroyderies, Jewels; etc. learn to sing, Dance, play on the Lute,
> leap, ride the great horse, shew feats of Activitie Prowess and Chivalrie,
> display their Magazines of Treasure, multiply and adorn their
> Attendants, expose the Glory of their Relations to the Ey, boast their
> Nobilitie and Descent, wish for Kingdoms, or vaster Empires, acquire all
> kind of Graces, practice all sorts of virtues, study all Arts of Learning,
> and especially shew an infinit unquenchable Love; and all this to appear
> more lovely, bec. the first and grand designe of Love is to be beloved;
> What may we think of God Almighty? By how much the more he loves,
> by so much the more doth he exceed in all. And while he studies to make
> him self infinitly Amiable, he doth not only Beautify his Person, but
> enlarge his Kingdom, increase his Retinue, Beautify his Palace, glorify
> him self with Heroick Acts, or rather with Divine and Heavenly ones,

enrich his Attendants, and make all the felicities and Pleasures of his
Court answerable to the greatness and Perfection of his Lov. Which Lov
especially he sheweth to be infinit, as well as his Power, Wisdom, Truth,
faithfulness, Goodness, Holiness, Blessedness and Glory; and all these
doth he freely sacrifice as it were at the feet of his Beloved. He adorneth
him self; not only with his Kingdom, Attendants and Treasures; but
with his infinit Perfections also; for, he is a voluntary Being, existing of
his own Pleasure; his Eternity and Immensitie are instead of all the
Nobilitie of famous Ancestors; His Wisdom beyond all Learning; his
goodness abov all virtue. Tho he is of necessity, bec. from all Eternity he
existed of his own Pleasure, yet bec. he existed of his own pleasure he
hath all in him that infinit Lov could invent or Desire: for he is the Cause
and the Son of his own Wisdom. And is willing not only to have infinit
Wisdom and Goodness and Power etc. but that the infinit Greatness of
all these should be manifest in his Beloved's Eys. for loving him self
infinitly, he infinitly desires to be Beloved of him self, and for that cause
perfectly discloseth all his Beauties, to him self for ever. And bec. He is
the Beloved he desires to make him self infinitly Beautifull, Rich,
Glorious, Blessed, that he might answer infinit Lov, with glories able to
justify the same as well as please it. And for this cause also doth he adorn
him self with all perfections forever. And both these he evidently
performeth by being Love alone. for perfect Love does not only consult
but finish its own Objects Welfare, and in becoming all thereunto it is
able: And therefore the Love of God is the more perfect, bec. it is infinit
and Eternal. It is not the Power, but the Act of Loving. Power to lov is
subject to Miscarriages; It is neither Wise nor Holy. But the Act of loving
in a most Wise and Holy manner, casteth out all fear. It is Wise and Holy
by its Essence. And tho it soundeth strange like a very Paradox, it is
freely Wise yet cannot be otherwise. an Act of Lov is of its own Pleasure
Gracious, Good, and Blessed, bec. it is an Act of Lov: The very same
reason makes it both. An Act of Love is the Power of Loving exerted
freely: and when it is exerted, it is by its Essence Good and Gracious to its
object. It cannot be without its own Pleasure: It cannot be an Act of Lov
without being Good and Gracious. Its Essence dependeth on it self and
all the Qualities Essential thereunto depend upon its Existence. which it
self dependeth upon its Choice and Pleasure. So that all the Necessities
under which we conceiv it to lie, depend upon its own Pleasure, and are
not Oppressions thereunto, but Liberties and pleasures. It is impossible
for Love to be without its Object in God, bec. Lov is its object.[28]

28. Traherne, *Works*, vol. 1, pp. 561–4.

What might the blessedness of God add to God's love and wisdom? The main perfections of God in the two passages from Traherne are: infinity or limitlessness, glory, love, beauty, eternity, wisdom, goodness, power, blessedness, happiness or felicity, justice, joy, faithfulness, holiness and grace. If one sees infinity and eternity as qualifiers of any perfection – God's glory is limitless and eternal, and so is every other perfection – then how do the rest relate to love and wisdom? Following biblical meanings of the terms, under love and wisdom (either singly or together) one might gather goodness, justice, faithfulness and grace, with some case to be made for beauty, power, happiness or felicity, joy and holiness. Yet beauty, power (in blessing and cursing), happiness, joy and holiness might fit better with blessedness, and so, especially, does glory.

Glory is particularly important in opening up the meaning of blessedness and making sense of it as a third leading perfection. It connects to what has been identified above as the heart of worship in glorifying or blessing God's name for God's sake. Blessing has other resonances too that complement love and wisdom. It signifies abundance and completeness without losing the dynamic of life and constant overflow towards others – the Trinity is a *perichoresis*, a round dance of mutual blessing inviting and inspiring people to bless God and each other and creation, and enabling creation itself to bless its Creator. The strongly interpersonal connotations of love fit it less well for rendering God's dynamic relation to non-human creation, and here blessing goes well with wisdom.

There is an unavoidable yet not arbitrary or empty vagueness in this interplay of attributes, and strict delimitation or definition is not appropriate. Traherne (together with many others in the theological and poetic traditions of Christianity) shows the potential of experimenting with terms in all sorts of combinations, and exploring to the limits their capacity to expand our appreciation of God through exuberant, imaginative conceptualising. It is worth quoting him at length again on the blessedness of God.

<blockquote>

The Blessedness of God Mani-
festeth his Kingdom to be
Infinit and Eternal

How the Holiness of God, how his Righteousness, how Glory
Conduceth to the Perfection of his kingdom, may be seen in other
places. Here we shall discover how this Blessedness doth influence it
</blockquote>

with a Necessity of Perfection, and how that Perfection cannot chuse but be Infinit, both becaus his Blessedness, and the nature of Perfection imports an Atchievement of all that can be don … But the Nature of Blessedness will open the Mysterie.

Felicitie consisteth in two Joys, the Joy of Communicating, and the Joy of receiving. Where the Blessedness is Infinit, the Communications and Receipts are so. The Receipts are Infinit, becaus of the Emanations: And the Joys, where the Receipts are Infinit Especialy when the Delights, which the Author takes in his communication are Endless, and the pleasure Infinit Which he feeleth in the Returns that are made unto him. The Blessedness of GOD is so Divine, that it is the Perfect Joy and Happiness of his Creatures. It is Eyther the Result of his Goodness, or the very same. For if all that is Good is Communicativ of it self, what is infinitly communicative is Infinitly Good, and Eternal Goodness is Eternaly Communicative. Whose property it is to Delight in its operations, and in the same Act to giv and Receiv all its Treasures. It gives them while it makes others to be Happy by them. It receivs them while it delights in their Happiness. Goodness is of a Nature so Mysterious, that it is as happy in giving as Receiving, and receives by giving. Nay our Savior affirms it to be more happy in giving, then Receiving. For our Lord hath said, It is more Blessed to give then to receiv. To giv is to Reign, oblige and Triumph, the Joy of giving is attended with an Increase of Authority, Confidence and Power. To receiv without Meriting, is to becom Subject to another, to forfeit ones Liberty, and be Engaged to Gratitude. Is it not a Strange Paradox, that Blessedness should be Relative, and regard others, which is so absolut a Being in it self? Is it not a Mysterious Surprizing Wonder, to see Men made Greater by giving, and less by Receiving? …

[God] giveth not his Works alone, but his Wisdom, Goodness, and Power, His essence, his Blessedness and Glory. And these he giveth by doing for us all, that Wisdom Power, and Goodness can perform. Making his Blessedness our Blessedness; His Joys our Joys His Treasures our Treasures. all which by making us in his Image, to lov one another, he hath miraculously improved, by making us like him to enjoy the Happiness of all in evry object of our Lov. If he giveth himself unto us, we may safely Conclude he hath done all that can fitly be atchieved for us. for what can he do more, then giv himself? Which is a gift so glorious, that in it all other Gifts are at once Contained. Loving us Infinitly, it seemeth as if our Blessedness were the Sole End of all Things. For it is with so much Care, and Earnestness intended, as if all his Happiness consisted in our Glory.

. . .

I know that his Essence is his Blessedness, but it is a Voluntary and Eternal Act, begetting, begotten, and proceeding to all Eternitie. An Act that is the Fountain, and the End of all things. The Wellspring and Fountain of the Beginning it self, the Beginning of evry Creature, the Life and Spirit in Evry Creature, the virtue of the Father, the Ground of their perfection, An Act Eternaly inriched with all Worlds, Eternaly Including all Beauties, infinitly Free, and yet as Infinitly Necessary, Instantaneous and yet still Eternal. The Blessedness of God is Infinit in it self, yet attended with all Circumstances of Delight and Glory. It is Simple, and undivided, yet Infinitly Multifarious: it is the Sole Cause of its own Happiness, yet accompanied with a concurrence of Causes, objects and Perfections on evry Side, that make it life the Happiness of Men upon Earth Composed of Mixture, tho Infintly more Excellent and pure. You see the Apostle mentions the Bride of GOD, the Famelie of God, the Kingdom of God, his Sons and Daughters. A fair Intimation that God is Infinitly Happy in him self, and in all his Creatures: in his Bride, in his Friends, in his Children, in his famelie, in his Subjects, and that he has Riches Honors and Pleasures like the Men of the World, tho exceeding all, of Infinit Value and Continuance and therfore more perfect then theirs.[29]

That is a meditation which is disciplined by reference to scripture and to the long tradition of philosophical, theological, liturgical and contemplative engagement with God, and which also improvises in the Spirit, daring to search afresh into God with a worship-centred, imaginative and intellectual passion. Blessedness is simultaneously an absolute perfection of God in God's essence (and God is to be blessed for God's sake) and also relational, comprehensively related to the whole creation that is blessed by God and therefore shares in God who makes 'his Blessedness our Blessedness'. *There is utter harmony between 'for God's sake' and 'for our sake'. The paradoxes of giving and receiving are explored,*[30] *and supremely that of giving oneself.* God 'gav even the whole Trinitie unto us' and is 'Infinitly Happy in him self in all his Creatures'. Through it all is the 'vehemency of the Lov of God'. What sort of wisdom might conceive and shape such a love and blessedness?

---

29. Ibid. pp. 321–5.
30. With reference to Ricoeur's critique above of those such as Jean-Luc Marion who try to think of God using the category of gift but without that of being, Traherne is a good example of one who takes up the language of being into rich, scripture-inspired thinking that avoids the dangers Marion fears.

God's wisdom

For Traherne, wisdom as a perfection of God might be taken as God's own knowledge, purposeful understanding and judgement, conceiving and informing the superabundance of God's life and activity, interrelating God's many perfections, and delighting in the radiant intelligibility of himself and of the creation. It is, to use one of his favourite adjectives, infinite,[31] and therefore beyond finite comprehension, but the generosity of God in sharing it means that Traherne's mind and imagination are constantly being opened up to new dimensions of it. Because it is inextricable from all the other perfections, to appreciate them with understanding is to appreciate God's wisdom. Hence wisdom recurs, scattered throughout his meditations, and at times as the central focus, as in the image, quoted above, of God's Kingdom in terms of Solomon's kingdom and the Queen of Sheba admiring Solomon's wisdom above all.

In a more sober and consistently scriptural mode, but with a comparable sense of the overwhelming richness and depth of each of the perfections of God, Barth specially connects God's wisdom with God's patience, and begins by reflecting on

> the fact that all further consideration of the divine attributes can but move in a circle around the one but infinitely rich being of God whose simplicity is abundance and whose abundance is simplicity itself. We are not speaking of a new object but allowing the one object, God, to speak further of Himself. We are continuing to contemplate the love of God and therefore God Himself as the One who loves in freedom. What end can there be to this development? We are drawing upon the ocean.[32]

While there are problems with Barth's discussion of God's wisdom, which will be raised below, it offers an exemplary summary of key elements from scripture and from Christian tradition. At its heart is the affirmation that God's wisdom consists in knowing why and for what purpose God loves, that God's being as love is intrinsically intelligible and purposeful, inexhaustibly rich in meaning, and makes the deepest sense. Drawing on the classic Protestant theologian H. Heidegger, he says:

---

31. For a subtle discussion of infinity, which displays Traherne's acquaintance with the science of his day, see ibid. pp. 331–6.
32. Barth, *Church Dogmatics*, vol. II, part 1, p. 406.

In God's wisdom, too, it is a question of what is worthy of God as God, what befits Him as He loves. It befits Him to affirm Himself and to carry through His plans. In this reside His holiness and righteousness. But in both these *moderatio* is also proper to Him (and here we are reminded of God's patience). By this they are both conjoined with His divine glory, rooted in it and related to it. In this relationship His holiness and righteousness, His whole being and doing, have truth, order, beauty, meaning, purpose and reason. In this foundation and relationship consists His wisdom.

The wisdom of God is the inner truth and clarity with which the divine life in its self-fulfilment and its works justifies and confirms itself and in which it is the source and sum and criterion of all that is clear and true.[33]

The ascription of 'truth, order, beauty, meaning, purpose and reason' to God as the content of his wisdom is combined with an account of Jesus Christ as the one in whom '**are hid all the treasures of wisdom and knowledge**' (Col. 2:3) and as the crucified one who has become for us '**wisdom from God**' (1 Cor. 1:30). The immersion of God's wisdom in the complexity, agony and distortion of existence represented by the cross is supported by the close connection of God's wisdom with his patience and by Barth's decisive judgement at the end of a long excursus largely on Proverbs and Job 28:

The place where we discover the wisdom of God, the place where it really exists and is known in the fear of God, is, if we give due weight to the Old Testament witness in its context and specific utterances, the place where God gives Himself to be recognised as Creator, Sustainer and Lord of the world. And that place is His holy and righteous, gracious and merciful dealings with Israel.[34]

Yet is there not some tension between the emphasis on Israel's history, Job and the crucified Jesus, on the one hand, and, on the other, the stress on clarity at the end of the previous quotation? This can be linked to a more substantial problem in the relationship between knowledge and wisdom in Barth's doctrine of God and in his theology more widely. Despite seeming to criticise H. Heidegger for subordinating God's wisdom to his knowledge,[35] that appears to be what Barth does. This is suggested quantitatively by the first 250 pages of the volume being devoted to our knowledge of God, and the encompassing concept for

33. Ibid. p. 426.   34. Ibid. p. 432.   35. Ibid. p. 426.

the whole discourse about the perfections being our knowing in correspondence to God's knowing, determining and revealing of himself.[36] Wisdom is given seventeen pages as one of the perfections and is given no encompassing role in the wider theology akin to that of knowledge. I have already noted (chapter 4 above) his playing down the wisdom theme in the book of Job in favour of a focus on truth and falsehood, and agreed with Ticciati's worry about failure to do justice to the shaping of Job through immersion in traumatic events and wrestling to come to terms with them. Other questions that might be raised concern his too complete identification of wisdom and Word, to the detriment of the former;[37] the relative absence of the Apocrypha's intertestamental wisdom (such as the Wisdom of Solomon and Sirach) from his theology, despite their influence on the New Testament; his neglect of wisdom as a theme in his massive christology (which, in terms of the classical 'offices' of Jesus Christ, concentrates largely on him as priest, king and prophet but not sufficiently as a sage 'greater than Solomon'); and his scant attention to traditions of Christian worship and prayer as distillations and performances of Christian wisdom.

There are issues here about the use of scripture. This is not so much a question of method as one of substantial difference in what David Kelsey calls a scriptural 'discrimen',[38] a basic intellectual and imaginative apprehension of scripture such that certain things are given prominence. The prominence Barth gives to knowing and knowledge, clarity, theology as *scientia*, truth and falsehood, and imperatives means that he pays less attention to wisdom and its moods, which include the indicative and imperative but also the interrogative, subjunctive and, embracing all, the optative mood of desire.

Barth, of course, insists on knowledge and wisdom being one in the simplicity of God, but the relative emphasis on them greatly affects the import of his theology. Wisdom is more patient of unclarity, and even resists the idealisation of clarity as the one satisfactory end of seeking to understand. Wisdom is less fixated on the indicative mood. My studies of Job and Jesus suggest that it is worth thinking of God's wisdom as having

36. As regards human knowing, I have not laid out my epistemology in this book. It is given in Ford and Hardy, *Living in Praise*.
37. See my discussion of this with special reference to Jüngel in 'The God of Blessing Who Loves in Wisdom', pp. 118ff.
38. David H. Kelsey, *The Uses of Scripture in Recent Theology* (London: SCM Press, 1975), p. 160 and *passim* thereafter.

in it something analogous to the other moods too. The other mood in God to which Barth does full justice besides the indicative is the imperative (each volume of the *Church Dogmatics* includes an ethics, rooted in the command of God) – even to the point of postulating obedience in God.[39] But what might correspond in God to Jesus' and our questioning and searching, and how do we read the many scriptural references to God's own questioning and searching? Is there anything analogous in God to experimentation, the testing of possibilities, as in the stories of Abraham and Isaac and of Job? And what about desire? God's desire so pervades the Bible that it must surely be seen as part of divine wisdom too. There are strong inhibitions in parts of the Christian tradition against celebrating and rejoicing in God's desire, but it is there – often in worship and song, and sometimes in strands of which Barth was at best reserved and at times suspicious, such as the monastic, ascetical and contemplative traditions.

Traherne is utterly uninhibited in this regard. He intelligently and exuberantly revels in contemplating God's desire and God's wisdom, among many other perfections, and delights in participating in them wholeheartedly. 'The fervor of his [God's] Lov, and the Extreme Ardor of his desire, wherewith he is carried to Infinit perfection, is his real puritie.'[40] Traherne treats infinite desire as a perfection, and his language of God bursts with desire-related language[41] – wanting, alluring, pleasing, yearning, longing. 'So much of the Life of God may be Esteemed Wanting, as there is Wanting in his Action of Infinit Perfection ... His own Wisdom, and power allured him: So did the Hallelujahs, and praises of all his Creatures.'[42]

So God's wisdom is to be thought of, analogously and in line with my interpretation of scripture and tradition, in terms of the five moods; but not only that. From chapter 1 there has been another more fundamental dimension of wisdom expressed in terms of cries. Traherne's daring to speak of God's infinite wanting and of God's passionate responding to the desires, sufferings and praises of creatures invites a further meditation on the cries of God. Few things are more conducive to amazement and adoration of God than to measure God's wisdom by the task of the

39. Barth, *Church Dogmatics*, vol. IV, part 1, pp. 192–7.
40. Traherne, *Works*, vol. 1, p. 328.
41. In this he is drawing on a long tradition, above all exemplified by Augustine, whose works he knew well.
42. Ibid. p. 329.

discernment of cries in our world. But even more is this so when God's wisdom is acknowledged in the very crying itself, as in the loud cry of Jesus from the cross.

This cry, which in chapter 1 was seen to be pivotal for Christian wisdom, is the ultimate intensity of a wisdom utterly committed to human existence whatever the consequences. It is the touchstone for wisdom in God. In it the 'for your sake' of Jesus cries out to a God whose own 'for my name's sake' he lovingly represents. God's 'for my name's sake' does not spare his Son in response to humanity's cries. But this is not just a transaction. Its secret is that God's desire is for one who in love gives a perfect 'for nothing' response – that of Jesus in his temptations and in Gethsemane on the Mount of Olives. The exultant crying out of Jesus in the Holy Spirit (Luke 10:21–22) springs from having been utterly trusted ('**all things have been handed over to me by my Father**') and thoroughly known ('**no one knows who the Son is except the Father**'), and this having been fully reciprocated by him. In the same Spirit (Stephen '**full of the Spirit and of wisdom**', Acts 6:3; see 6:10) we are invited into this relationship ('**But filled with the Holy Spirit, he gazed into heaven and saw the glory of God and Jesus standing at the right hand of God**' – Acts 7:55; '**Lord Jesus, receive my spirit**' – 7:59) and into a life, and possibly a death, where love and wisdom in the Spirit '**cried out in a loud voice**' (see 7:60).

In resonating with such a cry we learn the love and wisdom of God together, for the sake of a limitless overflow of blessing – '**. . . and, lifting up his hands, he blessed them . . . and they were continually in the temple blessing God**' (Luke 24:50, 53). One surprise blessing of Stephen's death was for Saul, later Paul – '**Then they dragged him out of the city and began to stone him; and the witnesses laid their coats at the feet of a young man named Saul**' (Acts 7:58) – who later writes about blessing, love and wisdom:

> 1 Corinthians 1:23–24 [23]Christ crucified . . . [24]the power of God and the wisdom of God . . .
> 1 Corinthians 2:7 God's wisdom, secret and hidden . . .
>> 2:10 for the Spirit searches everything, even the depths of God . . .
>> 2:16 we have the mind of Christ . . .
> 1 Corinthians 10:16 The cup of blessing that we bless, is it not a sharing in the blood of Christ? The bread that we break, is it not a sharing in the body of Christ? . . .
> 1 Corinthians 13:8 Love never ends.

A crescendo of cries is envisioned in heaven. The book of Revelation opens with a vision of the resurrected Jesus Christ in glory in heaven, his face 'like the sun shining with full force' and his voice 'like a trumpet' and 'like the sound of many waters' (Rev. 1:16, 10, 15). It is this voice that announces messages to the churches and then, again 'like a trumpet' (4:1), summons to the main apocalypse. Heaven is full of noise, with 'rumblings and peals of thunder', and with 'loud voices' mentioned many times. But the pervasive sound is of singing.

> Revelation 4:8–11 [8]And the four living creatures, each of them with six wings, are full of eyes all around and inside. Day and night without ceasing they sing, 'Holy, holy, holy, the Lord God the Almighty, who was and is and is to come.' [9]And whenever the living creatures give glory and honour and thanks to the one who is seated on the throne, who lives for ever and ever, [10]the twenty-four elders fall before the one who is seated on the throne and worship the one who lives for ever and ever; they cast their crowns before the throne, singing, [11]'You are worthy, our Lord and God, to receive glory and honour and power, for you created all things, and by your will they existed and were created.'

Singing is perhaps the most developed form of crying out. It is not necessarily the most powerful – there can be something more primal, raw and gripping about the cry from the cross or a shriek of delight. But the deepest human expressions of joy and grief have often been expressed in song. *Singing is a culture's way of remembering, taking to heart, indwelling and communicating its most passionate cries.*

The book of Revelation imagines life beyond the cries of suffering and grief.

> Revelation 21:3–5 [3]And I heard a loud voice from the throne saying, 'See, the home of God is among mortals. He will dwell with them; they will be his peoples, and God himself will be with them; [4]he will wipe every tear from their eyes. Death will be no more; mourning and crying and pain will be no more, for the first things have passed away.' [5]And the one who was seated on the throne said, 'See, I am making all things new.'

At the centre of this vision of newness is the one who has entered into death and brought new life, and he is addressed in a new song.

Revelation 5:9–14 [9]They sing a new song: 'You are worthy to take the scroll and to open its seals, for you were slaughtered and by your blood you ransomed for God saints from every tribe and language and people and nation; [10]you have made them to be a kingdom and priests serving our God, and they will reign on earth.' [11]Then I looked, and I heard the voice of many angels surrounding the throne and the living creatures and the elders; they numbered myriads of myriads and thousands of thousands, [12]singing with full voice, 'Worthy is the Lamb that was slaughtered to receive power and wealth and wisdom and might and honour and glory and blessing!' [13]Then I heard every creature in heaven and on earth and under the earth and in the sea, and all that is in them, singing, 'To the one seated on the throne and to the Lamb be blessing and honour and glory and might for ever and ever!' [14]And the four living creatures said, 'Amen!' And the elders fell down and worshipped.

Later there is an amplification of volume and musicality (waters, thunder and harpists) to signify the sound of a choir whose very identity is in 'hallowing the name': they are those who have died for the name of Jesus and of his Father, now singing a new song in their presence. It consummates the **'blessing and glory and wisdom and thanksgiving and honour and power and might'** (Rev. 7:12) that the angels and others had ascribed to God earlier – now such praise is being offered by those who glorified his name to the point of death:

Revelation 14:1–3 [1]Then I looked, and there was the Lamb, standing on Mount Zion! And with him were one hundred and forty-four thousand who had his name and his Father's name written on their foreheads. [2]And I heard a voice from heaven like the sound of many waters and like the sound of loud thunder; the voice I heard was like the sound of harpists playing on their harps, [3]and they sing a new song before the throne and before the four living creatures and before the elders.

The hyperbolic intensity of the book of Revelation, perhaps unequalled in the Bible, has at its core this meeting of the Lamb, Jesus Christ crucified, with the martyrs. *When the one who has cried out on the cross meets those who have cried out in martyrdom the result is an explosion of new song. This is the ultimate in hallowing the name: worthy lives, worthy deaths, and worthy, overwhelming, new and loud singing. '**Blessing and glory and wisdom**' – and also love – have henceforth to be understood by reference to this vision of a community before God of those who, having died for the sake of God's name, now live in the full presence of God and each other.*

The church as a school of desire and wisdom

Even in the book of Revelation there is deep concern about the worth of the church in the face of its call to bear the name of Jesus Christ and his Father worthily. Its second and third chapters are messages to seven churches of Asia Minor. The messages can be read as the visionary prophetic wisdom of Jesus for his churches, a set of specific discernments taking into account what is going on in the communities and their contexts. They combine knowledge (each begins 'I know'), judgement, instructions, guidance, encouragement and promises. The introduction to each message gives Jesus a title.

> Revelation 2:1 ... These are the words of him who holds the seven stars in his right hand, who walks among the seven golden lampstands ...
> 2:8 ... the words of the first and the last, who was dead and came to life ...
> 2:12 ... the words of him who has the sharp two-edged sword ...
> 2:18 ... the words of the Son of God, who has eyes like a flame of fire, and whose feet are like burnished bronze ...
> Revelation 3:1 ... the words of him who has the seven spirits of God and the seven stars ...
> 3:7 ... the words of the holy one, the true one, who has the key of David, who opens and no one will shut, who shuts and no one opens ...
> 3:14 The words of the Amen, the faithful and true witness, the origin of God's creation ...

Each title could be explored, but for now the point is that the first thrust of each message is to draw attention to the church's Lord, in whose name they are called to live and be faithful even to death. *The 'who' of this wisdom is primary, in line with the primacy of worship in the rest of the book.*
 At the end of each message is a promise.

> Revelation 2:7 ... To everyone who conquers, I will give permission to eat from the tree of life that is in the paradise of God ...
> 2:11 ... Whoever conquers will not be harmed by the second death ...
> 2:17 ... To everyone who conquers I will give some of the hidden manna, and I will give a white stone, and on the white stone is written a new name that no one knows except the one who receives it ...

2:26–28 [26]... To everyone who conquers and continues to do my works to the end, I will give authority over the nations; [27]to rule them with an iron rod, as when clay pots are shattered – [28]even as I also received authority from my Father. To the one who conquers I will also give the morning star ...

Revelation 3:5 ... If you conquer, you will be clothed like them in white robes, and I will not blot your name out of the book of life; I will confess your name before my Father and before his angels ...

3:12 ... If you conquer, I will make you a pillar in the temple of my God; you will never go out of it. I will write on you the name of my God, and the name of the city of my God, the new Jerusalem that comes down from my God out of heaven, and my own new name ...

3:20–21 [20]Listen! I am standing at the door, knocking; if you hear my voice and open the door, I will come in to you and eat with you, and you with me. [21]To the one who conquers I will give a place with me on my throne, just as I myself conquered and sat down with my Father on his throne.

Each promise is accompanied by versions of the cry: '**Listen to what the Spirit is saying to the churches!**' (2:7, 11, 17, 29; 3:6, 13, 22). Each promise also invites into a desire, both shaping it and giving permission to yearn confidently for what is being offered. The imagery is of unimaginably good objects of desire (eating from the tree of life in God's paradise; life that does not face ultimate death; hidden manna; authority and power over nations, like that of Jesus; glorious clothing; recognition by name before God and all the angels; eating with Jesus, reigning with Jesus) and also of discovering one's own true, mysterious identity (a new name known only to oneself) and of bearing God's name, Jerusalem's new name, and Jesus' new name. *Here is an orientation of desire that is ascribed to the Spirit and that embraces the Father, all nations, intimacy with Jesus in a meal-centred community, and a new, transformed identity – even a revelation of the new name of Jesus.*

So the visionary wisdom for these churches is rooted in worship and shapes their desires and hopes through promises. In between the opening identification of Jesus and the culminating orientation of desire comes the messages' engagement with the present life of the communities. The core concern is clear: '**you are enduring patiently and bearing up for the sake of my name**'; '**be faithful until death**'; '**you are holding fast to my name**'; '**your love, faith, service, and patient endurance**'; '**you have kept my word and have not denied my name ... you have kept my word of patient endurance**' (Rev. 2:3, 10, 13, 19; 3:8, 10). These are churches under great pressure and persecution (the horrendous violence in the rest of the book is a vivid image of their world), and living for the sake of the name of Jesus can mean suffering and dying.

What are the essentials in this situation? Many of them have been central to the church century after century: faithfulness, patience, love, service, relations with Jews (if that is what is meant by 2:9 and 3:9), relations with the rest of society (2:14, 20), and especially teaching (2:14, 15, 20; 3:3, 8) and the need to listen to what the Spirit is saying (see above). *That cry of Jesus to the church to listen, echoing the Old Testament cry, 'Hear, O Israel!', constitutes the church as a school of the wisdom of Christ, alert to his words and to his own embodiment of them.* That cry is repeated seven times and is juxtaposed with seven desire-shaping promises, suggesting that this is also a school of desire.

Marks of Christian desire and wisdom in the church

So the church can be seen as a school of desire and wisdom. This is an appropriate heading under which to recapitulate the various ways in which the church has figured in previous chapters. There it has been considered as a community of interpretation, in its relation with Judaism after the Shoah, and as a central concern of the Acts of the Apostles and 1 Corinthians. The christology of wisdom and desire in chapter 5 opens the way for an ecclesiology along similar lines. Other strands of the New Testament besides Acts, 1 Corinthians and the book of Revelation point in the same direction.[43] Historically and theologically the church is inextricably interwoven with scripture, tradition and worship and is the social location of the three together. It therefore needs to be, among other things, a school of wisdom, its understanding and practice shaped around the desire for wisdom in worship, wisdom in the interpretation of scripture and tradition, and wisdom in responding to God's promises.

If this were a full-scale ecclesiology those statements would need to be worked through in relation to scripture, church tradition and history, and a range of other models of the church besides that of a school of desire and

43. Indeed the possibilities for developing this theme are if anything richer with other New Testament books. The themes of living, praising, worshipping and knowing in Ford and Hardy, *Living in Praise* easily transpose into those of desire and wisdom, making its interpretation (in chapter 3) of Paul's Letter to the Philippians especially relevant to the present discussion. 2 Corinthians (see Young and Ford, *Meaning and Truth in 2 Corinthians*, chapters 6, 7 and 8), Ephesians (see chapter 5 in *Self and Salvation*), Romans, Colossians, 1 and 2 Timothy, Hebrews, James, the letters of Peter and the letters of John also have a great deal of promising material which could be drawn on in a fuller ecclesiology that sees the church as a school of desire and wisdom.

wisdom. What the present discussion requires is something less extensive but able to mediate between the previous chapters and the case studies of chapters 8–10 by focussing on the character and calling of the Christian community. This will be attempted by thinking through the four classic marks of the church understood as a school of desire and wisdom.

The classic marks of the church are unity, holiness, catholicity and apostolicity. Each is to be understood first of all as a blessing of God, a gift and a joy; then as a calling, to be desired and learned with others; and also as something to be realised through signs of God and God's purposes in the world.

(i) The church is a school of desire for unity

Psalm 133:1–3 [1]How very good and pleasant it is when kindred live together in unity! [2]It is like the precious oil on the head, running down upon the beard, on the beard of Aaron, running down over the collar of his robes.[3]It is like the dew of Hermon, which falls on the mountains of Zion. For there the LORD ordained his blessing, life for evermore.

Unity like that celebrated by Psalm 133 is a blessing from God, to be longed for, worked for and enjoyed. It is deeply connected with life, peace, trust and love, and most fundamentally with the unity of God: the one God wants those he created in his image to live in peace together, and the commandment to love God is inseparable from the commandment to love neighbours.

The embodiment of this is in a community that understands itself as the people of God. Perhaps the deepest issue for Christian unity is the question about the relation of the church to Israel, both the Israel of the Bible and the Jewish people down the centuries. Is it possible for Christians to understand themselves as the people of God in continuity with Israel without implying that Jews today are not?[44] Or, in George Lindbeck's terms, is it possible for the church to appropriate its identity

---

44. For a succinct discussion of this, see R. Kendall Soulen, 'Israel and the Church: A Christian Response to Irving Greenberg's Covenantal Pluralism' in *Christianity in Jewish Terms*, ed. Tikva Frymer-Kensky et al. (Boulder, CO: Westview Press, 2000). Soulen discusses Paul's 'determination to maintain the truth of two seemingly irreconcilable convictions: the gospel was God's power of salvation for everyone, Jew and Gentile alike, *and* God's promises to Israel were irrevocable, including that part of Israel that did not believe in the gospel. Unfortunately, subsequent generations of Christians resolved the conundrum much more simply by just dropping the second of Paul's two great convictions' (p. 170). Soulen's rejection of this supersessionism and his insistence on one covenant can be explored at greater length in his *God of Israel and Christian Theology* (Minneapolis: Augsburg Fortress, 1996). One of his main interlocutors, Michael Wyschogrod, develops a Jewish understanding of Jewish–Christian relations that parallels Soulen's in *Abraham's Promise: Judaism and*

as Israel without expropriating Judaism?[45] His convincing thesis is that this is both possible and in line with the New Testament. Not only is supersessionism (the replacement of Israel/Judaism by the church) to be rejected, but the church needs to reappropriate its understanding of itself as, in some sense, Israel. 'Sharing Israelhood' is vital for the health of the church as well as for its relationship with Judaism.[46] It is unlikely that attempts of churches among themselves to arrive at an appropriate form of unity will thrive unless they have all worked through their relationship to the one irrevocable covenant and calling of God (see Rom. 9–11) that is shared with Judaism, and to 'the primal schism' – the separation of Christianity from Judaism.

The New Testament gives many indications of a strong commitment to Christian unity, grounded in the conviction that this is essential to the church in the purposes of God. Luke–Acts (see above chapters 1, 2 and 5) offers the conception of unity that has perhaps become most widely shared. It is rooted in the sending of the Holy Spirit, in the preaching of the Gospel and in common baptism ('the sacrament of unity'[47]), and it is embodied in an apostolic, eucharistic worshipping community that shares a mission to the whole world.

John's Gospel presents the passionate desire of Jesus for unity among his followers at a point that gives it maximum emphasis. The prayer at the culmination of his farewell discourse with his disciples links unity with, on the one hand, his own relationship to his Father and, on the other, the relationship of his followers with the world.

> John 17:20–26 [20]'I ask not only on behalf of these, but also on behalf of those who will believe in me through their word, [21]that they may all be one. As you, Father, are in me and I am in you, may they also be in us, so that the world may believe that you have sent me. [22]The glory

Jewish–Christian Relations, ed. Michael Wyschogrod and R. Kendall Soulen (Grand Rapids, MI: Eerdmans, 2004), though neither denies what Soulen calls 'an irreducible element of dispute and even rivalry' (Christianity in Jewish Terms, p. 174).

45. There is a further major issue regarding the relation of Islam to both Judaism and Christianity. 'People of God' can be helpful as a heuristic concept in discussing this. From a Christian standpoint Katherine Sonderegger has argued convincingly that 'people of God' need not be strictly identified with the Christian church (in her paper 'The People of God' to the Society for the Study of Theology annual conference in Leeds, April 2006).

46. George Lindbeck, 'What of the Future? A Christian Response' in <i>Christianity in Jewish Terms</i>, pp. 357–66. For a fuller presentation of Lindbeck's ecclesiology see 'The Story-Shaped Church: Critical Exegesis and Theological Interpretation' in <i>Scriptural Authority and Narrative Interpretation</i>, ed. Garrett Green (Philadelphia: Fortress Press, 1987), pp. 161–78.

47. For an illuminating discussion of baptism in relation to church unity and the modern ecumenical movement by a leading ecumenist who is also a distinguished historian, see David Thompson, <i>Baptism, Church and Society in England and Wales</i> (Carlisle: Paternoster, 2005).

that you have given me I have given them, so that they may be one, as
we are one, [23]I in them and you in me, that they may become
completely one, so that the world may know that you have sent me and
have loved them even as you have loved me. [24]Father, I desire that
those also, whom you have given me, may be with me where I am, to see
my glory, which you have given me because you loved me before the
foundation of the world. [25]Righteous Father, the world does not know
you, but I know you; and these know that you have sent me. [26]I made
your name known to them, and I will make it known, so that the love
with which you have loved me may be in them, and I in them.'

Unity in love is there seen as the pivot between God and the world, and
at the heart of Jesus' desire.

Paul's concern for the unity of the church is a key theme in 1
Corinthians, as chapter 5 above described. But within the Pauline litera-
ture the most emphatic teaching on unity is in the Letter to the Ephesians.
The whole letter is relevant to this theme, but especially four elements.

First there is the description of the church as Christ's body, **'the
fullness of him who fills all in all'** (1:22). There is discussion of whether
the 'him' refers to Jesus Christ or God; but, if it is Christ, he is being
identified with the activity of God. The fact of the dispute itself makes a
point: as in John 17 there is the closest link between the church, Jesus
Christ and his Father.

Second, there is the radical conception in Ephesians 2 of Jesus Christ as
'our peace', breaking down by his death the dividing wall of hostility
between Jews and Gentiles, and creating in himself **'one new humanity'**
in a church being **'built together in the Spirit into a dwelling place
for God'** (2:22).[48] The deepest secret of Christian unity is this solidarity
through the death of Jesus (enacted in baptism), understood as given
already but to be grown into more and more.

Third, Ephesians 3 sets the death of Jesus in the context of **'the plan**
(οἰκονομία, 'economy') **of the mystery hidden for ages in God who
created all things, so that through the church the wisdom of God in
its rich variety might now be made known to the rulers and authorities in the heavenly places'** (3:9–10). This echoes an earlier description
of the mystery of the interrelatedness of all things in the purposes of God
understood through wisdom:

48. For my understanding of the implications of this for the church and Judaism today
see Ford, 'A Messiah for the Third Millennium'.

Ephesians 1:8–10 [8]With all wisdom and insight [9]he has made known to us the mystery of his will, according to his good pleasure that he set forth in Christ, [10]as a plan for the fullness of time, to gather up all things in him, things in heaven and things on earth.

Fourth, the practical implication of all this is a heartfelt plea to the Ephesian church:

Ephesians 4:1–6 [1]I therefore, the prisoner in the Lord, beg you to lead a life worthy of the calling to which you have been called, [2]with all humility and gentleness, with patience, bearing with one another in love, [3]making every effort to maintain the unity of the Spirit in the bond of peace. [4]There is one body and one Spirit, just as you were called to the one hope of your calling, [5]one Lord, one faith, one baptism, [6]one God and Father of all, who is above all and through all and in all.

That is the most comprehensive New Testament statement about unity, inextricably connecting the oneness of God with a church united in the Spirit, in Christ, in eschatological orientation, in faith and in baptism, that sustains its unity through practising humility, gentleness, patience and love. Such practices constitute the bonds and ethos of a community of peace. The verses that follow show the gifts that need to come together in order to enable a fuller and deeper unity, the desire being that '**all of us come to the unity of the faith and of the knowledge of the Son of God, to maturity, to the measure of the full stature of Christ**' (4:13) Again there is an echo of chapter 1, this time in its prayer for '**a spirit of wisdom and revelation as you come to know him, so that, with the eyes of your heart enlightened, you may know what is the hope to which he has called you**' (1:17–18). *This community is to understand itself as inhabiting a multifaceted unity within the mystery of God's 'economy', sustained through praying for and learning the wisdom of God in Jesus Christ and exercising the gifts and virtues of the Spirit.*

Two millennia later, the church is multiply divided. The one body of Christ is deeply wounded, torn apart, sometimes in physical violence. The twentieth century saw an unprecedented phenomenon: many religious communities, which until then had a competitive and even conflictual relationship moved, through the ecumenical movement, to a conversational and collaborative relationship, and in some cases to organic unity. The process required huge efforts at international, regional, national and local levels. It involved risky initiatives and courageous leadership, intensive study and discussion year after year, 'faith and order' as well as 'life and work' issues, new institutions, considerable funding and dedicated prayer.

Yet, at the time of writing, among the main Christian denominations that have participated in ecumenical dialogue and cooperation there is a sense that the process has slowed or even in some cases gone into reverse. What are the signs of hope? I mention one that illustrates my thesis. In January 2006 about 150 people from ten countries, three continents and eight churches came together for five days in Durham, England, to explore the theme of 'Catholic Learning and Receptive Ecumenism', with Cardinal Walter Kasper, President of the Pontifical Council for Promoting Christian Unity, as a leading contributor. The general idea was for each tradition to explore what it might, with integrity, learn from other traditions. This aim of responsible receptivity and mutual learning embraced history, doctrine, worship, ethics, polity, institutional life, politics and psychology. The specific focus was on what the Roman Catholic Church might learn from a range of other churches and from various forms of disciplined investigation. In my terms, it was an attempt to share wisdoms. There were two especially striking aspects of the conference. One was the presence of people from many churches who had dedicated many years and immense effort to ecumenism and who were able to communicate both their passionate desire for unity and their hard-won wisdom. The other was the power of the worship, combined with pain because of the inability of all to share in the same eucharist together. It was as if the cry of longing for unity, and for the wisdom that might enable it, met the cries of praise, thanks, intercession, penitence and anguish.

The result was a deepening and re-energising of the desire for unity together with an overwhelming, at times almost despairing, realisation that for each church and each person this means a practical working out of the wisdom of the cross. *The loud cry of Jesus from the cross, the cry of a torn body, is the touchstone for this wisdom. Like Job, it has only one hope against hope:* 'My God! My God!'

(ii) The church is a school of desire for holiness

It is this hope in God alone that is central to holiness. Of all the marks of the church holiness most obviously points to God. The '**Holy, Holy, Holy**' of Revelation 4:8, quoted above, takes up the cry of the seraphs in the theophany to the prophet Isaiah.

> Isaiah 6:3 And one called to another and said: 'Holy, holy, holy is the LORD of hosts; the whole earth is full of his glory.'

Holiness is first of all to do with the being of God – hence the addition in Revelation 4:8 of '**the Lord God almighty, who was and is and is to come**'. The Hebrew root of the word for holiness, *qds*, signifies separation, and is often associated with places (holy land, holy mountain, temple sanctuary) or times (above all the Sabbath). Through later usage, especially by the prophets of Israel, it gathered rich spiritual and ethical meanings to do with the sort of life and behaviour appropriate for God's people. The sense of otherness, of orientation to God as God, suits it to being a key concept in the wisdom of loving God for God's sake.

To desire holiness is to respond to the call of God to the people of God to be like God:

> Leviticus 19:2 Speak to all the congregation of the people of Israel and say to them: You shall be holy, for I the Lord your God am holy.

In the immediate context, that is connected with revering parents, keeping the Sabbath, avoiding idolatry, and other commands. What holiness requires of people has been very controversial throughout Jewish and Christian history, and also one of the deepest divisions between Jews and Christians. Since the church has taken over directly the scriptural injunctions to Israel, all the questions discussed above on unity relating to Christianity and Judaism are raised here too.

> 1 Peter 1:14–16 [14]Like obedient children, do not be conformed to the desires that you formerly had in ignorance. [15]Instead, as he who called you is holy, be holy yourselves in all your conduct; [16]for it is written, 'You shall be holy, for I am holy.'

Indeed, within each community, matters related to holiness have perhaps been the most frequently cited reason for schism. It is a perpetual problem that is inseparable from worshipping and seeking to obey a holy God. It requires continual discernment, a wisdom of holiness.

The desire for holiness, like the desire for unity, therefore must seek an appropriate wisdom which takes seriously both desires and also the powerful cries that articulate them. This can easily become detached from a living relationship with God, and in particular from the Joban '**fearing God for nothing**'. In the wisdom of holiness the hallowing of God's name for God's sake is a crucial niche of the ecology, helping to ensure that holiness differs from moralism and from the undiscerning repetition of either scripture or tradition. A further sign of the 'for nothing' can be 'the beauty of holiness', and the delight in aesthetic means of glorifying God.

As this chapter has suggested, the atmosphere within which such holiness flourishes is that of prayer and worship. In line with this, holiness calls for a transformation of desire (see chapter 5 above) and a life that is prepared to realise the love of God in smaller and greater matters (the latter including martyrdom). To be a school of such desire is to be a community in which prayer and worship are learned, faith in all its moods (indicative, imperative, interrogative, subjunctive and optative) is practised with a view to wise discernment, and exemplars of holiness (saints, martyrs, and less obvious models) are appreciated and imitated.

As with unity, the claim that the church is holy seems to be obviously contradicted by the reality of much church life in the past and present. Biblical Israel had the same problem of failing repeatedly to live up to God's call to holiness, as does Judaism. In both Christianity and Judaism the answer has not been to give up on holiness but to acknowledge the necessity of habitual repentance. The cry for holiness is first of all a cry of penitence, a response to the self-interrogating thrust of faith. In the church, the expectation of holiness is emphasised by the claim to have received the Holy Spirit – indeed most uses of the word 'holy' in the New Testament are related to the Spirit. But in no Christian church is this a simple claim to holiness. The Holy Spirit is quintessentially a gift of God, and one that is not simply possessed when given; rather, the mark of having received it is to ask for it continually, so that the all-pervasive, constitutive cry of the church is: 'Come, Holy Spirit!' And the further, classic mark of a positive answer is an intensification of the recognition of how far from the holiness of God one is.

(iii) The church is a school of desire for catholicity

Catholicity, or universality, like unity and holiness, is fundamentally connected with who God is. The God who creates all things also plans, as Ephesians says, **'to gather up all things in him, things in heaven and things on earth'** (1:10). The wisdom of catholicity has that breadth of embrace, and involves the crossing of many boundaries and dealing with many differences.

From the beginning of the story of Israel as God's chosen people the horizon of blessing embraces the whole world. Abram is promised: '... **in you all the families of the earth shall be blessed**' (Gen. 12:3). The church understands itself as one of the ways in which that promise is being fulfilled. Judaism participates in its fulfilment too, and its ways of doing so are a rebuke to any Christian totalitarian vision of catholicity embodied in a single universal organisation monopolising God's blessings. Indeed ecclesial catholicity is probably best understood as the church in dispersal, distributed in many places and spheres of life, relating to many 'others', complementing the gathered church.

This means that the wisdom of catholicity has to take urgent account of the cries of the world. The church that takes seriously its responsibility before God towards the world (including the natural world) is faced with a continual task of discerning among cries. To be a school of desire for catholicity, for the universality of God's compassion and love, is to learn this discernment together, in dialogue with many others beyond one's own community. Each of the remaining chapters of this book might be seen as an exercise in seeking such wisdom. Inter-faith wisdom is sought across church boundaries with Judaism and Islam in response to the desire for mutual understanding and peace from God. Academic wisdom is sought through an interdisciplinary collegiality alert to the yearning for meaning, knowledge and all-round educational formation. In response to the cries of those with mental disabilities the L'Arche communities are formed around the wisdom of friendship. In the midst of numerous countersigns, Christian commitment with others to peace among faiths, higher education and those with disabilities is a sign of ecclesial catholicity.

(iv) The church is a school of desire for apostolicity

God says to Abram: 'Go!' (Gen. 12:1), to Moses: 'Go!' (Exod. 3:16), to Isaiah: 'Go!' (Isa. 6:9), to Ezekiel: 'Go!' (Ezek. 3:1, 4, 11, 22). Jesus says to his disciples: 'Follow me!' (Luke 9:23), 'Do this!' (Luke 10:28, 22.19), 'Go!' (Matt. 28:19). Being sent is the central thrust of apostleship. Its roots, as with the other marks of the church, are deep in Israel being chosen as the people of God and being given a vocation, a mission, by God; and again, as already discussed in relation to unity, basic questions are raised about Judaism and the church, symbolised by the number of Jesus' core group of disciples being the same as the number of Israel's tribes, twelve.

Disciples (μαθηταὶ) means 'learners', and the twelve are also called 'apostles' (ἀπόστολοι, 'the sent ones').[49] Apostleship is the mark of the

---

49. Some strands of the New Testament name others as apostles besides the original twelve, and Paul also claimed to be an apostle. See Sean Freyne, *The Twelve: Disciples and Apostles: A Study in the Theology of the First Three Gospels* (London: Sheed & Ward, 1968); C. K. Barrett, *The Signs of an Apostle* (London: Epworth Press, 1970).

church most directly related to learning and teaching. The bitter disputes about claims to apostolicity in the church centre on authority over teachings and practices. A key issue has been 'apostolic succession': is the authentic lineage of authoritative teaching democratic (the consensus of the whole church), presbyteral (through elders, ministers or priests), episcopal (through bishops), or papal (through the Pope as bishop of the 'apostolic see' of Rome, looking back to both Peter and Paul, and having primacy among bishops)? These differences lead to very different approaches to teaching and passing on the faith, though most are agreed that, whatever the polity, the whole church (the extent of which is, of course, also disputed) shares in being apostolic. The ending of Matthew's Gospel has perhaps been the *locus classicus* in the New Testament:

> Matthew 28:16–20 [16]Now the eleven disciples went to Galilee, to the mountain to which Jesus had directed them. [17]When they saw him, they worshipped him; but some doubted. [18]And Jesus came and said to them, 'All authority in heaven and on earth has been given to me. [19]Go therefore and make disciples of all nations, baptising them in the name of the Father and of the Son and of the Holy Spirit, [20]and teaching them to obey everything that I have commanded you. And remember, I am with you always, to the end of the age.'

That combines authority and obedience; worship; sending the apostles; the centrality to the disciples' identity of the threefold name of Father, Son and Holy Spirit; handing on teaching; and the promise of communion with Jesus. But it also locates the authority in Jesus, who is distinguished from the community as a continuing authoritative presence, and it notes the occurrence of doubt even among the disciples in the presence of the risen Jesus. The final note is eschatological, orientation towards the longed for consummation at 'the end of the age'. So it is simultaneously indicative, imperative, interrogative and optative, and sends the 'learners' out to teach 'all nations' by making more 'learners' to share in their apostolate.

To desire apostolicity is therefore to take part in a community that is involved in the histories of all nations, with learning and teaching happening above all for God's sake, in God's name, intrinsic to which is the naming of Jesus and the Holy Spirit. A wisdom of apostolicity will not be able to avoid hard decisions about disputed matters of authority and succession (the sign of which is membership in one denomination rather than another); but it will also see those disputes in the context of the unity of God and of baptism in God's name, the location of authority in Jesus over against all his disciples, and the longing for unity at 'the end of the age'. The disputes are neither the first nor the last word, and they are always conducted in the presence of the one living Word.

It is also worth remembering Matthew's parabolic vision of the ending, when the criterion of judgement between 'sheep' and 'goats' is whether they have had compassion on strangers, those without clothing, the hungry, the thirsty and those in prison. The church as a school of desire for apostolicity is inseparable from learning to obey the commands of Jesus, above all the command to love God and the neighbour. Jesus' **'I am with you always'** is to be set alongside **'I was hungry and you gave me food ... Truly I tell you, just as you did it to one of the least of these who are members of my family, you did it to me'** (Matt. 25:35, 40). This is the test of apostolic schooling, the wisdom of love and compassion in action. The final chapter of this book will consider L'Arche as an attempt to realise it.

Christian theology as wisdom

This chapter has considered the central reality of Christian theology, the God of blessing who loves in wisdom. The nerve of wise Christian love is loving God for God's own sake, blessing and hallowing God's name. This love calls on all our capacities, including our minds. Christian theology is one exercise in the mind's love for God and the neighbour. Before trying to practise theology in three case studies (chapters 8–10 below) it is worthwhile considering further the topic indicated by the Introduction's title, 'Theology as wisdom'. The intervening chapters have taken soundings in wisdom theology through interpreting scripture and, to a lesser extent, Christian tradition. But this exercise is part of a long tradition of conceiving theology as wisdom or in closely related terms. In conclusion I will briefly highlight some of the landmarks in that tradition.[50]

First it is necessary to recognise a false dichotomy which modern and late modern study of theology has often made. On the one hand, it is frequently acknowledged that, in the early period of Christianity, philosophy had a major role to play in the development of the tradition; on the other hand, the role of wisdom in that development is far less commonly

---

50. I am grateful to Dr Paul T. Nimmo for assisting with the research for the rest of this section.

recognised. This position fails to note that, as Wilken says, 'the ancients did not make the distinction we do between wisdom and philosophy'.[51] Rather, 'in antiquity, the terms were often interchangeable. Philosopher could designate a wise man and *sophos* a philosopher. Philosophy was as much concerned with life as it was with ideas.'[52] While the early traditions in the New Testament can be rather suspicious of φιλοσοφία and earthly σοφία (see for the former Colossians 2:8; and for the latter 1 Corinthians 1:18–2:7, 2 Corinthians 1:12, Colossians 2:23 and James 3:15), Christian apologists in the middle of the second century began to find it in their interests to describe Christianity as a philosophy.[53]

One of the first theologians to embrace the portrayal of the Christian faith as a philosophy was Justin Martyr. He ventures that 'philosophy is, in fact, the greatest possession, and most honourable before God, to whom it leads us and alone commends us' (*Dial.* 2).[54] Throughout his apologetic work, Justin attempts to forge connections with other, non-Christian philosophers, arguing that Christians 'on some points ... teach the same things as the poets and philosophers whom you honour, and on other points are fuller and more divine in our teaching' (*Apol.* 1.20). The account of his conversion, however, renders it beyond doubt that Justin uses the term 'philosophy' in a very broad sense. He recounts how 'straightway a flame was kindled in my soul; and a love of the prophets, and of those men who are friends of Christ, possessed me; and whilst revolving his words in my mind, I found this philosophy alone to be safe and profitable. Thus, and for this reason, I am a philosopher' (*Dial.* 8). *This interconnectedness between love, scripture, Christian community and philosophy stands in the closest proximity to what throughout this book has been termed wisdom.* Indeed, Carol Harrison notes, in the time of the early church as a whole 'the idea of wisdom was a common denominator in any attempt to come to grips with the question of truth, in philosophical as well as Christian circles'.[55] For

51. Robert L. Wilken, 'Wisdom and Philosophy in Early Christianity' in *Aspects of Wisdom in Judaism and Early Christianity*, ed. Robert L. Wilken (Notre Dame and London: University of Notre Dame Press, 1975), p. 144.
52. Ibid.
53. Wilken points out this endeavour was aided by the pagan philosopher-physician Galen, who began to call Christianity a 'philosophical school'. Wilkin observes that 'to be considered even a third-rate philosophical school was a step upward in social acceptance from the time Pliny and Tacitus thought Christianity a first-rate superstition', in ibid. p. 160.
54. The translations used here for the works of Justin Martyr are those found in *The Ante-Nicene Fathers*, vol. 1. *The Apostolic Fathers with Justin Martyr and Irenaeus* (Grand Rapids, MI: Eerdmans, 2001 – reprint), found online at http://www.ccel.org/ccel/schaff/anf01.html.
55. Carol Harrison, 'Augustine, Wisdom and Classical Culture' in *Where Shall Wisdom Be Found?*, ed. Stephen C. Barton (Edinburgh: T. & T. Clark, 1999), p. 125.

early Christians, wisdom and truth 'converged in their shared goal, the attainment of wisdom or possession of truth, for they believed that it was here that the ultimate good, or happy life, was to be found'.[56]

One culmination of this early wisdom dimension of theology comes in the person of Augustine, whose *Confessions* recount a search for wisdom that leads through a variety of philosophical schools before reaching a terminus in Christianity. He tells how, on reading at nineteen the exhortation to philosophy in Cicero's work *Hortensius*, 'Worthless suddenly became every vain hope to me; and, with an incredible warmth of heart, I yearned for an immortality of wisdom, and began now to arise that I might return to Thee' (*Conf.* iii.4(7)).[57] He continues, 'How ardent was I then, my God, how ardent to fly from earthly things to Thee! Nor did I know how Thou wouldst deal with me. For with Thee is wisdom. In Greek the love of wisdom is called "philosophy", with which that book inflamed me' (*Conf.* iii.4(8)). Ultimately, Augustine arrives at what he calls 'the true and divine philosophy' (*Letter* 2), and writes in respect of the two commandments of the Gospel, 'All philosophy is here, – physics, ethics, logic: the *first*, because in God the Creator are all the causes of all existences in nature; the *second*, because a good and honest life is not produced in any other way than by loving, in the manner in which they should be loved, the proper objects of our love, namely, God and our neighbor; and the *third*, because God alone is the Truth and the Light of the rational soul' (*Letter* 137.5).[58] Robert Dodaro comments that, for Augustine, '*ratio sapientiae* consists in the faith, hope, and love through which the mind reflects on God and on those eternal things (*res aeternae*) that pertain to God, such as true virtue and happiness, as well as eternal rest'.[59] The underlying conception of wisdom at play here thus once again combines the elements of *scripture, creation, ethics, love and worship.*[60]

56. Ibid.
57. The translations used here for the works of Augustine are those found in *The Nicene and Post-Nicene Fathers*, Series 1, vol. 1. *Augustine: Confessions and Letters*, and vol. 3. *Trinity; Doctrinal and Moral Treatises* (New York: The Christian Literature Publishing Co., 1886 and 1890), respectively found online at http://www.ccel.org/ccel/schaff/npnf101.html and http://www.ccel.org/ccel/schaff/npnf103.html.
58. Harrison writes in this connection: 'That he was thereby able to argue for universal access to wisdom through a humble following of Christ, rather than by the rational efforts of those with minds capable of such reflection, is perhaps even more important than the philosophical issues at stake', 'Augustine', p. 137.
59. Robert Dodaro, *Christ and the Just Society in the Thought of Augustine* (Cambridge: Cambridge University Press, 2004), p. 165.
60. While Augustine (echoing Aristotle) continues to make a distinction between wisdom and knowledge – see *Trin.* 12.14 (22), where Augustine writes that 'action, by which we use

In the medieval period, there were two distinct, though not mutually exclusive, approaches to the relationship between theology and wisdom. On the one hand, there was a more mystical track, represented by such theologians as Bonaventure. In his Commentary in Four Books on the Sentences of Peter Lombard, Bonaventure asks, 'Whether this book or theology is for the sake of contemplation, or that we become good, or whether it is a speculative or practical science?' (*Comm.*, Book I, Questions on the Foreword, question 3).[61] The answer he gives is that 'Theological science is an affective habit and the mean between the speculative and practical, and for (its) end it has both contemplation, and that we become good, and indeed more principally, that we become good' (*Comm.*, Book I, Questions on the Foreword, conclusion to question 3). In his reasoning, he explains that the intellect considered in itself is perfected by the habit of speculative science while the intellect considered as extended to work is perfected by the habit of practical science: however, 'if we were to consider it in a middle manner as born to be extended to affection, it is thus perfected by a middle habit, between the purely speculative and practical, which comprises both; and this habit is called wisdom ... *For wisdom is of doctrine according to its name*, in the sixth (chapter) of Ecclesiaticus. Whence this (habit) is for the sake of contemplation, and that we become good, however principally, that we become good' (*Comm.*, Book I, Questions on the Foreword, response to question 3). For Bonaventure, therefore, the virtue of wisdom overcomes the Aristotelian divorce of speculative knowledge and practical work, and does so by means of love. He writes that 'we should dispose ourselves to ascend into God so as to love him *with our whole mind, with our whole heart and with our whole soul* ... In this consists both perfect observance of the Law and Christian wisdom' (*Itin.* 1.4).[62]

On the other hand, there was also a more scholastic investigation of the question, exemplified by such theologians as Thomas Aquinas.

temporal things well, differs from contemplation of eternal things; and the latter is reckoned to wisdom, the former to knowledge' – it is fundamental to his entire theological enterprise that wisdom and knowledge are held together in the one true Mediator, Jesus Christ – see *Trin.* 13.19(24), where he posits that 'the Word made flesh, which is Christ Jesus, has the treasures both of wisdom and of knowledge'.

61. The translation used can be found on-line at 'The Franciscan Archive' – http://www.franciscan-archive.org/bonaventura/opera/bon01012.html.
62. The translation used is that of Ewert Cousins, found in Bonaventure, 'The Soul's Journey into God' in *Bonaventure*, The Classics of Western Spirituality Series (Mahwah, NJ: Paulist Press, 1978), p. 61. For Bonaventure, it is the knowledge that Christ died on behalf of humanity that moves the Christian towards this love (*Comm.*, Book I, Questions on the Foreword, response to question 3).

Aquinas writes in the very first section of his *Summa Theologia* that 'sacred doctrine essentially treats of God viewed as the highest cause – not only so far as He can be known through creatures just as philosophers knew Him – "That which is known of God is manifest in them" (Romans 1:19) – but also as far as He is known to Himself alone and revealed to others. Hence sacred doctrine is especially called wisdom' (*Summa Theologia* 1a.1.6).[63] Precisely because it concerns itself with God, 'wisdom exercises judgment over all the other intellectual virtues, directs them all, and is the architect of them all' (*Summa Theologia* 1a2ae.66.5). Aquinas recognises a 'twofold wisdom' exercised in matters of judgement, the first stemming from virtue, and the second from learning, but ultimately attributes both to God: the first as a gift of the Holy Spirit, and the second through the principles obtained from revelation (*Summa Theologia* 1a.1.6 ad 3).[64] Later in the *Summa*, Aquinas again refers to this twofold nature of wisdom, noting that 'wisdom is not merely speculative, but also practical' (*Summa Theologia* 2a2ae.45.3), although he does assert the superiority of the latter, writing that 'since it [practical wisdom] attains to God more intimately by a kind of union of the soul with Him, it is able to direct us not only in contemplation but also in action' (*Summa Theologia* 2a2ae.45.3 ad 1).[65] Thus Aquinas seems to end up with a similar nexus of concepts surrounding wisdom as Bonaventure does: *love of God, union with God, revelation, and a union of the theoretical and the practical. The task of theology is thus one part of the exercise of wisdom in love.*[66]

---

63. The translation used is that of the Fathers of the English Dominican Province, found on-line at http://www.newadvent.org/.

64. Aquinas observes that 'wisdom, to which knowledge about God pertains, is beyond the reach of man, especially in this life, so as to be his possession: for this "belongs to God alone" (Metaph. i, 2): and yet this little knowledge about God which we can have through wisdom is preferable to all other knowledge', *Summa Theologia*, 1a2ae.66.5 ad 3.

65. For Aquinas, it belongs 'to the wisdom that is an intellectual virtue to pronounce right judgment about Divine things after reason has made its inquiry, but it belongs to wisdom as a gift of the Holy Ghost to judge aright about them on account of connaturality with them', *Summa Theologia*, 2a2ae.45.2. 'The latter wisdom is the result of the love [charity] of God, which unites the believer to God', *Summa Theologia*, 2a2ae.45.2. Under the rubric of wisdom are thus held together both knowledge and love.

66. In the *Scholium* of the Quaracchi Editors to the text of Bonaventure, *Comm.*, Book i, Questions on the Foreword, question 3, it is remarked that Bonaventure here touches 'upon the question debated among the scholastics, whether theology is *wisdom*, which is commonly affirmed, see Alexander of Hales, *Summa.*, p. i., a. 1, m. 1.; (Bl.) John Duns Scotus, *Sent.*, Bk. i, Prolog., q. 3; St. Thomas., *Sent.*, Bk. i, Prolog., a. 1, q. 3 [and] *Summa.*, i., q. 1, a. 6; Bl. (now St.) Albert the Great, *Sent.*, Bk. i, d. 1, a. 4, ad 1; Richard of Middletown, *Sent.*, Bk. i, Prolog., q. 5, ad 3; Giles the Roman, *Sent.*, Bk. i, Prolog., p. 2, q. 1; (Bl.) Peter of Tarentaise, *Sent.*, Bk. i, Prolog., q. 1; Henry of Ghent, *Summa.*, a. 6. q. 2; Durandus, *Sent.*, Bk. i, Prolog., q. 1. in fine'. On Aquinas' theology as wisdom see Levering, *Scripture and Metaphysics*, especially chapters 1–4 and 6.

After this period, the conception of theology as wisdom, and what that might mean, becomes more difficult. Denys Turner comments that when Denys the Carthusian looks back at the figure of Hugh of St Victor in the twelfth century, he saw relived the 'Augustinian ideal of a comprehensive, unified conception of Christian wisdom as serving validly only the purposes of Christian love'.[67] However, Turner notes that 'Denys cannot look much later than the late thirteenth century for a mirror of this ideal. Indeed, it is possible to perceive as early as the first few decades even of that century the first unravelling of this complex skein of knowledge and love.'[68] The progressively scholastic approach to theology in the burgeoning universities of Europe slowly eroded the patristic and medieval sense of the interconnectedness of theology, wisdom and love. Turner asserts that 'This growing sense of distance between what knowledge can achieve and what is achieved by love, corresponding with a tendency to assign the mystical to the experiential and affective, the intellectual to the detached and cognitive, drives an exegetical wedge between the Psalmist's "taste" and his "see", between what is *sapida* and what is *scientia*.'[69] And Mark McIntosh concurs that by the later Middle Ages, 'instead of perceiving knowing and loving as one coinherent activity in God, they come to appear as strangers, rivals, even enemies struggling for dominance in the drama of the inner self'.[70]

The work of St John of the Cross reflects this growing sense of distance between the realms of knowledge and love, to the detriment of a more holistic concept of wisdom, in its division of the discipline of theology. He writes that 'though some may be altogether ignorant of scholastic theology by which the divine verities are explained, yet they are not ignorant of mystical theology, the science of love, by which those verities are not only learned, but at the same time are relished also' (*A Spiritual Canticle of the Soul and the Bridegroom Christ*, Prol.6).[71] John also posits that 'contemplation, whereby the understanding has the loftiest knowledge

67. Denys Turner, 'Wisdom Within or Without' in *Where Shall Wisdom Be Found?*, p. 143.
68. Ibid. p. 143.
69. Ibid. p. 144. Turner is here indicating the (flawed) medieval etymology that saw the word *sapientia* (wisdom) as deriving from the words *scientia* (knowledge) and *sapida* (of pleasing taste) – and thus being a knowledge that tastes or savours; ibid. p. 143. Aquinas quotes Isidore of Seville positively after this fashion, declaring that just as 'the taste is quick to distinguish between savors of meats, so is a wise man in discerning things and causes', *Summa Theologia*, 2a2ae.46.1.
70. Mark McIntosh, *Mystical Theology* (Oxford: Blackwell, 1998), p. 71.
71. The translation used is that found at the website of the Christian Classics Ethereal Library, at http://www.ccel.org/ccel/john_cross/canticle.html.

of God, is called mystical theology, which signifies secret wisdom of God; for it is secret even to the understanding that receives it' (*Ascent to Mount Carmel*, II.viii.6).[72] It is thus clear that, for St John of the Cross at least, there remains no bifurcation of knowledge and love in true wisdom. Nevertheless, within this divided labour of theology, there appears to emerge an implicit prioritisation of the interior, individual and affective dimensions of Christian wisdom over its exterior, communal and cognitive dimensions.

In general, however, the practice of scholastic theology and the practice of mystical theology seem to have drifted ever further apart. McIntosh observes that by the sixteenth century, 'mystical writers no longer authorize their statements by appeal to scriptural or traditional authorities, but by appeal … to the "I", the particular experience of the speaker'.[73] This situation had clear ramifications for Christian wisdom, particularly in respect of the importance (or otherwise) of such matters as scripture, tradition, community and ethics, all of which had been held together in earlier construals of Christian wisdom which stressed the coincidence of knowledge and love in God. It is little wonder that the internal relationship between academic theology and mystical theology became at best strained and at worst antagonistic.

Moreover, the notion of Christian wisdom in general soon encountered a new external challenge in the form of scientific discovery. Rémi Brague observes that, after the Middle Ages, 'New observations and the theories forged to account for them ended up in a vision of the physical universe that could no longer be reconciled with the ancient and medieval image of man's place in the cosmos.'[74] As the explanatory power of the natural sciences increased, so the position of the Christian God and Christian wisdom came under increasing scrutiny. Jürgen Moltmann observes that 'Th[e] unity of theology and the sciences was shattered with the birth of modern times.'[75] Daniel W. Hardy correspondingly

72. The translation used is that found at the website of the Christian Classics Ethereal Library, at http://www.ccel.org/ccel/john_cross/ascent.html.
73. McIntosh, *Mystical Theology*, p. 68. Correspondingly, he observes, 'language for talking about the indescribable wonder of God (who cannot *be* experienced *in se*) becomes the language of having a wonderfully indescribable experience of God', ibid. p. 68.
74. Rémi Brague, *The Wisdom of the World*, trans. Teresa Lavender Fagan (Chicago and London: University of Chicago Press, 2003), p. 186. Brague proceeds to sketch some of the consequences of this cosmographic shift for metaphysics, anthropology and ethics; ibid. particularly pp. 188–211.
75. Jürgen Moltmann, *Science and Wisdom*, trans. Margaret Kohl (Minneapolis: Fortress Press, 2003), p. 8.

argues that, with the development of the sciences, 'consciousness and the world which it studied lost contact with the presence of wisdom in consciousness and materiality. Reference to the wisdom of God present in materiality was forgotten.'[76] Celia E. Deane-Drummond similarly recounts that 'with the rise in Enlightenment thinking scientific knowledge gradually became separated from wisdom',[77] and concludes: 'Once science becomes fragmented into specialities containing mere information, as is the case in modernity, it loses touch with its deeper philosophical roots in wisdom.'[78] The gradual process by which the place of Christian wisdom within the realm of the material and scientific was progressively eroded only served to confirm the already existing internal disjunction within Christian wisdom of fact and value, of knowledge and love. McIntosh notes in this regard that 'coincident with the apparent divine withdrawal from the cosmos, mysticism in modernity also withdraws into this inner castle, the world of the inner self – a world whose claims to wisdom, authority and truth could easily be marginalized by religious and academic authorities, even as they have been suborned and co-opted by modern individualistic consumerism'.[79] In this eventuality, the possibility of a holistic view of Christian wisdom which would include both the internal and the external, the individual and the communal, knowledge and love, seems remote.

The final word in this all-too-brief survey of theology and wisdom should, however, perhaps reflect some of the more positive recent developments in attempting to heal this division within Christian wisdom. Deane-Drummond's own constructive work, for example, includes the desire to recover the theological motif of wisdom in order to respond appropriately to the new advances in the biological sciences.[80]

76. Daniel W. Hardy, *God's Ways with the World* (Edinburgh: T. & T. Clark, 1996), p. 256. Hardy continues: 'It was replaced by reference to man's own consciousness of the world, rationalized either through particular pursuits (in the separate sciences) or by a general theory of rational consciousness (as in Descartes, Locke, Kant and Hegel)', ibid.
77. Celia E. Deane-Drummond, *Creation Through Wisdom* (Edinburgh: T. & T. Clark, 2000), p. 7. By contrast, she argues, 'Classical science was rooted in philosophy or love of wisdom. Wisdom was integrated into the search for knowledge, and was understood as integrated into life itself', ibid. p. 233.
78. Ibid. pp. 233–4. This contention is repeated from a secular point of view by Mary Midgley, who laments the loss of background thinking about what really matters in knowledge, that is, the loss of the sort of large-scale thinking which is an aspect of wisdom: 'When knowledge is secluded in this way and equated with information, understanding is pushed into the background and the notion of wisdom is quite forgotten', in *Wisdom, Information, and Wonder* (London and New York: Routledge, 1989, 1991), p. 45.
79. McIntosh, *Mystical Theology*, p. 69.
80. Deane-Drummond, *Creation Through Wisdom*, p. 234.

Moltmann, in not unrelated fashion, advocates a 'Wisdom theology', in which 'God is perceived from the life and orders of nature, and then recognized again in human wisdom about life'.[81] Hardy has also written constructively of the role of the Christian tradition in conceptions of wisdom, arguing that 'If wisdom is also concerned with certain goals for rationality and knowledge which lie beyond what they are, preeminently with the achievement of goodness and beauty, or with their achievement in human life in the world, then rationality and knowledge are not to be dissociated from these goals or "values".'[82] On a very practical level, Anne E. Streaty Wimberly and Evelyn L. Parker have written compellingly about the need for seeking wisdom in Christian communities, suggesting that 'Christian wisdom formation has its source in God. It relies on our faith in God, openness to God, discernment of God's desire for our lives, and a commitment or sense of duty to sojourn toward the good and true that comes from our engagement in personal and corporate spiritual disciplines.'[83] In each case, there is evident an approach to Christian wisdom which not only embraces the personal, interior realm of love and contemplation but also re-embraces the material, communal, scriptural and ecclesial dimensions of knowledge and practice.

The chapters which follow seek to contribute to this constructive and holistic endeavour through three case studies that explore relations between faiths, universities (the contemporary world's main institution for advancing knowledge) and communities of friendship centred on people with learning disabilities.

---

81. Moltmann, *Science and Wisdom*, p. 148.
82. Hardy, *God's Ways with the World*, p. 236.
83. Anne E. Streaty Wimberly and Evelyn L. Parker, 'Introduction' in *In Search of Wisdom: Faith Formation in the Black Church*, ed. Anne E. Streaty Wimberly and Evelyn L. Parker (Nashville: Abingdon, 2002), p. 13. In the same volume, and picking up a recurring theme in *this* volume, Anne E. Streaty Wimberly and Edward P. Wimberly posit that 'Wisdom is hewn in the throes of the language of lament. Through this language we cry out about disappointing and even devastating relational realities, disturbing events in past and present life, aging- and health-related issues, other unexpected and new circumstances, and fears about the unknown future. Wisdom formation is about learning the language of lament, which really is about learning to take our complaints and the realities of life directly to God', in 'Wisdom Formation in Middle and Late Adulthood' in *In Search of Wisdom*, p. 132.

8

An inter-faith wisdom: scriptural reasoning between Jews, Christians and Muslims

If Christian theology can fruitfully be seen as seeking wisdom, what about its relationship to other faiths? This chapter[1] addresses that question through a case study of the practice of scriptural reasoning, understood as a wisdom-seeking engagement with Jewish, Christian and Muslim scriptures. Its origins, practices, understandings and social settings are described and discussed, with some concluding remarks on its possible contribution to the public sphere in the twenty-first century. The Bible has been the main resource for Christian wisdom through the previous seven chapters, where it has also been related to traditions of Christian worship, scholarship and theology, with some attention to Judaism. The thrust of those chapters makes further engagement with Judaism and with other faiths not only unavoidable but desirable and even urgent. In particular it follows from the eighth thesis for the interpretation of scripture, *Christians need to read the Bible in dialogue with diverse others outside the church*, and by its accompanying maxim and appeal: *Let conversations around scripture be open to all people, religions, cultures, arts, disciplines, media and spheres of life. Let us read for the sake of friendship with all!* (see p. 87 above).

Core identities in conversation

There are many convergent reasons why it is sensible for inter-faith engagement among Jews, Christians and Muslims to make their

1. This chapter is a slightly altered version of 'An Inter-Faith Wisdom: Scriptural Reasoning between Jews, Christians and Muslims' in *The Promise of Scriptural Reasoning*, ed. David F. Ford and Chad C. Pecknold (Oxford: Blackwell, 2006), originally published in *Modern Theology* 22, no. 3 (July 2006), pp. 345–66.

scriptures a primary focus. Each tradition's scripture is at the heart of its identity. This is so in rather different ways, but recognising those differences can be a source of illumination to each.[2] Scriptures are formative for understanding God and God's purposes; for prayer, worship and liturgy; for normative teaching; for imagination and ethos; and so on. Religions meet new situations and are challenged to change over time, and if a new development is at all important it is inevitable that debate about it will appeal to scripture. Many of the bitterest disputes within and between all three faiths centre on appeals to scripture. So an attempt to deal with the core identity of any of the three will inevitably involve its scripture.

This is sometimes taken as a reason for avoiding scriptures in dialogue situations. The Tanakh, the Bible and the Qur'an are the main platforms of those within each tradition who stand against dialogue and in favour of self-protective or aggressive confrontation. Each of these scriptures has texts that can be used to legitimate violence, claims to superiority, blanket condemnations, cruel punishments, suspicions, oppressive morality, and hostility to those who are not believers in God as identified by one's own tradition. Their scriptures are where the particularity of each is evident 'warts and all', and have been widely used in polemics between them as well as in attacks on each by secular critics. Even for many of those who do believe it right to engage in dialogue and collaboration, the scriptures are where they find what is most distinctive, most difficult and least negotiable. So to study together anything other than very carefully selected passages might seem a recipe for increasing tensions and meeting many impasses.

2. See Gavin Flood, 'The Phenomenology of Scripture' in *The Promise of Scriptural Reasoning*. Flood writes, 'The second term of my title, "scripture," is a category whose contents have been widely contested in the history of Abrahamic religions but a category that at a simple level I take to refer to the texts, oral and written, of historical traditions that set them aside from other texts because of the claims they make on human communities. Usually it is claimed that these texts bear witness to a revelation: in the case of the Qur'an the text is the revelation of God mediated through the Prophet, in the case of the New Testament the text bears witness to the revelation of Christ. Other scriptures are understood in other ways. For the atheistic Mimamsakas the Veda is revelation (*sruti*, that which has been heard by the sages) which is authorless while the Tantrikas have a hierarchy of revelation from a hierarchy of cosmic levels, their own texts transcending the restricted revelation of the Veda. While, of course, the Hindu texts are very different from the Jewish, Christian or Moslem texts, the category "scripture" meaningfully applies across traditions although accounts of what scripture is will vary greatly. We might say that scriptures comprise primarily injunctions to act along with accompanying prohibitions and narratives. Some traditions have emphasised the injunctive nature of their scriptures (such as the Mimamsaka claim that the Veda is primarily concerned with injunction (*vidhi*) while others have emphasised the narrative dimensions (such as more recent narrative theology). It is important that common questions can be asked across the divides of tradition about the nature of scripture, questions which will be answered in different ways' (p. 160).

Yet, despite the problems, the attractiveness of this approach is considerable. If it were to succeed it could not only bring core identities into conversation; it could also sustain them there. Within each tradition, scriptures are a focus of endless study, conversation and dispute, and around them have grown up enduring forms of collegiality. *One of the critical things lacking in relations between Jews, Christians and Muslims is such centres of long-term collegiality where ways of study, understanding and application can be worked at and passed on across generations.* The study of their scriptures has been overwhelmingly intra-traditional, supplemented in varying degrees by academic study in uncommitted environments. Yet, given the fundamental nature of the issues between them (with roots going back many centuries), given the necessity of engaging with scriptures if those issues are to be satisfactorily dealt with, and given the richness and complexity of each scripture and its associated traditions, then the only appropriate way is that which each faith has followed itself: *the creation of groups, traditions, networks and institutions able to form readers dedicated to study and discussion.*

These are matters which require more than one person and more than one lifetime. They have to be handled by communities who can learn together how to go about this novel and urgent task.[3] There are almost no places in the world at present where collegial conversations are sustained jointly around these three scriptures and traditions of interpretation. In a few universities the scriptures of each tradition are studied alongside each other, but that has very rarely led to deep interplay between all three. Yet there are some initiatives in this direction, and I will devote the rest of this chapter to discussing one in which I have been privileged to take part.

Scriptural reasoning: an introductory description

This initial description of scriptural reasoning (and, even more, the discussion in later sections) is offered as only one portrayal of something that has already evoked many other descriptions and is constantly producing more.[4] Because scriptural reasoning draws people of very different

---

3. See ibid. p. 169: 'Traditional communities of textual reception change through history and new communities of reception emerge. Scriptural reasoning might be seen as one such new community, true to the spirit of dialogue but grounded in text and hermeneutically sensitive.'

4. Nicholas Adams, 'Scriptural Difference and Scriptural Reasoning' – chapter 11 in *Habermas and Theology* (Cambridge: Cambridge University Press, 2006), available on-line at http://etext.lib.virginia.edu/journals/jsrforum/writings/AdaHabe.html; Peter Ochs,

commitments and disciplines into engagement with each other it is a phenomenon which is bound to be described differently even (perhaps especially) by those who know it best: part of its approach is to resist 'authoritative overviews' of the three scriptures and traditions of interpretation that are being brought into conversation, and so its own character likewise calls for diverse descriptions. This has been described by Ben Quash as its 'dramatic' character, with many voices that cannot be integrated into a monologue.[5] What follows in this and the following sections portrays and interprets it from the standpoint of a Christian academic participant whose main academic areas are biblical interpretation and contemporary critical and constructive theological thought, and whose chief interest in this chapter is in the wisdom it might yield for inter-faith engagement today.

Scriptural reasoning had its immediate origins in the early 1990s in 'textual reasoning' among a group of academic Jewish text scholars (mostly of Tanakh and Talmud), on the one hand, and philosophers and theologians on the other hand, who were concerned that there was little fruitful engagement between their sets of disciplines.[6] They began to meet together to study texts from scripture and Talmud in dialogue with Western philosophy, in particular those Jewish philosophers who had themselves tried to cross this divide, such as Hermann Cohen, Franz Rosenzweig (perhaps the most embracing influence), Martin Buber, Emmanuel Levinas and Eugene Borowitz. The text scholars were trained in both traditional Jewish interpretation and the methods of the modern Western academy, and the philosophers and theologians were likewise students of Jewish thought as well as of Western thought from classical

'Reading Scripture Together in Sight of Our Open Doors' in *The Princeton Seminary Bulletin* 26, no. 1, new series (2005), pp. 36–47; Aref Ali Nayed, 'Reading Scripture Together: Towards a Sacred Hermeneutics of Togetherness' in *The Princeton Seminary Bulletin* 26, no. 1, new series (2005), pp. 48–53; Basit Bilal Koshul, 'Affirming the Self through Accepting the Other' in *Scriptures in Dialogue: Christians and Muslims Studying the Bible and the Qur'an Together*, ed. Michael Ipgrave (London: Church House Publishing, 2004), pp. 111–18; Randi Rashkover, 'Cultivating Theology: Overcoming America's Skepticism about Religious Rationality' in *CrossCurrents* 55, no. 2 (June 2005), pp. 241–51; Chad Pecknold, *Transforming Postliberal Theology: George Lindbeck, Pragmatism, and Scripture* (New York: T. & T. Clark; London: Continuum, 2005); Ben Quash, 'Holy Seeds: The Trisagion and the Liturgical Untilling of Time' in *Liturgy, Time, and the Politics of Redemption*, ed. Chad Pecknold and Randi Rashkover (Grand Rapids, MI: Eerdmans, 2006). For further resources, see also the website of the *Journal of Scriptural Reasoning* Forum at http://etext.lib.virginia.edu/journals/jsrforum/.
5. Ben Quash, 'Heavenly Semantics: Some Literary-Critical Approaches to Scriptural Reasoning' in *The Promise of Scriptural Reasoning*, originally published in *Modern Theology* 22, no. 3 (July 2006), pp. 403–20.
6. For the best account of textual reasoning by participants and commentators, see *Textual Reasonings*, ed. Peter Ochs and Nancy Levene (London: SCM, 2002).

Greece up to the present. The name they gave to what they did, 'textual reasoning', simply referred to the two sides that were brought together: the interpretation of traditional texts and the practices of philosophical and theological reasoning. A core question they shared was about Judaism after the Shoah,[7] leading them to interrogate both the modern Western context within which the Shoah had been possible and also the resources – premodern, modern and postmodern[8] or contemporary – for responding to it within Judaism.

One perhaps surprising conclusion[9] that many of them came to was that post-Shoah Judaism needed both to appropriate afresh its scriptures and traditions of interpretation and at the same time to engage more deeply with others who are wrestling with the meaning of their faith today, especially Christians (see p. 141 above) and Muslims. This latter conclusion had not been arrived at abstractly. It was rooted in some of the group already having found congenial Christian thinking going on, especially in Yale around Hans Frei and George Lindbeck.[10] Their Christian postcritical, 'postliberal' hermeneutics, which had learnt much from Karl Barth, had many resonances with Rosenzweig's approach to Judaism.[11] In addition, at Drew University in the late 1980s and early 1990s there was a scriptural interpretation group, that grew out of a course on Kant and scripture, around the Jewish thinker Peter Ochs (who had previously been at Yale and knew Frei and Lindbeck) that included Christians and later Muslims. So when the textual reasoning group, whose first co-chairs were Ochs and the philosopher David Novak, began in 1991 there were already within it the seeds of later Abrahamic developments.

These began to be cultivated when some Christian academics (including Daniel Hardy and myself) began to attend the lively, learned and

7. See Peter Ochs, 'Textual Reasoning as a Model for Jewish Thought after the Shoah' in *Filosofia e Critica della Filosofia nel Pensiero Ebraico*, ed. P. Amodio, G. Giannini and G. Lissa (Naples: Giannini Editore, 2004) pp. 233–72.
8. In the early years they used 'postmodern' in self-description, but as that term has become overused and ceased to have much specific meaning they have tended to drop it. My own preferred term for the modernity that has been traumatised by the Shoah and other twentieth-century horrors and disasters is 'late modernity', with 'chastened modernity' for those aspects of it that have tried best to learn from the twentieth century – see David F. Ford, 'Holy Spirit and Christian Spirituality', and above, chapter 4, pp. 121–52.
9. Ochs, 'Reading Scripture Together in Sight of Our Open Doors', pp. 36–47.
10. For a good gathering of the types of thinking that fed into this pre-history of scriptural reasoning see *The Return to Scripture in Judaism and Christianity: Essays in Postcritical Scriptural Interpretation*, ed. Peter Ochs (Mahwah, NJ: Paulist Press, 1993).
11. Randi Rashkover, *Revelation and Theopolitics: Barth, Rosenzweig and the Politics of Praise* (New York: T. & T. Clark; London: Continuum, 2005).

argumentative textual reasoning sessions at the annual meetings of the American Academy of Religion in the early 1990s. This led into 'scriptural reasoning', which was first Jewish–Christian[12] and then in the late 1990s became Jewish–Christian–Muslim. There were large questions to be tackled if this was to work. They were wrestled with in two settings, a summer meeting of a small group for a few days of intensive scripture study, with discussion of the various dimensions of scriptural reasoning (see the sections to follow below); and a larger group that eventually met twice a year, in Cambridge and wherever the American Academy of Religion was meeting.[13]

The four key strands that were brought together in these ways were: Jewish textual reasoning as already described; Christian postliberal text interpretation (whose main theological reference point was Karl Barth, in particular as interpreted by Frei in Yale); a range of less text-centred Christian philosophies and theologies, both Protestant and Catholic; and Muslim concern simultaneously for the Qur'an and for Islam in relation to Western modernity (especially understood through the natural and human sciences and technology).

In what follows I will think through this young movement from various angles – its collegiality, its institutional relations, its ways of coping with the meaning of scriptures, and its significance for public education and debate.

An Abrahamic collegiality: not consensus but friendship

At the centre of the collegiality of scriptural reasoning is reading and interpreting selected texts from the Tanakh, Old Testament/New Testament and Qur'an in small groups, whose inspiration is the Jewish

---

12. For a Jewish account of Christian theological engagement with Judaism that includes discussion of various strands that have fed into scriptural reasoning see Peter Ochs, 'Judaism and Christian Theology' in *The Modern Theologians: An Introduction to Christian Theology since 1918*, ed. David F. Ford with Rachel Muers (3rd edn, Oxford: Blackwell, 2005), pp. 645–62.
13. Out of these have grown a variety of elements, including: a unit in the programme of the annual meeting of the AAR, groups in various parts of the world, a grassroots body called the Children of Abraham Institute (CHAI), the online *Journal of Scriptural Reasoning*, a research group based at the Center of Theological Inquiry in Princeton focussing on medieval scriptural interpretation in Judaism, Islam and Christianity, a scriptural reasoning programme at St Ethelburga's Centre for Peace and Reconciliation in London, postgraduate programmes in the University of Virginia, and contributions to inter-faith gatherings in Qatar, South Africa, Karachi, London, Durham, Berlin, Georgetown, see Jeffrey W. Bailey, 'Sacred book club – reading and much else – scripture across inter-faith lines', *Christian Century* 123, no. 18 (2006), pp. 36–42.

practice of *chevruta* study,[14] and also (when there is more than one group) in plenary sessions, which often have the purpose of pursuing more theoretical, philosophical, theological and 'public issue' questions related to the text study and occasionally discussing matters relating to the group's process, governance and future development.

In scriptural reasoning done between academic Jews, Christians and Muslims[15] the priority of small-group study means that each one is first of all bringing to the table his or her own scripture, a much-studied and much-loved book. They also bring what Aref Nayed has named their 'internal libraries':[16] not only all they have learnt through tradition-specific activity in study, prayer, worship and experience but also what they have learnt through whatever academic disciplines they have studied – and also, of course, elements from a range of cultures, arts, and economic, political and social contexts.

A recurring image used to describe the social dynamics of this encounter is that of hospitality – and the resources of each scripture on hospitality have often been a focus for study. Yet this is three-way mutual hospitality: each is host to the others and guest to the others as each welcomes the other two to their 'home' scripture and its traditions of interpretation. As in any form of hospitality, joint study is helped by observing certain customs and guidelines that have been developed through experience over time. These are the prudential wisdom of the practice of scriptural reasoning and, like most such customs, are best learnt by apprenticeship that sees them being performed and imitates them or improvises upon them. Put in the form of maxims, a selection of those most important for collegiality would include:

- Acknowledge *the sacredness* of the others' scriptures to them (without having to acknowledge its authority for oneself) – each believes in different ways (which can be discussed) that their scripture is in some

14. *Chevruta* (fellowship) study is an ancient rabbinic method of studying Jewish texts that continues into the present. By engaging with a text in very small group settings, students learn through interaction both with the text and with each other. The method not only facilitates and deepens their education, but can also forge and strengthen relationships among students. The traditional setting for *chevruta* study was the *yeshivah*, a Jewish institution for the advanced study of religious texts. In scriptural reasoning the usual group size is between six and nine, allowing for two to three members of each faith tradition.
15. The other main types so far have been among Jews, Christians and Muslims from congregations (who may or may not have academic training) and among academics who include others (usually specialists in one of the scriptures or traditions) besides Jews, Christians and Muslims.
16. In plenary discussion at a scriptural reasoning conference in Cambridge, June 2003. See Aref Ali Nayed, 'Reading Scripture Together: Towards a Sacred Hermeneutics of Togetherness'.

sense from God and that the group is interpreting it before God, in God's presence, for God's sake.[17]

- The 'native speakers' hosting a scripture and its tradition need to acknowledge that they do not exclusively own their scriptures – they are *not experts on its final meaning*; guests need to acknowledge that hosts are to be questioned and listened to attentively as the *court of first (but not last) appeal*.
- Do *not* allow *consensus* to be the dominant aim – that may happen, but it is more likely that the conclusion will be a recognition of deep differences.
- Do not be afraid of *argument*, as one intellectually honest way of responding to differences – part of mutual hospitality is learning to argue in courtesy and truth, and each tradition as well as each academic discipline embraces complex practices of discussion and dispute.[18]
- Draw on *shared academic resources* to build understanding – members of different faith communities may be trained in the same field or share a philosophy (pragmatism, critical realism, phenomenology, idealism).
- *Allow time* to read and reread, to entertain many questions and possibilities, to let the texts unfold within their own traditions of interpretation and in (often unprecedented) engagement with each other, to stick with a text without premature resolution of its difficulties, and to sound the depths.
- Read and interpret with a view to the fulfilment of *God's purpose of peace* between all – this shared hope (however differently specified) can sustain endurance through inevitable differences, misunderstandings, confrontations and resentments.
- Be open to *mutual hospitality turning into friendship* – each tradition values friendship, and for it to happen now might be seen as the most tangible anticipation of future peace.

Many of those maxims are embraced in the following account by Nicholas Adams:

> Scriptural reasoning is a practice of 'publicising' deep reasonings, so that others may learn to understand them and discover why particular

---

17. In a situation, such as the second one described in note 15 above, in which some participants are not in any sense members of one of the three faith communities, scriptural reasoning is only likely to work well if those in this fourth category, together with those who are Jewish, Muslim or Christian, conform to certain norms, such as imaginative understanding and respect for how the others take their scriptures, willingness to be as vulnerable as the others in exposing their basic convictions to argument, and unwillingness to claim either an overview or a neutral vantage point.
18. See Quash, 'Heavenly Semantics': 'High quality argument may in the end be a better "product" of scriptural reasoning (if that is a suitable term to use at all) than any agreed statement would be, and a more desirable thing to transmit to those who enter the tradition which this practice generates' (p. 68).

trains of reasoning, and not just particular assumptions, are attractive or problematic. *Scriptural reasoning makes deep reasonings public.* It sees them not as particularistic obstacles to debate, but as conditions for conversation, friendship and mutual understanding. Without deep reasonings, there are no religious traditions to speak of. Depth is not obscurity, however: the acknowledgement of depth is a recognition that it takes time to plumb. Scriptural reasoning models the discovery that making deep reasoning public is not only risky – because one makes oneself vulnerable when revealing what one loves – but time-consuming. It is a non-hasty practice, and is thus a kind of beacon in our time-poor world ... Each of the three Abrahamic traditions has its own rules for interpreting scripture (and internal disagreement about these rules), and, even if there is overlap between them, it is not the overlap that makes scriptural reasoning possible. The significant point of contact is a shared acknowledgement that scriptural texts are sacred, together with a shared desire to do scriptural reasoning. The most striking thing about the context of scriptural reasoning is not consensus but friendship. To use the word *chevruta* [related to 'friendship'] to describe the meeting of Muslims, Jews and Christians is itself surprising, and the actual friendships that are formed through such study do not lessen the surprise. Consensus can be measured and managed ... Friendship is altogether more confusing, and even the most sophisticated philosophical accounts of it somehow repeat the absurdity of the hopeless lover who tries to persuade the other to love him by using arguments. Abstract description of friendship is nearly as pointless as thirstily trying to make sense of water. Friendship is nonetheless the true ground of scriptural reasoning, and who can give a good overview of that? The traditions have different understandings of friendship with God, friendship with members of one's own family, one's own tradition and with strangers. Somehow, the recognition that each worships the one true God moves scriptural reasoning beyond an interaction determined by conventions for showing strangers hospitality. Showing strangers hospitality is a significant enough miracle. Yet scriptural reasoning does not quite reproduce this context: when members of three traditions meet together to study shared scripture, who is the guest and who is the host? In a way that is difficult to be clear about, the participants in scriptural reasoning all find themselves invited, not by each other, but by an agency that is not theirs to command or shape. There is an 'other' to the three traditions, and that seems in an obscure way to make friendships possible.[19]

---

19. Nicholas Adams, from chapter 11 of *Habermas and Theology*.

The picture of a collegiality of intensive study and conversation that emerges from such description might be seen as a boundary-crossing liturgy. This gathers in hospitality and friendship members of academic institutions whose primary communities are synagogue, church and mosque. Its quasi-liturgical character is appropriate, since it is likely that study of scripture which acknowledges the presence of God (variously identified) comes as close to worshipping together as faithful members of these three traditions can come with integrity.

A further question arising from this is about the institutional location of this collegiality of scriptural reasoning.

House, campus and tent

In the sort of scriptural reasoning I have been discussing,[20] the participants are simultaneously members of a synagogue, church or mosque ('houses'), of a university ('campus'), and of a scriptural reasoning group ('tent'). What is the relation of the tent to the house and campus? They are clearly very different types of location.

House

The houses are the main homes of the three scriptures and their traditions of interpretation. Synagogues, churches and mosques are of course themselves diverse, not least in how their scriptures are understood and acted upon. Scriptural reasoning has in fact drawn participants from various strands of Islam, Judaism and Christianity, and the setting of inter-faith interpretation can open the way for fresh dialogue within each community. Yet it is not part of any of the traditions to engage in joint study of their scriptures with the others. *So scriptural reasoning is a complex combination of what is at the core of each tradition with what is novel for each.* As with any innovation it needs to be discussed and tested, not least with reference to scripture.

Is there a valid justification for scriptural reasoning from within Judaism, Islam and Christianity? Many are possible, some of them incompatible even within one faith tradition, though the practice of scriptural reasoning can proceed without agreement on its rationale. There are of course some within each tradition who would dispute its validity, but so long as faithful members of each tradition in fact practise it and justify it

---

20. See note 15 above on other types.

in tradition-specific ways the presumption must be that it can have a place in relation to each house. I will offer three brief examples of how it might be justified from within each of the traditions, while recognising that very different justifications are also possible, and that the practice does not demand overall agreement.

From within Judaism, Steven Kepnes writes:

> The solitary Jew who reads the New Testament and the Qur'an in this age of Holocaust, five Arab-Israeli Wars, terrorism and Israeli occupation, reads with fear and trembling. The solitary Jew who reads these books simply as cultural documents can easily find horrible portraits of Jews as hypocrites, Christ-killers, perverters of Allah's word and enemies of his messenger. Here, one sees sources of anti-semitism and legitimations for mass murder.
>
> But the solitary Jew who reads these texts as she would read the Torah, that is, as scripture, finds something different. Now these texts appear as far more complex. The language becomes poetry, the textual meanings more multiple. As scripture, as the living word of God and the foundation and future of a religious community, the New Testament and the Qur'an appear as texts of hope addressed to a people's suffering. Like the Torah, these texts come with good news for a people that is confused and brought low by sickness, poverty, and a world that is in the process of bewildering change. When these texts are read as parallel texts to Torah, with a focus on God's relation to another people that he chooses to gift with revelation and healing, the Jews in these texts fade into the background so that others can take center stage.
>
> But scriptural reasoning is not a solitary practice, it is a collective practice of reading and dialogue. And when Jews and Christians and Muslims read their scriptures together in face to face reading encounters, whole new dimensions open up. The reading encounter, which is the true hallmark of scriptural reasoning, places those very people to whom God gifted with a revealed text in front of their scripture as its witness and host. In shared moments of being guest in another person's religious home the reality of revelation and healing is all the more vibrant. From this point of heightened vibrancy spiritual bridges are built. New paths for God-wondering are forged and energies of reason and spirit released for the healing not only of the rifts between the different scriptural communities but for the healing of the entire world.[21]

---

21. Personal communication in response to my request. For a fuller account by Kepnes see 'A Handbook of Scriptural Reasoning' in *The Promise of Scriptural Reasoning*, pp. 23–39.

From within Christianity, there is an obvious justification for Christians reading with Jews, since they share so much scripture; and the Qur'an includes many references pointing to Jewish and Christian scriptures. An overall Christian justification might be constructed from the previous seven chapters. The wisdom interpretation of scripture has already been quoted at the opening of this chapter, with its eighth maxim of reading in dialogue with diverse others outside the church. The most embracing theological rationale for scriptural reasoning is the concern to understand 'all things' with reference to God, which must include other faiths and their scriptures. The basic ethos is that of the final maxim: 'Let us reread in love.' Scriptural reasoning aims at rereading in a community of friendship the three scriptures alongside each other. All of this is in line with the conceptions of Jesus Christ, the Holy Spirit, God, tradition and church offered in earlier chapters.

Of special relevance is the interpretation of the book of Job in chapters 3 and 4 above. That shows a passionate searching which simultaneously diagnoses the problems of a tradition and also wrestles with God in the midst of the anguish of historical existence in order to arrive at a fresh, tested wisdom for the future. But this is not given in a formula: its way of wisdom is to imitate Job's searching and being searched, to question the pathologies of tradition, to celebrate God for God's sake and creation for creation's sake, and to be part of 'a long-term community of worship, generosity and compassion' (see p. 119 above). Scriptural reasoning is a way of wrestling with a deeply rooted and urgent twenty-first-century issue connected with past, present and likely future traumas, and one inseparable from the possibility of long-term human peace and flourishing.

From within Islam, Basit Koshul writes:

> Is there any Qur'anic warrant for Muslims to sit down with Jews and Christians to discuss matters of common concern – with the scriptures from the three traditions providing the framework for the discussion? The Qur'anic warrants for such a position are many – I will offer one by putting together two different ayahs from the Qur'an.

> Say, 'People of the Book, let us arrive at a statement that is common to us all: we worship Allah alone, we ascribe no partners to Him, and none of us takes others besides Allah as lords.' If they turn away, say: 'Bear witness that it is we who have surrendered ourselves unto Him.' (3:64).

> Here Muslims are asked by the Qur'an to extend an invitation to Jews and Christians to arrive at a common understanding. But it must be

acknowledged that this understanding need not be based on scriptures – it could be based on some abstract, universal concept such as 'human dignity' or 'state of nature' or 'universal reason' etc. etc. The following ayah explicitly identifies the basis on which this understanding is to be based:

Say, 'People of the Book, you have no true basis [for your religion/ arguments] unless you uphold the Torah, the Gospels and that which has been sent down to you from your Lord.' (5:68).

Taking these two passages as the starting point, the case for a Qur'anic warrant for scriptural reasoning can be further detailed. To begin with, these passages demonstrate that not only is the Qur'an conscious of the Biblical tradition, it is in active conversation with it. Whether it is affirming the authenticity and verity of the Blessed Prophet's ministry (e.g. 26:197, 7:156–7), critiquing certain practices and beliefs among the Jews and Christians (e.g. 57:48, 2:111) or calling upon the Jews and Christians to come into dialogue and working relationship with Muslims (3:65–8), the Qur'an repeatedly turns to the Bible in support of its position. While the Qur'an does criticize the Jews and Christians who do not accept its message, its strongest words of condemnation are reserved for those who fail to uphold the teachings of the Torah and Gospels. The fact that the Qur'an itself is in conversation with the Torah and Gospels is reason enough for Muslim scholars to participate in scriptural reasoning where Jewish and Christian scholars are attached to their respective scriptures not only because of academic interest but also because of personal commitment. But the Qur'an offers other reasons for engagement with the Biblical traditions.

Even though it does not state so explicitly, there is reason to believe that the Qur'an sees engagement with Jews and Christians as not only leading to a better understanding of the non-Muslim scriptures and communities, but also leading to a better understanding of the Qur'an on the part of the Muslims. The number of references to the history, beliefs, practices, etc. of Jews and Christians in the Qur'an is not insignificant. One issue that a conscientious Muslim reading the Qur'an must ask him/herself is the following: How accurate is my understanding/reading of the passages that refer to the Jews and Christians? Given the fact that our reading of a text is always from a particular perspective and through a particular lens – with the perspective and lens shaping the text that is being read – it is obvious that a Muslim's reading of the passages about Jews and Christians is shaped by particular historical, cultural, political and obviously theological lenses. A most efficient way to address this issue is for a

Muslim to read the passages dealing with Jews, Christians, Torah, Gospels, etc. in the company of the people/subject being addressed. As a matter of fact this is the suggestion made by the Qur'an itself. This Qur'anic approach offers a gold standard by which the Muslim community should measure itself on how its image of non-Muslim communities is shaped. Scriptural Reasoning is a forum where Jews and Christians can (and always do) speak for themselves when the Qur'anic text is addressing them. This helps them not only gain a better understanding of the Qur'an (as the Muslims are gaining a better understanding of the Torah and Gospels) it has the potential of helping them gain a better understanding of their own scriptures:

Behold, this Qur'an explains to the children of Israel most [of that] whereon they hold divergent views; and, verily, it is a guidance and a grace unto all who believe [in it.] Verily, your Lord will judge between them in His wisdom – for He alone is Almighty, All-Knowing (27:76–8).

In short there are many references to the Torah and Gospels in the Qur'an, and there is there no shortage of examples where the Qur'an directly addresses the Jewish and Christian communities. This is another way of saying that there is ample warrant for the practice of Scriptural Reasoning in the Qur'an. Scriptural Reasoning is not only an extremely (perhaps uniquely) valuable means for gaining insight into the wisdom of the Qur'an (and by extension the Torah and Gospels because the Qur'an sees itself as a continuation of the same phenomenon). SR is also an extremely (perhaps uniquely) valuable means for bringing the Divine Speech to life in the world because it is a place where Jews, Christians and Muslims are brought together by their love of their respective scriptures, which is matched by their desire to see a world where justice and harmony are the norms rather than tyranny and strife.[22]

As those accounts suggest, the matter goes deeper than justification of the validity and permissibility of scriptural reasoning. There is also a case to be made for the positive enhancement of each house. The origins of scriptural reasoning, as recounted above, included a specifically Jewish group of 'textual reasoning'. This intra-traditional dynamic has been repeated within the other two traditions. There are Muslim quranic reasoning groups and Christian biblical reasoning groups that were begun by those already participating in scriptural reasoning. It is as if

22. Personal communication in response to my request.

the intensity of study and conversation around the three scriptures increases the need of participants for a comparable 'in-house' intensity. *Far from inter-faith engagement being in competition with involvement in one's own tradition, the depths of one evoke the depths of the other.* So part of the promise of scriptural reasoning is to be a stimulus to 'house' members to study and interpret their own scriptures and traditions of interpretation with new energy.

Such renewal need not happen only among those who also take part in scriptural reasoning – for many reasons inter-faith study is more restricted in numbers than in-house study and likely to remain so. Scriptural reasoning might be seen as one niche in a house's ecosystem which is more likely to flourish if within other niches there is lively, faithful and thoughtful study of the house's own scripture. 'Thoughtful' indicates the presence in each house of traditions of reasoning and argument in relation to their scriptures, and of institutions where there is transgenerational collegiality dedicated to sustaining and developing these. It is especially important that such places are seeking wisdom both within and across their own boundaries.

For those who take part in scriptural reasoning an issue raised by its non-competitive dynamic is about the balance of inter-faith and intra-faith study. One way of approaching this is in terms of time. Scriptural reasoning ideally requires a long time at any one session, but that does not mean it has to happen very frequently. This is a matter for discernment within each community. Judging from experience so far, the ideal periodicity of the practice of scriptural reasoning is not that of one's daily in-house scripture-saturated prayer, scripture study/recitation, meditation, and suchlike; nor that of one's weekly (or more frequent) gathering for community worship, instruction, and suchlike; rather its optimal rhythm seems to be of less frequent meetings, perhaps monthly or quarterly. During its development its main participants met twice or three times a year. Yet, however frequent the meetings, as in most groups the value is proportionate to regularity, which is all the more important if gatherings are seldom.

The other essential feature of a group that meets relatively seldom is the quality of communication between meetings, both within itself and more widely. Here electronic communication has greatly helped. Scriptural reasoning has a website and an electronic journal so that those in the wider community of the houses and campuses can listen in and respond to what is going on; and email ensures that there can also be regular communication among direct participants. The combination of face to face meetings with electronic interaction produces a new dimension of collegiality uniting 'richness' with 'reach'.[23] As the 'houses' too become better networked and alert to such possibilities a practice such as scriptural reasoning has the potential to help those who seek to develop rich scripture study within as well as across the boundaries of their own house.

Campus

Just as the 'traditional and untraditional' nature of scriptural reasoning tests the character of any mosque, synagogue or church and provokes various responses, so its 'scriptural and reasoning' nature is a sensitive matter in universities. As the ideal 'house' for scriptural reasoning is one that acknowledges an internal justification for this new practice and then uses it to go deeper simultaneously into its own scripture and the scriptures of others, so the ideal university in the present state of our complexly 'religious and secular' world might be described as 'inter-faith and secular', a campus where there is shared ground among those of many faiths and none.

The next chapter will explore the contemporary university as a place of wisdom-seeking, setting it in a historical context reaching back to its medieval beginnings by way of the University of Berlin. That account culminates in arguing for the desirability of an inter-faith and secular university, and elsewhere I have developed this conception at greater length.[24] That would ideally integrate key elements that shape it as an academic institution (interdisciplinarity, the integration of teaching and research, all-round educational formation, collegiality, polity and control, and contribution to society) with hospitality to the religious and the secular together. In this way a plurality of wisdom traditions could contribute to its conversations, deliberations and decisions in the interests of education and research that have a fundamental concern for the long-term flourishing of humanity and its environment.

23. The Jewish textual reasoning group has drawn on Jewish traditional resources to think about the significance of their intensive electronic interaction with each other, seeing it as a form of 'oral Torah'.

24. See David F. Ford, 'Faith and Universities in a Religious and Secular World (1)' in *Svensk Teologisk Kvartalskrift* 81, no. 2 (2005), pp. 83–91, and 'Faith and Universities in a Religious and Secular World (2)' in *Svensk Teologisk Kvartalskrift* 81, no. 3 (2005), pp. 97–106.

Yet even without the realisation of such an ideal, there are some universities where the religious and secular dimensions are both taken seriously. They provide conditions where questions raised by the religions, between the religions and about the religions can be pursued through a range of academic disciplines in both critical and constructive ways.[25] Those conditions include above all the creation of an institutional space that might be described as 'shared ground' or 'mutual ground'. It is to be contrasted with both 'neutral ground' and 'contested ground'. Neutral ground is what a secular society or institution often claims to provide in matters of religion. A problem is that the conditions for entering it are usually secular in the sense of requiring particular religious identities to be left behind: norms, concepts and methods have to be justifiable in non-religious terms.[26] Contested ground is where there is no agreement about how to constitute it. Historically, neutral ground is a solution to otherwise irresolvable conflict, especially over religious matters; its high cost is seen in the ill match between secular universities and our religious and secular world. They are predominantly secularist in an ideological sense; and in a multi-faith and secular world, where the vast majority of people are directly related to a religious tradition, and where each major religious tradition is in complex relationships with other religions and with secular forces and worldviews, the largely secularised universities are unable to respond academically. They do not on the whole educate people able to engage intelligently in this multi-faith and secular world, nor do they foster the high-quality religion-related study and debate across disciplines necessary to make thoughtful critical and constructive contributions to the public sphere or its various dimensions (political, economic, cultural, technological, religious). Neutral ground is best seen as sometimes necessary, but temporary and in the long term an unsatisfactory solution to the need for places of peaceful engagement that respect the integrity of all participants and encourage them to contribute from the riches of their traditions.

---

25. For a brief account of the field of theology and religious studies in such a setting see David F. Ford, *Theology: A Very Short Introduction* (Oxford: Oxford University Press, 1999, 2000), especially chapters 1 and 2; for a discussion of the field with reference to several countries and types of institution, see *Fields of Faith: Theology and Religious Studies in the Twenty-first Century*, ed. David F. Ford, Ben Quash and Janet Martin Soskice (Cambridge: Cambridge University Press, 2005).

26. See *Fields of Faith*, Part 1, 'The End of the Enlightenment's Neutral Ground'; also Jeffrey Stout, *Democracy and Tradition* (Princeton: Princeton University Press, 2003) for a secular critique of the neutral public sphere in the United States.

Mutual or shared ground[27] is the preferable solution. It is to be found in various forms in a range of universities, especially in Britain and North America. It is the most congenial space for scriptural reasoning, since it might be seen as a wider version of scriptural reasoning's practice of mutual hospitality. Scriptural reasoning can both benefit from an environment of shared ground and also in its own small way try to enrich it. Its ability to gather Jewish, Muslim and Christian academics from many disciplines into a form of collegiality that is productive in academic as well as other ways can be a sign to secularised universities that academic integrity is not in tension with all forms of religious conviction.

Yet it can also easily act as a provocation to those in the university who are still rightly sensitive to the dangers of religious domination, dogmatism and divisiveness. The practice of scriptural reasoning in university settings, even those that offer shared ground, must meet strong challenges from several sides. Can it practise relevant disciplines (which can range through a great many faculties) to the highest standards of the various international 'guilds' of academic peers? Can it relate across these disciplines? Can scriptural reasoning be taught well in universities according to appropriate norms and standards? Can it give plausible theoretical accounts of a hermeneutics that critically and constructively draws together the three scriptures and their premodern, modern and late modern traditions of interpretation? Above all, what about its 'reasoning'? How does it relate to the *Wissenschaft* that was so important in the founding of the University of Berlin? This ideal has since pluralised in various directions in different fields, though without losing a family resemblance that generally still exerts a strong pressure towards academic accountability in rational terms.

In the course of trying to meet such challenges there are inevitable counter-challenges which the university must meet – it is the character of shared ground that the questioning is mutual. This is sometimes a matter of confronting common academic prejudices and *idées fixes*. These include: a modern parochialism that cannot take the premodern seriously in matters of truth; an incapacity to appreciate intellectual achievement in the area of religious thought; a failure to respect the large numbers of religious academics who are at least as intelligent,

---

27. See *Fields of Faith*, Part 11, 'Meetings on Mutual Ground' and the perceptive discussion by Nicholas Adams, Oliver Davies and Ben Quash in ibid. chapter 13, 'Fields of Faith: An Experiment in the Study of Theology and the Religions'.

well-educated, sophisticated and critically alert as their secular colleagues; an insistence on religious and theological positions meeting standards of rationality that are by no means accepted throughout the university; or a blindness to the complexly religious and secular character of our world. It also has potential implications for how disciplines are conceived, researched and taught, especially those that have to do with the religions. And it brings into the seminar room ways of approaching substantive matters, such as God, revelation, the nature of scripture, faith, tradition, ethics, politics, and so on, that can differ greatly from usual approaches.

Overall, scriptural reasoning is a small sign of something more wide-spread but still contested in the academic world: the emergence of new 'religious and secular' settlements that provide mutual ground for exchanges across many boundaries. Whether such ground expands is likely to be the major factor in its university future.[28] But it is important that, for all its flourishing in some university environments, it is not simply assimilable to any university setting or model. It has its own character which will now be described.

Tent

Academic scriptural reasoning sessions have been carried on in hotels, conference centres, universities, seminaries and private homes. 'Tent' is an image for the space of study and conversation wherever they actually happen. It has scriptural resonances of hospitality (see Genesis 18) and divine presence (see Exodus 40), and with the whole Middle Eastern culture of nomads and desert travel in which the Abrahamic scriptures are rooted. It suggests the fragility of a network of Jews, Muslims and Christians who are part of the well-established structures of houses and campuses but who also gather in this lightly structured setting. It is of a different order from a house or a campus, suggesting (at least in our culture) a place that is not one's permanent home, and not in competition with the others as religious or academic institutions.

A tent is also connected with being between locations. This 'in-betweenness' is a significant metaphor in various ways for scriptural reasoning. *It is concerned with what happens in the interpretative space between the three*

---

28. For the sake of brevity I have not covered a range of other institutional settings where scriptural reasoning can be practised, such as seminaries (some of which are closely related to or even integrated with universities), or institutions with Muslim, Jewish and Christian chaplaincy but no academic study of religion or theology. Each raises issues which require discussion with reference to their specific conditions.

scriptures; in the social space between mosque, church and synagogue; in the intellectual space between 'houses' and 'campuses', and between disciplines on the campuses; in the religious and secular space between the houses and the various spheres and institutions of society; and in the spiritual space between interpreters of scripture and God. These are spaces inviting movement in different directions and discouraging permanent resting places, and are suited to the tent's lightness, mobility and even vulnerability. Yet in addition there is resilience and durability in a good tent, and it can be used at short notice and in conditions and locations that are unsuited to large buildings. It also allows for an intimacy of encounter that may be harder to achieve in more institutionalised settings.

A further resonance is with leisure activity. This may seem odd for something that is taken seriously and is the focus for a good deal of work. But it is in line with the appropriately peripheral character of scriptural reasoning within both house and academy. Within the house, as discussed above, studying scriptures with those of other houses can never have the focal importance of studying one's own scriptures. Within the academy, too, scriptural reasoning is non-focal with regard to any particular academic's field (at least at present).[29] Scriptural reasoning does not encourage anyone to become an 'expert' in scriptural reasoning, as if it were possible to know all three scriptures and their traditions of interpretation in a specialist mode. It is an advantage to try to learn each other's languages, both literally (especially Hebrew, Greek and Arabic) and metaphorically (customs, history, traditions of thought and practice, and so on), and it is helpful if some members of one house have made a special study of another house; but none of this is essential for scripture reasoning. The usual pattern is for participants to be especially proficient in their own tradition and to be able to 'host' discussion of their scripture. But at least one of the other traditions is generally outside one's academic specialty, and so study of that, together with study of all three together, is more like a leisure or amateur activity, something peripheral to whatever one writes most of one's books about. This does not mean that books cannot be written about it, but they are likely to be jointly authored or else, like the present chapter, acutely aware of the limitations of one perspective on something that intrinsically requires at least three.

---

29. It is of course possible to imagine it as an academic specialty in which one person might fill an academic post devoted to it. This would require a careful job description to avoid the impossible demand for threefold expertise, and the ideal would be a team of at least three.

Scriptural reasoning's tent can be pitched within the grounds of a house or a campus, but it has to be wary of becoming too much at home there, for different reasons in each case. Within a specific 'house' – under the auspices of a church, mosque or synagogue – the obvious danger is of the host inhibiting full mutuality between the three as hosts and guests, since the ground is 'owned' by one party. Within a campus there is more possibility of fully mutual ground, though it is probable that for historical reasons any particular university will be weighted towards one or two of the three. There are other possible problems with universities: policy, curricula, appointments and funding are not necessarily in the hands of those who appreciate a practice such as scriptural reasoning; university and even departmental politics can swing in different directions; and universities are not always unselfish enough to share in something that is at home in many places, including some of which they might not completely approve.

For these and other reasons scriptural reasoning has tended not to become too dependent on any particular house or campus, however good the camping there; but it is very young, and, if it continues, new institutional forms more integrated with houses or with campuses or other settings may be generated by it in time.[30]

Coping with superabundant meaning

When the three scriptures and the traditions of interpretation that they have inspired are put alongside one another one is faced with three unfathomable oceans, three universes of meaning.

Not only that, but within and beyond the traditions there is a further universe of academic study dedicated to these three scriptures and their histories of interpretation, drawing on philology, literary theory and criticism, history, theology, philosophy, psychology, psychoanalysis, social anthropology, sociology, political theory and ideology, postcolonial theory, art history, media studies, cultural studies, music and liturgy.

---

30. Historical parallels would suggest that a driver of new forms is likely to be divisions among scriptural reasoners leading to different schools of thought and varying relationships with religious communities, universities and other settings.

Not only that, but each of the universes is expanding daily as unprecedented numbers of people in all three traditions (billions worldwide), and beyond them, continue to search for meaning in these scriptures and in the responses to them.

Now in addition one can try to imagine the possibilities of the three in interaction with each other, and the further multiplicity of interconnections that open up.

Finally, one can imagine the three, in interaction with each other, exploring issues in contemporary life, and seeking wisdom for each tradition, for the three in their relations with each other, and for the flourishing of our world.

That overwhelming superabundance of meaning is clearly beyond any individual human comprehension, any encyclopaedic mind, or any series of volumes, or computer database. This is not just because of the problem of sheer quantity. Much of the meaning – the interconnecting that is only possible for a well-trained memory and mind, the making of judgements that have taken into account an appropriate range of factors, the discernment that grows out of years of prayer and meditation, the capacity for self-awareness and self-critique that require spiritual as well as intellectual maturity, the immersion in community life that shapes a sense of what rings true, the education in a discipline that has accumulated and tested learning over centuries – is embodied in people who have been formed over long periods, and whose way of understanding is inseparable from who they are. Even such people can hope to cope with the abundance only if they are in sustained collegial relationships with each other. Further, the essential responsibility towards the future is only possible if the collegiality includes apprenticeships across generations.

So a necessary condition for coping is groups and networks of people of different generations who embody the main dimensions of the seeking and finding of meaning. *The most vital of all these dimensions is that of living, wise embodiment of the core identities of Islam, Judaism and Christianity.* This is the most obvious and simple reason for the impossibility of overviews or comprehensive expertise: *no one can live and think bearing more than one of these core identities at the same time.*

Within this collegiality, how is the abundance coped with? The basic way is through each coming with their scriptures and 'internal libraries' and engaging in reading, listening and interpretation in conversation with the others. Within that I would identify in particular three fundamental and coinherent elements.

Plain sense with midrash

The first task of an interpreter of scripture is to try to do justice to its plain sense. There is of course much discussion about what the plain sense is, but the sorts of things that need to be taken into consideration are the manuscript evidence; the lexical meanings of words in their semantic fields; the significance of syntax, figures of speech, genres, contexts, and resonances with other texts; sequences and habits of thought and expression; the relation of sense to reference; implicit pre-suppositions; and (most complex of all) different ways of construing and relating those things in different strands of the tradition and in the various schools and disciplines of interpretation today.

The latter points to the insufficiency of the plain sense in certain crucial respects. Its polyvalence, surplus of meaning and openness to multiple interpretations frequently generate an abundance of possibilities. This laying out of many interpretations may be sufficient if one's interest is phenomenological, surveying these fascinating possibilities without con-cern for any current relevance or application. But, if one believes that these texts can be retrieved as sources for understanding and living today (and scriptural reasoning includes at least three sets of people who do believe that about their own scriptures), and that that involves the search for their contemporary meaning and the risk of application, then more is required. One Jewish way of naming this 'more' that has been the topic of much discussion in scriptural reasoning is 'midrash', and Christian and Muslim traditions have their equivalents of this.[31] Midrash discovers in the text a sense for the time and place of the interpreter.

Midrash can seem idiosyncratic, an improvisation on the text that may seem to maintain only a tenuous relation to its plain sense. But in any scriptural tradition something like midrash is unavoidable if the mean-ing of the text is to be 'performed' today. Its combination of recognition of the plain sense with discernment of an applied sense is at the heart of what I call a wisdom interpretation of scripture.[32] This is the central way

---

31. See chapter 2, pp. 53–8 above for discussion of extended senses in Christian interpretation. For a Jewish understanding of midrash in relation to scriptural reasoning see Ochs, 'Reading Scripture Together in Sight of Our Open Doors'. On Muslim interpretation see Aref Ali Nayed, 'Reading Scripture Together: Towards a Sacred Hermeneutics of Togetherness'.

32. See chapter 2, pp. 79–89 above, and also David F. Ford, 'Reading Scripture with Intensity: Academic, Ecclesial, Inter-faith, and Divine' in *The Princeton Seminary Bulletin* 26, no. 1 (2005), pp. 22–35.

in which scriptural reasoning copes with the abundance of meaning: *by trying to take as much as possible of it into account, by always giving priority (as Judaism, Christianity and Islam traditionally do) to the plain sense, and by risking a contemporary extended, midrashic sense that has emerged out of wisdom-seeking conversation across traditions and disciplines.* This contemporary sense is a performance of interpretation for now. It does not seek to be normative knowledge or to be the only valid interpretation or to be demonstrable and invulnerable; rather it seeks to be wise. It is not so much about mapping the ocean (though maps help) as about diving in search of the pearl of a deep sense that rings true now.

Theory

Midrash copes with the abundance of meaning through first-order interpretation seeking to improvise wise contemporary senses of specific texts. A complementary, second-order strategy is the development of theory. Indeed one might say that as midrash has been the characteristic outcome of the small *chevruta*-style text-study scriptural reasoning groups, so theory has been the typical product of plenary sessions. The larger setting is less suited to close study of texts, but better at trying to distil into concepts and theories a second-order description of what has gone on in a number of smaller groups and discussing their wider connections and implications.

Theory, often closely connected with particular philosophies, theologies, social sciences or natural sciences, is also prominent in published writings on scriptural reasoning. The second-order 'moment' of concepts interconnected in theory is suited to written presentation.

On the other hand, it is extremely hard to do justice in print to the complex oral exchanges of small groups studying three scriptures at once, and even harder for one person to do so. An early draft of the present chapter attempted to give an example of scriptural reasoning focussed on texts from Tanakh, Bible and Qur'an that had been discussed during a five-day conference. It faced some problems that in combination I judged to be insuperable. The chief one was the impossibility of condensing hours of discussion (often apparently fragmented or centrifugal) around these texts into anything that would fit in a chapter. A second problem was that the oral character of the exchanges, together with their context in the biographies of the members, in the history of the group and in all the other things that were going on in the conference (including a good deal of theoretical and political discussion), repeatedly made specific interpretations, if reproduced in writing, seem not only bare but even misleading. They cried out for 'thick' description, for substantial annotation, for explanation, and for sensitive characterisation of each 'voice' if justice were to be done to what had actually gone on. It is not surprising that there has been considerable discussion among those taking part in scriptural reasoning about the importance of developing forms of rich, multidimensional description and the use of social (or cultural) anthropology to assist in this. A third problem was that I became acutely aware that my account of the discussion around these texts was that of a certain Christian interpreter and needed to be complemented by accounts from the other participants – this would be possible, but not in the space available here.

So I decided not to try to give an example of actual text interpretation, and to remain content for now with introducing scriptural reasoning from various angles. The practical conclusion is not that it is impossible to be more descriptive but that it is not possible now in just one chapter; therefore as scriptural reasoning continues there needs to be more work on appropriate forms of description. But even so, as regards actually learning scriptural reasoning, one should probably not have too high expectations of such work. It is in the nature of an intensive, dialogical social practice that it is best learnt by initiation into the group, followed by apprenticeship.

What might be an appropriate fixed form for presenting conversation around these three sets of texts? The printed page is especially limited – it is stretched to its limits in presenting the rabbinic debates around scripture in the Talmud, which are probably the nearest traditional equivalent to scriptural reasoning – and they are only coping with one scriptural 'ocean of meaning'. It may be that an interactive electronic medium with the possibility of pursuing several different lines of thought from the one word or verse (as through hypertext) and of holding on screen several text boxes, any of which can be searched with reference to the other (and variant translations called up at will), would do better, not least because it might be able to draw users into the creative process rather than just reproducing one past instance of it. But, like Talmud, any attempt to reproduce the results of face to face interplay is likely to be difficult, underdetermined, and in need of long apprenticeship in order to follow the allusions, moves and leaps. One is reminded of Plato on the dangers and disadvantages of writing over against live conversation: a writing cannot respond to questions and cannot adapt to particular audiences, and so is inferior to oral διαλέγεσθαι (conversation, dialogue or dialectic).[33] But it can do better at presenting theory in sets of interconnected ideas.

Theory's second-order discourse is also relatively well suited to the individual authorship that is the norm in specialist academic publishing in theology, philosophy, and other arts and humanities subjects. Again, Plato is instructive. His earlier works were fully dialogical, trying to catch the dynamics of Socrates in conversation. After the *Phaedrus* the dialogue form is minimal, the readers for whom his works are written seem to be philosophers or trainee philosophers, and the theoretical sophistication of the works increases. For Plato, philosophy was learned and developed through face to face conversation in the context of a whole way of life, and his later writings are aids to that process rather than attempts to produce a literary imitation of it in dialogue form.[34] In the centuries that followed, the living heart of his philosophical tradition was the conversational teaching of the Academy in Athens.

With regard to scriptural reasoning, this underlines the emphasis above on its collegiality; and, while it reduces any expectation that it will be done justice by theoretical accounts, it also makes theory modestly complementary to discussion of scripture. *The unreproducible density and dynamics of conversation in small groups gathered around scriptural texts may be central to its practice and to the quality of its collegial scriptural wisdom, but that quality also needs the contribution of theory to sustain intellectual rigour and creativity.*

At the beginning the most influential theoretical contribution was Peter Ochs' use of C. S. Peirce's semiotics and relational logic, and that has continued to be a fruitful resource.[35] It has Christian counterparts in Oliver Davies[36] and Chad Pecknold[37] and a Muslim appropriation is seen in Basit Koshul, who also draws on the social theory of Max Weber and the philosophy of Muhammed Iqbal.[38] Nicholas Adams has engaged in critical

33. See Plato, *Phaedrus* 275c, 275d, 275e, 276c, 277d.

34. See Charles H. Kahn, *Plato and the Socratic Dialogue: The Philosophical Use of a Literary Form* (Cambridge: Cambridge University Press, 1996), pp. 376–92.

35. See Peter Ochs, *Peirce, Pragmatism and the Logic of Scripture* (Cambridge: Cambridge University Press, 1998), and 'Scriptural Logic: Diagrams for a Postcritical Metaphysics' in *Modern Theology* 11, no. 1 (January 1995), pp. 65–92.

36. Oliver Davies, 'The Sign Redeemed: A Study in Christian Fundamental Semiotics' in *Modern Theology* 19, no. 2 (April 2003), pp. 219–41; *The Creativity of God: World, Eucharist, Reason* (Cambridge: Cambridge University Press, 2004), especially chapters 2, 4, 5, 6; for reference to scriptural reasoning see e.g. p. 121.

37. Pecknold, *Transforming Postliberal Theology*.

38. Basit Bilal Koshul, 'Affirming the Self through Accepting the Other'; 'Studying the Western Other, Understanding the Islamic Self: A Qur'anically Reasoned Perspective' in *Iqbal Review* 46, no. 2 & 4 (April and October 2005), special issue, pp. 149–74.

discussion with Jürgen Habermas in dialogue with German Idealist philosophy from Kant to Schelling and Hegel,[39] while Randi Rashkover has given theoretical consideration to the original Jewish–Christian dimension to scriptural reasoning.[40] Other important theoretical contributions have been made by Gavin Flood, Timothy Winter, Ben Quash, Robert Gibbs and Daniel Hardy.[41]

Such variety shows the capacity of scriptural interpretation to stimulate conceptual thinking in dialogue with pragmatism, idealism, phenomenology, social theory, legal theory, scientific theory, ethical theory, philosophy of language, philosophy of history, systems thinking, feminist theory and hermeneutical philosophy. The very diversity also resists any theoretical overview – there can be no overall master theory where so many conceptual descriptions and analyses engage with each other. The intersection of such theoretical accounts also intensifies the conversation around scriptural texts and their implications.

So the effort to 'make deep reasoning public' (Adams, above) simultaneously leads deep into scriptures and deep into theories, interweaving premodern, modern and late modern discourses.

Analogous wisdoms

A further dimension of coping with the superabundance of meaning is the relating of these mutually informing discourses of theory and scriptural interpretation (plain sense and midrash) to their practical implications in various spheres of life – which is, of course, a leading concern of the rabbinic sages in their midrash and of comparable strands in Christianity and Islam. *The condition for wise Abrahamic practicality is that each tradition allows itself to have its own wisdom questioned and transformed in engagement with the others. This means recognising them as analogous wisdoms with the potential of worthwhile interplay.*

Collegial wisdom-seeking by Jews, Christians and Muslims can go on in other ways than through conversation around their scriptures, but considering each scripture is essential to any wisdom that might claim to

39. Adams, *Habermas and Theology*; see also Nicholas Adams, 'Beyond Logics of Preservation and Burial: The Display of Distance and Proximity of Traditions in Scriptural Reasoning' in *Iqbal Review* 46, no. 2 & 4 (April and October 2005), special issue, pp. 241–8.
40. Rashkover, *Revelation and Theopolitics*.
41. See the following chapters in *The Promise of Scriptural Reasoning*: Flood, 'The Phenomenology of Scripture'; Timothy Winter, 'Quranic Reasoning as an Academic Practice'; Quash, 'Heavenly Semantics: Some Literary-Critical Approaches to Scriptural Reasoning'; Robert Gibbs, 'Reading with Others: Levinas' Ethic and Scriptural Reasoning'; and Daniel Hardy, 'Conclusion', on the way these can be understood together.

be in line with each tradition. Above all, attention to the scriptures helps ensure that emergent wisdom is related to God and God's purposes in history and for the future. Within scriptural reasoning perhaps nothing has been theologically more fundamental than the threefold sense that study and interpretation are happening in the presence of God and for the sake of God, in the midst of the contingencies and complexities of a purposeful history, and in openness to God's future and for the sake of God's purposes. Yet precisely in the understanding of God, history and eschatology lie some of the most profound and stubborn differences – the Christian description of which is in terms of God as Trinity, and an account of creation, history and the future in which Jesus Christ is both central and ultimate.

How might this situation of deep differences with regard to analogous categories be coped with wisely? Christian participants in scriptural reasoning have not found it helpful to concentrate on arriving at doctrinal agreement with Jews and Muslims on the Trinity, christology and eschatology (or at agreement on analogously distinctive Jewish or Muslim beliefs and practices). Not only would success in that be virtually inconceivable but insisting on it may in most contexts be an unwise path, leading deep into the marshes created by centuries of misunderstandings and polemics. A well-worn path into inter-faith cul-de-sacs is to focus on 'secure disagreements' which complacently reinforce the identity of each with minimal mutual exploration, learning or challenge.

Rather, what has been found fruitful is continual engagement with the scriptures that have contributed both to such doctrines and to the shaping of a whole way of life (including worship, ethics, institutions and so on). This can lead to conversations and understandings that do not ignore the disagreements but also do not get stuck in them. Ways of handling fundamental disputes can be worked out, essential to which is each tradition trying to discern and share its own wisdom of dispute (or its inadequacies in this regard).[42] And intrinsic to that discernment is the wise interpretation of scripture in many 'moods'. That is an urgent quest within each tradition and one in which each can benefit from the others.

---

42. See Quash, 'Heavenly Semantics', pp. 59–76: 'I sometimes catch myself imagining what it would mean for my own church (the Anglican Communion) if it saw its task not so much as achieving agreed statements as improving the quality of disagreement, and if it saw part of its best and most generous legacy to future Anglicans as being the transmission of these high-quality debates. To be given a debate might be as enriching as to be given a doctrine. That is after all what is achieved by the passing on of midrash in Judaism.' Chapters 3 and 4 above have presented the book of Job as shaped around a high-quality debate.

Scriptural reasoning in the public sphere

What about the possibilities of scriptural reasoning in the public sphere?

The main point is an extension of what was said about scriptural reasoning in universities – which are indeed part of the public sphere. Once it is recognised that we are in a multi-faith and secular world and that secular worldviews and principles have no right to monopolise the public sphere in the name of neutrality, then we need ways of forming the sort of 'mutual ground' that allows each tradition to contribute from its core belief, understanding and practice. That requires many bilateral and multilateral engagements, and among those is trilateral dialogue between Jews, Christians and Muslims. Earlier sections have described scriptural reasoning as allowing rich and deep encounter that both does justice to differences and also forms strong relationships across them. It is a new collegiality that might have an impact on the public world in several ways: by being a sign of reconciliation; by being a site where Jews, Christians and Muslims can work out in dialogue the considerable ethical and political implications of their scriptures; and by encouraging analogous practices among Jews, Christians and Muslims in positions of public responsibility.

Secularised societies have generally failed to mobilise religious resources for public wisdom and for peace. Religions have often reacted against them, faced with a choice between assimilation or confrontation. But there is another possibility: mutually critical engagement among all the participants aimed at transforming the public sphere for the better. For Jews, Christians and Muslims committed to this the best way forward might be through simultaneously going deeper into their own scriptures and traditions, deeper into wisdom-seeking conversation with each other and with all who have a stake in the public good, and deeper into activity dedicated to the common good. So one promise of scriptural reasoning is the formation of people through collegial study, wise interpretation and friendship who might be exemplary citizens of the twenty-first century, seeking the public good for the sake of God and God's peaceful purposes.[43]

---

43. Potential contributions to a Stout-like public space might be found in such works as: Peter Ochs, 'Abrahamic Theo-politics: A Jewish View' in *The Blackwell Companion to Political Theology*, ed. William Cavanaugh and Peter Scott (Oxford: Blackwell, 2003); Adams, 'Scriptural Difference and Scriptural Reasoning'; Robert Gibbs, 'The Rules of Scriptural Reasoning' in

Conclusion

For all its potential usefulness in enabling understanding, peace, collegiality and much else, scriptural reasoning's deepest and most comprehensive rationale in all three traditions is that it is done for God's sake. It can be instrumental; but before God it is above all an end in itself, worth doing because it celebrates the name of God in the company of others who are doing something comparable. As such, for Christians (and analogously for Jews and Muslims in ways that open up fascinating questions of similarity and difference), it exemplifies the wisdom of God, as explored in the seven chapters above, in circumstances that are perhaps unprecedented in history. It represents an extension and testing of the sort of theology described in the Introduction: scriptural-expressivist; postcritical; concerned with desire and discernment and with learning in the Spirit in many moods; pursued in an academic collegiality that is rooted in worshipping communities; and dedicated to God and the Kingdom of God.

Scriptural reasoning also resonates strongly – even shudderingly – at its core with the cries of our world. One of Steven Kepnes' suggested 'Rules for Scriptural Reasoning' is:

> Scriptural reasoning begins with the scriptural sense that the human world is broken, in exile, off the straight path, filled with corruption, sickness, war and genocide. Scriptural reasoning practitioners come together out of a sense of impoverishment, suffering, and conflict to seek resources for healing.[44]

Perhaps the most acute articulation of this has been by the person who has been most important in developing scriptural reasoning, Peter Ochs. In the course of offering philosophic warrants for scriptural reasoning he supplements the account I have so far given of 'the cry', analysing it in Peircean logical categories.[45] His key maxim is: 'Care for those who cry!'

The Journal of Scriptural Reasoning 2, no. 1 (May 2002), available on-line at http://etext.virginia.edu/journals/ssr/issues/volume2/number1/ssr02-01-gr01.html, and Robert Gibbs, Why Ethics? Signs of Responsibilities (Princeton: Princeton University Press, 2000); Chad Pecknold, 'Democracy and the Politics of the Word: Stout and Hauerwas on Democracy and Scripture' in Scottish Journal of Theology 59, no. 2 (2006), pp. 198–209; Mike Higton, Christ, Providence and History: Hans W. Frei's Public Theology (New York: T. & T. Clark; London: Continuum, 2004); Rashkover, Revelation and Theopolitics; and see Bailey, 'Sacred book club'.
44. Steven Kepnes, 'Rules for Scriptural Reasoning' in The Promise of Scriptural Reasoning, p. 24.
45. The conclusion of his argument is: 'Diagrammed in the terms of Peirce's logic of relatives, a cry may therefore be characterized as an indexical sign of pain or suffering. The force of such

which he finds exemplified in all three scriptures,[46] and he differentiates scriptural reasoning's way of responding to this from other modern, postmodern and postliberal projects.[47] His climactic example is the revelation of God to Moses at the burning bush (Exodus 3 in the context of the whole of Exodus 1–20) where the cry of suffering Israel is the stimulus for a paradigmatic redemption. 'We do not hear the cry as mere cry, but only as what "reached Me [God] so that I now do this".'[48] *Scriptural reasoning is a joint response by Jews, Christians and Muslims, inspired by the reading of their scriptures, to the cries of a suffering world, including their own communities, and it is committed, for God's sake, to being part of God's compassionate response to those cries.*

a sign depends on the world of signs within which it is received . . . [W]e may now characterize such "worlds of signs" as the *semiotic conditions according to which we know the world and how to act in it*. For present purposes we may note three sets of conditions: *material and formal* (the *language* through which we know the world), ontological (the *practices and relationships* through which we know the world), and *interrogative* (the space-time specific questions or problems to which our activity of knowing and acting now responds). According to scriptural reasoning, *the ontological meaning of a cry is set by Scripture's model of creation and command*: in this world created by God, a cry means, *at once*, that someone somewhere is in pain; that there is also somewhere a redeemer, or someone who can and will respond to hear and heal that pain; and that we who are in earshot of the cry are obligated to hear it and join in that work of healing. To worship the creator God of Israel is to retain the hope that, ultimately, each cry will be heard and the conviction that each of us is obliged to share in the hearing. According to scriptural reasoning, *a cry is thus defined materially and formally as at once a sign of need and an imperative to act*: a fact that carries with it not only a value but also a behavioural command. This is why the cry is received, finally as interrogative: *the conditions of command are necessarily here-and-now*, as if to say: "You who hear this cry are obliged to inquire into and act in response to its space-time specific conditions." This is why, finally, the meaning of a cry cannot be defined once-and-for-all or atemporally or as a condition of "being in general": it is a condition of *this being*, here' – Peter Ochs, 'Philosophic Warrants for Scriptural Reasoning' in *The Promise of Scriptural Reasoning*, pp. 130–1.

46. Ibid. p. 131.

47. Ibid. Ochs distinguishes between what he calls 'the dyadic logics of suffering and oppression and the non-dyadic, or illustratively triadic, logics of caring for whose who suffer and of repairing the conditions of suffering and oppression'.

48. Ibid.

9

An interdisciplinary wisdom: knowledge, formation and collegiality in the negotiable university

The twentieth century saw the greatest expansion of higher education in history. Universities multiplied and expanded around the world.
This has accompanied an explosion of knowledge and a multiplication of
disciplines and subdisciplines. Academics are part of a global network of
teachers, scholars and researchers, linked through books, journals, electronic communications and a great deal of face to face interaction in visits
and conferences. University students were estimated to have passed the
100 million mark in 2003, and 2 million of them were studying outside
their home country.[1] Universities during the past century have become
more involved in the economy, in government, in many areas of civil
society and in most professions, and they now educate large numbers of
those who are in leadership and other key positions in most societies in
the world. As common phrases like 'information society', 'learning culture' and 'knowledge economy' suggest, the role of institutions of higher
education, being centrally concerned with information, learning and
knowledge, is of increasing importance.

The increases in institutions, disciplines, academics, students and
influence have gone along with massive transformations in universities.
There are now many types of university, and, even among those with long
histories that have sustained some continuity with their past, those that
have flourished have also undergone and continue to undergo huge
changes. At the same time, there has been considerable differentiation,
and universities by no means have a monopoly of the expanded fields
of teaching at higher levels or conducting research. Indeed, the case for

1. International Finance Corporation, quoted in the 'Special Report on Higher Education'
in *The Economist*, 26 February 2005.

universities in line with the model of the nineteenth-century University of Berlin as institutions of teaching and research, covering the range of arts, humanities and sciences, and valuing the academic freedom of both academics and students, has had to be made afresh in competition with several other models.

The opening decades of the twenty-first century are a pivotal time for universities. Many forces, internal and external, seek to shape them, and major reconfigurations of higher education are happening at all levels – international, national and institutional. The most obvious challenge is that of the globalisation and commodification of higher education and advanced research. They are now 'big business', and the educational equivalents of conglomerates and international corporations are emerging. In what follows I am looking at only one 'niche' in this global environment: the 'world class'[2] university that combines teaching and research across a wide range of disciplines.

Most such universities owe a good deal to the tradition begun in the Middle Ages in universities such as Paris and renewed and developed by the University of Berlin. Within this tradition I take three main points of reference: the medieval origins; the foundation of the University of Berlin and the problems of that model today; and the University of Cambridge since the nineteenth century. In relation to the modern university six key elements are identified: uniting teaching and research; all-round educational formation; collegiality; polity and control; contributions to society; and, pivotal to the whole conception and involving each of the other five, interdisciplinarity.

The examination of Berlin and Cambridge suggests that current pressures amount to a crisis for this type of university. Will this sort of institution, which attempts to integrate the six key elements in the interests of a long-term intellectual and social 'ecology', be able to survive, flourish and help shape the wider global intellectual and cultural environment in the twenty-first century? One obvious way ahead is what is happening at present: a multitude of adaptations and negotiations which try to cope with pressures from various stakeholders and developments inside and outside universities. This is normal and unavoidable.

---

2. The main criteria used in the *Times Higher Education Supplement* World University Rankings are: peer review, number of citations per faculty member, ratio of students to staff, number of international students and staff, and the opinion of global recruiters. In the Shanghai Jiao Tong University Academic Ranking of World Universities, the criteria are: Quality of Education, Quality of Faculty, Research Output, Size of Institution.

But the surprise of the medieval origins and especially the surprise of nineteenth-century Berlin invite thought about another possibility. What if something like Berlin were to happen in the twenty-first century?

It may be that in retrospect this period could prove to be as seminal as the opening decades of the nineteenth century. There might even be a burst of institutional creativity that could shape a twenty-first-century model of the university analogous in richness of conception and breadth of influence to the University of Berlin. If that were to happen it would have to learn lessons from the history of universities. It is particularly hard to imagine it occurring without certain parallels to Berlin – for example in combining renewal of the best from the past with future-oriented innovation, in intensive conversational and adversarial engagement alert to many dimensions simultaneously (intellectual, historical, educational, political, economic, ethical and religious), and also, perhaps, in the need for one institution to be the symbolic embodiment of the new model.

Such a pioneering model might, as in Berlin, be conceived by a government or civil service that has people of the quality of Wilhelm von Humboldt who are open to the best available ideas; or it might come from a group with a vision which unites with major private funders (a more American pattern); or it might emerge from the transformation of an existing institution that has advantages such as already being of international stature and able to attract funds, having sufficient independence to reshape itself, and being able to generate a high-quality debate that leads through deliberation to decision and action. The scale of the challenge is such that it would probably be most fruitful if at least those three possibilities were explored (and it may be that the first is already happening in China). I will only pursue the third because it is closest to the University of Cambridge, my main contemporary case study, but I hope that that will have sufficient analogies with other types of university in Europe, North America and elsewhere to make it of wider interest. In particular I hope that the basic constructive question underlying the historical, descriptive and prescriptive elements of the discussion will be broadly relevant, together with some of the answers. The question is: *What is the wisdom needed for shaping universities in the twenty-first century?*

Surprising institutions

Each of the three points of reference in the history of universities discussed below might be described as surprising in relation to its context.

There is about them something of the quality of novelty combined with rightness that is associated with discoveries, inventions and leaps of understanding in many disciplines. Likewise, they share with such innovations the invitation to go further and be open to more surprises, and this chapter will also explore that possibility.

Medieval origins

The medieval university was a distinctive invention without close parallels among its institutional predecessors. The story of its origins is well told by the contributors to *A History of the University in Europe*,[3] and I have discussed aspects of it at greater length elsewhere.[4] For present purposes its most important features were those that had most long-term influence.

These include what Rüegg discerns as the seven core values of the medieval university: rational investigation of the world; ethical values of modesty, reverence and self-criticism; respect for the dignity and freedom of the individual; rigorous public argument appealing to demonstrated knowledge and rules of evidence; the recognition of the pursuit of knowledge as a public good irreducible to economic interest; the need for continual self-criticism in the course of improving our knowledge; and the value of equality and solidarity.[5] These values were rooted in Christian teachings about such matters as: God as creator of a world order accessible to human reason; human imperfection; humanity in the image of God; the deep connection under God between knowledge and virtue; the importance of self-correction and penitence in seeking the truth; and the corporate, collegial nature of education and the search for knowledge and understanding. A striking aspect of the core values is that most are widely held today not only by those who share their Christian roots (the doctrinal teachings mentioned are all still in various forms part of most

---

3. *A History of the University in Europe*, vols. I–IV, general editor Walter Rüegg (Cambridge: Cambridge University Press, 1992–). On the origins see vol. I, *Universities in the Middle Ages*, ed. H. De Ridder-Symoens (1991), especially chapter 1, 'Themes' by Walter Rüegg (pp. 3–34).
4. David F. Ford, 'Faith and Universities in a Religious and Secular World (1)' in *Svensk Teologisk Kvartalskrift* 81, no. 2 (2005), pp. 83–91 and 'Faith and Universities in a Religious and Secular World (2)' in *Svensk Teologisk Kvartalskrift* 81, no. 3 (2005), pp. 97–106. While the present chapter concentrates largely on the contemporary university and its core concerns (summed up in the six elements listed, and referring to the University of Cambridge as its main current institutional example) it is complemented by these two articles which pay more attention to historical interpretation and the role of religion and only mention in passing the six elements and Cambridge.
5. Rüegg, 'Themes', pp. 32ff.

Christian theologies) but also by a great many others who follow other faiths or none. There may be very different rationales for adopting them, but in practical terms the medieval principles continue to hold good, at least as ideals, across much academic life.

It is also striking how the fundamental goals of the medieval university have continued to be relevant.[6] These can be summed up as: *first, understanding and truth for their own sake; second, formation in a way of life, its habits and virtues; and third, utility in society – study oriented towards practical use and employment in various spheres of life.* These three were present from the start; so also was the tension between them. There have been many variations in emphasis in different university systems and periods, but, as will become evident below, many of the most important debates and decisions about the shaping and priorities of universities continue to revolve around how to balance the claims of these three. Three further features have also been of enduring importance: scholarly self-government, institutional space for tension and debate, and collegiality.[7]

Overall, the medieval university might be seen as an achievement of Christian wisdom that had learnt much from other wisdoms, especially those of Judaism, of ancient Greece and Rome, and of Islam.[8] It worked out in practice the implications of some core Christian doctrines by creating a setting that let those very doctrines be debated in fresh ways and that opened up a new intellectual space for a range of disciplines. It combined a wisdom concerned with knowledge and practices (in faculties of theology, law, medicine and the liberal arts) with an institutional, collegial wisdom that shaped an enduring, transgenerational community. It was a complex, internally differentiated institution that held in tension a variety of faculties, types of theology, colleges, fundamental goals and core values, and had a polity that had the potential to deliberate about the appropriate balances within those tensions. It was also extraordinarily successful in propagating itself in the centuries that followed: 'No other European institution has spread over the entire world in the way in which the traditional form of the European university has done.'[9]

---

6. On these see *A History of the University in Europe*, vol. 1, especially chapters 1–4 and 13. For further reflection on the goals see Ford, 'Faith and Universities in a Religious and Secular World (1)', pp. 87–8.

7. See Ford, 'Faith and Universities in a Religious and Secular World (1)', pp. 87–8.

8. For a brief summary of this interplay and reference to sources see ibid. pp. 86–7.

9. Rüegg, 'Foreword' to *A History of the University in Europe*, vol. 1, p. xix.

The University of Berlin (the Humboldt University)

The second point of reference, the foundation of the University of Berlin in 1810, takes a leap over many centuries. During them there had been many developments in universities,[10] but by the end of the eighteenth century European universities were not generally flourishing.

Late medieval scholasticism had centuries earlier been largely supplanted by humanism in various forms, which deeply affected both Protestant and Roman Catholic higher education. The religious divisions of Europe had been accompanied by considerable university expansion, and many of these institutions had thrived. But in the seventeenth and eighteenth centuries many new developments in philosophy, history, political thought, economics, the natural sciences and technology occurred outside universities. Their social settings were salons, conversational circles, societies, academies, associations, *contubernia, convivia, sodalitates*, networks of correspondents and journal contributors, and many close friendships. The universities were generally aligned with one church or another, backed by state power that was increasingly centralised and concerned to control education and religion along with other spheres. Their theological education was subject to strict orthodox constraints; what had begun as lively humanist dialogue with original classical sources had become largely antiquarian and oriented to the learning of authorities; and their teaching of mathematics and the sciences was not oriented to research and generally failed to keep up with what was happening in the new societies, academies and other associations.[11] There were economic factors too that led to university decline: they were no longer a route to the best careers, and had not connected with expanding areas of the economy.

Yet there were initiatives in higher education in eighteenth-century Europe that heralded the future. These were largely of two types: specialist institutions, often for training in particular professions; and

10. The full story is of course much more complex than can be done justice to here. The best available account is in *A History of the University in Europe*, both vol. I, and also vol. II, *Universities in Early Modern Europe (1500–1800)*, ed. H. De Ridder-Symoens (1996). For a brief summary of developments in the early modern period (taken as 1500–1800) under the headings of differentiation, professionalisation and expansion see Ford, 'Faith and Universities in a Religious and Secular World (1)', pp. 88–9.
11. The poor record of universities in regard to the scientific revolution should not, however, be exaggerated. For a balanced assessment which gives much credit to universities see Roy Porter, 'The Scientific Revolution and Universities' in *A History of the University in Europe*, vol. II, pp. 531–64.

university reforms, as in Halle and Göttingen.[12] Those two paradigms of specialist institutions and reformed universities became the competing models in the nineteenth century.

The first was associated with France, where the Revolution abolished universities and started afresh with 'special colleges subjected to severe, often military discipline, strictly organised and controlled by an enlightened despotism that governed to the last detail the curriculum, the awarding of degrees, the conformity of views held concerning official doctrines, and even personal habits'.[13] This might be seen as realising one vision of what modernity is about: making a clean sweep of the past and beginning from scratch, rationally working out what is required and implementing it in a systematic plan.

The second model, represented above all by the University of Berlin, might be seen as embodying an alternative vision of modernity.

Founded in 1810, it was named the Humboldt University after the scholar and statesman Wilhelm von Humboldt,[14] who persuaded the King of Prussia to adopt a conception largely thought out by the theologian Friedrich Schleiermacher, against a background of discussion and argument with others, especially the philosopher Johann Gottlieb Fichte. The idea of a new type of university was generated in the midst of one of the most creative periods in intellectual history, whose leading thinkers over several decades included Kant, Goethe, Lessing, Hamann, Schelling, Schopenhauer and Hegel, besides Schleiermacher and Fichte.

It was by no means inevitable that the Prussian government should choose to follow this course. The sorry state of many German universities and the powerful example of France's *tabula rasa* solution meant that

12. Notker Hammerstein, in 'Epilogue: The Enlightenment' in ibid. pp. 638–9, writes: 'What happened at Halle and Göttingen and the university reforms which followed them in the German-speaking countries could be continued, after the French Revolution and the challenge of the Napoleonic age, by important innovations that in many respects established a new model for university education and training and for the practice of academic science and scholarship. Although the reforms embodied in the University of Berlin were original in their emphasis and indeed presented a new understanding of research, scientific progress and the value of science in the broadest sense, they built on a foundation of earlier developments, theories and techniques. It then became evident that universities were appropriate sites for the sciences and for scholarship, for providing the intellectual foundation for the confidence of the modern state in its legitimacy and its capacities, and for the education and training needed by modern societies.'
13. Walter Rüegg, 'Themes' in *A History of the University in Europe*, vol. III, *Universities in the Nineteenth and Early Twentieth Centuries*, ed. Walter Rüegg (2004), pp. 4–5.
14. See Wilhelm von Humboldt, 'Über die innere und äussere Organisation der höheren wissenschaftlichen Anstalten zu Berlin' (1809/10), translated in 'On the Spirit and the Organisational Framework of Intellectual Institutions in Berlin', *Minerva* 8, no. 2 (April 1970), pp. 242–50.

there were many advocates of specialist institutions, and the government was in fact seriously considering following that route and abolishing its universities. Yet Humboldt, Schleiermacher[15] and others were able to envision an institutional surprise: one that simultaneously had deep roots in the medieval university, that learnt from the best of the contemporary German universities,[16] that could offer an institutional home for both traditional and new disciplines, that allowed a considerable amount of academic freedom in learning, teaching and researching, that met both religious and secular needs (clergy, civil servants, teachers, doctors, lawyers, scientific research) in a society which was complexly religious and secular,[17] that set the university at the apex of the educational system and its forms of accreditation, and that established a professional career structure for academics.

This might be seen as one of the great achievements of a type of modern wisdom which is the main alternative to that of the French Revolution described above. Simultaneously, it is strongly intellectual in a way that learns from many fields in their most advanced forms; it takes account of social, political, economic, moral and religious dimensions of learning and life; it critically appropriates the premodern (both Hebraic/Christian and Hellenic – Humboldt and many others in Germany in this period had a special fascination and reverence for ancient Greece); it celebrates modernity's passion for freedom of inquiry and for rationality in scholarship and science (*Wissenschaft*); it promotes educational formation (*Bildung* – Humboldt's vision of *allgemeine Menschenbildung*, 'overall education' and *allseitige Bildung der Persönlichkeit*, 'formation of a well-rounded

---

15. See Friedrich Schleiermacher, 'Gelegentliche Gedanken über Universitäten in deutschem Sinn' (1808), translated in *Occasional Thoughts on Universities in the German Sense: With an Appendix Regarding a University Soon To Be Established*, ed. Terrence Tice, trans. Edwina G. Lawler (Lewiston, NY: Edwin Mellen Press, 1991).

16. Some of these, such as Halle and Göttingen, had something of a golden age in the eighteenth century, and it is possible (as does my colleague Nicholas Boyle, in a personal communication) to play down the 'surprise' element in Berlin by seeing it more as a reform of the eighteenth-century German system. If Berlin was in greater continuity with some of its German predecessors this brings it more into line with the 'slower surprises' of Cambridge through which it transformed itself over the centuries (see below).

17. To use this adjectival pairing is to indicate a society in which: (a) some institutions are secular in the sense of not being under religious control, (b) some institutions are under religious control, (c) some institutions that used to be under religious control are no longer under religious control, and (d) some institutions that have been secularised in this sense nonetheless contain religiously committed people, show varying degrees of hospitality to those people and their religious activities, and in some cases include institutional components that are under the control of religious groups or institutions. I am grateful to Jeffrey Stout for his insights in this connection.

personality'[18]); and it embodies its vision practically in an organisation that works and lasts. This is in fact both ancient and modern wisdom, and is both religious and secular.

With regard to the latter, how to cope with religion is perhaps the core challenge to Western modernity, and one that has returned on a global scale in the twenty-first century. The French Revolution's solution was to try to abolish Christianity and even for a time attempt to replace it with a religion of reason. The University of Berlin tried both to do justice to reason and to engage constructively with religion as it was found in Prussia at that time. There was a passionate debate between Fichte (first Rector of the University of Berlin), whose concept of *Wissenschaft* (fully rational scientific and scholarly method) excluded theology from the university, and Schleiermacher, who also advocated *Wissenschaft* but saw it as contributing to (though not dominating) theology and the professional training of clergy in the university. Hans Frei's account of this describes Schleiermacher resisting any overarching systematic framework or theory of *Wissenschaft* for the University of Berlin since this could not do justice to 'the irreducible specificity of Christianity at the primary level of a "mode of faith", a cultural-religious tradition, and a linguistic community'.[19] Transcending systems, even those by which one is most strongly persuaded; doing justice to immersion in the messiness and 'irreducible diversity' of history; and negotiating practical settlements that cannot fit neatly within any system: these might be seen as capacities of wisdom that have been especially desirable since the Enlightenment and the French Revolution. They have often been notable in their absence among champions of both religious and secular systems and, as will be discussed further below, the world of the twenty-first-century university, with its massive global religious and secular problems, has just as great a need of them.

The context in which this wisdom was able to be received and acted upon by those with the power to do so is also very important. The French Revolution not only had traumatised and transformed France, it had also shaken the foundations of European civilisation. Napoleon had

---

18. Rüegg, 'Themes' in *A History of the University in Europe*, vol. III, p. 23.
19. Hans W. Frei, *Types of Christian Theology*, ed. George Hunsinger and William C. Placher (New Haven and London: Yale University Press, 1992), p. 114 – this is Frei's redescription of Schleiermacher's position. For a fuller, overlapping account of the religious aspect of Berlin and its implications see Ford, 'Faith and Universities in a Religious and Secular World (1)', pp. 89ff.

developed further the revolutionary policy in higher education. He had also humiliatingly defeated Prussia in 1806–7 and his occupation had a devastating impact on its universities. So Humboldt and Schleiermacher were thinking in the aftermath of a massive civilisational, national and university trauma, and their wisdom has something of the character of the wisdom I described in the book of Job (chapters 3 and 4 above) and its later analogies in Jewish responses to traumas. Perhaps this context of humiliation by France partly explains why Prussia did not follow the French model, attractive though it was, and why, in the interests of national pride, Prussia was motivated to seek something that was both new and yet strongly in contrast with the French model. The traumatic interruption also made radical innovation more acceptable and practicable.

The University of Berlin became the dominant model in Europe, the United States, and elsewhere (it was later especially influential in Japan), though some countries followed the French pattern.[20] Despite many twentieth-century developments, the main features of the Berlin model are still characteristic of those that, in various 'league tables', are judged to be the best universities in the world.[21] It is a model that has many variations in different countries, and also has, both in its original conception and in its various embodiments, been shown to have considerable problems. These have become especially evident in the late twentieth and early twenty-first centuries as the globalisation of higher education and research has intensified. But any re-envisioning of the university in the twenty-first century must appreciate the achievement of Berlin and attempt to do at least as well in today's situation. My attempt to do that will set alongside Berlin the University of Cambridge, an institution that both has learnt from Berlin and also has other features that make it a worthwhile case study in pursuit of something like a new 'Berlin surprise'.

---

20. For the story of the spread and details of the developments in different countries, see Christophe Charle, 'Patterns' in *A History of the University in Europe*, vol. III, pp. 33–80.
21. In October 2005, the *Times Higher Education Supplement* listed the top ten universities in the world in the following order: Harvard University, Massachusetts Institute of Technology, University of Cambridge, University of Oxford, Stanford University, University of California (Berkeley), Yale University, California Institute of Technology, Princeton University, Ecole Polytechnique. In August 2005, meanwhile, in the Shanghai Jiao Tong University Academic Ranking of World Universities, the top ten universities in the world were listed in the following order: Harvard University, University of Cambridge, Stanford University, University of California (Berkeley), Massachusetts Institute of Technology, California Institute of Technology, Columbia University, Princeton University, University of Chicago, University of Oxford.

The University of Cambridge

Christopher Brooke begins his preface to the final volume of his history of the University of Cambridge[22] as follows: 'It might be said, with some exaggeration, that in 1870 the University of Cambridge was a provincial seminary; in 1990 it is a major academy of international repute.'[23] The surprise of Cambridge lies partly in this transformation, but that was only one of a number of reinventions since it began in 1209, and perhaps the greatest surprise is that capacity for repeated renewal in an ancient institution.[24]

Cambridge today appears to be both older and newer than the University of Berlin.

On the one hand, it is a niche in a long-term intellectual and social ecology within which it has preserved and adapted features of the medieval university, such as colleges, that Berlin has never had. It is worth reflecting on this ecology.

Education is transgenerational and takes place best in environments that have been developed, reflected upon and reformed over a long time. Knowledge is cumulative, and new knowledge requires testing, sifting, refining and passing on as part of a coherent discipline or set of disciplines, a complex process that takes time and requires continuity and collaboration. Those disciplines, or aspects of disciplines, which it is more difficult to describe as accumulating knowledge (such as philosophy) may have all the more need to sustain a long tradition of thinking and discussion that can recall the positions and arguments of the past. The intellectual values nurtured in study, teaching and research, such as truth-seeking, rationality in argument, balanced judgement, integrity, linguistic precision and critical questioning, are long-term ideals, norms and practices. The creation and sustaining of physical and social settings where they actually flourish is an extraordinarily demanding task, and the timescale involved is nearly always transgenerational. The socially

22. *A History of the University of Cambridge*, general editor Christopher N. L. Brooke: vol. I, *The University to 1546* by Damian Riehl Leader; vol. II, *1546–1750*, by Victor Morgan with a contribution by Christopher N. L. Brooke; vol. III, *1750–1870*, by Peter Searby; vol. IV, *1870–1990*, by Christopher N. L. Brooke (Cambridge: Cambridge University Press, 1988, 2004, 1997, 1993).
23. Ibid. vol. IV, p. xv. Brooke goes on to qualify this by noting that the dominance of the clergy among the alumni was already in decline in 1870 and that 'provincial' is hardly adequate for the university of Newton, Bentley and Whewell. One might add that Darwin had published his *Origin of Species* in 1859.
24. See David F. Ford, 'Knowledge, Meaning and the World's Great Challenges: Reinventing Cambridge University in the Twenty-first Century' in *Scottish Journal of Theology* 57, no. 2 (2004), pp. 182–202.

and personally embedded nature of the values means that they are rarely well learnt except through face to face contact in settings structured and shaped through experience of embodying the values and resisting whatever undermines or distorts them. The values and their settings are continually under threat from many angles, and decades of building can be demolished in a very short time.

A great deal more might be said about the long-term nature of the intellectual and social ecology of which higher education is a part. So it can be helpful to look at an institution such as the University of Cambridge that has survived and adapted many times. There is also the possibility that such an institution has preserved features from the past that might offer resources for further renewal in fresh circumstances. In other words, being more ancient than Berlin need not mean being 'out of date': if it has succeeded in adapting in order to become a modern research university it may also have elements that predate Berlin and can be helpful for the future.

On the other hand, Cambridge's manner of responding to very recent challenges and opportunities makes it appear in many ways 'newer' than the Berlin model, at least in its contemporary German form.[25] This is seen most obviously in its role in generating new industries and businesses, in forming partnerships with the private sector, and in seeking its funding from a variety of sources besides the state.

Cambridge also represents a different model for change than either the French Revolution or the University of Berlin.[26] Cambridge's periodic

---

25. Speaking of the current 'crisis' in German higher education back in 2001–2, the then President of the Humboldt University in Berlin, Jürgen Mlynek, poses the question, 'If the Humboldtian model is now outdated, where then is the new model, and above all, where then is the educational–political dream team comparable with that of von Humboldt, Schleiermacher and Fichte?' Having mentioned the key features of the Humboldtian model, he then expresses the hope that there will result 'an intensive exchange of thoughts on how its [the model's] words are to be filled with life', see http://www.hu-berlin.de/presse/zeitung/archiv/01_02/num_6/editorial.htm. There are thus energetic efforts being made to reform the Berlin model, both in the Humboldt University itself and within the whole German-language university system (and its analogues in other countries, such as Norway and Sweden). These are a hopeful sign in global higher education, just as are similar efforts in some universities in the United States, and in the vast university system of China (the two other systems that I have had the opportunity to observe first-hand). In what follows, my concentration on Cambridge is justified partly by its intrinsic interest, partly by the extent of my own involvement in it, and partly by my contention that it can, either directly or by analogy, offer something distinctive to the quest for a wisdom appropriate to universities today.
26. Parts of what is said about the University of Cambridge will also be found in the published versions of the 2003 Gomes Lecture in Emmanuel College Cambridge, most readily accessible in Ford, 'Knowledge, Meaning and the World's Great Challenges'.

reinventions of itself, seen in attempts to change through recapitulating and renewing the traditions that have been most valued, and occasionally in more fundamental transformations, are very different from the 'blueprint' systematic approach of the French and German innovations.[27] Because of its democratic, self-governing character,[28] together with its federal, collegial dimension, it has been a site of an immense amount of dispute and negotiation. My main interest is in the character of the historically immersed wisdom that might, at its best, be discerned in all this and in the developments that might be called for now. It is a wisdom that is best viewed in the shape of the institution and its practices as they have emerged from the complexities of its history, but I see it at the beginning of the twenty-first century facing what might be its greatest challenges ever. Can it yet again recapitulate and renew some of the best in its past while being open to appropriate innovation suited to unprecedented conditions?

Before tackling that directly I will discuss the challenges facing both it and Berlin today.

Six key challenges

This section will identify and discuss six issues fundamental to the survival and flourishing of a world class university in the Berlin tradition in the twenty-first century. Each discussion will point to the profound problems that face such a university, and reference will be made to both Berlin and Cambridge in the diagnoses. As regards prognoses and prescriptions, reference will be mostly to Cambridge.

Uniting teaching and research

Just over a century after the foundation of the University of Berlin there were two other major institutions in Berlin that had been founded by the state purely for research, on which Charle comments:

> The foundation of the Imperial Physical-Technical Institute in Berlin in 1887, and of the Kaiser-Wilhelm-Society in 1911, which brought together state, industry and research in institutes outside the

27. See especially *A History of the University of Cambridge*, vols. I–IV.
28. Though see Christopher Brooke, ibid., *passim* on the complexity of the actual exercise of power in Cambridge through its many centuries of existence.

universities, represented a major step in the division of labour between research and teaching ... The German university and academic system as a whole, if one ignored the *concours*-system and the elite universities in the form of the *grands écoles*, was getting perilously close to the Napoleonic model which in its origins it had rejected totally.[29]

By the beginning of the twenty-first century such independent research institutes, whether sponsored by government or by non-government sources, were conducting the majority of scientific research, and in other fields too there were many non-university research centres. In this situation the question is not about the necessity of always combining research with teaching but about whether there should be some places where the two go together even though it is taken for granted that they can be carried on separately. How might the uniting of the two be justified?[30]

Granted that there can be perfectly good reasons for research and teaching to be carried on separately and that there are many fine institutions where this happens,[31] and also granted that there are often pressures on researchers to give up on teaching or on teachers to give up on research, the question is whether there is a strong case for a world class university to be committed to keeping the two together. Within the long-term perspective mentioned above, the question is whether the intellectual and social ecology, of which higher education is part, is well served by institutions where teaching and research are combined.

I would summarise the case in terms of the deep affinity and mutual reinforcement between the habits, values and orientations of good teaching and good research. Both require intellectual values of truth-seeking, rationality in argument, balanced judgement, integrity, linguistic precision and critical questioning. Both involve disciplined, patient attention to the natural or social world, to texts that have abundant meaning, to alternative hypotheses or interpretations, to

29. In Christophe Charle, 'Patterns', in *A History of the University in Europe*, vol. III, pp. 60–1.
30. What follows is an amended excerpt from my Gomes Lecture 'Knowledge, Meaning and the World's Great Challenges'.
31. In the USA 'there are over 3000 institutions of higher education. Only a few hundred are recognizably universities and of these not more than 200 are research-based. Moreover, even in the leading research-based universities, most teaching is not done by researchers but by short-term contract workers' – Gerard Delanty, 'Ideologies of the Knowledge Society and the Cultural Contradictions of Higher Education' (Paper delivered to the conference 'Changing Societies, Changing Knowledge', Selwyn College, Cambridge, 9–10 January 2003), *Policy Futures in Education* 1, no. 1 (2003), p. 78.

complexities that resist our simplifying, and to particularities that defy our generalising. And each at its best releases new energy and offers moments of sheer joy. Most academics who are passionate about their fields have caught the passion from their teachers. Dedication to teaching is certainly a matter of relishing the interaction with good students and passing on in gratitude something of what one has been given; but it is also a recognition that, besides the contribution to many spheres of life made by one's students, those who continue in one's own field as academics are likely to contribute to it far more than oneself. So any concern for future research in one's field beyond one's own individual contribution supports *the wisdom of cultivating lineages of researchers who are also teachers*. Without such lineages it is hard to imagine a healthy long-term intellectual and social environment.

But beyond the need for continuing to support new thought and research in specific fields, today's situation makes the case for the cross-fertilising of teaching and research even stronger. With so many jobs being knowledge-intensive, and with continual change in knowledge, information and skills requiring not only habitual new learning but also the perceptive integration of the new with the old, there is a sense in which 'we are all researchers now'. Research skills can best be learnt through apprenticeship to those who are at the forefront of their field – if they are willing, and enabled, to teach them.

In the Berlin tradition the teaching of students, except for a few doctoral candidates, has generally been more distant from any model of such apprenticeship than that of Cambridge. This has partly been due to Cambridge's retention and development of the medieval college, of which more will be said below. But Cambridge's marriage of teaching and research has come under increasing pressure.

The university does well by all the official criteria of research assessment and teaching quality. Yet that is hardly an adequate measure, not least because those appraisal procedures generally do not take into account (and are even disruptive of) the interrelation of teaching and research. In Cambridge, where teaching and research are at present quite closely related, sustaining and developing that marriage requires both the conviction that it is the best way forward (based on a case such as that presented above) and a creative response to short-term economic and academic arguments against it, involving answers to the questions just raised. It is a marriage whose flourishing therefore demands long-term perspectives with accompanying funding, values and wisdom.

All-round educational formation

The French model of formation was tightly controlled and focussed on specialist training; the German model allowed students great freedom in choosing their course of study, and in Humboldt's conception aimed at a broad formation, or *Bildung*. Rüegg's verdict at the beginning of the twenty-first century is that

> the higher education systems of continental Europe have never been able to combine the general education of undergraduate students with scientific teaching à la Humboldt, as they do in the best Anglo-American universities.[32]

The Berlin pattern as developed in continental Europe was far better at educating researchers than it was at non-specialist education. Despite the ideals of its founders, its major contribution, building continual innovation into the university, was often in tension with the general formation of most of its students and even with the marriage of research and teaching discussed in the previous section.

The case for a dimension of all-round education being part of university life is strong from many angles. Universities educate a majority of those who go on to hold leadership or other key positions in most spheres of life, and this makes something more than a specialist training desirable. How are appropriate values, intellectual virtues, good judgement, and broad understanding of people, institutions and society to be formed? In a 'learning society' and 'knowledge economy' which changes fast, it is likely that people will change jobs many times and, again, too specialist an education will not be sufficient. The sheer complexity of our society and its institutions requires the ability to make significant connections and appraisals in more than one area. That is an intellectual and ethical task, but also imaginative and aesthetic. The pluralism of a culture in which core values and identities are so varied, confronting people daily in the media and other ways, requires the ability to think about such matters if one is not to be easy prey to manipulation or constantly thrown off balance. Overall, the health not only of the economy but also of democratic polity and its accompanying civil society depends on a well-educated population. There are very few other institutional settings where a wide range of fields, professions and applications come together, so if the university fails here, the flourishing of society is at stake.

32. Walter Rüegg, 'Themes', in *A History of the University in Europe*, vol. III, p. 12.

The dimension of formation through university education is one of the least discussed at present. It is clear to me from participation as a student in universities in Ireland, England, the United States and Germany not only that each of them forms students differently but that the differences are by no means only to do with ways of teaching and learning. Perhaps even more important is the overall environment, the institutional culture that enables certain sorts of experience and growth. In discussing the Berlin model above, Rüegg's verdict was quoted, that 'the best Anglo-American universities' have done better at general education. That leaves a wide range of models to choose between, but, if Cambridge is included among them, how is its approach to be described and assessed, and the challenges to it identified?

Cambridge does not mostly do it through its formal courses of study,[33] which for undergraduates are quite specialised and for postgraduates are even more specialised. Lectures across the university are open to all, but most do not use this as a way of broadening their education. The main Cambridge approach is to combine quite intensive study within one field with a rich environment in other ways.

The key formative element is the college, a centre for residence, social life with students and academics from all disciplines, small-group teaching, tutorial assistance, meals, sport, the arts, groups and societies of many sorts, and religion. Colleges will be discussed separately below, but for now their significance for *Bildung* is the issue. Within certain constraints (which have over the years greatly diminished) there is a great deal of freedom to take different paths within a setting providing high-quality possibilities. Berlin reacted against a collegiality that had a strong *in loco parentis* religious ethos and that exercised quite comprehensive control over students. Cambridge colleges only gradually gave up that ethos, through long and sometimes painful processes of negotiated adaptation, but what was retained has the advantages of face to face communities with a rich culture and a different kind of freedom from the German one that concentrates on freedom to learn and teach. Cambridge students find themselves part of a multidisciplinary community with several other dimensions, most of which they can opt out of, but many of which are found by most students to be worth their free participation.

---

33. There are of course subjects that are broad and interdisciplinary in themselves, such as my own field of theology and religious studies, but most undergraduate courses are more specialised than that.

The main element that is not to be opted out of is also a critical difference from the Berlin model (and from most others): small-group teaching, often one to one or with only two students to one teacher. This intensive, face to face, disciplined conversation centred on specific academic tasks is for most students the core of their education. It is a formation through something like apprenticeship in a subject, with a direct relationship and accountability that is yet separate from the examination process (which is conducted by the university).[34] It is rare for a student to graduate without having come to know well at least one fellow of their college. The companionable, supportive college 'home base' for learning face to face with individual accountability combines with the wider world of the university lectures, seminars, examinations, central resources such as libraries, and open academic events of many sorts to make, at its best, a learning environment that both nurtures and challenges.

Other resources for formation also come from the wider university, with its vast number of groups and societies devoted to everything from sport and dance to politics and religion. Of special importance in relation to the conceptions of *Bildung* at the time the University of Berlin was founded is the role of the arts, especially music and drama. They flourish at both college and university levels, and link into the wider arts world of Cambridge, London, Britain and elsewhere.

Overall, as regards intellectual formation the picture is of learning patterns that form intellectual virtues, values and skills which can shape a lifetime of further learning, and that involve informal, sociable cross-disciplinary engagement, shaping a horizon in which other disciplines make sense. The wider picture is of numerous possibilities of involvement with physical, intellectual, political, artistic and religious activities.

How does all this measure up to the statement above that opened this section on the rationale for all-round education? The answer is that it achieves it in part, and that mainly through optional participation. One point of concern is the small extent to which interdisciplinarity, thinking about how one's own main discipline relates to nearer and more distant neighbours, is built into most courses of study. Another is the scarcity, either in formal courses or in the wider environment, of preparation for

34. Historically, this sort of teaching is quite recent, beginning in nineteenth-century Oxford and developed over nearly two centuries. It is the subject of continuous discussion in colleges and faculties.

wider responsibilities in national and global civil society. The general
ethos is that education is for personal development and advantage, and
even the wider implications of one's own field of study for the public
good are rarely considered.

This is mirrored in the lack of any university-wide, or even faculty-
wide, discussion of such matters to do with the common good. The last
time this happened across the university was during the student unrest of
1968, a bitter experience owing both to the low quality of much debate
and to the political reprisals and increased government control that
followed. Since then the general trend has been towards expansion of
university education in the direction of serving the economy, with students seen primarily as consumers of a product that serves their career
prospects. This will be taken up below under the heading of contribution
to society, but its implications for all-round education have been serious.
Is it possible for a university both to serve legitimate economic goals and
also to offer an all-round education that respects truth, knowledge
and understanding for their own sake, and that forms students in responsibility towards the public good? It is my contention that this is
both desirable and possible, but that, as in early nineteenth-century
Berlin, there are contrary possibilities that could easily win out, and the
twenty-first century might well end without a new surprise analogous to
the achievement of Humboldt and his friends and allies. Their
allgemeine Menschenbildung met its own problems, many now shared
with Cambridge and elsewhere, but the possibility of their solution
today has not so far appeared. It may be that Cambridge's retention and
adaptation of the medieval college pattern gives it an advantage in facing
this challenge. Such colleges are easily portrayed as expensive luxuries by
those whose main concern is education in the service of careers and the
economy. But they conserve a set of extraordinarily favourable conditions
for all-round formation.

The inattention to all-round formation underlines what is perhaps the
most glaring weakness of contemporary higher education: its inability to
cope adequately either with the 'who?' question that the issue of formation raises or with the related 'why?' question. There is much attention to
questions of 'what?' and 'how?' but the categories used in relation to
formation tend to be narrowed to the cognitive and practical, and there is
little debate about the adequacy of the rationale for this. One way of
putting the challenge of 'who?' and 'why?' is that education should aim
to form wise people committed to the common good. That is not an item

on the agenda of Cambridge or most other higher education institutions, yet it arises implicitly in many forms, and this chapter suggests that it needs to be made an explicit issue in discussion, negotiation and deliberation relating to universities.

Collegiality

The University of Berlin revived and renewed aspects of the medieval university, but it did not have anything like the medieval university colleges.[35] These, especially as they developed in Oxford and Cambridge, integrated into a residential community life academics and students pursuing a range of disciplines. Colleges could provide settings for cross-disciplinary and transgenerational conversation and collaboration. Berlin's freedom of teaching and learning, together with its seminars and institutes, to some extent played a similar role in fostering such conversation. But the lack of structured settings for collegiality across disciplines and generations became a more serious problem in the face of specialisation and the fragmentation of fields, together with greatly increased numbers of students and academics. Many universities influenced by the Berlin tradition, especially in the United States,[36] have tried to address this, sometimes by imitating aspects of Oxford and Cambridge colleges. But it is hard to argue that either they, or indeed their English models in their present form, are what is required for the twenty-first century.

The challenge here goes to the heart of the attempt to envisage an appropriate long-term social and intellectual ecology for universities today. The intellectual values central to university education and research[37] are socially embedded, and they thrive best when rooted in physical and social settings dedicated to them; conversation and collaboration across disciplines need to be part of ordinary academic life; and there is all-round formational value in different generations and practitioners of diverse disciplines being part of a face to face community while also relating to the whole university environment.

35. On the medieval university colleges see Jacques Verger, 'Patterns', in *A History of the University in Europe*, vol. 1, pp. 6off.
36. For example, the collegiate system in Yale and elsewhere.
37. For example, 'truth-seeking, rationality in argument, balanced judgement, integrity, linguistic precision, and critical questioning'. – See Ford, 'Knowledge, Meaning and the World's Great Challenges', p. 187.

This problem with the social aspect of the Berlin model may not be accidental with regard to its core conception. Wilhelm von Humboldt was explicit about departing from the medieval university by having a conception of freedom that was closely associated with solitude. The ideal was of highly motivated individual students and academics who found 'die Einsicht in die Wissenschaft' (insight into *Wissenschaft*) through and within themselves, and whose main connection with each other was purely intellectual.[38] This tendency towards individualism fails to do justice to the social dimensions of learning, teaching, research and personal formation.[39]

Since the Cambridge colleges represent something completely lacking in the Berlin model and help to meet some of its deepest problems, it is worth discussing them further. This will be done with a special emphasis on their contribution to the pivotal issue of interdisciplinarity, which will be the final element discussed below.

Colleges are long-term environments of conversational culture centred on meals. If Randall Collins is right in contending that at the heart of intellectual creativity is intensive, disciplined face to face conversation and debate between contemporaries and across generations, then they are well suited to enabling such conversation.[40] He marshals a large amount of data to show that this was so in the days before printing, it continued after printing, and it still holds true in an age of rapid travel, mass communications and computers. The face to face aspect can obviously be fulfilled through travelling to meet others, but it also points to the wisdom of having 'home' environments where contact with those in one's own and other fields is habitual. Colleges at their best sustain habits of internal hospitality favourable to conversation among those in different fields, together with external hospitality to those from other colleges, institutions and countries.

The simple core element here is that colleges gather together from different generations and from all disciplines *people* who are dedicated to learning, teaching and research. Knowledge and understanding inhere primarily in people, rather than in the storage facilities of books and computers. The problem of an aggregate of unrelated disciplines is not

38. Rüegg, 'Themes' in *A History of the University in Europe*, vol. III, p. 21.
39. See Walter Horace Bruford, *The German Tradition of Self-cultivation: Bildung from Humboldt to Thomas Mann* (Cambridge: Cambridge University Press, 1975).
40. Randall Collins, *The Sociology of Philosophies: A Global Theory of Intellectual Change* (Cambridge, MA: Harvard University Press, 1998), Introduction and *passim*.

met by some comprehensive system of knowledge accounting for them all – even were that possible it would soon, like Berlin's idealist concept of *Wissenschaft*, be considered out of date; rather *it is met by developing further a collegial culture*. This at its best provides dozens of micro-environments in the university where different things can be grown and where new things can be tried and sometimes fail (without having too disastrous results).

'At its best' is an important qualification. The twentieth century was a period of unprecedented collegial creativity in Cambridge – between the 1950s and 1970s eleven new colleges of diverse types were added.[41] Even so, the colleges have been outstripped in many ways by the far more massive expansion of faculties and research institutes. Many Cambridge academics, especially those on research contracts, are not members of a college, and, for those who are, their college is a dining club (the significance of whose meals and conversation has already been stressed) but its academic potential may not be realised. The core challenge to the colleges is to actualise far better than they do at present the quality of collegiality required to foster interdisciplinarity and the interplay between teaching and research.

Colleges are only one set of collegial niches in the environment, the others being more like those in other universities. These include all the faculties and departments, the centres and institutes, the longer- and shorter-term partnerships, and the numerous teams, groups, projects, societies, syndicates, lecture series and one-off events. Most of the disciplinary and interdisciplinary academic life of the university happens in these settings, often in the context of intense conversation and collaboration. One limitation is that nearly all of it is confined to one field or a few closely related fields, thus

41. Christopher Brooke in a letter (22 January 2002) to the author wrote: 'Between the 1950s and 1970s we actually did found 11 new colleges in Cambridge – 11 of the 31 are either totally new foundations or converted institutions of that period; a very remarkable achievement. Let us observe two contrasts: of the other 20 colleges 14 are medieval academic chantries – founded to support (mostly) graduate students and pray for their founders and benefactors; two were late 16th century puritan foundations – with purposes so little different from the pre-reformation colleges that the greater part of the statutes of Emmanuel was copied (almost word for word) from St John Fisher's for Christ's! – the 17th college was Downing founded (very oddly) by the Court of Chancery in 1800; and out of several 19th century attempts, three survived, your own Selwyn, and Newnham and Girton. That is to say, there is no period except the mid-14th century when founders have been so active as in the 1950s–70s . . . Four pressures particularly inspired the flurry of foundations. 1. The needs of university teaching staff . . . 2. The urge to gender equality . . . 3. The urgent need to provide for research students . . . 4. Visiting scholars – a major feature of the Cambridge scene, brought here by the immense prestige of our labs and the best working University Library in Europe.' See also Brooke, *A History of the University of Cambridge*, vol. IV, especially chapter 18.

raising again the challenge of more thoroughgoing interdisciplinarity. The very success of such settings can build up a life of their own that has little interest or energy to devote to university-wide debate and deliberation. The resulting fragmentation puts one of the biggest question marks against the contemporary university: if it cannot sustain interdisciplinary and cross-generational collegiality in teaching and research, why have it at all, apart from possible advantages in economies of scale?

Polity and control

The University of Berlin represents a particular balance of emphasis on what might be seen as the three main aims of universities since their medieval beginnings: knowledge, truth and understanding as worth-while in themselves; the formation of students; and utility. Perhaps its most remarkable feature was the extent of its dedication to the first aim while yet being completely dependent upon a state that also required educational formation and usefulness. The monarchical, increasingly bureaucratic Prussian state set up and financed an institution that allowed academics and students a considerable amount of freedom: there was a high degree of internal self-government by academics. Deeply embedded in the system was the conviction that the free exercise of critical rationality was sacrosanct. One consequence of this was that the state renounced control over inquiry and its results (though it did appoint professors);[42] another was that it protected the university from any other forces that might want to exercise such control.

In the context of European universities of the time this meant above all freedom from church control. Was this a secular university? If by that is meant the absence of ecclesiastical control, then it was. But if it is compared with the revolutionary French system of ideological, anti-religious secularism, this is better described as 'religious and secular': Prussia had a state church, and the university had a theology faculty whose main aim was to educate its clergy but which also became a leading centre in the German-speaking tradition of Christian scholarship and constructive thought that led the world in academic theology for nearly two centuries. It was a settlement that tried to do justice both to religion in the form of Christianity and also to the danger that religious domina-tion had been shown to pose to academic freedom.

---

42. There were also instances of interference in other ways, compromising the sacrosanct nature of academic freedom.

In the two hundred years since the University of Berlin was founded the issue of control has continually resurfaced. One problem has been the considerable power of professors and their tendency to become a privileged, conservative elite who can afford to be unresponsive not only to those who might want to infringe their academic freedom but also to students, other academics and even to new developments in their fields. More fundamental has been the vulnerability of universities to abuse of state power, most terribly during the periods of National Socialist and Communist rule. But the decisive issue today is perhaps about economic power, and the appropriate way for a university to be run in the global context of free market capitalism. And the decisive question is what involvement government should have in that running in order that the university might both meet its aims of knowledge, formation and utility, and remain sufficiently responsive to forces of change.

There are at present many battles around the world over the control of universities. Most universities outside the United States are controlled by governments; the best in the world are private foundations; the main trends are towards increasing private or joint control, and the development of transnational universities or international associations of universities. It may be that most government universities will go the way most state industries have already gone, becoming private with varying degrees of state control and accountability. I have already suggested some of the problems and advantages of the Berlin pattern of state control combined with a good measure of academic self-government. The main alternative is the American one of private foundations with large endowments governed by boards of trustees on which business and professional people, often distinguished alumni, hold most power, and with differing degrees of academic self-government. In Berlin academics are state employees with considerable corporate and individual academic freedom. In American private universities academics are employees in the private sector, usually with little control over their institution, but the more senior have contracts that give them individual tenure. I do not want to enter into the advantages and disadvantages of this system but to discuss briefly the situation in Cambridge.

Cambridge University is a self-governing democracy of 'all those who are university officers engaged in teaching and administration, all fellows of colleges, and all members of faculties'.[43] This body has to approve

43. Brooke, *A History of the University of Cambridge*, vol. IV, p. 351.

all major changes to statutes and ordinances, and otherwise the university is run by boards, faculties and groups of faculties composed mostly of academics. Each college within the university is a self-governing corporation with separate endowments.

The greatest single change of the past hundred years has been the growth (in budgets, students, staff, buildings and endowments) of the university's faculties and research institutes, especially in the sciences, dwarfing the income and other resources of the colleges. The correlate of this has been increased dependence on state funding for teaching and research. The state has exercised more and more power over the whole British higher education system through its financial control, with increasing emphasis on the contribution universities make to the British economy. Yet the level of dependence on state funding is falling, with the proportion of income from student fees, research contracts, knowledge transfers and endowment going up. This is especially true of Cambridge, and the university's policy is to increase as much as possible its non-state income. So there is a variety of funders and stakeholders in constant negotiation with each other.

The ideal aimed at is a preponderance of endowment sufficient to ensure financial independence similar to that of leading American universities, while retaining academic self-government. Financial independence is not likely in the medium-term future, and the 'mixed economy' has its advantages, ensuring that many interests are genuinely represented in negotiations and deliberations. But it is striking that even the state recognises the importance of endowment and its link with independence.[44] The message is clear: there is a direct relation between freedom and endowments, so if a university prizes its freedom it ought to make building endowment a priority.[45] Endowment is especially important for a world class university which does not wish to be tied to the

---

44. A government minister said in 2003 at the launch of a new initiative in higher education: 'First of all, we should face up to the truth that genuine university freedom comes through building endowment, rather than any other device. Universities in this country need to build up their endowments.' Charles Clarke, the Education and Skills Secretary, in a speech in the House of Commons, 22 January 2003.

45. This too was the judgement of Humboldt. He wanted to set up his university with an endowment of land sufficient to ensure its financial independence, but this was rejected by the Prussian government; see Heinrich Deiters, 'Wilhelm von Humboldt als Gründer der Universität Berlin', *Forschen und Wirken – Festschrift zur 150-Jahr-Feier der Humboldt-Universität zu Berlin 1810–1960*, vol. 1. *Beiträge zur wissenschaftlichen und politischen Entwicklung der Universität* (Berlin: VEB Deutscher Verlag der Wissenschaften, 1960), pp. 31–2. The financial independence of government that he had wanted for Berlin was achieved by some of the universities that followed his model, especially in the United States. That too has proved to

educational and research needs of one nation and to the predominantly short-term priorities of governments, fee-paying students and those who pay for research. The prospect for Cambridge if it were to succeed in building up its endowment to levels comparable with leading American universities is that it could conceivably have the best of all worlds: genuine self-government and a large measure of financial independence, together with accountability to a range of stakeholders, none of whom has preponderant power over it.

Yet for that to come about, three interrelated things are essential: to obtain the endowment; to show that it can govern itself well; and to have a well-thought-through, convincing conception of its own identity and mission (the latter will be discussed below). The issue of effective self-government is crucial at present. Most British universities have business-style line management systems in which academics corporately have little say, and the state generally favours this. There is strong state pressure for Cambridge 'management' to improve and meet standards laid down by the government. Yet its democratic decision-making has often been suspicious of innovation and easy prey to blocking by sectional interests.

Change in large institutions is one of the most difficult things to achieve satisfactorily. In a self-governing institution such as Cambridge it requires broad participation, mature deliberation, persuasion that there is a better, wiser way, and enormous skills in negotiation among stakeholders. In between the extremes of those who resist any change and those who favour strongly centralising solutions there appears to be a consensus that I would summarise as follows: this is a large and expanding institution whose governance and management have not kept pace with the complexity of both internal and external factors, including money; it requires a better balance between continuing self-governance, central leadership and management; it needs strategic planning in which academic, political and financial considerations go together; above all it needs a vision and strategy that is clearly in the service of the flourishing of its long-term environment of teaching and research, interdisciplinarity, collegiality and contribution to society. When that formidable challenge is set alongside the other five discussed here it is clear why something on the scale of the Berlin surprise is required if Cambridge is to meet them.

have its dangers, but on balance the lesson of history seems to be clear: von Humboldt's instinct for financial independence was wise, and any attempt to repair, renew and develop further the Berlin model for the twenty-first century needs to take this seriously.

Contributions to society

It is helpful to approach the contributions of a university to society in terms of those three basic aims of knowledge, formation and utility. The temptation today is to concentrate on the third, frequently in fairly narrow terms – 'knowledge transfer' for national economic gain, or 'transferable skills' for use in employment. The University of Berlin was partly a reaction against tendencies in early modern universities towards too great concern with utility. It represented a powerful redress in the direction of *Wissenschaft* and *Bildung*. The main contributions of the university to society were to be, first, knowledge and rational understanding across the range of disciplines, and, second, well-educated people (for church, civil service, teaching, law, medicine, the sciences, and other areas of work). The utility to society was to come primarily through fulfilling those aims.

It was a major achievement to persuade a state that knowledge pursued in academic freedom was for the public good. Such persuasion is an ongoing task, both inside and outside universities, and a core problem with the heritage of Berlin today is that there is little comparable to the immense energy of thinking and advocacy that went into its foundation (see below on the discussion of university reform in the nineteenth century and today). The broader issue is about the role of reason, understanding, knowledge and truth in our culture and civilisation, and the confidence that they might contribute to a wisdom of human flourishing. The Berlin ideal reached back to the medieval *amor scientiae* (love of knowledge) and also drew on the explosion of inquiry and knowledge in modernity, giving a prominent place to research and innovation. It could be seen as an institutionalised challenge to the whole society to transcend itself through inquiry, advancement of knowledge and education.[46] Its prime contribution to society therefore might be seen as a ministry of truth, knowledge and meaning.

Its other main contribution, that of *Bildung*, was in some tension with this insofar as it related to training for professions and other employment, a tension most noticeable in the position of theology as both *wissenschaftlich* and concerned with clergy education. This led, as explained above, to a settlement proposed by Schleiermacher that proved fruitful in many ways, and there were comparable settlements in other

---

46. The idea of the university as institutionalising the possibilities of a society transcending itself in these ways I owe to Daniel Hardy.

areas. In the two hundred years since then, even within the direct line of descent of the University of Berlin there have been the most varied settlements in this sphere. The problems with the Berlin tradition of *Bildung* discussed above, together with the huge changes in politics, economics, culture and religion, mean that twenty-first-century universities have to rethink not only their rationale for combining teaching and research but also how their teaching is related to the public good. The other problems with the Berlin tradition converge here too. The sorts of knowledge and understanding that are most widely relevant and instructive are often interdisciplinary, and the university is challenged to draw together its various disciplines in the interests of dissemination. Collegiality too has significance here: the way an institution organises and conducts itself is both formative for its members who go into other spheres and also itself a contribution to society.

What about the remaining aspects of utility, which are often the most prominent in public debate today, such as knowledge transfer to economically profitable ends? At the beginning of the twenty-first century the partnership between universities and industry or other commercial sponsors is perhaps the single most important element in the reshaping of universities. *When this is added to many other types of benefaction, sponsorship or persuasive pressure (from politics, professions, cultures and subcultures, class interests, gender interests, or religions) the 'negotiable' character of the university becomes more obvious, and it is also more urgent both for it to have a vigorous culture of negotiation and also, pervading that, for it to have a strong, internally negotiated sense of its own identity and purposes.* An adequate understanding of utility must include the long-term intellectual and social ecology of society benefiting both from truth, knowledge and understanding pursued whether or not they are directly useful, and also from the formation of students who are educated in a well-rounded way.

The Cambridge tradition since its foundation has largely emphasised formation, and its main activity has been educating people, inseparable from which was its contribution of them to society, especially to the church. During the past two centuries it has gradually complemented its concerns for mathematics, classical scholarship and theology with a full range of modern disciplines and has also embraced Berlin's emphasis on innovation in knowledge through research. Recently, it has also gone far beyond Berlin in becoming involved with business and industry, fostering 'Silicon Fen' and its science parks, and entering a host of collaborative and sponsorship relationships. The latter are prime examples of the negotiable university, and also of the worries surrounding it. Is the university compromising its integrity with regard to knowledge and formation? Is it being bought? Is it too dependent on such sources of funding? Can it do justice both to the state insistence on 'knowledge transfer' and on students being formed with 'transferable skills' (meaning 'of use in employment') and also to its priorities of knowledge and formation?

The general response to such questions is that the university needs to have a well-worked-out conception of itself, its values and purposes to bring to the negotiations (especially in order to be able to recognise what are compromises and when they are needed). Part of that is thinking through a richer concept of utility than is usual in public debate about higher education and then trying in every way possible to persuade others of it.

Even starting from the idea of 'knowledge transfer' one is soon led into a broader concept of what society needs. Elsewhere I have described this in relation to the Cambridge Genetics Knowledge Park.[47] A responsible attitude to knowledge transfer, rooted in commitment to the flourishing of future generations, must move into issues of meaning, values, ethics and long-term commitments. *There are very few places in society where there is even an attempt to consider all those together. Part of the value of universities to society is that they can be independent places of debate and deliberation about such matters in the interests of the long-term ethical and intellectual ecology of our civilisation.*

The independence is not only to allow an integral approach, debate of controversial issues and long-term commitments; it is also important in allowing for 'blue skies' research and theorising. This links back to the first priority of valuing knowledge for its own sake and being encouraged to go where the questions lead. The 'moment' of singleminded pursuit of truth has to have its own integrity. It need not by any means exclude or be in competition with the further 'moment' that asks about significance and use, but it is important to maintain the freedom of the first moment – and even whole departments that are dedicated to it.

I have already characterised part of what a university can contribute to society in terms of a 'ministry of meaning' in many spheres; through and beyond this there are innumerable links by individuals and groups with businesses, public and voluntary bodies, schools, the media, professions,

47. Ford, 'Knowledge, Meaning and the World's Great Challenges', pp. 191ff.

and areas of regional, national and international life. All of this goes on, but its scope and richness are rarely acknowledged in public discussion and policy, and the ridiculously crude criteria and metrics usually used in assessing the value of universities to society are a severe threat to this contribution.[48]

Interdisciplinarity

The Berlin model has at its heart a vision of teaching and research conducted in faculties that are differentiated yet also interrelated. Its conception of this interrelation of faculties is centred on *Wissenschaft*. Frei also describes the way in which the original Berlin idea of *Wissenschaft* included

> A self-involving perspective on the totality of things natural, cultural, and transcendent: a *Weltanschauung*. The idealist view of *Wissenschaft*, in other words, included or presupposed a whole-making outlook that served at the same time to justify that universal validity. Here was a claim to a comprehensive unity of all specific knowledge which at the same time insisted that each specific area had its relative autonomy – a comprehensive unity at the same time cognitive or noetic, aesthetic, and moral, based on a conviction of the unity, accessibility, and self-accessibility, or privileged status, of the human subject in its relation to all else.[49]

Yet this term, which has also 'been rendered in English variously as "science", "knowledge", "philosophy", "theory of science or explanation" or "theory of reason or understanding"', underwent considerable changes:

> In German usage, it changed drastically from the vast sense that it carried at the time when the new university was being planned and

48. For example, in his speech quoted above, Charles Clarke named as the three 'great missions' of universities 'research, knowledge transfer and, perhaps most important of all, teaching' (speech in House of Commons, 22 January 2003). The restriction of the middle dimension to knowledge transfer is disturbing and characteristic, and the Cambridge Genetics Knowledge Park (see previous note) points to its inadequacy. It is in line with a range of reductionist criteria increasingly applied to the performance of universities and other bodies. As Onora O'Neill shows in her Reith Lectures, published as *A Question of Trust: The BBC Reith Lectures 2002* (Cambridge: Cambridge University Press, 2002), one of the problems with inappropriate and unintelligent criteria is that they act as perverse incentives, undermining or distracting from high-quality performance and significant contributions. In relation to universities this is especially damaging in the area of contributing to society. No credit is given, for example, for involvement in schools, for a wide range of consultative roles, or even for many types of publication in print and other media that widely disseminate knowledge and understanding.
49. Frei, *Types of Christian Theology*, p. 108.

begun, to a much more limited sense two generations later, when it became difficult to give the word a fields-encompassing definition except in the most formal and vacuous sense, unless of course one reserved it for one kind of endeavour alone, such as the 'hard' sciences.[50]

This narrowing and fragmenting of the meaning of one emblematic term (accompanied by periodic but not generally successful attempts to reverse the process) continued into the present century, and is a sign of the crisis of unity that faces the successors of Berlin today. In the absence of philosophical idealism,[51] or of any other coherence found through philosophy or through any other discipline or family of disciplines, there is no agreement about what holds the disciplines of the university together. Yet the key pointer to why the university should embrace many disciplines, and how their unity might be conceived, comes from the original University of Berlin: as Frei pointed out, it was actually not consistent even with its own comprehensive notion of *Wissenschaft*, but represented the outcome of vigorous, complex negotiations between diverse conceptions.

It is now generally acknowledged that the explosion of knowledge and publication in all fields, and the development of new disciplines and subdisciplines, has not been matched by their interrelation. Yet many of the most significant and exciting possibilities in the advancement of knowledge and understanding are interdisciplinary, and there are strong impulses, coming both from within disciplines and from outside them, towards increasing interrelation. This offers perhaps the strongest rationale for the very existence of universities. Top-level specialist teaching and research go on in many other settings, but universities that maintain a broad range of disciplines are a different sort of environment, one with greater potential for interaction and cross-fertilisation.

Yet the bias of the Berlin model and its variation in Cambridge is heavily towards the single discipline or at best a set of closely related disciplines. It is hard to say that even a fraction of the cross-disciplinary potential is realised. Is it possible to have a fruitful academic culture of interdisciplinarity, both in teaching and in research, while avoiding the obvious dangers – above all the loss of rigour and depth in the course of

50. Ibid. p. 97.
51. For an account of idealism as the ideology of the university revolution pioneered by Berlin, see Collins, *The Sociology of Philosophies*, chapter 12.

seeking breadth and connections? *This is perhaps the pivotal question facing universities as such. Their distinctive mark is not so much teaching and research as teaching and research in relation to a broad range of fields. If the range goes they may still be called universities but there has been a fundamental change of academic identity and a loss of contribution to society and civilisation.* The desirability of creating settings where this range can be engaged with is generated both from within each field and from the wider society. The desirability becomes overwhelmingly greater when the long-term intellectual and social ecology of our civilisation is taken into account. Yet the challenge of fulfilling this is immense and is becoming more difficult.

As might be expected with such a pivotal issue, it connects with all the other dimensions of the university. Overall, it is unlikely that the many pressures towards becoming a set of largely separate institutes will be resisted unless there is a well-thought-through and strongly articulated conception of the university to which interdisciplinarity is intrinsic. To seek 'excellence in teaching and research' is not sufficient, yet that is the height of ambition of most parts of the university most of the time.

In interdisciplinarity we therefore see the distinctive academic challenge of the twenty-first century. Only the university that meets this creatively will offer something comparable to the achievement of the Berlin surprise over the past two centuries. But, among the many differences from Berlin, the one that stands out with regard to the interrelation of fields is the role of an overarching conception of *Wissenschaft*. The intellectual framework of Berlin was that of idealist philosophy and its embracing epistemology. If anything is clear about the twenty-first-century academy it is the absence of any such epistemological consensus. This need not mean complete relativism as regards what counts as knowledge and methods of attaining it,[52] but it does pose huge problems for the recognition of one field by another (or sometimes of one aspect of one field by another aspect) and for cross-disciplinary conversation, let alone collaboration.

Yet Berlin also hints at a way through this dilemma. In fact it was not monolithic in its epistemology. Insofar as it followed Schleiermacher, it was eclectic and arrived at a settlement that allowed for other approaches to knowledge within a dynamic institutional setting. It embodied a

---

52. I would guess that the vast majority of academics in all fields are hostile to thoroughgoing relativism as something that would radically undermine their teaching and research; nevertheless relativists represent prophetic challenges on the boundaries of most fields, and especially in cross-disciplinary discussion.

wisdom of negotiation in the interests of a conception of academic life that recognised reality as transcending the embrace even of its own favourite discipline, philosophy, and of its philosophy's favourite system, idealism. The lesson from this is not to emulate Fichte's attempt to make one philosophy govern all fields but to emulate Schleiermacher's and Humboldt's wisdom of negotiation.

Towards a wisdom of negotiation

It may be even more difficult for us to achieve this now than it was for them, and there is no guarantee that either the people or the requisite conditions (see below) will come together to enable it to happen, but the first essential is to discern the nature of the challenge. This culture would take into account the whole 'ecology' of factors involved – teaching and research, all-round education, interdisciplinarity, collegiality, contribution in the broadest sense to society, polity and power relations – and thereby amount to a vision of reinvention. In addition, it would be alert to the global state of various disciplines and how they are developing, for there is no way that the negotiations can be carried on adequately without the participation of academics active in the relevant disciplines. Moreover, it would keep together a rich conception of the core identity of the university with the variety of practical 'low-level' factors that can help or hinder interdisciplinarity. And finally, it would feed and test its wisdom of negotiation through participation in intensive conversations – local, national and international – about both interdisciplinarity and the other five elements.

A vision of the twenty-first-century university and its realisation

The vision emerging from the previous section can be summarised as a negotiable and negotiating university that

- marries research with teaching across a wide range of disciplines;
- offers an all-round education aiming to form students in a wisdom that seeks the common good;
- cultivates forms of collegiality where intensive interdisciplinary and transgenerational conversation and collaboration take place in teaching and research;
- contributes broadly to society;
- is well-endowed, self-governing and accountable to many stakeholders;

- is interdisciplinary in its academic life, in its contributions to society, and in its discussions about its own practices, polity and purposes.

There can be no universal template for such a university, and with regard to its possibility I have used the University of Cambridge as my main case study. I will now reflect on the conditions for its realisation, again with Cambridge as the main university in mind.

A twenty-first-century trauma?

The Humboldt University was seen as partly a response to trauma: the upheaval of the Enlightenment, the scientific revolution and the French Revolution, followed by the Prussian experience of defeat and humiliation by Napoleon. Is there anything analogously traumatic that might open up the current University of Cambridge to the sort of transformation that seems to be required by the challenges discussed above?

The two leading nineteenth-century contenders for the label of traumatic transformation are, first, the removal of religious tests, as a symbol of the transformation of Cambridge from a purely Anglican establishment whose colleges were staffed by celibate and mostly clerical fellows to a university open to those of any faith or none;[53] and, second, the expansion of the examined curriculum to embrace subjects other than mathematics, classics and theology, and especially the development of the natural sciences, together with accompanying changes in teaching provision, the role of research, and the relationship of the university to the colleges. Yet, despite dramatic moments, especially centred on government commissions and legislation, it is hard to describe such changes as traumatic.[54]

In the twentieth century both World Wars had an impact,[55] but I would argue that only the late twentieth-century combination of political and economic bids to shape British universities, beginning with Mrs Thatcher after 1979, should properly be called traumatic. The level of government control, both direct and indirect, has been unprecedented, as has the level of involvement with major non-government sponsors. Free market capitalism, especially in the aftermath of the collapse of European and Soviet Communism, has drawn higher education into

---

53. See Searby, *A History of the University of Cambridge*, vol. III, chapters 7–10; and Brooke, ibid. vol. IV, chapters 4, 5, 13, 14, 17.
54. See Searby, ibid. vol. III, chapters 12–14 on university reform and the Graham Commission; and Brooke, ibid. vol. IV, chapters 3 and 11 on university reform, the second Royal Commission and the Asquith Commission.
55. See ibid. vol. IV chapters 10 and 16.

the global economy. In addition, religion has become globally prominent in ways that have surprised many – especially Western intellectuals. Cambridge was relatively untouched by Fascism and Communism, but is now facing the full impact of late modern capitalism. It is also responding to the global resurgence of religion.

In some respects, trauma is not an appropriate term for what is happening: there has been nothing like military defeat and foreign occupation to open the Cambridge imagination to radical possibilities and to focus the mind and will on reinventing the university. Yet it may be that the characteristic form of trauma in our time is that of complex, multifaceted and overwhelming change that cannot be associated with any single event. Perhaps the emblematic trauma of the twenty-first century will be environmental disaster brought about by human agency, as in the destruction of species, pollution and climate change. This sort of long drawn out catastrophe is comparable (and, in relation to the global forces involved, often closely related) to traumatic change in intellectual and social 'ecologies'. None of them can be dealt with adequately by immediate, short-term responses. They require collaborative, thoughtful engagement on many fronts, and the wisdom to follow through knowledge and understanding into decision and action. A global society faced with such catastrophes needs places where such informed, collegial thoughtfulness and dispute can happen. It needs places where it can work at repairing and transcending its current understanding, formation and solutions.

The core challenge here is to seek wisdom in the midst of the conditions of radical, multilevelled change. Clearly the university is not the only institution to face this, but it might have some advantages in responding if it can both learn from its past and transcend it. Is it imaginable that Cambridge might do this creatively enough to offer one possible model for a 'new Berlin' in the present century?

The prime condition for realisation – a seventh challenge
In general terms it is unlikely that major university reform will occur unless at least three dimensions come together: a favourable political, economic and cultural context; material provision for institutional renewal; and convincing ideas about reshaping the university.[56]

56. Collins, in *The Sociology of Philosophies*, reads the history of philosophical creativity in terms of such categories, and I have adapted them to deal with this instance of institutional creativity.

As regards the first, Berlin University was founded in the aftermath of Prussian defeat by Napoleon on a wave of patriotic enthusiasm that saw education as one of the main ways of building up the traumatised nation.[57] As regards the second dimension, the persuasion of the Prussian king released the necessary material provision.

Are there favourable conditions for university reform today with regard to those two dimensions? I have suggested that this is a pivotal time, with major reconfigurations of higher education already happening both nationally and internationally, along with continual expansion. Institutions are reinventing themselves in negotiation with stakeholders, and there is considerable dissatisfaction with many features of inherited patterns. At the same time the demand for graduates and research increases, and there is general agreement about the worthwhileness of high-quality universities (together with debate about how to describe that quality). There is also a sense of extended trauma as the intellectual, cultural and spiritual ecology copes with pressures of commodification and globalisation. As regards material provision, the supply of public and private money for universities has greatly increased: in most countries the question is not whether to spend on higher education but where to focus the spending. So the first two conditions are fulfilled today.

That leaves the third dimension: convincing ideas. I have elsewhere described the intensive conversation, debate and controversy over decades, embracing an extraordinary array of intellectual leaders (including Kant, Hamann, Herder, Goethe, Schiller, Schelling, Hegel, Fichte and Schleiermacher) that generated the conception of the University of Berlin.[58] There does not seem to be anything comparable happening today. This therefore would appear to be the prime condition that is

---

57. Many other changes (such as the abolition of serfdom, introduction of equality before the law and the limiting of aristocratic privileges) contributed to shaping a context that might be described as politically liberal and reformist within the constraints of a fairly absolutist, undemocratic system. The new Prussia wanted a well-organised system of education and its accreditation, and the university fitted well as the apex of this. It also wished to avoid the French *tabula rasa* approach, and so was open to what was in effect a renewal and reform of the medieval university in line with modern principles. The wider context was the increasing role of education in developing nation states, which recognised that their economic welfare was correlated with their level of education. The industrial and scientific revolutions had demonstrated the crucial role of knowledge, and the discoveries of 'rapid-discovery science' lent prestige to the intellectual enterprise. There was also a widespread sense of the 'shaking of the foundations' in the aftermath of the French Revolution, and openness to an approach that promised to probe and hopefully re-establish the foundations.
58. See Ford, 'Faith and Universities in a Religious and Secular World (2)'.

lacking for a surprise (or, if a somewhat less innovative view is taken, a reform) on the analogy of Berlin.

It seems that few academics and administrators within universities around the world have been able to transcend the considerable pressures of sustaining their institutions in order to rethink them in fundamental ways. Taking the six challenges discussed above as the criteria for what is 'fundamental', one looks in vain for thinking about them as a whole.[59] Nor have other major stakeholders in politics, business, culture and the professions been able to contribute creatively to reimagining universities. Yet they are often insistent on the universities meeting their requirements, and their pressures add to the urgency of universities doing their own creative thinking. The lack of university-led constructive thinking has left the field open for others to pursue their own, usually very partial, goals. *At the least, universities need a strong self-conception in order to resist such pressures; at best, they need it in order to be able to invite other stakeholders to contribute to a vision of the future of universities that has taken the measure of the six challenges.*

The seventh challenge, therefore, is to inspire and sustain creative thinking and discussion that have the kind of intellectual and institution-building capacity which helped to generate the University of Berlin. This is the prime condition for being able to meet the other six challenges.

Is it imaginable in Cambridge? It would certainly be a surprise were it to happen. In between the majority who pragmatically get on with business as usual, coping *ad hoc* with issues as they arise, and the few who would advocate some sort of systemic revolutionary change it is difficult to imagine passionate seeking for a wisdom of negotiation in relation to all six challenges. Yet it is worth trying to envisage what might help enable it.

Ideally there would be university-wide discussions,[60] but, if Berlin is a precedent, the debates require smaller, more intensive face to face conversations, preferably in groups that intersect with each other. These would make considerable demands on participants, in extending and

59. As regards Britain, Gordon Graham has described the vacuum in critical thinking about the subject of the university itself, see the quote in Ford, 'Faith and Universities in a Religious and Secular World (2)', p. 101.
60. Mike Higton's University of Exeter 2004 Boundy Lectures *Thinking about the University*, Lecture 3, 'Being a University', makes a well-argued case for university-wide conversations; see the excerpt in Ford, 'Faith and Universities in a Religious and Secular World (2)', p. 105.

receiving intellectual hospitality across many boundaries and in the sheer size and complexity of the issues. It might be that these issues are now perceived as sufficiently important and fascinating to arouse the energies of enough academics in a collaborative effort.

This chapter has grown out of conversations and experience of universities as much as out of the written sources referred to, and it is written in the hope that it might help to stimulate further conversation in Cambridge and elsewhere. To advance this purpose two things now remain: to ask where universities might find sources of wisdom in their thinking about reform; and to inquire how my own field might contribute.

Where might this wisdom be found?

In the earlier chapters of this book wisdom has been seen as uniting knowledge and understanding with imagination, good judgement and decision-making. It responds to the cries of humanity, is involved with complexities and intractable realities, tries to appreciate the most significant connections and differences between discourses, disciplines, cultures, periods, philosophies, worldviews and religions, and takes responsibility for seeking the long-term flourishing of the natural and human world.

Within education, wisdom is classically the most comprehensive ideal, beyond information, knowledge, practice and skills. Learning and teaching wisdom is a social activity, involving traditions and communities together with all sorts of interactions among them. In considering university reform, the scope and interconnection of the issues, such as response to radical change, formation in intellectual virtues and values, interdisciplinarity, collegiality, power and control, the uses of knowledge, and the role and quality of thinking, teaching and research in our civilisation, mean that considering them cannot be detached from frameworks of overall meaning and from our convictions about what it means to be human, about justice and truth, about the nature of (even the existence of) the common good, and much else.

One general answer, therefore, to the question as to where the wisdom for reshaping the university might be found is: *in the resources of traditions and communities that seek wisdom and have developed overall frameworks and core convictions.* The richest wisdom traditions need to be drawn upon and developed further to meet new challenges. What might this mean?

It obviously means understanding how and why each discipline and family of disciplines has been shaped and reshaped over time,[61] and likewise each university and type of university, in particular the one being reconceived. But these ongoing histories are themselves the sites for much wider conversations and controversies, and there can be no hiding in specialisms from the necessity to face such large issues as meaning, truth, goodness and beauty. They are at least implicit in high-level discussion of university reform, and it is better for them to become explicit. The failure to do so makes universities far more vulnerable to unexamined assumptions, values and philosophies coming from specific disciplines (economics and management studies being today among the most influential – often in forms that are at some remove from the best in those fields) or from politicians, benefactors, sponsors of research, students or other stakeholders. The impoverishment of academic thinking about universities is in part due to its inability to acknowledge the scope of the task: *that it calls for a wisdom about large issues which themselves often have long histories.* Those who conceived the University of Berlin knew this well.

Once the broad nature of the task is recognised, how is it to be carried out? The first thing to be faced is the diversity of the 'wisdoms' in play. An element in the reluctance of universities to ask the large questions about themselves is the fear that fundamental differences will lead to conflict or paralysis, and that it is more sensible to carry on pragmatically doing what is possible without opening up irresolvable questions. This fear and reluctance are reinforced by pressures of routine teaching, research and administration, by the power of bureaucracies, and by the short-term interests of most stakeholders.

As an alternative, one would have to imagine a set of engagements within and across wisdom traditions and their contemporary communities of discourse. *It is crucially important that these wisdom traditions be academically mediated.* Attempts to apply to universities understandings and judgements derived directly from traditions and discourses that have not been mediated through relevant academic disciplines and discussion are likely to be manipulative and dangerous. This applies to principles and policies derived from political, economic, cultural and religious

---

61. One way of seeing the continual discussion within each field of itself is as the working out of a 'local' wisdom appropriate to its own content, purposes, boundaries and interrelations with other fields.

positions, for all of which there is a temptation to try to shape universities to their own ends without travelling the arduous road of investigation and rigorous discussion that alone can allow ideas to be applied with integrity in universities.

Those formed through various academically mediated wisdoms would thus come into critical and constructive conversation with each other about the large questions in the context of a common concern for universities. They would not assume that it is possible or necessary to share a common framework nor would they have to reach consensus on all their other differences, but they would need to develop a culture of negotiation, both about the large questions and about the best ways to realise any negotiated settlement. Such a culture would probably require 'set texts' relevant to the key questions facing it (some of which, as in the years leading up to the foundation of the University of Berlin, would be new texts written for these discussions), that might act as common reference points in discussion. This is standard practice within many subject areas, and it would be odd if it could not be adapted to help inform university-wide conversation and deliberation. *The hope is that shared problems and institutional loyalties, shared texts and the collegiality of conversation around them, and the shared goal of finding wisdom for a negotiable university that is able to accommodate a broad range of disciplines, responsibilities and wisdom traditions, would together generate a particular wisdom for each university, though one from which others in analogous institutions might learn.*

Which traditions and communities would take part in this wisdom-seeking conversation? The essential one is that of the modern research university itself, which I have been considering as a tradition rooted in the medieval university, renewed and reformed in the University of Berlin, and now exemplified in many forms, including that of the University of Cambridge. Like any tradition it requires constant re-examination and the discovery of resources for its further reform. Within the contemporary university there are diverse traditions whose interaction has already shaped it. These include philosophical schools, such as idealism, empiricism, critical realism, hermeneutics, and so on; various ethical and political positions; science-based understandings such as Darwinism and behaviourism; social scientific frameworks such as functionalism; different religions in their academic mediations; and hermeneutics of suspicion that critique, deconstruct or ironise all of the above.

That incomplete list (not to mention the combinations possible between its constituents) is a reminder of the difficulty of initiating and sustaining this conversation. In addition to taking part, each of them is being asked to become both guest and host to the others and also to be open to self-reformation and transformation. Yet in practice not all will have the motivation, creativity and energy to play an active part – just as, in the discussions preceding the University of Berlin, a relatively small number of circles dominated the attention space.[62] In line with that, the probable general answer to the question as to where the wisdom might come from is: *from at most five or six intensive conversation circles who draw on various traditions and sets of disciplines and enter into wisdom-seeking discussion and argument with each other.*

Might such circles actually happen? The local Cambridge conditions of a collegial, conversational, interdisciplinary culture are clearly in tension with the demands on busy people of teaching, research and administration. It seems unlikely that many of the academics and administrators who might contribute most would take this as a high enough priority in very busy lives. Perhaps it is only conceivable as a daring initiative agreed by both the university and its colleges and funded sufficiently to liberate the time of key people. It is just possible that the desire to reinvent Cambridge in order to meet the six challenges might be strong enough to release the enormous amount of energy required. If such conversations were to lead to a re-envisioning of the university there would be the final challenge of realising it through deliberation, persuasion, negotiation, voting and implementation. Imagining this stretches credibility yet further, and one stark fact of Cambridge's history since the nineteenth century stands out: it has usually been government pressure that has brought about fundamental change. At the time of writing this again seems a possibility. If there were to be strong political pressure, with associated negotiation and legislation, the impoverished state of the university's thinking and deciding about itself would leave it vulnerable to the imposition of conceptions that are far less capable of meeting the six challenges than what it might have worked out for itself. So fears about the future might reinforce recognition of the seriousness of the six challenges so as to motivate a corporate effort at reconception by the university and colleges.

---

62. Collins, *The Sociology of Philosophies*, pp. 38, 42, 81–2, 380ff, 791–2, 876, 880 and *passim*, offers convincing evidence for his 'law of small numbers', which says that at any one time the 'knots of argument' that can successfully claim attention number between three and six, though at certain exceptionally creative times (and the period of Berlin's foundation was one such) there may be a few more for a while. If there were a Cambridge debate about reforms for the twenty-first century where might the best conversations occur?

The last task of this chapter is to ask what, within such a process aimed at reconceiving the university to meet the six challenges, the contribution of theology and religious studies might be.

A developing settlement: theology and religious studies in Cambridge

Cambridge has had considerable Christian input, even since its nineteenth-century constitutional opening up to non-Anglicans and non-Christians. In the centuries before that, the character of the university and its colleges was formed entirely within a Christian milieu, first pre-Reformation and then Anglican. The leading members of its golden age of theology in the last quarter of the nineteenth century, Lightfoot, Westcott and Hort, were all actively involved in the debates about university reform. Many of the main shapers of the university and of its colleges in the twentieth century were lay or ordained Christians.[63]

The picture that emerges is of a 'religious and secular' university that has worked out a variety of settlements which have resulted in an environment not easy to categorise. Mostly the Christian involvement has not been labelled as such but has been as voices and votes in the various sites of debate, deliberation and decision, and usually on both sides of major issues. This 'distributed' influence, largely lay, sits uneasily with any dualism of the religious and non-religious, and on university and college questions it has been rare for divisions to be along confessional lines. Indeed one of the striking aspects of Cambridge since the deep conflicts over the constitutional position of religion were resolved has been the extent and variety of the Christian contribution. The leading historian of the University in recent years, Christopher Brooke, in his chapter on 'The Dons' Religion in Twentieth-Century Cambridge', looks at how his selection of five laypeople – Catholic, Baptist, Presbyterian, Congregationalist/Methodist and Anglican – worked out their faith in the University, and emphasises both the importance and the complexity of this aspect of contemporary Cambridge history.[64]

In the twentieth century there have been considerable numbers of students and dons from other faiths, whose contribution has yet to be

---

63. This is one of the striking features to emerge from Brooke, *A History of the University of Cambridge*, vol. IV: see especially Prologue, chapters 4, 5, 11, 13, 14, 17, 18.
64. Ibid. chapters 13, 14.

researched. With regard to discussion of Cambridge's future, the potential is there for a range of faith traditions, each with its own wisdom about knowledge, education and collegiality, to play a role in debates about the university.

The Faculty of Divinity is the chief place to look for a 'focussed' contribution through academic engagement with religious traditions. In line with many other British universities, Cambridge has followed neither the German pattern of confessional theology faculties nor the dominant American model (especially in state-funded universities and colleges) of religious studies, but has chosen to unite theology and religious studies. It followed its own path towards this. Its academic posts, filled exclusively by Anglicans in the nineteenth century, were opened first to other Christians and then without restriction, so that the staff now has members who are Christian, Jewish, Muslim or of other faiths and none. In the last quarter of the twentieth century and the early twenty-first century its undergraduate and masters degrees were named 'theology and religious studies', and its capacity to teach and research in other traditions than Christianity increased, as did its study of theology and religions with the help of sociology, anthropology, psychology and the natural sciences.[65] There was much internal discussion, and contributions were made to national and international debates about the field.[66]

Many of the participants in these developments had first-hand knowledge of institutional settings in Germany, the United States and elsewhere, so the reshaping of the field was partly in conscious response to other patterns. Three distinctive features have been a concern for scholarly engagement with various religious traditions in their multifaceted particularity (historical, textual, intellectual, psychological, sociological, artistic, ethical, political), together with critical and constructive thinking in relation to them, and attempts to bring each into dialogue with other religious and secular traditions. What might the contribution of such a faculty be to envisioning the twenty-first-century university?

---

65. Other developments included a Centre for Advanced Religious and Theological Studies, a revised curriculum, the construction of a faculty building, and new forms of academic collaboration with the expanding Cambridge Theological Federation (Anglican, Methodist, Roman Catholic, Orthodox, United Reformed, and a Centre for Jewish–Christian Relations).
66. Notably through a process of seminars and international consultation leading to the publication of *Fields of Faith. Theology and Religious Studies for the Twenty-first Century*, ed. David F. Ford, Ben Quash and Janet Martin Soskice (Cambridge: Cambridge University Press, 2005).

Perhaps its main importance is in embodying a negotiated and still developing settlement in which several disciplines and wisdom traditions are participants. It is a setting in which there can be contributions from diverse individuals and communities that have profound disagreements with each other, and is therefore not a neutral institutional space but one constituted by 'mutual ground'.[67] It goes beyond the 'Christian' medieval university and the 'Christian and secular' University of Berlin towards an 'inter-faith and secular' settlement that might well be a concept with which the whole university could identify. There are many religious universities in the world and also many secular universities. Given the character of the twenty-first-century world as both religious and secular in complex ways, it makes sense for there to be some universities which reflect this character, where diverse traditions are mediated academically and encouraged both to engage with each other and to help shape the university.[68] *The twentieth century showed the terrible destructiveness that both secular ideologies and religious faiths can inspire; the twenty-first century needs some universities where there can be wisdom-seeking study and conversation about what divides and unites people, and where some from diverse communities might be formed in thoughtful collegiality.*

In such a setting, when the future of the university is at issue, there is a challenge to each tradition to contribute what it can. This chapter concludes with a brief indication of what, in line with this and previous chapters, might come from the Christian tradition to help inspire and guide university renewal and reform.

A Christian contribution to the life and renewal of the university

The most obvious Christian contribution to a wisdom for university renewal arises from the medieval Christian origins of universities. As described above, the core values of the medieval university were rooted in a Christian understanding of God, creation, created human being, human reason, virtue and sociality, human imperfection and the need for penitence, safeguards and self-correction, and a range of values such as modesty, reverence and rigour in argument. Neither universities nor

67. On neutral and mutual ground see ibid. Introduction, Part I and Part II.
68. For a development of the idea of the inter-faith and secular university see Ford, 'Faith and Universities in a Religious and Secular World (2)'.

theology have stayed the same, and the challenge today is, in dialogue with medieval theology and values, to work at an analogous Christian theology for the twenty-first-century university. It is unlikely that a simple repetition of medieval theology will suffice today, and this sets *a task of reinterpreting, testing and constructively rethinking Christian theology and its implications for universities*.

That is part of a wider task that previous chapters have seen as intrinsic to seeking Christian wisdom today: engagement with premodern, modern and contemporary understanding and wisdom so as to discern their truth and their worth for today. Any Christian involvement in the sort of intensive conversations and deliberations envisaged in previous sections will be continually challenged to propose and defend such discernments in dialogue with well-conceived and well-supported alternatives. The main danger is that Christian theology will not be able to respond adequately. Even where it has faced the questions about how those medieval teachings and values are to be understood and revised today it has often done so in intellectual settings that are Christian in ways that have not been fully engaged in and tested through wider academic debate. *The required theology needs to be both Christian and academically mediated (which by no means need involve dictation by reigning academic fashions), and this requires intensive conversation both among Christians and between them and others*.

The first seven chapters of this book focussed on a few of the main topics on the intra-Christian agenda. Chief among these was the interpretation of scripture. Intrinsic to that were the 'regimes of reading' that have shaped the study of scripture in the Western academy and beyond. The better a Christian theology is exercised in the ways of such readings the better resourced it will be to engage in the sort of reinvention of universities that can embody a wisdom that is deeply involved with the realities of current existence in the interests of future flourishing.

More specifically, chapters 1–7 attempted to distil a scriptural wisdom, and that might be developed to constitute a core for Christian thinking about universities. The following elements are especially worth noting:

- The discernment of cries, which for universities means continual attention to cries both for knowledge and understanding and also for wise education and for responsiveness to the sufferings and needs of society.
- The radical, interrogative Joban searching for wisdom, together with immersion in the complexities of historical existence and fearless critique of tradition, which allows also for critique of modernity and its pathologies, including those sponsored by universities.

- The need for wisdom in the midst of, and following, trauma, which for universities in the twenty-first century means above all the comprehensive challenge of the commodification of education, research and knowledge, threatening the long-term intellectual, cultural and spiritual ecology.
- The power of desire and the need for its purification and wise orientation, which is worked out in universities through continual negotiation of the balance between truth and knowledge for their own sake, all-round formation in wisdom that seeks the common good, and utility to society.
- The wisdom of loving God for God's sake, which in universities might provide a Christian rationale to inspire and champion the love of truth and knowledge for their own sake – this being perhaps the goal of universities that is most under threat in the twenty-first century. There are other ways of championing it, but arguably in a religious and secular world they are greatly weakened if this taproot of the medieval *amor scientiae* is cut off.
- The church as a school of desire and wisdom, called to affirm, critique and transform universities, above all by forming its members in worship, collegiality, love of and witness to truth and wisdom, and generous service of the world.

A Christian contribution needs both deep engagement with distinctively Christian sources and also comparable engagement with other sources (this being grounded ultimately in God's involvement with all sources). Chapters 8–10 of this book give some case studies of this double engagement. Scriptural reasoning in particular was presented as a model of wisdom-seeking study and conversation in the contemporary university, alert to academic disciplines and also to the contributions of three scriptures and their traditions of interpretation. The present chapter has been thought through in continuity with the rest of the book, but mostly has tried to present its understanding and analysis in terms that are not explicitly Christian. Yet the further development of it in any particular setting would undoubtedly call for more explicit discussion of basic rationales, goals and values by both Christian and other contributors. The founders of the University of Berlin did not shy away from such fundamental thinking and the conflicts into which it led; nor is it likely that those seeking a rich enough wisdom for the twenty-first university will be able to avoid doing so.

10

An interpersonal wisdom: L'Arche, learning disability and the Gospel of John

L'Arche is founded on the need for an intelligent, wise love, so that each person may discover who they are and grow to greater maturity. Love is at the heart of the Christian message.

JEAN VANIER[1]

They cry out to us and there is a vulnerability in their cry. They need us to walk with them, to support them, to believe in them, and to reveal to them their gift. There is an immense power in their cry, which is a cry for friendship, for recognition and for acceptance. In listening to their cry and in responding to it by becoming their friends and companions on the journey, we discover that, in reality, we need them as much, if not more, than they need us. Just as we call forth the adult in them and help them to assume greater independence, they call forth the child in us and awaken in us the qualities of the heart.

TIM KEARNEY[2]

The spirituality of L'Arche is based on the revolutionary 'upside-down' vision of the Beatitudes, on the paradox that our spiritual health and healing lies not in the pursuit of power, but in the welcome and integration of weakness, both in ourselves and the other:

Blessed are the poor in Spirit
Theirs is the kingdom of heaven.
Blessed are those who mourn
For they shall be comforted.
Blessed are the gentle,

1. Jean Vanier, 'Hope in Europe: Becoming More Human' in *Faith in Europe? The Cardinal's Lectures*, ed. Cormac Murphy-O'Connor (London: Darton, Longman and Todd, 2005), text available on-line at http://www.rcdow.org.uk/cardinal/default.asp?content_ref=370.
2. Tim Kearney, 'Introduction' to *A Prophetic Cry: Stories of Spirituality and Healing Inspired by L'Arche*, ed. Tim Kearney (Dublin: Veritas Publications, 2000), p. 17.

For they will inherit the earth ...
Blessed are the peace-makers
For they shall be called sons and daughters of God.
(MATTHEW 5:3—9)

    The gift of this 'upside-down' spirituality is well expressed in the words of Jim Cargin, an assistant who has journeyed in L'Arche for the past twenty years, and who wrote to me recently after a year's sabbatical: 'It is true that each person's life is of infinite value; that there is a mysterious blessing in weakness and poverty, and that God is close to the broken-hearted. I do see L'Arche as a sign of hope, being a means of healing, and a prophetic movement of God's Spirit in our times, in our society. As such, it calls attention to the freeing action of God in Jesus, affirming our deepest identity as Beloved, children of a loving Father, who always calls us to true maturity'.

TIM KEARNEY[3]

L'Arche is a federation[4] of about 130 residential communities around the world. The basic pattern is that of a household in which people with learning disabilities[5] live together with assistants, some of whom are there for a year or two while others are committed in a long-term covenant relationship with L'Arche. It began in 1964 when Jean Vanier, helped by a Dominican priest, Père Thomas Philippe, invited Raphael Simi and Philippe Seux to leave the large institution in which they were living and make a home with him in Trosly-Breuil, a village near Compiègne.[6]

    Besides growing in numbers of communities L'Arche has changed in many ways. It has become rooted in all five continents and so embraces many cultures and languages. It began as male and celibate and came to have mixed gender households and married couples as members. Its structures and governance have undergone developments to cope with its global scope (for example, through federal and regional bodies, assemblies, coordinators and financial arrangements). It has had to cope with

3. Ibid. p. 18.
4. The International Federation of L'Arche Communities, headed by two International Coordinators and an International Board. For general information see www.larche.org.
5. The terminology is always a sensitive matter, ranging from 'the mentally handicapped' through 'people with learning difficulties' and 'people with developmental disabilities' to 'the mentally challenged' and 'the differently abled'. In L'Arche 'core members' is common.
6. See Kathryn Spink, *The Miracle, the Message, the Story: Jean Vanier and L'Arche* (London: Darton, Longman and Todd, 2006). For his own account of L'Arche see Jean Vanier, *An Ark for the Poor: The Story of L'Arche* (Toronto: Novalis; London: Geoffrey Chapman; New York: Crossroad, 1995).

very different attitudes to disability and also with diverse systems of regulation, bureaucratic supervision, funding and healthcare. Its way of handling religious boundaries has also changed. Beginning as Catholic (though always open to core members who were not Catholic), it first became ecumenical with other Christian churches, and a good deal of thought and effort has gone into linking communities with local churches as well as into engaging with church leaders. As it spread to countries where other religions are in the majority L'Arche came to have communities that are largely Muslim or Hindu, and in traditionally Christian countries communities have become more diverse.

The result of such developments is that, growing out of its basic concern to build communities around people with disabilities, L'Arche has had to face many of the leading issues of our time. How construct an international federal polity that allows each region to have a full say and guards against distortions or abuses of power? How handle money in a federation where there are great inequalities of wealth among communities? How deal with increasing regulation in developed countries, applied by bureaucracies which see L'Arche as a 'care provider' that has to conform to their standards and are not concerned about enabling this sort of community life? How much energy should go into gaining political support for the disabled? How far should 'professional carers' shape the ethos and 'good practice' of L'Arche? How appreciate cultural differences without being divided by them? How handle sexual relations in a residential community of unmarried people? Owing to the disabilities, the death rate in L'Arche communities is higher than average: how deal with dying, death and bereavement? What about authority, commitment, faithfulness, forgiveness, celebration, work and overwork, leisure, education, and so on? And in a community in which there are people of many faiths and none, what is the role of faith in community life?

A wisdom-seeking community faces a major transition

Such questions, many of which call urgently for answers in practical, day-to-day forms, inevitably turn L'Arche into a wisdom-seeking community. Most of this happens locally as each community grapples with the questions, often under considerable pressures. There is a good deal of communication among communities, and various sorts of gathering at regional and international levels – for celebration, consultation and deliberation, education and training, renewal and prayer.

I have been part of a group of theologians who have 'accompanied' L'Arche for more than a decade through taking part in smaller and larger gatherings, visiting communities, consulting and writing.[7] L'Arche has been concerned that its wisdom-seeking embrace a wide range of people and groups from beyond the community. But it has also been clear that its main reference point has been Jean Vanier, both in his embodiment of what L'Arche means and also in his learning from the life of L'Arche around the world and his sharing of that through friendships, continual travelling, talks, retreats and writings.[8]

Vanier's own formation is well described in his biography by Kathryn Spink. He is French-Canadian, his father having been Governor-General of Canada, and was shaped through French and English culture. He joined the Royal Naval College in Dartmouth during the Second World War, becoming a naval officer, and later studied and wrote a doctorate on Aristotle's understanding of happiness. He also met Père Thomas, a Dominican priest with a spirituality profoundly shaped by the Beatitudes. Père Thomas became a guiding influence on Vanier, and it was from this relationship that the initiative to begin L'Arche came. So the strands that came together in Vanier included a deep Catholic spirituality that was also strongly biblical, a naval training, a university education that engaged with classics and classical philosophy, and the interplay of the French and English dimensions of Western civilisation.

A feature of the years since beginning L'Arche has been Vanier's openness to new developments and influences. It was by no means inevitable

---

7. The main joint publication has been Frances Young, *Encounter with Mystery: Reflections on L'Arche and Living with Disability* (London: Darton, Longman and Todd, 1997), and participants have individually written more. Mine include *The Shape of Living* (London: HarperCollins, 1997; Grand Rapids, MI: Baker Books, 2000, 2004; London and Grand Rapids: Zondervan, 2002), chapter 4; and 'Wilderness Wisdom for the Twenty-first Century: Arthur, L'Arche and the Culmination of Christian History' in *Wilderness: Essays in Honour of Frances Young*, ed. R. S. Sugirtharajah (London: T. & T. Clark, 2005), pp. 153–66.

8. E.g. *An Ark for the Poor: The Story of L'Arche*; *Becoming Human* (London: Darton, Longman and Todd, 1999); *Community and Growth*, 2nd edn (London: Darton, Longman and Todd, 1989); *Finding Peace* (London: Continuum, 2003); *Made for Happiness: Discovering the Meaning of Life with Aristotle* (London: Darton, Longman and Todd, 2001); *Man & Woman, He Made Them* (London: Darton, Longman and Todd, 1988); *Our Journey Home* (London: Hodder & Stoughton, 1997); *Seeing Beyond Depression* (London: SPCK, 2001); *Tears of Silence*, revised edition (London: Darton, Longman and Todd, 1991); *The Broken Body: Journey to Wholeness* (London: Darton, Longman and Todd, 1988); and with his sister Thérèse Vanier, *Nick: Man of the Heart* (Dublin: Gill and Macmillan, 1993) and *One Bread, One Body* (Leominster: Gracewing, 1997). A specially valuable theological work to which Vanier contributed is *Critical Reflections on Stanley Hauerwas' Theology of Disability: Disabling Society, Enabling Theology*, ed. John Swinton (New York: The Haworth Pastoral Press; London: Victoria, 2005).

that L'Arche should become international or ecumenical or inter-faith, or that its federal structure and overall ethos (with regard to faith, community, relations with professionals and bureaucracies, and so on) should develop as they have done. Vanier learnt from many sources and was open across his own boundaries, but at the heart of this was his dedication to and friendship with people with disabilities. One of the principal distinctive marks of both Vanier and the culture of L'Arche is recurrent testimony to the transformative effects of friendships between core members (those with disabilities) and the assistants and others who live in community with them. In a sense, they have led L'Arche across national, gender, racial, cultural, linguistic and religious boundaries, with friendships usually being pivotal.

The centrality of Vanier in beginning, learning, forming and continuing to play a leading role in discerning the understanding and practice of L'Arche now poses L'Arche a major question about the transition to the next generation. Vanier was born in 1928 and has now withdrawn from organisational roles in L'Arche. He lives in the mother community at Trosly-Breuil in northern France, continues to write and travel, and is undoubtedly the single most important human link within the worldwide federation and between it and the rest of the world. But what about L'Arche after Vanier? During the past decade there has been an increasing sense that that question has to be faced, and Vanier has encouraged this. The responses have been various, but I will concentrate on two that best illustrate the search for wisdom: the 'Identity and Mission' process from 2002–2005 (which will be reflected upon with the help of the writings of Vanier and others); and, especially, Vanier's own contribution through his commentary on the Gospel of John.

The 'Identity and Mission' process 2002–2005

As the fortieth anniversary of the beginning of L'Arche approached, the coordinators of the federation, after consultation, began a federation-wide, three-stage process called 'Identity and Mission'. Each of the nine zones around the world participated, with more than a hundred 'reflecting groups' meeting over three years.[9]

9. One source for what follows is the Annual Report of the International Coordinators, Jean Christophe Pascal and Christine McGrievy in March 2005, published on the L'Arche website, but with the permission of the Coordinators I have also had access to a mass of material sent to them by the reflecting groups.

The first stage, called 'Once Upon a Time', was about sharing the stories of members, communities and L'Arche as a whole, trying especially to distil from them fundamental convictions, perceptions and purposes, and to identify the essential elements of L'Arche. It was, in other words, an attempt to discern a historically grounded wisdom in the forty years of L'Arche. When the group and regional reports were gathered and considered together there was a convergence on the belief that God had called L'Arche into being and was experienced as gentle, compassionate and vulnerable, and continually faithful and involved. The large number of individual and community stories and their distillations were found to fall under three headings: *Relationships, Transformation* and *Sign*. The consensus on essential elements of L'Arche named them as:

> People with developmental disabilities and others sharing life together
> Relationships that are a source of mutual transformation
> Faith life and trust in God.

In line with these basic elements, others were:

> Acceptance of weakness and vulnerability
> Competence and quality of care
> Cultural and religious diversity
> Membership of an International Federation
> Openness to and engagement with the world.

The second stage, called 'Welcoming Our Shadows', faced L'Arche's failures and the pitfalls and obstacles that have hindered or distorted the living out of the basic convictions and essential elements. In other words, this was an attempt to discern the negative aspects of L'Arche's history as they affect the present. Six major failures and obstacles were identified:

1 Difficulty in recognising and naming God as central to daily life together, and the tendency for faith to remain a private matter.
2 Insufficient understanding of the founding story of L'Arche, limiting the community's flexibility, creativity, vision and sense of identity, and hindering the story's potential to challenge and transform.
3 Structures and patterns that do not effectively develop or sustain commitment, vocation and membership, and that do not sufficiently foster the interrelationship of community life, faith life and service provision.
4 Lack of clarity about authority and ambivalence about giving authority to leaders.

5 Difficulty in recognising, admitting and handling limits.
6 Many hurt and broken relationships, often because of lack of loving
   and honest communication.

The third stage was called 'Go Out into the Deep'. It concerned the
future orientation of L'Arche, how its vision is to be incarnated afresh
in a new time, and what risky initiatives might be taken in order to be
true to the vision. As with each of the other stages, the reflecting
groups produced dozens of reports, themselves already a distillation
from group conversations. The reports were then considered together
and a provisional mission statement and set of priorities agreed. This
mission statement for the federation is:

- To make known the gifts of people with developmental disabilities
  revealed through mutually transforming relationships.
- To engage in our diverse cultures, working together to build a more
  human society.
- To foster an environment in communities that is inspired by the core
  values and our founding story, and responds to the changing needs
  of our members.

The priorities included communication; empowerment of people with
disabilities; reflecting on founding stories and core values; encouragement and support of members; space for reflection, prayer and spiritual growth; healthy patterns and rhythms of living; seeking a common
understanding of being a community of faith that embraces people of
many religious traditions and none; inter-faith reflection; inculturation
and involvement with diverse cultures; developing a culture of discernment; leadership models; training; integration of faith, community and
professional lives; participation in international bodies and forums; and
'to announce and be a witness to the vision of our common humanity'.

What sort of wisdom?

Such, in bare summary form, are the results of the three years. They leave
to the imagination the effects within each of the communities of this
intensive, structured conversational process. The group reports make
frequent reference to the personal and communal heart-searching and
renewal that was stimulated. It might be seen as an example of corporate
wisdom-seeking: taking into account the past, present and future, both
personal and communal; facing complexities, ambiguities and problems;

drawing on many sources of understanding and discernment – religious, cultural, scientific, professional, and especially the experience of assistants and those with disabilities living in community together; conversing in a setting of trust and openness; and having the results distilled and tested in relation to other groups from various parts of the world.

The L'Arche Identity and Mission process, when seen in the light of other L'Arche literature, both exemplifies key elements of wisdom discussed in previous chapters of this book and also opens them up in fresh ways.

The cries of Raphael, Philippe and Innocente

Chapter 1's focus was on wisdom and cries. As the quotation from Tim Kearney at the opening of this chapter says, L'Arche is rooted in response to the cries of those with disabilities. L'Arche's distinctive wisdom comes through being gripped by those cries, discerning their meaning, and judging what response is appropriate to them. The opening quotation from Jean Vanier speaks of the founding of L'Arche 'on the need for an intelligent, wise love', and his writings frequently speak of this as evoked by listening with the heart to the cries of those with disabilities.

A mark of this is its radical particularity. Each person cries in his or her own voice, and each responds in his or her own way. To grasp the particular reality of these events of crying out and responding above all demands testimony. What was left out of the previous section's summary account of the Identity and Mission process was the testimonies, the multitude of stories that were told over three years in the reflecting groups. The first stage's 'Once Upon a Time' was largely narrative in form, and the undistilled reports of the groups make clear that the main topics were the founding story of L'Arche, the founding stories of specific communities and the testimonies of group members, all interpreted in relation to sacred stories, above all of Jesus. The second stage's concentration on the shadow side of L'Arche again had testimonies as its main food for discussion, drawing out further aspects of the stories and especially alert for cries of suffering. The third stage's focus on L'Arche's mission and its priorities was an attempt to discern a future orientation in line with, yet also improvising upon, those testimonies and the reflections upon them.

Throughout, this was a process carried on within earshot of the cries of the disabled. In *Community and Growth*, his most substantial book until the recent commentary on John's Gospel, Jean Vanier interweaves his own testimony to the foundation of L'Arche with a story from the Ivory Coast, together with reference to Jesus, as he describes the cry that he hears at the heart of human life.

> When I came to Trosly-Breuil, that small village north of Paris, I welcomed Raphael and Philippe. I invited them to come and live with me because of Jesus and his Gospel. That is how L'Arche was founded. When I welcomed those two men from an asylum, I knew it was for life; it would have been impossible to create bonds with them and then send them back to a hospital, or anywhere else. My purpose in starting L'Arche was to found a family, a community with and for those who are weak and poor because of a mental handicap and who feel alone and abandoned. The cry of Raphael and of Philippe was for love, for respect and for friendship; it was for true communion. They of course wanted me to do things for them, but more deeply they wanted a true love; a love that sees their beauty, the light shining within them; a love that reveals to them their value and importance in the universe. Their cry for love awoke within my own heart and called forth from me living waters; they made me discover within my own being a well, a fountain of life.
>
> In our L'Arche community in the Ivory Coast, we welcomed Innocente. She has a severe mental handicap. She will never be able to speak or walk or grow very much. She remains in many ways like a child only a few months old. But her eyes and whole body quiver with love whenever she is held in love; a beautiful smile infolds in her face and her whole being radiates peace and joy. Innocente is not helped by ideas, no matter how deep or beautiful they may be; she does not need money or power or a job; she does not want to prove herself; all she wants is loving touch and communion. When she receives the gift of love, she quivers in ecstasy; if she feels abandoned, she closes herself up in inner pain – the poorer a person is, old or sick or with a severe mental handicap or close to death, the more the cry is solely for communion and for friendship. The more then the heart of the person who hears the cry, and responds to it, is awoken.[10]

By attending to such cries in a community that seeks ways of wise loving, L'Arche is committed to the continual discernment of cries that chapter 1 began to explore.

---

10. Vanier, *Community and Growth*, pp. 97–8.

Reading scripture with these saints

L'Arche has been deeply shaped by Christian scriptures, and some of its communities by other scriptures too. Some key passages have recurred in the writings of Vanier and others and point to leading features of its vision and ethos. The Beatitudes (Matt. 5:1–11; Luke 6:20–23; see the second quotation from Tim Kearney at the beginning of this chapter), with their blessings on the poor, those who mourn and weep, the gentle, the pure in heart and the peacemakers, point to the centrality in the Kingdom of God of those who are usually marginalised, and have been headline texts encouraging a community that honours those with disabilities. It has been the same with Paul's description of the church in Corinth as containing many who are 'low and despised in the world'.

> 1 Corinthians 1:27–28 [27]But God chose what is foolish in the world to shame the wise; God chose what is weak in the world to shame the strong; [28]God chose what is low and despised in the world, things that are not, to reduce to nothing things that are . . .

Those with disabilities are among the lowest and most marginalised in most societies, are the least 'wanted', the least desired, people. Increasingly, foetuses are aborted if disability is detected. If God chooses 'things that are not' then these are signs of 'not being', communities of the sorts of people whose abortion is widely encouraged. To desire them for their own sake, to have them as the focus of respect, love and friendship in a covenant community, to honour their names and tell their stories, is a radical challenge to the church as well as to the rest of society. Later in Paul's letter the description of the church as the body of Christ, in which the weaker and less presentable members are of vital importance to it and the gifts of all members are needed, has been a constant reference point for L'Arche.

> 1 Corinthians 12:20–27 [20]As it is, there are many members, yet one body. [21]The eye cannot say to the hand, 'I have no need of you,' nor again the head to the feet, 'I have no need of you.' [22]On the contrary, the members of the body that seem to be weaker are indispensable, [23]and those members of the body that we think less honorable we clothe with greater honour, and our less respectable members are treated with greater respect; [24]whereas our more respectable members do not need this. But God has so arranged the body, giving the greater honour to the inferior member, [25]that there may be no dissension within the body, but the members may have the same care for one

another. [26]If one member suffers, all suffer together with it; if one member is honoured, all rejoice together with it. [27]Now you are the body of Christ and individually members of it.

The Gospels above all have been the key texts for L'Arche. Besides the Beatitudes, there are teachings about compassion, forgiveness, humility, gentleness, being like children, prayer, service, hospitality, wealth, generosity and above all about the Kingdom of God. The parables of the Kingdom, with their surprises about who is important in God's eyes, have received special attention, above all the pictures of God's ultimate celebratory feast at which are present '**the poor, the crippled, the blind, and the lame**' (Luke 14:21). Overall, each element of what chapter 2 called the hermeneutics of incarnation, crucifixion, resurrection and Pentecost can be seen operative in L'Arche and its literature in distinctive ways. The bodiliness of Jesus' incarnation, his utterly physical involvement in vulnerability, healing, feeding, suffering, dying and rising, is of special significance in a community where much communication is non-verbal and the routines of bodily care give primacy to the sense of touch. The themes of incarnation, death, resurrection and the Holy Spirit have been most thoroughly opened up through the Gospel of John, to which a later section will be devoted.

The final, comprehensive maxim at the end of chapter 2 was 'Let us reread in love'. The desire for love of God and neighbour among the disabled and the assistants of L'Arche communities might be seen as their ideal core perspective on scripture, and the next section will examine this further. The other nine maxims of chapter 2 could also be explored in their L'Arche forms, but I will select just three for comment.[11]

The 'cry' form of the seventh thesis and maxim is: 'Let us become apprentices of saints!' L'Arche has plenty of 'saints' who have worked out their interpretations of scripture in community and articulated them in writing and orally. But a striking mark of their interpretations is that they ascribe so much of their insight to their disabled fellow-members. 'People with a handicap truly lead the assistants deeper into faith; they become our teachers.'[12] These other 'saints', many of whom cannot read

---

11. For an experimental treatment relating to another, the second maxim on reading scripture theodramatically for the sake of God and God's purposes in history, see Ford, 'Wilderness Wisdom for the Twenty-first Century', which discusses an oral statement by Jean Vanier about Arthur, the disabled son of the theologian Frances Young: 'I wonder whether that is anything close to a dream I have – the whole of the history of Christianity is culminated in Arthur.'

12. Vanier, *Community and Growth*, p. 97.

or write, are at the heart of L'Arche's wisdom interpretation of scripture. In biblical terms that is in line with Paul's idea quoted above of wisdom that comes from those judged foolish, and with his later description of how the Holy Spirit works in the body of Christ, enabling fruitful new forms of mutuality and reciprocity.

This leads into the eighth maxim: 'Let conversations around scripture be open to all people, religions, cultures, arts, disciplines, media and spheres of life.' L'Arche, centred on communities in which the disabled and assistants share, draws into its search for wisdom around the world people who come under that range of categories. With regard to scripture, the most obvious question is about those in traditions other than Christianity with different scriptures, but there is also a question about those of different Christian traditions of interpretation. Its Christian initiators have generally sought through L'Arche to go deeper into the resources of their own traditions, to encourage others to do the same with their traditions, and to engage in conversation and deliberation with them in order to arrive at fresh wisdom in the interests of a better future together.[13] This is in line with what happens in scriptural reasoning, as

---

13. In a section called 'The bread of pain' on how to handle divisions about eucharistic sharing among Christians in L'Arche Jean Vanier writes: 'To live ecumenism, each person is called to live and deepen what is essential to their faith in Jesus: to be in communion with the Father and to grow in love for others. But they must live and deepen what is specific to their own church too. True ecumenism is not the suppression of difference; on the contrary, it is learning to respect and love what is different. The members of the community must then be grounded in their own tradition and love it. [Note – This connects with chapter 2's first six maxims for a wisdom interpretation of scripture.] It means also that they feel truly called by Jesus to eat the bread of pain in order to further that unity.' Vanier goes on to talk about anticipating 'the bread of unity' by cultivating all that unites Christians: 'in particular baptism; the Word of God; the cross of Jesus and carrying our cross; living in the Holy Spirit, prayer and the presence of Jesus. Together, all the members are called to holiness and love. If they cannot celebrate the Eucharist together, they can celebrate the washing of each other's feet, living it as a sacrament.

'In L'Arche, if we cannot eat at the same eucharistic table, we can all eat together at the table of the poor. "When you give a banquet," says Jesus, "invite the poor, the crippled, the lame and the blind, not your friends or relations or rich neighbours" (Luke 14:13–15). If we cannot drink together from the same eucharistic chalice, we can all drink together from the chalice of suffering (see Matt. 20) caused by division among Christians and by the rejection of the poor and the weak. These are the specific gifts of L'Arche.

'We can discover also the intimate link between the broken body of Christ in the Eucharist and the broken and suffering bodies of our people. We can discover that the poor are a path to unity. As we are called to love them, and to be loved by them, we are in some mysterious way brought together in the heart of Christ.'

He then goes on to apply the same principles to inter-faith matters:'What I have said of interdenominational communities can also be said, but in a different way, about inter-religious communities. Here the bread of pain is perhaps even greater. We have to discover how to celebrate our common humanity. We must discover the cycles of nature and the presence of God in all the beauty of our universe. We must learn how to celebrate a common prayer to God, the Father of us all' (*Community and Growth*, pp. 203–4).

described above in chapter 8. That is about wisdom interpretations of their scriptures by Jews, Christians and Muslims together, and comparable forms of interpretation go on among Hindus, Buddhists, Sikhs and others. For all of these L'Arche offers a context in which their scriptures can be read differently and also together. Where, and with whom, we read scripture is a crucial matter. L'Arche is a place where people with disabilities from many religions open the way for themselves and their co-religionists to engage more deeply together in the search for a wisdom of common humanity and peace. A strong connection can be made between, on the one hand, listening to the testimonies to life in L'Arche and then going beyond them to a practical wisdom that can shape life there in the future; and, on the other hand, listening to the plain sense of scripture and then going beyond it to making wise connections with other parts of scripture, with the rich traditions of its interpretation, with other religious and non-religious traditions, with life today, and with questions about the future.[14]

The ninth maxim is: 'Read scripture in the Spirit, immersed in life, desiring God's future, and open to continually fresh rereadings in new situations.' Its cry is 'Let us read in the Spirit for the sake of the Kingdom of God!' L'Arche is a fascinating laboratory for fresh scriptural interpretation partly because it has ventured into one new situation after another, and at any one time is involved in diverse contexts around the world while also trying to be true to its core values and founding story and to stay in communication. Again, Vanier's commentary on the Gospel of John, yet to be discussed, is the best example. He gathers together over fifty years of rereading that Gospel, most of them in the context of L'Arche, showing how this helps sound new depths in the Gospel, and at the same time he holds up to L'Arche and the rest of the world an invitation into a mystery of love and wisdom.

Job, Jesus, Paul and L'Arche

The main scriptural focus of chapters 1–7 was on Job, Jesus and Paul. Cries and responding to them went to the heart of the wisdom of all three. There are abundant further resonances with L'Arche too.

The correspondences identified between Job and Jesus in chapter 6 can embrace key features of L'Arche too. Besides the passionate crying out, there is the transformation of desire amidst the contingencies and

---

14. This connects to chapter 2's fourth maxim: 'Let us read for plain sense, open to other senses!'

sufferings of human existence. God's desire for Job and Jesus is found mirrored in Paul's testimony to God's choosing of the weak, the low, the despised, the less respectable, 'things that are not'. If these are at the heart of a community there is a challenge to many of the reigning desires of our society, and an attempt to educate desire in different ways.

Vital to L'Arche's transformation of desire is the significance of friendship. Friendship gone wrong is central to the dialogues of Job – the friends who fail in compassion and wisdom. In the Synoptic Gospels Jesus is the friend of the marginal – of the sick, the tax collectors, the prostitutes. In John's Gospel Jesus calls Lazarus his friend: '**Our friend** (φίλος) **Lazarus**' (John 11:11). Vanier's commentary makes a good deal of this and of other details in the story, offering one of his most explicitly L'Arche-influenced readings, while making clear its subjunctive character ('This is of course only a supposition . . .'[15]). Lazarus is called ἀσθενής, meaning sick, without strength, feeble or insignificant, and Vanier suggests: 'In the language of today, we would probably say "who was disabled".'[16] He adds up the hints – he lives with two unmarried sisters who are devoted to him; their home is described by Luke as '**the home of Martha**' (Luke 10:38); he is present but never speaks.

> As I read all this I cannot help but come to the conclusion,
> which of course comes from my experience in L'Arche
> with people with disabilities,
> that Lazarus has a handicap and probably a serious one.
> The word *asthenés* can imply this.
> Were the two sisters unmarried in order to look after him?
> The words of his sister, 'the one you love is sick,'
> seem to me significant.
> To me, these words imply
> 'the one that you visit and bathe,
> the one you love with tenderness and affection,
> is in danger of death'.[17]

It is in relation to Lazarus that the crucial theme of friendship with Jesus is introduced:

> This is the first time in the Gospel of John
> that we hear of Jesus' love

15. Jean Vanier, *Drawn into the Mystery of Jesus through the Gospel of John* (London: Darton, Longman and Todd, 2004), p. 196.
16. Ibid. p. 195.   17. Ibid. p. 196.

for individual people,
the first time that John, speaking of Jesus,
uses the Greek words *agape* and *philia*.
Agape is a preferential love for someone;
a love whereby we seek his or her welfare.
Philia implies the same reality
but with a connotation of mutuality and friendship.
In later chapters, we will hear a lot
about the preferential love of Jesus
for his Father and for his disciples.
Up until now, however, the men whom Jesus chose to follow him
are called disciples, not friends.
There is an inequality between them,
an inequality which Jesus came to level into the mutuality
and equality of genuine friendship.
It is only later in this gospel that Jesus calls them 'friends'.[18]

That L'Arche-inspired midrash on Lazarus as *asthenés* and *philos* is one of the most direct examples of what will be discussed more fully below, Vanier's wisdom interpretation of John in the light of L'Arche, and vice versa.

Perhaps the most fundamental correspondence between Job, Jesus, Paul and L'Arche is what previous chapters have called 'wisdom after trauma'. So many of the disabled in L'Arche have histories with multiple traumas – of the disabilities themselves, of rejection, isolation, and combinations of physical, emotional, mental, social and spiritual anguish that amount to what Simone Weil calls *malheur*, affliction (see p. 104 above). As Weil saw, one of the most difficult things is to pay full attention to someone in such affliction. How can we bear to stay with it, look on it, take the cries to heart? She connected this required quality of attentiveness with the attention at the heart of prayer and of study. Part of the wisdom sought by L'Arche is about growing in attentiveness to deeply damaged people. At a communal level, it is a kind of attentiveness similar to that needed to try to do justice to the Shoah – and in chapters 3 and 4, as we followed Micheal O'Siadhail's attempt to do this in *The Gossamer Wall: Poems in Witness to the Holocaust*, the focus repeatedly shifted between individuals and the wider picture of a traumatised people. Vanier's communities have led him into attentive friendship

18. Ibid. pp. 195–6, emphasis added.

with many traumatised individuals and also into prophetic attention to the pathologies of societies in which such affliction happens and where many of us turn away and close our ears to disability.

Yet as with Job, Jesus and Paul, the trauma is not the last word. The very extremity of involvement in suffering elicits from each cries that can become a measure of the mystery of a God who remains the God of blessing. The conclusion of chapter 3 might just as well have been written about L'Arche – or about the picture Paul gives of the church at its best:

> The epilogue [of the Book of Job] shows the enjoyment of riches and other blessings in a long-term community of worship, generosity and compassion. *The cries of suffering have not been forgotten, silenced or ignored; cries of joy and gratitude have greeted the many blessings; and the generative centre of the whole way of living is the cry of awe: 'now my eye sees you'* (Job 42:5) (see p. 119 above).

I will take up that final reference to God below, but first turn to the way L'Arche relates to traditions of church and world and the possibilities of their transformation.

Opening up the protective 'packages' of individuals, church and world

Because it responds to cries, L'Arche can never be very neat. The cries of those with disabilities have summoned it across national, gender, cultural, denominational and religious boundaries, and the urgency of love and compassion has not been able to wait for resolution of all the problems, or attend to all the loose ends. Within L'Arche communities, for all the importance of order and pattern in daily life,[19] there are continual reminders of the relativity of such order, as behaviour, emotion and communication, as well as food and drink, fail to stay within their 'proper' categories and containers.

It is easy to see how such messiness, together with the facing of affliction, can be a threat to many people. Deep fears and insecurities are opened up in contact with L'Arche, and assistants are often profoundly disturbed by their experiences. It has been a continuing problem for L'Arche how to care for assistants as well as for those with disabilities.

---

19. One striking feature of the communities is the extent to which many are able to live by a calendar formed by events of special religious importance (mostly those of the Christian liturgical year, but also those of other faiths) and by events (especially birthdays) of significance to individual members.

L'Arche has developed its own psychological and counselling wisdom, drawing on professionals and on its own experience, in order to cope with the problem. For assistants, living in community is often a major challenge, let alone sharing that community with the disabled. The large number of testimonies to this overwhelming experience often tell of transformations of self through intensive involvement with others in community, but there are also some whose overwhelmings are less positive.

The basic response to the searching challenges to personal identity provoked by L'Arche is clear throughout Vanier's writings, signalled by the title of his major work, *Community and Growth*. Vanier recognises that living in these communities frequently leads people into personal crises, as it has more than once led him, but he also sees such crises as giving an opportunity for growth and transformation. Subheadings of that book indicate the way he combines realism with confidence in the possibilities of growth through minor and major traumas: 'Community, a place of healing and growth'; 'Community and forgiveness'; 'Called by God just as we are'; 'Share your weakness'; 'From "the community for myself" to "myself for the community"'; 'Inner pain'; 'Leave your father, your mother, your culture'; 'From heroism to dailiness'; 'Times of trial: a step towards growth'; 'Growth in individuals and growth in community'; 'The risk of growth'; 'Growth as nourishment'.

The goal of growth that is held up again and again is that of wise love. Vanier is especially concerned with the barriers that divide people from each other and from God, the numerous forms of closure, woundedness and self-protectiveness that inhibit, subvert or prevent growth in love. He analyses these acutely, drawing on observations over many years. His fundamental conclusion is that the radical security needed to grow in wise love in the face of our own barriers and those of others is rooted in God's love and the gift of God's Spirit.

> We must help each person to live more and more clearly and deeply from an inner confidence of being loved by God just as they are.
> I sometimes tend to behave as if everyone could live in community and grow through their own efforts towards universal love. With age and experience of community life, perhaps too with a growing faith, I'm becoming conscious of the limitations and weaknesses of human energy, the forces of egoism and the deep psychological wounds – fear, aggression and self-assertion – which govern human life and raise up all the barriers which exist between people. We can only emerge from

behind these barriers if the Spirit of God touches us, breaks down the barriers and puts us on the road to healing.[20]

This leads directly into reflection on 'another dimension' of growth centred on Jesus, and what he writes on this resonates with John's Gospel, explaining why commentary on that Gospel has been his culminating work.

> Jesus was sent by the Father not to judge us and even less to condemn us to remain in the prisons, limitations and dark places of our beings, but to forgive us and free us, by planting the seeds of the Spirit in us. To grow in love is to allow this Spirit of Jesus to grow in us.
>
> Growth takes on another dimension when we allow Jesus to penetrate us, to give us new life and new energy.
>
> The hope is not in our own efforts to love. It is not in psychoanalysis which tries to throw light on the knots and blocks of our life, nor in a more equitable reorganisation of the political and economic structures which have their effects on our personal lives. All this is perhaps necessary. But true growth comes from God, when we cry to him from the depths of the abyss to let his Spirit penetrate us. Growth in love is a growth in the Spirit. The stages through which we must pass in order to grow in love are the stages through which we must pass to become more totally united to God.[21]

Such a vision of growth in love for each other and for God, in response to our crying from the depths, connects with what has been said in discussion of Job, Jesus and the church of Corinth, but its Johannine thrust also opens further dimensions yet to be addressed.

The packaged protectiveness that can prevent individuals and communities being open to growth can also affect the church and other institutions.

The Roman Catholic Church was the seedbed of L'Arche: Pope John Paul II warmly affirmed it,[22] and there are strong links in many countries with Catholic parishes, dioceses, organisations, religious orders, priests and lay people. Yet L'Arche has not wanted to become an official Catholic organisation, and its constant movement across boundaries and attempts

---

20. Vanier, *Community and Growth*, pp. 132–3.   21. Ibid. p. 133.
22. In recognising Jean's work, Pope John Paul II stated, 'Over the past 30 years L'Arche has grown to become a dynamic and providential sign of the civilization of love.' This statement is quoted on the L'Arche website for the United States – http://www.larcheusa.org/jeanvanier.html.

to form communities that are both ecumenical and inter-faith has led to some tensions with its origins. L'Arche exemplifies some of the great debates among Catholics at present concerning their identity as Christians and their relations with non-Catholics. Among the symptoms of this are the differing responses of various Catholic religious orders and movements to L'Arche. It has tended to be closest to contemplative orders, Jesuits, Franciscans, the Little Sisters of Jesus and others who live alongside the poor. It has been more distant from those whose work of service does not lead them into living alongside those they serve, and also from those whose efforts to renew the Catholic Church emphasise a strong centre of authority in the Vatican together with well-defined 'packages' of teaching, and clear boundaries entailing sharp distinctions between insiders and outsiders, orthodox and unorthodox, leaders and led.

Those in the second group appear to be threatened by L'Arche's fostering of friendship between assistants and the disabled, by its complexifying of boundaries, by its federal, distributed, 'flat' structure, by its resistance to neat sets of ideas or teachings, and by its willingness to be led by its concern for those with disabilities into 'messy' situations where the security of predefinition is not possible as new ways forward are explored. L'Arche's prophetic wisdom offers a classic challenge to the Catholic and other churches at such points, one that is in line with the resistance of Job to the 'packages' offered by his friends and of Jesus to the religious authorities of his day. This is another concern that Vanier's commentary on John's Gospel takes up, where it is especially marked in his sharp words about clinging to security in groups and to the ideologies that legitimise these closed identities.[23]

Such ideological closure exists as much in the secular as in the religious sphere, and L'Arche often sits uneasily there too. One form of it, found especially in more developed countries, occurs when regulatory control becomes over-dominant. Regulation is obviously legitimate in wanting to ensure human rights, health, safety, protection against abuse, education and work for the disabled, proper qualifications and remuneration for carers, funding and accountability. The problems come in the reactions of the bureaucratic mindset to what does not easily fit its

---

23. E.g. Vanier, *Drawn into the Mystery of Jesus through the Gospel of John*, pp. 163ff, 177ff. Vanier recalls his own journey beyond the limitations of his early Catholic, Western and naval formation into being influenced by Asia, by other churches, by other religions and by those of no specific religious tradition (pp. 180–1).

categories. Around the world, and especially where there are state welfare systems, L'Arche is trying to work out ways to maintain its commitment to communities with faith and friendship at their heart while also negotiating with bureaucracies about forms of regulation and accountability. As often with L'Arche, there is a representative aspect, relevant to other areas, of this demanding labour that tries both to comply with appropriate regulation and also to resist the excesses of control, security and surveillance in the interests of a community that fosters trust, intimacy, physical touch, love and risky change.

In the image of this God

One challenge for a theologian seeking wisdom in L'Arche is to pursue today what von Rad (see p. 226 above) saw as the continually renewed effort of wisdom in Israel to discern how to be human before God and to do this afresh from the heart of faith in God. How might the God identified in previous chapters be understood in relation to L'Arche?

A response by communities in India during the discussion of L'Arche's Identity and Mission included a meditation on loving people not because of what they do, or what they have, but for themselves, for who they are.[24] This connects with 'fearing God for nothing', the hermeneutical key to the book of Job suggested in chapter 3, which was further developed in later chapters, culminating in chapter 7's discussion of loving God for God's sake.

L'Arche's approach to those with disabilities embodies a way of being human before God that is a fresh sign of who God is. God desires a relationship with us for our own sake and for this to be reciprocal. But who are we? We are created in God's image, the image of a God who loves us for our own sake. We are fully ourselves as we are loved for our own sake and as we love God and others for their own sakes. L'Arche seeks to be a sign of this humanity and this God. The poor, the despised, the disfigured, the disabled are especially suited to being at the heart of such a sign. There is little worldly incentive to embrace them in love and friendship, yet their deepest secret is that they are created, chosen and delighted in by God for their own sake. Chapter 4 suggested that 'God's own "for nothing" is the wisdom of one who risks a relationship without guarantees, and who gives human existence the terrifying dignity of a life and death drama in which wisdom and foolishness really matter.' It really

---

24. Unpublished material provided by L'Arche.

matters whether the disabled are loved for their own sake; it is the difference between a life of wise love before God and one that misses this joyful fulfilment of creation. Like the crucifixion, L'Arche is both a scandalous sign and a mystery of love. The demands and risks of the relationships in L'Arche are in line with all its members being in the image of a God who risks 'for nothing' relationships with creation in the desire that creation might be fulfilled in a love that has the wisdom of the cross at its heart.

L'Arche is, of course, one among many such signs. Chapter 7 ranged from Abraham and Isaac to Shadrach, Meshach and Abednego, and from Jesus to the Gulag, to gather other signs. They culminated in a vision of heaven crying out and celebrating in new songs the names of God, the new name of Jesus, and the new names of those who have been witnesses for God. L'Arche may be the first community in history that has told the stories of those with disabilities and has honoured their names.

'When the one who has cried out on the cross meets those who have cried out in martyrdom the result is an explosion of new song' (see p. 251 above). There are analogous explosions of song, and also of laughter, in L'Arche. They are communities of celebration.

> Celebration is a moment of wonder when the joy of the body and the senses are linked to the joy of the spirit. It unites everything that is most divine and most human in community life ... At the heart of celebration, there are the poor. If the least significant is excluded, it is no longer a celebration. We have to find dances and games in which the children, the old people and the weak can join equally. A celebration must always be a festival of the poor, and with the poor, not for the poor ...
>
> Visitors are often astonished at the joy they sense at L'Arche. Their impression surprises me too, because I know how much suffering some people in our communities are carrying. I wonder then if all joy doesn't somehow spring from suffering and sacrifice. Can those who are rich and live in comfort and security with everything they need, and refuse to be close to those who are suffering, be truly joyful? Isn't there a lot of unconscious guilt in them which closes them up? Joy comes from openness. But I am sure that poor people can be joyful. At times of celebration, they seem to overcome all their suffering and frustration in an explosion of joy. They shed the burden of daily life and they live a moment of freedom in which their hearts simply bound with joy. It is so too with people in community who have learnt to accept their wounds, limitations and poverty. They are forgiven; they are loved.

They have discovered liberation; they are not frightened of being themselves; they do not have to hide away; they are free with the freedom of the Spirit.[25]

That joy in life for life's sake is a third dimension, inseparable from joy in God and joy in each other, in the ecology of blessedness that was celebrated in chapter 7 in the ecstatic language of Thomas Traherne.

School of desire and wisdom, sign to a religious and secular world

The penultimate section of chapter 7 discussed the church as a school of desire and wisdom and as part of a religious and secular world. How might this apply to L'Arche?

L'Arche is an organisation which does not fit the usual categories. It is easier to say what it is not than what it is. It is not a church, a religious order, a movement, a social service agency or a residential care network, though it shares features with each of those. Yet 'school of desire and wisdom' suits it well. Its capacity to educate desire and its commitment to seeking wisdom have already become clear. Its main form of learning is by apprenticeship and accompaniment, like the disciples of Jesus. *The primary apprenticeship is to those with disabilities – they are seen as the main source of teaching.* The leading verbal form that L'Arche wisdom takes is the sort of testimony described above. This points to it being above all a wisdom learned through specific history, alert to events, surprises, and above all to particular people.

This is closely linked to learning to relate to God, with each assistant encouraged to seek spiritual accompaniment and take part in retreats and worship if they are open to that. The Charter of L'Arche says in the first paragraph on 'The Communities':

> L'Arche communities are communities of faith, rooted in prayer and trust in God. They seek to be guided by God and by their weakest members, through whom God's presence is revealed. Each community member is encouraged to discover and deepen his or her spiritual life and live it according to his or her particular faith and tradition. Those who have no religious affiliation are also welcomed and respected in their freedom of conscience.[26]

---

25. Vanier, *Community and Growth*, pp. 315, 319–20.
26. The next paragraph of the Charter reads: '1.2 Communities are either of one faith or inter-religious. Those which are Christian are either of one church or interdenominational.

The flourishing of L'Arche also requires other forms of learning and wisdom. Many types of academic and professional knowledge and skills are relevant – medical, psychological, organisational, financial, cultural, sociological, historical, theological, and so on. Many sorts of experience are also relevant – the practical skills of living with disability, being an assistant, organising a community, coordinating L'Arche regionally or internationally, coping with problems in specific areas, relating to various churches and to other religions, and so on.

All of this not only amounts to education in desire and wisdom; the combination of elements means that there is continual interplay between the religious and the secular. These are faith communities (welcoming those of any faith and none) in close engagement with their societies. The fourth section of the Charter, headed 'Integration in society' commits them to openness to the world around them, including the world of work, and to working closely with families, professionals, governments and other organisations, as well as with religious communities. Spanning these spheres, it sees its vocation to be a sign to both church and world. Its Charter says that it is 'not a solution but a sign, a sign that society, to be truly human, must be founded on welcome and respect for the weak and the downtrodden' and, 'in a divided world, L'Arche wants to be a sign of hope . . . unity, faithfulness and reconciliation'.[27]

One might add to that: *a sign of wisdom*; and one that challenges many conceptions of who can be wise, what wisdom is, and from whom it may be learnt.

Drawn into the Mystery of Jesus through the Gospel of John

The above brief recapitulation of earlier chapters' discussion of wisdom in dialogue with L'Arche has several times referred to Jean Vanier's commentary on the Gospel of John and has quoted what it says about Lazarus. In what follows I will try to characterise this unusual form of commentary so as to open up its distinctive contribution to Christian wisdom.

'There is such life and wisdom contained in this gospel that no one person can discover or hold on to it all', Vanier writes in his Foreword.[28]

Each community maintains links with the appropriate religious authorities and its members are integrated with local churches and other places of worship' (see Vanier, *An Ark for the Poor*, p. 119, and Appendix 1, p. 118).

27. Ibid. pp. 117–18.

28. Vanier, *Drawn into the Mystery of Jesus through the Gospel of John*, p. 8.

The sense of superabundant meaning, truth and wisdom recurs through his commentary, rooted in John's conception of God.

> John 6:12 'Pick up all that has been left over so that nothing may be lost.'

Vanier comments:

> They fill up twelve baskets full!
> At Cana, Jesus transformed an excessive amount of water
> into delicious wine.
> Here he multiplies five loaves of bread and two fish
> into an excessive quantity of food.
> That is God.
> God gives abundantly, signifying that God loves us abundantly.[29]

That interplay of significance between the wine, the bread, love and God is a response to John's multilevelled narrative, encouraging meditation that finds more and more. Vanier calls his style 'meditative prose' and it is printed like poetry, inviting readers to savour it a line at a time. It is open-textured, a recognition in form of the open, often deceptively simple prose of John's Gospel. Here large, simple words and symbols are presented – among Vanier's favourites are *dwell* (μένειν), *cry* (κράζειν; κραυγάζειν), *love* (ἀγαπᾶν; φιλεῖν), friend (φίλος), *life* (ζωή), joy (χαρά), *I am* (ἐγώ εἰμι), *trust, believe* (πιστεύειν). They are capacious, richly resonant in many directions, and they inevitably connect with different readers in different ways. Vanier draws on a lifetime's experience, especially in L'Arche, in order to explore them, and his style invites his readers to do the same in their own ways. His 360 pages open up John and L'Arche together, besides many other themes such as the nature of a consumer society, the dangers of the quest for certainty, the importance of the sense of touch, or the relation of intuition and reason.

How might his form of interpretation be further described and evaluated? I would make three main points about it, all connected with discussions in this and earlier chapters.

John's wisdom for transition to the next generation
First, there is Vanier's suggestion as to why John's Gospel was so late to be written and so different from the Synoptic Gospels. I quote it at some

---

29. Ibid. p. 120.

length because of the parallel I discern with Vanier's own reasons for
writing his commentary on this Gospel late in life.

> One may ask why the Gospel of John did not find its final form
> until some sixty years after the death and resurrection of Jesus.
> Why is it so different from the other three gospels,
> which John obviously knew?
> During all those years he must have told over and over again
> what he had lived and seen about Jesus
> and what he had heard from Jesus.
> But why did he wait so long for the gospel to become complete?
> We can only make suppositions, of course.
> Mine is that there was a special need at the end of the first century
> to make better known what I call
> the mystical element of this gospel,
> which was lived and announced in a special way
> in the community over which John presided.
> This mystical element is the call of Jesus
> for his followers to become one with him
> and to live with him as a beloved friend.
> The message of Jesus was beginning to spread
> throughout Asia Minor, Greece and other parts of the world.
> Followers of Jesus were becoming more numerous.
> The structures of the church were being put into place
> and the theology of the church was developing.
> History has shown that as a group grows larger,
> discords and conflicts arise,
> rules and regulations become necessary,
> and then structures can take precedence over the spirit.
> The mystical and the spiritual tend to take a back seat.
> No wonder John wanted to complete his Gospel![30]

One might develop this further in relation to Vanier's own position
in L'Arche. Vanier's suggestion is that the Gospel of John was the result
of longer reflection on the events of the 'first generation' that are told in
a more straightforward way in the first three Gospels. It is as if the
transition of generations, together with expansion and institutionalisa-
tion, calls for a deepening, a more reflective grasp, of those events, so
that coming generations may be helped to appreciate their richness and
to live creatively beyond them. Their wisdom needs especially to be

---

30. Ibid. pp. 12–13.

distilled for this time of transition. L'Arche during its first forty years
has produced many accounts that might be compared to the first three
Gospels, above all testimonies in the form of stories that are crucial for
understanding its origins, development, character and spirit. It has also
expanded and built an organisation. But there is in addition a need for
mature reflection and deepening, for which John's Gospel is a classic
model.

That gospel is acutely aware of the importance of the transition
beyond the founder, Jesus. It has a long set of 'farewell conversations'
in chapters 13–17. There is important, counter-intuitive teaching: '**It is
better for you that I go away …**'; '**You will do greater things …**';
'**I still have many things to say to you, but you cannot bear them
now. When the Spirit of truth comes, he will guide you into all
the truth.**' This amounts to a promise of superabundant fruitfulness
in the second generation, if only the disciples will receive the Holy
Spirit and take on the full responsibility that is inseparable from love.
John's Gospel seems to be written to help a community make this
transition.

What Vanier identifies in the passage quoted above, and at greater
length throughout his commentary, is the substance of John's contribution. What can allow L'Arche in the twenty-first century to deepen
its life, strengthen its unity, develop its mission, innovate in the Spirit,
and avoid such pitfalls as backward-looking nostalgia for the 'heroic
early days', or fundamentalist repetition of the founder's teaching and
actions, or (at the other extreme) forgetfulness of the founding story
and inspiration of the community? Vanier's answer is: fresh rereading
of the Gospel of John that at the same time reflects on L'Arche. His
commentary is distilled from this: *it is a wisdom of love and friendship with
Jesus and with those he loves, a communion of heart that is nothing less than
indwelling in the Spirit the love that unites Jesus and his Father*. What Vanier
has attempted is to leave in this written testimony a rereading of the
'plain sense' of John inextricable from a midrashic rereading of L'Arche
in Johannine terms. There are insights into John that are hard to
imagine without Vanier's living and praying in L'Arche for forty
years (the example of the interpretation of Lazarus already given
above is one of many). There are also insights into L'Arche, and especially into what it most deeply needs if it is to flourish in the next
generation, that are unimaginable without his fifty years of meditation
on John.

Vanier's wisdom interpretation

This leads into the second point: the commentary is, in my terms, a wisdom interpretation of John. All ten of the maxims at the end of chapter 2 could be exemplified in it. Likewise the hermeneutics of incarnation, crucifixion, resurrection and the giving of the Spirit are in it. As regards scholarship, Vanier knows a range of ancient and modern commentaries on John, but his aim is not to contribute something original to biblical scholarship. Rather he tries to be alert and sure-footed in the territory of New Testament academics, drawing on a selection of them.

John's Gospel is the most puzzling of the four. Nearly everything about it is subject to dispute – dating, authorship, contributions of later editors, community of origin and its opponents, relation to the other three Gospels, relation to Judaism, relation to Greek thought, culture and religion, historical veracity, and literary structure. Vanier's sure-footedness is seen in the fact that he generally avoids statements or speculations that cannot be supported by some reputable scholarship. But the extent of scholarly uncertainty and disunity allows for some latitude, which he sometimes takes. His main concern, however, is to meditate on the Gospel with reference to the present. Chapter 2 defined wisdom interpretation as an engagement with scripture whose primary desire is for the wisdom of God in life now, and Vanier's commentary fits that.

Such wisdom interpretation was also characterised in terms of its discernment of cries and its articulation in many moods of faith and understanding. Vanier's commentary, like his writing about L'Arche elsewhere, is pervaded by reference to cries, in this case the cries of Jesus as well as the cries of those he meets and the cries of the suffering in our time. Likewise the other moods all feature. He is especially critical of the misuse of and overemphasis upon the indicative mood of affirmation and the imperative mood of control.

> Nicodemus had certitudes. He knew the law.
> Clearly, theological certitudes and laws are important and necessary.
> We need to know Scripture.
> We need a community of faith, a place of belonging.
> We need church.
> We need teachers.
> We need a vision that flows from those of the past who have lived and loved Jesus.

All this gives us a solid foundation
that enables us to love in truth
and to live a deep spiritual and mystical life.

But certitudes and law can also close us up in ourselves
in the self-satisfaction of knowledge,
of feeling righteous and superior.
They can prevent us from listening to people,
and being open to new ways of God.
They can wound the childlike attitudes of wonderment
and stifle the longing for the Spirit.
Those who live only out of certitudes and the law,
who hide behind the law,
tend to control others,
fearing all that is 'new' will lead to a loss of control.
They fear change and risk stifling the Spirit
in their own hearts and in the hearts of others.
Certitudes and power are seductive.
They give security and a feeling of existing, even an identity;
we are *someone* if we have certitudes and power.[31]

There the interrogatives of wonderment and the optative desire for the Spirit are victims of dominant indicative and imperative certainties. Earlier in his reflections on John 3 Vanier noted the description of Nicodemus as one who *knows*, and the response of Jesus in proposing 'the way of "*not knowing*", of being born from "*above*"'.[32]

John 3:8 The wind blows where it chooses and you hear the sound of it, but you do not know where it comes from or where it goes. So it is with everyone who is born of the Spirit.

In the story of Nicodemus it is the surprises and subjunctive possibilities of new-born children and of the uncontrollable Spirit that break free of the constrictions of limited certitudes.

But Vanier has his own favourite indicatives, chief among which is the supreme one that embraces all others and relativises them within an infinite horizon: **I am.**[33] He also has his favourite imperatives. **'You also must wash one another's feet'** (John 13:14) has become the mandate for L'Arche's quasi-sacramental liturgy of footwashing. It is

---

31. Ibid. pp. 78–9.   32. Ibid. p. 75.
33. E.g. ibid. pp. 98, 122, 157–8, 307–8. See pp. 210–13 above.

'an intense moment of communion through the body',[34] a subversion of most practices of command,

> a new way of exercising authority
> through humility, service and love, through a communion of hearts,
> in a manner that implies closeness, friendliness, openness and
>   humility.[35]

Above all there is the imperative of love.

> John 13:34 'I give you a new commandment, that you love one another.
> Just as I have loved you, you should love one another.'

> Here Jesus is calling his disciples not only to love others as they love
>   themselves
> but to love as he – Jesus – loves them.
> That is what is new.
> He is creating a holy, sacred covenant between them.[36]

That love command is as near as an imperative can come to an optative – Jesus sets love before his disciples as the content and goal of their desiring, 'a road to fullness of life and joy'.[37] The deepest thirst in us is 'our desire and need to love and be loved'.[38] This is a participation in the desire of Jesus, who 'reveals his desire to be with us all, in love'[39] and who dwells in the love of his Father.

> John 17:24 'Father, I desire that those whom you have given me may
> be with me where I am, to see my glory which you have given me in
> your love for me before the foundation of the world.'

Accompanying this is the desire for wisdom: 'Our intelligence needs and yearns for wisdom',[40] and the keynote opening of the Gospel, the Prologue, is a 'hymn of the wisdom of God'.[41] The interpretation of scripture ideally combines the two, rereading in wise love.

The summit of love: contemplative interpretation

The third and final point about Vanier's interpretation is the most remarkable. It is implied in much that has been said above, but deserves to be singled out as the most important characteristic of all. It is difficult to

---

34. Ibid. p. 231.   35. Ibid. p. 233.   36. Ibid. p. 251.   37. Ibid. p. 253.
38. Ibid. p. 59.   39. Ibid. p. 303.   40. Ibid. p. 125.   41. Ibid. p. 18.

articulate. A preliminary statement is required: *the matters Vanier deals with correspond in significance and scope to those of John's Gospel.* This may seem what any commentator would do: obviously one comments on the matters John writes about. But in fact commentators rarely measure up to the dimensions of this Gospel in what they say, and least of all in their contemporary parallels and applications. Their capacity, and above all their spiritual capacity, is judged by how far they do justice to this abundance of meaning which overflows all capacities. Because that meaning is not confined to the time or place it was written but, on account of its content (the God of all creation – past, present and future), reaches into the present and the future, it therefore calls for corresponding love and wisdom now if justice is to be done to it. So a further statement, still preliminary, can be ventured: *Vanier benefits from the hermeneutical assistance of L'Arche, which has stretched and transformed his conception of love and wisdom into something that is nearer to John's than that of most commentators.* But there is something more.

Vanier indicates it in his meditation on John 17. In the culminating statement of the book on the theme of love he finds this prayer pointing to 'the summit of love', beyond love as service, and even beyond love as giving one's life for others:

> In this prayer, the friends of Jesus are called to an even greater love,
> to become one with each other
> as the Father and the Son are one in the Spirit.
> It is something totally new,
> a unity that can in no way be achieved by human means.
> It is an openness and tenderness to each one,
> that flows from the deepening transformation in God.
> Friends of Jesus are no longer just walking towards God,
> serving one another,
> they are *together, one in God,*
> because *God is in them.*[42]

Here is the deepest root of Vanier's interpretation and of its authority. *It is interpretation 'in the Spirit' which, in the language of classic Christian theology and spirituality, springs from contemplative union with God.*

> John 17:23 'I in them and you in me, that they may become completely one, so that the world may know that you have sent me and have loved them even as you have loved me.'

42. Ibid. p. 298.

Conclusion: love's wisdom

Song of Songs 8:6–7 [6]Set me as a seal upon your heart, as a seal upon your arm; for love is strong as death, passion fierce as the grave. Its flashes are flashes of fire, a raging flame. [7]Many waters cannot quench love, neither can floods drown it. If one offered for love all the wealth of his house, it would be utterly scorned.

Colossians 2:2–3 [2]I want their hearts to be encouraged and united in love, so that they may have all the riches of assured understanding and have the knowledge of God's mystery, that is, Christ himself, [3]in whom are hidden all the treasures of wisdom and knowledge.

Love, the love of God inextricable from the love of people, is the summit of Jean Vanier's wisdom, shaped especially by scripture and L'Arche. This summit is the most appropriate place to conclude a book on Christian wisdom. It offers both a vantage point from which to look back on the previous chapters and also a site for the culminating scriptural meditation on the Song of Songs.

The descriptions applied to the theology of this book in the introduction included 'scriptural-expressivist'; postcritical (drawing on the premodern, modern and late modern); a theology of desire and discernment; and a theology of learning in the Spirit. Since love has been a recurrent theme in the discussion of wisdom, it could also most comprehensively be called a theology of the love of wisdom and of the wisdom of love.

The 'God of blessing who loves in wisdom' both cries out to humanity and hears their cries. The richest wisdom has been found in God's love of creation for its own sake and a responsive human love of God for God's sake and of other people for their own sake. Wise living before this God involves a faith that above all acknowledges being desired and loved by God, like Jesus at his baptism, and that in response desires and loves God.

Within this relationship of desire and love, immersed in the challenges and risks of the drama of existence, there is a life of being affirmed and affirming, being instructed and instructing, being questioned and questioning, being surprised and exploring new possibilities; and all this calls for a continual discernment of cries.

The wisdom interpretation of scripture that informs this faith has as its encompassing maxim: 'Let us reread in love!' This takes scripture's own core commandments of loving God and neighbour (which includes loving with all one's mind) as the motive, criterion and goal of wise reading. Can there be such rereading even in the face of trauma? The slow wrestle with the book of Job, which extends through chapters 3 and 4 and beyond, answers that by attempting it. Previous regimes of reading can be drawn on today, and Job can yield wisdom for coping with the recent trauma of the Shoah. Jesus Christ can be seen as one who embodies the love of God for God's sake and teaches the transformation of desire that that requires. His loud cry on the cross, the Easter acclamation 'He is risen!' and the ongoing petition of the church 'Come, Holy Spirit!' are at the heart of the hermeneutics of crucifixion, resurrection and Pentecost through which scripture and history are read. The church can be understood as a school of desire and wisdom, its tradition too needing to be continually reread in love. The core dynamic of Christian wisdom is learning to live together in the Spirit of Jesus Christ, the Spirit of love for a God who is praised, thanked and blessed 'for his name's sake'.

What happens when the rereading is done with Jews and Muslims? The discussion of scriptural reasoning suggested that the secret of this Abrahamic collegiality is its primary orientation towards friendship rather than consensus. It is a wisdom-seeking that flourishes best when it is done in love. And what of universities? I have described them as motivated from the beginning by the love of knowledge (*amor scientiae*), formation of students and usefulness to society, and as flourishing best when their overarching ethos is the desire for integration of those three motives focussed through wise interrelation of a range of disciplines. Here the love of wisdom is primary, but the importance of collegiality can be seen as an acknowledgement of the interpersonal dimension of academic life that can find its fulfilment in a wisdom of love. Insofar as the university takes seriously the phenomena of human life and the religious traditions, it is also appropriate for it to inquire into, among other matters, the reality of love; and, insofar as the university is open in its wisdom-seeking, collegiality and formation to learning from its own

Christian origins in medieval Europe and from other religious and secular sources, it can embrace a concern for the wisdom of love.

The culmination of the wisdom of love has been seen in the L'Arche communities and in Jean Vanier's reading of the Gospel of John. When Vanier reaches his 'summit of love' he turns to the Song of Songs to find words for it:

> [I]t is the friendship of lovers, their wedding feast of love when the
>   bride and beloved become one in the sharing of their lives,
> giving themselves to one another
> and together giving themselves to God and to others.
>
> In love each one is unique and precious;
> each one has his or her place;
> each one receives and each one gives;
> each one has a grateful heart.
> There are no more barriers;
> each delights in the other,
> each is a delight for the other
> because in each one is seen the face of God.
>
> *Arise my love, my fair one*
> *And come away;*
> *For now the winter is past*
> *the rain is over and gone.*
> *The flowers appear on the earth;*
> *the time of singing has come ...*
>
> *My beloved is mine and I am his.* (Song 2:10–12, 16)
>
> Each one is different
> and each one is needed
> for the completion of humanity in God.
> We are bonded together:
> vulnerable, one to another,
> open, one to another.
> Together we reflect the infinite beauty of God,
> the unity in God.
> Together we cry out our thanks to God and to others.
>
> We cry out together our desire for God to be glorified
> as the source and the end of all beings
> ...
>
> We struggle to keep welcoming people,

to love those whom we do not like or who do not like us.
We struggle to love those who are different or who appear to be rivals.
We struggle to love our enemies, those who hurt us.
We struggle not to judge and condemn people.

Peace comes as we enter this struggle,
as we work for unity
in our family and community,
in our church and between all followers of Jesus,
and between all our brothers and sisters in humanity.[1]

Vanier knows the power of enmity, hatred, fear, indifference, trauma and death to prevent or destroy the possibility of the mutual love and delight celebrated in the Song of Songs. His response has been to found and live in communities of friendship and celebration.

Similarly Micheal O'Siadhail faces the reality of the Shoah in *The Gossamer Wall: Poems in Witness to the Holocaust*; and in its final section, 'Prisoners of Hope', he refuses to let the last word be ironic disillusionment or despair, crying out in hope:

Show us again some end to shape our storyline.
A feast of rich food and well-aged wine ...
Isaiah's imagination stretches somehow to cope;
In Jeremiah's darkest scroll a jazz of hope
That stirs even in the deepest cries of silence:
Then shall the young women rejoice in the dance.[2]

That is above all a hope for love, and is followed through in *Love Life*, the book O'Siadhail wrote immediately after *The Gossamer Wall*. And there, like Vanier, he turns to the Song of Songs.

Fragrance of your oils.
L'amour fou. Such sweet folly.
Your haunting presence
Distilled traces of perfume.
Resonances of voice
Dwell in my nervous body.
My skin wants to glow,

1. Jean Vanier, *Drawn into the Mystery of Jesus Through the Gospel of John* (London: Darton, Longman and Todd, 2004), pp. 299–300.
2. Micheal O'Siadhail, *The Gossamer Wall: Poems in Witness to the Holocaust* (Newcastle: Bloodaxe Books; St Louis: Time Being Books), p. 116.

All of my being glistens.
Divine shining through.
Your lips like a crimson thread,
Your mouth is lovely . . .
You're all beautiful, my love.
Honeyed obsession
Of unreasonable love.
Pleased, being pleased,
I caress this amplitude,
Eternal roundness.
Voluptuous golden ring.
Sap and juices sing
Eden's long song in the veins.
Spirit into flesh.
The flesh into the spirit.
A garden fountain,
A well of living water,
Flowing streams from Lebanon.[3]

That, like the Song which it quotes, is, in Cheryl Exum's words about the
Song, a 'poem about erotic love and sexual desire – a poem in which the
body is both object of desire and source of delight'.[4] As O'Siadhail's
sequence of love poems moves on from falling in love through commitment and into a long marriage, the erotic is taken up into other
intensities and into the day-by-dayness of ordinary life together. Yet
the Song continues to resonate, culminating in a final concatenation of
sonnets.

My love, my love along the slopes of Gilead,
This is our Eden before the bitter apricot.
How unimaginable now our story if we had
Never met, never shaped each other's plot.
Fracture and hurt of a once bruised youth,
Sores healed by wine and oil and spice.
Kiss of life. Shulammite's mouth-to-mouth.
My wounds bound up in second paradise.
Over and over. Season by season by season,

3. 'Long Song' in Micheal O'Siadhail, *Love Life* (Newcastle-upon-Tyne: Bloodaxe Books,
2005), p. 13.
4. Cheryl Exum, *Song of Songs: A Commentary* (Louisville, KY: Westminster John Knox Press,
2005), p. 1.

I'm older than my mother's crimson moment.
Our slow grown plot of risks and pardon
As father cries how things would be different,
If things were again. O heart's secret treason!
My sister, my bride . . . I come to your garden.[5]

The movement between those two poems shows something of what Paul Ricoeur perceives in the Song of Songs. Whereas Cheryl Exum, like most modern scripture scholars, primarily explores the Song as an erotic love poem, Ricoeur wants to 'oppose a multiple, flowering history of reading, set within the framework of a theory of reception of the text, to this unilinear conception of the "trajectory" of explication of the Song of Songs. This is a history where not just ancient allegorical exegesis finds a place, but also modern scientific exegesis, and – why not? – even new theological interpretations, whether related or not to the older allegorical exegesis.'[6]

Ricoeur takes four 'fragments' of the history of reading the Song: analogical transference, with a special focus on liturgical usage; Origen's interpretation pivoting between typology and allegory, which he critically retrieves; modern 'allegorical' commentary, which he devastatingly criticises; and the modern abandonment of allegorical interpretation, which is both explained and sympathetically criticised in order to complement it by drawing on premodern approaches and by exercising a postcritical theological imagination. Ricoeur's justification of his position need not be repeated here,[7] but his key insight is vital. He emphasises 'the metaphorical dimension of a poem dedicated to erotic love, which is raised by its literary structure beyond any exclusive social-

---

5. 'Crimson Thread' in *Love Life*, p. 116.
6. Paul Ricoeur, 'The Nuptial Metaphor' in *Thinking Biblically: Exegetical and Hermeneutical Studies*, ed. André LaCocque and Paul Ricoeur (Chicago: University of Chicago Press, 1988), p. 265. As Ricoeur says, 'for many commentators, these allegorical interpretations are only referred to in their introductions as examples of the prescientific antecedents of an investigation of the text that owes everything to the historical-critical method' (ibid.). Exum too relegates it to her introduction, but her method is by no means limited to the historical-critical, and her commentary benefits from a wide variety of other approaches, especially feminist and other gender-related analyses: 'To my knowledge, the present commentary is the first to examine systematically gender differences and the role they play in the presentation of the relationship between the lovers in the Song' (*Song of Songs*, p. 81). Yet Ricoeur's attempt to differentiate his own approach still applies to Exum's rich array of methods, none of which is allegorical or theological in his sense.
7. Note especially his argument in 'The Nuptial Metaphor', pp. 267–74, his use of Ann-Marie Pelletier's work (pp. 276–7, 279, 280, 285, 290–1), and his qualified affirmation of Origen (pp. 281–5).

cultural context. These features ... seem to me to have as their effect – I do not say, intention – precisely to decontextualize erotic love, and to render it in this way accessible to a plurality of readings compatible with the obvious sense of the text as an erotic poem.'[8] He uses the phrase 'nuptial bond' for a love that is free and faithful and may be sexual but need not be, just as it may be matrimonial but need not be. He argues from a range of literary features that in the Song the nuptial is found in the erotic but can also be distinguished from it. 'All these features taken together constitute the indication of the nuptial in the erotic and, by implication, make possible and plausible a disentangling of the nuptial from the erotic and its new reinvestment in other variations of the amorous relation.'[9] The nuptial, equidistant 'between sexual realism and matrimonial moralism', is freed to become 'the analogon for other configurations of love than that of erotic love'.[10]

O'Siadhail's sequence of love poems, which begins with the Song contributing to his evocation of the passionately erotic, culminates in the sonnet from 'Crimson Thread' (just quoted) with a Song-soaked celebration of the matrimonial. The very last sonnet intensifies this.

> Dew, spice, honey, wine and milk,
> Bone of my bone, flesh of my flesh
> Wear again for me the damson silk
> I take as given and still begin afresh.
> *Awake o north wind, come south wind. ...*
> Never enough just to have rubbed along.
> Promise of promises nothing can rescind.
> All or nothing. All is Solomon's Song.
> *I come to my garden, my sister, my bride.*
> *Eat friend, drink and be drunk with love*
> And every moment I think I'm satisfied
> Wakes me to desires I'm dreaming of.
> In Solomon's blue curtain a cord of covenant,
> A crimson thread until the crimson moment.[11]

The rest of the poem associates 'the crimson moment' with death. That too is not alien to the Song of Songs. 'Only once [8:6–7 – quoted at the beginning of this chapter] does the poet offer an observation about the

---

8. Ricoeur, 'The Nuptial Metaphor', p. 268.   9. Ibid. p. 268.
10. Ibid. p. 274.   11. 'Crimson Thread' in *Love Life*, p. 117.

nature of love in general, and it is of the utmost importance for understanding the Song of Songs ... Though death is mentioned only once, and
that near the poem's end, everything in the poem converges upon and
serves to illustrate the affirmation that love is as strong as death.'(Exum)[12]
Ricoeur agrees with Exum, calling 8:6–7 'the sapiential crown' of the
Song, and its 'sapiential denouement'.[13] He parallels it with 'that other,
also sapiential denouement that says, "This is why a man leaves his
father and mother ... and clings to his wife and they become one flesh"
(Genesis 2:24). Does not the seal of the Covenant in Song of Songs 8:6
have the same sapiential flavour? In both cases, we do not know who is
speaking: the masterless voice of Wisdom? A hidden God? Or a discrete
God who respects the incognito of intimacy, the privacy of one body with
another body?'[14]

*Ricoeur has taken us into the explicitly theological, beyond Exum's erotic and
O'Siadhail's matrimonial, yet without denying either.* He refuses to cut off the
'flowerings' in the history of the Song's interpretation, allowing for the
ramification of meanings without playing down its erotic sense. His
method of proceeding, developed in the final section of his chapter,
centres on the Song's intertextuality, the multiple resonances between
the Song and other parts of the Bible (such as that with Genesis just
noted) and the possibilities of manifold 'seeing as' through rich, generative metaphors – above all the nuptial metaphor as an analogy for
divine–human relations.

Ellen Davis' remarkable commentary on the Song goes much further,
intertextually and theologically, than Ricoeur. The Song, she says, is 'the
most biblical of books. That is to say, the poet is throughout in conversation with other biblical writers.'[15] She makes a strong case for the appropriateness of its categorisation with Proverbs, Ecclesiastes and Job as
wisdom literature. If the present book were to have engaged with
Proverbs and Ecclesiastes to the extent that it has with Job, Davis' commentary on these along with the Song would have been the ideal starting
point, and would have led immediately into such topics as the significance of the female figure of wisdom, guidelines for healthy sexuality,

12. Exum, *Song of Songs*, pp. 2–3.
13. Ricoeur, 'The Nuptial Metaphor', pp. 270, 299–300.   14. Ibid. p. 300.
15. Ellen F. Davis, *Proverbs, Ecclesiastes, and the Song of Songs* (Louisville, KY: Westminster
John Knox Press, 2000), p. 231.

the relation of wisdom to creation and ecology, and the shaping of ordinary living before God in such matters as the use of the tongue, work, family life, friendship, money, power and knowledge. Her daring, multilevelled reading of the Song of Songs relates it to three basic problems.

First, there is the asymmetry of power between woman and man, which is met by their embrace 'in the full ecstasy of mutuality'.[16] Second, there is the alienation between humanity and nature, which is met by the lovers' garden of delight and the earth 'alive with birdsong and rampant bloom'.[17] Third is the distance from and loss of intimacy with God, met by that garden being represented as what Eden was meant to be, 'the place where life may be lived fully in the presence of God'.[18] And like Exum and Ricoeur, Davis too recognises the climactic significance for the Song of connecting love with death in 8:6–7. In her interpretation of it her marriage of scholarship and theology remints for today a classic Christian wisdom of death and dying.

> Love is the one thing in this life that *may* – if we let it – consume us as fully as death *will* one day consume us. Death consumes us even against our will, but we must yield to love. But for those who do yield, love consumes like fire; it is 'a raging flame.' A literal rendering of the Hebrew reads 'a flame *of the Lord*.' Hebrew writers sometimes use the divine name as an intensifying term. The comparable English idiom (though drawn from the opposite end of the spiritual spectrum) would be 'a hell of a flame.' So the NRSV translation suggests: 'a raging flame.' Yet our poet's habits and the image itself suggest there is here a deliberate echo of the religious tradition. Israel knows God as 'a consuming fire' (Deut. 4:24; Heb. 12:29; see also Isa. 31:9; Zech. 2:5). Love and death, love and flame of God – together these comparisons may help us to see that love, which comes to us as a gift from God, is not undone by death. Rather, love is the best preparation for what Christians have traditionally called a holy death.
>
> How can that be? Because love teaches us to give of ourselves, ever more deeply, to God and neighbour. It enables us to give in costly ways, yet at the same time joyfully. To the extent that we give ourselves up in love, we are protected against the fear of death, which otherwise enslaves every human being (Heb. 2:15). It is a simple truth but hard to hold fast. Those who have already been consumed by love can never be annihilated.[19]

---

16. Ibid. p. 232.   17. Ibid.   18. Ibid.   19. Ibid. p. 297.

The summit of this wisdom is the love of God for God's sake. Generations of Jews and Christians have been given their language for this love by the Song. Of such love, Davis writes:

> It does not come from anything God has done for us, but simply out of delight in who God is. It arises in us spontaneously because our souls were made for the love of God. One great modern teacher and mystic, Rabbi Abraham Isaac Kook, has suggested that all the rich imagery of the Song of Songs exists precisely for the sake of making vividly real this rare love which does not derive from material benefits. His teaching draws attention to one important aspect of the Song: namely, that the lovers' mutual delight is completely nonutilitarian ... The Song shows us only the essence of love, isolated moments of pure desire and delight in the presence of the other.[20]

This resonates with that most probing and radical of questions, '**Does Job fear God for nothing?**' (Job 1:9), though now in the form of desiring and loving rather than fearing God.[21]

There is a further parallel between Job and the Song. Both are shot through with cries. *Even more than Job, the Song is an exclamatory poem, almost pure crying out.* It is a drama of desire expressed in passionate cries, and its wisdom is a wisdom of cries. To read, reread and internalise the Song is to find a textbook for the school of desire and wisdom, inspiring and instructing the heart and mind in attention to cries and in the articulation of cries. It may or may not be that the reader has a human lover, but the divine lover is not similarly contingent. The alertness and articulateness that may be learnt through the Song are core practices in relating to God. The cries of love are an opening up to receive love and its wisdom, a training in active receptivity.

> Song of Songs 1:2 Let him kiss me with the kisses of his mouth!
>   1:15 Ah, you are beautiful, my love; ah, you are beautiful; your eyes are doves.
> Song of Songs 2:14 O my dove, in the clefts of the rock, in the covert of the cliff, let me see your face, let me hear your voice; for your voice is sweet, and your face is lovely.

---

20. Ibid. pp. 235–6.
21. On the connection between love and fear, Davis in her commentary on Proverbs 1:7 quotes John Donne: 'As he that is fallen into the king's hand for debt to him, is safe from all other creditors, so is he, that fears the Lord, from other fears. He that loves the Lord, loves him with all his love; he that fears the Lord, loves him with all his fear too; God takes no half affections' (Sermons 6:109): ibid. p. 29.

Song of Songs 3:5–6 ⁵Iadjure you, O daughters of Jerusalem, by the
gazelles or the wild does: do not stir up or awaken love until it is
ready! ⁶What is that coming up from the wilderness, like a column of
smoke, perfumed with myrrh and frankincense, with all the fragrant
powders of the merchant?
Song of Songs 4:10 How sweet is your love, my sister, my bride! how
much better is your love than wine, and the fragrance of your oils than
any spice!
    4:16 Awake, O north wind, and come, O south wind! Blow upon my
garden that its fragrance may be wafted abroad. Let my beloved come
to his garden, and eat its choicest fruits.
Song of Songs 6:10 Who is this that looks forth like the dawn, fair as
the moon, bright as the sun, terrible as an army with banners?
Song of Songs 8:3 O that his left hand were under my head, and that
his right hand embraced me!

Such are the exclamations, questions, imperatives, invitations and, above
all, the longings of love.
    The final cry of the Song is a surprising one.

8:14 Make haste, my beloved, and be like a gazelle or a young stag
upon the mountains of spices!

Ellen Davis' comment on it, correcting 'make haste' to 'flee', is a fitting
wisdom interpretation:

How different is the effect of that cry – 'Flee!' – from the ending we
expect in a love story: 'and they lived happily ever after.' Fairy tales
end with a picture of static happiness; we are not encouraged to
think what more might have happened to Sleeping Beauty and the
Prince. Who can imagine them struggling to grow together,
experiencing pain as well as joy, anger and disappointment, as all
real-life lovers do? The Bible, by contrast, is relentlessly realistic, if
also wildly hopeful. The Song does not end with the lovers sitting
together in the garden. They are still in motion, still straining with
desire, still hoping for something that is not yet given: a word, a
moment of presence. The Song ends on a note of separation,
uncertainty, anticipation of their next meeting. It is a realistic
picture of young love. And is it not also a true picture of our life
with God? For the answer to that, we must appeal to the experience
of those who are closest to God, the biblical writers and the saints
throughout history who have left us their common testimony: God
never fully satisfies us in this world but instead continually

stretches our desire toward heaven. Not satisfaction but the expansion and purification of holy desire is the surest sign of God's presence with us. So the art of the spiritual life is the art of learning to live with longing, with the eager expectation that God's presence will be felt yet again in our hearts, in our midst, and always in new ways.[22]

That is faith in the optative mood, evoked by the divine call and desire. It searches the heights and depths of our fragile existence, always learning and discerning, and never past being surprised. It is a faith whose source, hope and delight is the God of blessing who loves in wisdom.

22. Ibid. p. 302.

Index of citations

Subject index

Abraham, testing by God 231
Abrahamic faiths *see* inter-faith wisdom;
    scriptural reasoning
abundance 172, 242
  in Acts 65, 66
  in Job 107, 109, 115–20
  in John's Gospel 56, 373, 375, 379
  and post-Holocaust wisdom 141–2
action, prophetic 29, 31
Adams, Nicholas 280, 298
Adorno, Theodore 141
aesthetics, and holiness 261
affirmation 46, 59, 200, 235
affliction
  and attentiveness 364–5
  and decreation 104, 107
  in Job 104–7, 114
  and reader 122
  see also cries; Holocaust; trauma
allegory, and Song of Songs 74, 385–6
Alter, Robert 108, 114, 116, 117
American Academy of Religion 278
Amery, Jean 121
Anna 17, 49, 156, 171, 199
anti-intellectualism, and divine wisdom
    180–2
apophaticism 44, 62, 215, 220–1, 240
apostleship, in Paul 187–8
apostolicity of the church 249, 262–4
apprenticeship
  in L'Arche communities 371
  to the saints 86, 360–1
  in scriptural reasoning 279, 294, 297–8
  in universities 318, 321
Aquinas, Thomas 215, 216, 220, 238,
    267–8, 269
Arius, and divinity of Christ 7, 218–21
The Art of Reading Scripture 79–89
askesis 13

asking, and desire 159
Athanasius 218–20, 223
attentiveness 364–5
attributes of God *see* perfections of God
Augustine of Hippo
  and apophatic tradition 215
  and attributes of God 236
  and meanings of scripture 83, 88
  and philosophy and wisdom 266
authority
  in the church 196, 208, 220, 263–4
  and Jesus 263–4, 378
Azariah 231–2

Babel, Tower of 112, 139, 142, 143
Balthasar, Hans Urs von 82, 222
baptism, and unity of the church 256, 257
baptism of Jesus 157–8
  and affirmation by God 17, 21, 29, 49,
    59, 380
  and God as Trinity 210
  and Holy Spirit 157, 164, 200
Barmen Declaration 218, 219
Barrett, C. K. 181
Barth, Karl
  and Christian midrash 160
  and christology 160, 169, 218
  and Job 169–70
  and perfections of God 8, 236, 239–44,
    245–8
  and scripture 247, 277, 278
  and theodrama 82
  and Trinity 222
Barton, Stephen C. 14, 204–5, 207
Bauckham, Richard 81–2
Beatitudes, and L'Arche communities 350–1,
    353, 359
Begbie, Jeremy S. 11
Being, and God 214–17

saints, as guides to interpretation 85–6,
    203, 360–1
Satan
  in Job 97, 98, 99, 101, 102, 117, 133
  and temptation of Jesus 162, 172
Schleiermacher, F. D. E. 222, 310–12, 313, 315,
    330, 335
scholarship, and hermeneutics 69–76, 376
scholasticism 216, 267–70, 309
science
  and theology 270–2
  and universities 309, 337
Scotus, Duns 216
scriptural reasoning 9–10, 148, 273–82,
    361, 381
  and analogous wisdoms 299–300
  and apprenticeship 279, 294, 297–8
  and Christianity 284
  and collegiality 275, 278–82, 287, 288, 294,
    298, 301, 381
  and communication 287
  and core identities 53, 273–5, 294
  description 275–8
  frequency 287
  institutional location 282–93
    synagogues, churches and mosques
      282–8, 293
    universities 288–91, 293, 349
    venues 291–3
  and interpretive theory 296–9
  and Islam 278, 284–6
  and Judaism 283
  in public sphere 301
  and superabundant meaning 293–300
scripture
  and Barth 247
  and discernment 158
  inter-faith study see scriptural reasoning
  Jewish 52, 58, 60, 145
  in L'Arche communities 359–62
  and plain sense 295–6, 362, 375
secularity
  and universities 288–91, 301, 311, 326,
    345–7
  and wisdom literature 228
Shadrach, Meshach and Abednego 231
Sheba, Queen of 26–7
Shoah see Holocaust
Simeon 17, 49, 156, 199
Sirach
  and God for God's sake 227, 233
  neglect of 247
Solomon
  and Song of Songs 27
  and wisdom 26–7, 60, 134, 153, 174
Sonderegger, Katherine 256

song 250–1, 370
Song of Songs
  allegorical and liturgical reading 74,
    385–6
  and desire for love 11, 158, 382–91
  and poetry 386–7, 389
  and Solomon 27
  theological reading 75
Soulen, R. Kendall 255
Spinks, Kathryn 353
stakeholders, and universities 305, 328–9,
    336, 339, 340
state
  and control of universities 327, 328–9,
    337, 344
  and knowledge transfer 328, 330, 331,
    332, 333
Stephen, St 173, 233
  cries 42, 63, 249
  and Holy Spirit 42, 63, 173, 249
  and prophetic wisdom 42, 60,
    63, 65
subjunctive mood 48–9, 78, 79, 247
  and Job 102–4, 116, 119, 122, 129, 133
  and John's Gospel 363, 377
suffering
  and cries of discernment 19–20, 171
  devaluation 126–8
  and divine justice 123–5, 129
  and friendship see friends of Job
  and poetry 10, 94–5, 106–7, 110–11,
    112–13, 142
  see also Job (book); Job (character);
    L'Arche
supersessionism 151, 255, 256
surprise
  and Kingdom of God 48–9, 377
  and post-traumatic wisdom 103, 142
  and scripture 202
synagogue, as home of scripture 282–8
Szymborska, Wislawa 141

Talmud, in textual reasoning 276
Tanakh
  academic study 169, 276
  and core identities 274–5
  see also Old Testament; scriptural
    reasoning
teaching, and research 316–18, 336
Temple, in Luke 199, 201
temptation of Jesus
  and desire 157–9, 161
  and discernment 44
  and Holy Spirit 158
  and identity of Jesus 17, 19
  and passion of Jesus 162, 163